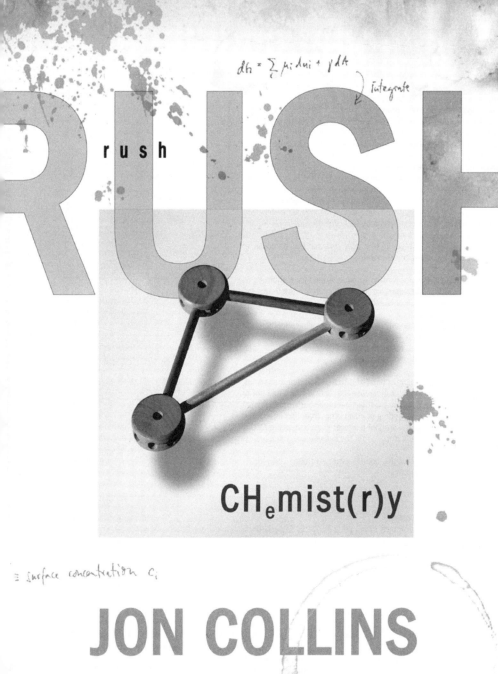

$$dh = \sum_i \mu_i \, dn_i + \gamma \, dA$$

integrate

RUSH

rush

CH$_e$mist(r)y

$\equiv$ surface concentration c_i

JON COLLINS

$$d\gamma = - \sum_i c_i \, d\mu_i \qquad (3)$$

a binary solution in contact with air

$$G = \sum_i \mu_i n_i + \gamma A \qquad (4)$$

complete differential

$$\sum_i \mu_i \, dn_i + \sum_i n_i \, d\mu_i + \gamma \, dA + A \, d\gamma \qquad (6)$$

Helter Skelter publishing

This edition published in 2005 by
Helter Skelter Publishing
Southbank House, Black Prince Road, London SE1 7SJ.

Copyright 2005 © Jon Collins.

Cover design and artwork by Hugh Syme.
Inner workings by Chris Wilson at CMWcreations.com

Printed in Great Britain by CPI, Bath.

All lyrics quoted in this book are for the purposes of review, study or criticism.

The right of Jon Collins to be identified as author of this work has been asserted in accordance with the Copyright, Design and Patents Act, 1988.

A CIP record for this book is available from the British Library.

ISBN 1-900924-85-4

Photography credits:
Jimbo Barton: Pages 115-118, 120, 122, 124, 126
Beetle Magazine: Pages 44, 46, 48
Matthew Bigwood: Cover/sleeve author photograph
   (please visit www.matthewbigwood.co.uk)
Brian Collins: Pages 195-196, 197 (upper), 198-200
   (please visit www.rockshotz.net)
Jon Collins: Pages: 7, 8, 9, 12, 14-15, 53, 61, 163
   (lower), 172
Ken Clutsam: Page 57
John Gulbus: Page 40
Iniskillin Winery: Page 184
Bernie LaBarge: Page 163 (upper)
Michael Mosbach: Pages 192, 197 (lower)
Stephen Tayler: Pages 135-139, 141, 143-145,
   147-149
Unknown: Pages 23, 43, 102, 170

Every effort has been made to contact the copyright holders of photographs used in this book, but some were unreachable. We would be grateful if the photographers concerned would contact us.

$$dh = \sum_i \mu_i \, dn_i + \gamma \, dA$$

integrate

CH$_e$mist(r)y

$\equiv$ surface concentration c_i

$$d\gamma = - \sum_i c_i \, d\mu_i \qquad (3)$$

a binary solution in contact with air

$$G = \sum_i \mu_i n_i + \gamma A \qquad (4)$$

complete differential

$$\sum_i \mu_i \, dn_i + \sum_i n_i \, d\mu_i + \gamma \, dA + A \, d\gamma \qquad (6)$$

To T.V., I.S. and M.O.
They were nobody's heroes.

Contents

Preface

Seems to me its chemistry...

Since their inception, Canadian rock trio Rush had the cards of popular music stacked against them. Today, to many, it is like they never existed – and yet, the wall-to-wall platinum and gold discs and the shelves stuffed with awards at their management offices in Toronto tell a different story. Rush have enjoyed success on a scale that many more famous stars would die for, and consistently achieved this success across more than two decades. Many of today's more eligible rock bands, from Godsmack to the Manic Street Preachers, claim some kind of inspiration from the trio that no pundit has ever really managed to categorise, and Rush continues to draw crowds in every corner of the world they visit. And yet, and yet... there is no place for the band on the podium of mainstream music, alongside the rock illuminati – the Zeppelins, Queens and Nirvanas. The band has never been inducted into the Rock and Roll Hall of Fame, nor is it likely to make the cover of *Rolling Stone* magazine.

While it is rare for Rush to be heard on the radio, when the band first reached out in the early seventies, it was radio – through characters such as Cleveland's WMMS-FM programme director Donna Halper, CHUM-FM DJs David Marsden and Don Shafer in Toronto, Mercury label representative Cliff Burnstein and the like – that gave the band its first break. It is no coincidence that these same characters are recognised mavericks in the industry, even today working against the current to deliver more than musical opiates for the masses. Lucky perhaps that Rush should fall in with these people but the relationships were not theirs alone, the management company SRO's joint chiefs of staff, Ray Danniels and Vic Wilson being no strangers to the maverick tendency.

In an industry driven by radio play, perhaps success cannot be judged by sales of records, tickets or t-shirts alone. On the surface, the arguments are simple – Rush's music was never truly appropriate for widespread radio, so they say, and there is little point denying that the esoteric musical style and very literary lyrics that characterise the music, have appealed largely to a dispossessed subset of male listeners, themselves in search of more than yet another, rejigged regurgitation of the twelve bar blues. While there was always a place for such music, it wasn't going to be Rush that broke through the mass-appeal conservatism that was rife in the biz. This would come a decade later with the arrival of grunge, spearheaded by the punk-influenced, but distinctively hard rocking, likes of Nirvana and Pearl Jam.

A common argument is that Rush's music was far too complex for "ordinary people" to get; this has been the basis for many a critic's withering review. If there's anything we can learn from the current popularity (on both sides of the Atlantic) of more progressive bands such as Radiohead and Muse, or even sci-fi rockers The Flaming Lips and The Mars Volta, it is that the final target for music, the listening public, is a lot more discerning than is generally assumed. Rush may have roused the ranks of the dispossessed, but this is in no small part because this audience refused to bow to what the majority of labels and radio programme directors were telling them. As if to cock a snook at mass marketing, Rush took this audience and made it its own. More than perhaps any band in the history of recorded music, Rush achieved success fundamentally and absolutely on its own terms.

Rush are more than a phenomenon. They are a statement, which runs something like this: Music journalists, you were wrong. Observers of mainstream culture, you were wrong. By complaining about the music, the screeching vocals, the supposed political statements, you did your industry a disservice. You felt you could dictate what people listened to, and you failed.

One Little History

Oh, Canada...

"Our population density is a little string running across the country," explains photographer, conference organiser and Toronto resident Bruce Cole. "If you go south you're in the United States, if you go north it's too cold. It's a ribbon running from the Pacific to the Atlantic, and probably 95% of the population lives in that ribbon. If you can figure out how to make a dime in Canada, you can make a dime anywhere." Ain't

that the truth – and nowhere was it truer than in the Canadian music business of the early seventies. With Toronto's burgeoning café culture, a veritable pot-boiler of musical talent was there for the taking but few indeed were the bands that freed themselves from the shackles of playing to the Canadian ribbon.

Rush was one such band, learning that the only way up was the hard way – treading the boards, playing an inordinate number of gigs per year and having the vision to assemble a management team that was prepared to share the uphill struggle against public

Well-spent youth: kids of today, making music on Toronto's street corners.

indifference and press castigation. The original line-up of singer/ bassist Geddy Lee, guitarist Alex Lifeson and drummer John Rutsey came from the same suburb, went to nearby schools and shared similar upbringings in aspiring, hard-working families, instilling an ethic that they carried with them into the rehearsal rooms and onto the stage, as they played night after night in front of every possible audience.

The first album, 'Rush', was a self-funded project, recorded at night and between gigs to keep costs to a minimum. It might have been derivative but it was enough to secure a certain level of interest from radio, leading to that all-important record deal – which was nearly drowned at birth as John announced that a life in music wasn't for him. Fact was, John wasn't happy with the increasingly progressive stylings the other two were adopting. Though initially he came across as a hick, it was fortunate in the extreme that the remaining pair stumbled upon Neil Peart – he shared the work ethic and the desire to stir things up musically, and he could write lyrics to match.

With the follow-up, the rock solid 'Fly By Night', the band achieved a certain local notoriety that it very nearly blew with its desire to push outward artistically, as illustrated by the third album, 'Caress Of Steel', which boasted the band's first fantasy-fuelled, musically complex, side-filling piece. Though it might not have seemed so at the time, perhaps the popular failure of the release was serendipitous: the band picked themselves up, dusted themselves off and created the anger-fuelled, dystopian concept album, '2112', which showed how much they had learned about both their art and their public. '2112' started the band on a journey, an exploration of anti-communistic individualism. In commercial terms, the musical progression between '2112' and its musically complex, sci-fi, rock and fantasy successors – 'A Farewell To Kings' and 'Hemispheres' – took Geddy, Alex and Neil to a place where they were absolutely free to do what they wanted, but internally, the strain was starting to show. Now they were there, it was time to stop, think and decide where to go next. The next part of the journey would bring the band back into the real world and into the commercial mainstream.

Making memories: the 'glittering prizes' on display in the SRO foyer.

The subsequent pairing of 'Permanent Waves' and its critically acclaimed follow-up 'Moving Pictures' remain the band's biggest selling albums, and some would say this period signals the pinnacle of their career. It was certainly the high point of their fame, or their notoriety. From this point on, it would have been very difficult to do any wrong if Rush kept to the track that they had forged. Indeed, from the perspective of their increasingly loyal audience subsequent albums 'Signals', 'Power Windows' and 'Hold Your Fire' were pearls of wisdom, delivered from a position of power. Within the studio however, the track was becoming increasingly worn. The band were at a stage where they could turn the handle and churn out an album, whether they enjoyed making it or not, and in the knowledge it would sell - that was no good thing.

'Presto' and 'Roll The Bones' injected new vigour into the band, bringing them into the nineties and away from the comfort zone of multilayered production. This led on to 'Counterparts', following which a five-year gap would pass before the band returned to the studio. Whatever came next, it would have no link with the past: sure enough, 'Test For Echo' was a new departure for the band. The dual personal tragedy of the death of Neil's daughter and wife forced another hiatus on the band. That is, it was a hiatus in hindsight, given that the thought of reforming was the last thing in anyone's minds. Remarkably enough, the album that did eventually emerge after this long sojourn, 'Vapor Trails', shared a number of connections with 'Test For Echo', not least a heavier sound, a raw edge and a near absence (a total absence, in the case of 'Vapor Trails') of keyboards.

Over the past three decades several factors have conspired in Rush's favour, not least a single-minded determination from the three members of the band to rise to the challenges put before them. Ever since Neil, Geddy and Alex first became associated in 1974, the threesome have quietly faced down one challenge after another – the dogged hard work to succeed against all odds being replaced almost overnight by the pressures of dealing with success, the difficulties of sustaining their creativity followed by the mid-life issues of balancing family life with a touring schedule. Over the past five years, the trio have demonstrated the ability to withstand even the most calamitous circumstances, from Neil's bereavements to Alex's day in a Florida court. Every time, Rush have come back fighting, as determined as ever.

To answer why this should be, one need look no further than the source of the chemistry within the band. You could not find three more different people than the gregarious Alex, the careful Geddy and the bookish Neil, but since the beginning they have shared a deeply held aspiration to create and to perform. Such hopes offer plenty of contradictions, not least the paradox of achieving recognition and finding oneself like a startled rabbit, caught in the limelight of one's own making. A failure to deal with the fruits of success has led to the demise of many bands, and Rush would likely have broken up 20 years ago were it not for a third characteristic, an amalgam of humility, humanity and friendship that has enabled the threesome to ride out the disagreements and help each other through the crises and traumas. In the chemical reaction that is Rush, these characteristics were the tempering agents, ensuring a slow and steady effervescence over three decades.

Individuals they may have been, but they have not been acting single-handedly. Over the years the band has assembled an enviable network of assistants, not least their own management organisation SRO, but also in the shape of producers such as Terry Brown, Peter Collins and Rupert Hine. Live performances are a collaboration with a tightly knit, devoted crew which has been handpicked since the very beginning, characters such as tour manager Liam Birt and lighting wizard Howard Ungerleider quietly going about their own business, everybody to the bus drivers and riggers being treated with equal respect. More than one role has been handed down from father to son, and albums have been dedicated to those who have passed on – just like one would expect from a family business.

So, what of the individuals? What can we learn about the people that make up the power trio, Alex, Neil and Geddy, a.k.a. (for reasons only they know) Lerxst, Dirk and Pratt? When asked, numerous collaborators and cohorts have answered the same thing – that these are three ordinary people with a desire to make music, as nice a bunch of guys that you could hope to meet. Ordinariness is a state of mind, and one which doesn't always come naturally – indeed, as Rush hit the heights of its popularity in the eighties, the players went to great lengths to preserve a semblance of normality.

Xmas 2004 at the SRO/ Anthem office.

In any case, what is normal? Is it normal to know your aspirations as a teenager, to the extent you are prepared to pack in your education and follow your heart? Is it normal to rehearse your instrument to the point of obsession, such that those around you can no longer tell the difference between two takes of a song? While all three band members were quite happy to party and let their hair down on occasion, none ever really succumbed to the trappings of rock stardom – it wasn't in the plan. This was not the behaviour of ordinary people, nor was it the behaviour of ordinary rock stars. Normal, schormal – perhaps it has been the achievement of normality in the face of the crazy rock 'n' roll circus that has been the biggest struggle of all – but they achieved it when so many have failed.

This is no glowing, rose-tinted, partial history, where any cracks have been filled, repainted and then carefully glossed over. "Accuracy is the key," says Canadian folk artist and SRO stable mate to Rush, Mendelson Joe. It is undeniable that there have been difficulties making certain albums: Alex admits he can barely listen to 'Signals', and Geddy reserves a similar comment for 'Grace Under Pressure'; there have been disagreements, arguments, endless debates, doors have been slammed, things have been thrown. To deny this would be to deny the humanity of the key players; equally, so would be the act of blowing things out of proportion. Neither then is this intended as a tome that digs unnecessarily into the band's private lives or delights in salacious details, not that there are many to be had. Bands that have lived the fantasies of fame to the full, such as Led Zeppelin and Motley Crüe, get the biographies they deserve, and so should Rush.

Not that the threesome were boring. If there is one word that could be used to sum up the experiences Rush shared with their collaborators, it would be "fun." Fun in the studio, making and crashing model aircraft, the inane conversations at the dinner table, the drunken giggling coming back after a night out, the practical jokes, the failed attempts to achieve the patently impossible. Fun on tour – from setting up support bands and each other, to little touches such as loading Geddy's vending machine with the latest souvenirs. Fun, fun, fun, fun, fun has kept the band sane, kept the channels of communication open through the hard times, lifted the occasional dark mood and countered the infrequent ideas of pride or arrogance.

Thirty years is a long time to be doing anything, let alone with the same three people, which is achievement enough. In addition, Rush have created a legacy of music that has touched the hearts of many thousands of people, without compromising their own integrity. In doing so, they can feel justly proud.

Acknowledgements

You've got to be a little obsessive to write a book, but after a while the thing starts dictating, rather than being dictated – I confess there was a time where I wondered what I'd bitten off. Every interview I found seemed to reference three others; every person I spoke to recommended a handful more people who I absolutely had to interview. So it developed, until I found two years had passed and it seemed I was still nowhere near the end. I felt something like M. Mangetout (a.k.a. Michel Lotito) must have felt, when he realised just how much metal there was on a Cessna... It goes without saying (but I'll say it anyway) that the people around you have to be very understanding, and I take off my hat, my coat and my boots to my family, Liz, Ben and Sophie, who have persevered and put up with me throughout.

This book would not be what it has become without the help and support of a number of people who have worked closely with Rush throughout the years. Special mention and heartfelt thanks go to Rupert Hine, who agreed so positively and readily to an interview when I was just getting things off the ground. Donna Halper was also there at the start, with her insights and sage words about the early days. Hugh Syme has done an amazing cover and has been inordinately helpful, and Howard Ungerleider invited me for an interview at Wembley Stadium that led to a gold mine of information from a cross section of the crew. Terry Brown, Peter Collins, Peter Henderson and Paul Northfield, thank you for all your help and for reviewing the text. Thanks also go to Adam Ayan, Barry McVicker, Barry Miles, Bob Roper, Brian Lee, Dave Meegan, Fin Costello, Rich Vinyard, Jaymz Bee, Steve Margoshes, Mark Kelly, Kooster McAllister, Patrick McLoughlin, Scott Alexander, Robert Scovill, Nick Kotos, Norman Stangl, George Graves, Neal Graham, Guy Charbonneau, Scott K Fish, Rob Wallis and Paul Siegel, Frank Opolko, Brad Madix, Geoff Barton, Peter Collins, Lorne Wheaton, Lou Pomanti, Russ Ryan, Neil Warnock, Stephen Tayler, Larry Jordan, Craig Blazier, Brett Zihali, Cliff Burnstein, David Marsden, Jorn Anderson, Mendelson Joe, Ira Blacker, James 'Jimbo' Barton, Peter Cardinali, Greg Hermanovic, Eric Hansen, Ronnie Hawkins, Andrew MacNaughtan, Bernie Labarge, Brian Collins, Tony "Jack Secret" Geranios, Glen Wexler, Rick Britton, Chris Stringer and John Fillion. Thanks to David Stopps, for kicking off a whole chain of events. Huge thanks to Pegi Cecconi at SRO, who has been an evenhanded proponent of this project since the start. And last but certainly not least, thank you to the many people who have co-ordinated the interviews and meetings, and put up with my small talk, at SRO and elsewhere.

Meanwhile, back home I cannot thank enough my good friends and reviewers. Particular thanks to Shane "Phone" Faulkner, who has helped me more than he could ever know, and Karin Breiter, Carole Bergen and Jane Moyer, for being there at the start (remember the green glass!). Thanks also to Mark Tiplady, Mark Dempster, Fraser Marshall, Dean Pedley, Dave Rogers and Mark Kennedy, who have fact-checked the text. None of this would even have started if it hadn't been for my publisher Sean Body, who innocently asked, "What's next?" and who has given the manuscript all the attention it deserves. Thanks to John and Julia, for putting me up (as ever) at short notice, and thanks of course to my Uncle, Les, for taping a copy of 'A Farewell To Kings' for my sister, Nicky (who, thinking little of it, passed it on to me). Thanks and a big hug to Christine Cooper, because I can. Good luck H and D.

I'd like to tip my hat to all the journalists and authors who have contributed to the corpus of Rush-related literature in the past – not least Steve Gett and Brian Harrigan's books, and the more recent tome from Martin Popoff, but also the many, many interviews that have been conducted through the years. I gained some small insight into what it meant to be an immigrant family in post-war Toronto, from the deeply moving 'Fugitive Pieces', by Anne Michaels.

All errors are my own – there will undoubtedly be some, for which an Errata section has been set up at www.rushchemistry.com. Some old interviews and articles contain contradictory information – what you have in your hands right now is, to the best of my knowledge, the most accurate version of the story so far. Because Rush operated as a family, it has sometimes been difficult to determine exactly who did what. Where necessary, I have used the term "they" to mean the band, the producer, the management and record label, and indeed just about anybody! Finally, to distinguish between the two my own interviews are reported in the present tense, and past interviews are quoted in the past tense.

This book has been written, typed and dictated in some of the strangest of places – notably on trains, planes and in automobiles. Special mention goes to The Snooty Fox in Tetbury, The Organic Shop Café, Cirencester Brewery Arts and the AV8 Bistro at Kemble Airfield. Thanks to all of you – now you know what I was up to.

Jon Collins, July 2005

Foreword

The model Chipmunk I built was a symbol; the beginning of the end of my tenure with RUSH. A magnificent, Canadian designed, control-line stunt plane bearing the number 8 on the starboard wing signifying the eighth record for the band and myself, one in a series of ten musical adventures. As Alex's radio-controlled high-wing soared into the heavens the little Chipmunk roared in a circle three times then buried itself in the long grass; amusing, yes, but never the less poignant.

This book lays bare the entire story, providing insight and anecdote, detailing events otherwise missed or overlooked and above all following a truly unique musical journey.

Broon

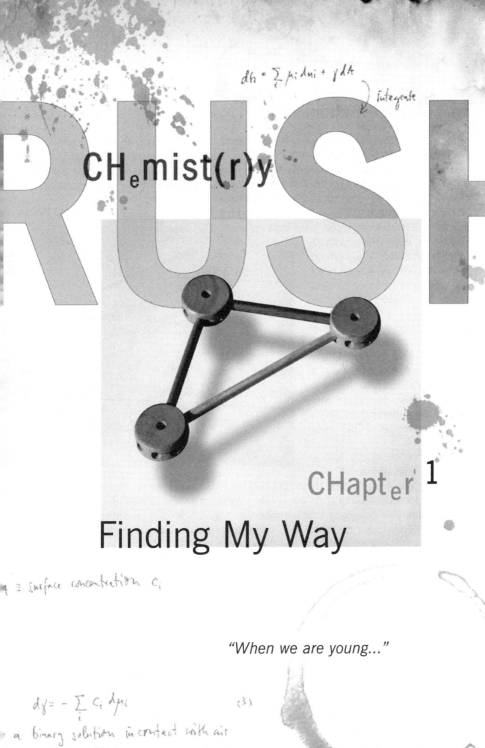

$dh = \sum_i \mu_i d n_i + \gamma dA$

integrate

CH$_e$mist(r)y

CHapt$_e$r 1

Finding My Way

$\gamma \equiv$ surface concentration c_i

"When we are young..."

$d\gamma = - \sum_i c_i d\mu_i$ (3)

a binary solution in contact with air

$G_i = \sum_i \mu_i n_i + \gamma A$ (4)

complete differential

$= \sum_i \mu_i d n_i + \sum_i n_i d\mu_i + \gamma dA + A d\gamma$ (6)

"What can this thing be that I've found?"

In The High School Halls

It is the first day of a new semester, at Fisherville Junior High, in the Willowdale district of Toronto. For the arriving class of 1964 everything is very new and unfamiliar, including most of the other students. In the melee of sights and sounds, eleven-year-olds Gary Weinrib and Alex Zivojinovich are just two boys among the many, working their way towards their first ever history class. Gary hides his trepidation with a quiet calm, a focus on getting there, while Alex's quick mind is churning as he takes it all in, seeking an opportunity to cover his inner fears with a joke, a sideways observation, an ice breaker. He doesn't need to – his brash paisley shirt is message enough to those around him. The two boys enter the classroom together, but they don't say hello. For now, each is satisfied with a glance, the quick scan that takes place in a moment. One nods at the other as they pass the door and familiarise themselves with the surroundings of their new classroom.

In the high school halls - Fisherville junior high

Over the weeks that follow, Gary and Alex get to know a little more about each other. They don't become pals straight away: Alex is a little too outgoing, too maverick for Gary, who prefers avoiding trouble to making it. Over time however the pair develop a mutual understanding, crack jokes and discuss shared themes such as music and sport; girls have yet to make an impact on the pre-teens. While Alex is taking viola lessons and Gary is learning piano, the boys agree that the guitar is the coolest instrument of all. Later, they discover that they were born within four weeks of each other, Gary on 29 July 1953, and Alex on 27 August.

Neither has any reason to imagine that they will be spending a large part of the rest of their lives together.

Alex and Gary's immigrant status was one subject that required no discussion. Many of the children at Fisherville Junior High had an ethnic background, so it just wasn't relevant. Alex's parents, Ned and Mellie Zivojinovich had come to Canada from a region that is now part of Serbia[1] in the mid-fifties. They ended up in the mining town of Fernie, British Columbia in the Rocky Mountains north of Vancouver, where Ned found work as a coal miner. Theirs was not an easy life, not just due to Ned's hard labour for little money; the newcomers spoke little English, and as a result were treated as second class citizens by more established residents. Much of this went over the heads of young Alexander and his two older sisters, who were brought up speaking the language of their parents' homeland. As the youngest child, he never wanted for attention.

When Alex was five, his father suffered a back injury which brought an abrupt end to his working in the mine. There was nothing else keeping the Zivojinovich family in Fernie, so Ned and Mellie decided to move to the more cosmopolitan Toronto. They settled in the aptly named Pleasant Avenue, Willowdale, a tree-lined suburban street that was a far cry from the hardships of the North. Ned and Mellie took on a number of jobs to pay the rent, including (for Ned) plumbing and working as a boiler engineer. For Alex, the move meant starting a new primary school and having to speak English. "I wasn't totally non-English speaking," he recalled, "But it just wasn't important." Until he started to make friends with English speakers, that is – across the road lived John Rutsey, also born in 1953, who became a firm friend. By the fourth grade they were going to the same school.

Round the corner from Pleasant Avenue lived the Weinribs, Manya and Morris. Gary's Jewish parents had somehow survived the horrors of Nazi-occupied Poland, spending four years in a sequence of concentration camps before their release from Bergen-Belsen and Dachau (respectively) at the end of the Second World War. Like many of their peers, as the shadow of post-war communism loomed in 1947 they chose to brave the New World rather than trying to rebuild their shattered past at home. Originally heading for New York, they took a detour to Canada because "someone said it was nice." It was – very nice in fact. Determined to make the best of the move, on arrival Manya changed her name to Mary and decided to set up a variety store, selling everything and anything from coat hooks to casseroles, bringing in enough money to support a growing family – oldest child Gary, his brother Alan and younger sister Nancy. Little has been said about Morris, but it is known that he played the balalaika, an eastern European folk instrument based on the lute.

Gary's primary school years were spent at Faywood Public School in Downsview,

In the high school halls - Faywood

on the other side of Toronto's Jewish district. At Faywood he became good buddies with a young Rick Moranis and Dave Thomas. Already the pair were reputed to be writing comedy scripts, but Gary found himself turning to music. "I feel like it kinda chose me, in a way," he remarked. Gary had impressed his parents at an early age by picking out Nancy's practice pieces on the piano after listening to her playing. Of course, nobody expected him to be a musician when he grew up, least of all himself – Gary wanted to be a scientist. Wishing the kinds of lives on their children that they had been denied, his mother and father willed him to be a doctor. All the same, Gary badgered his folks for piano lessons of his own.

Meanwhile for Alex, the pressure to take up music came top down, first with viola lessons. How many eleven-year-old boys do you know that choose to take up viola?

Where Alex was up front and cocky on the surface, Gary was introspective and shy.

When the pair first became acquainted, neither expected to become close friends. Before long however, music became the fellows' mutual companion, and each found in it an outlet for their individuality. They each took particular inspiration from the UK Blues Invasion, comparing notes on performers such as Cream and The Yardbirds. Music was their first love, as Geddy put it, "My entire pre-adolescence and adolescence were spent with headphones on."

Bassist Chops

When he was a child, Geddy nearly chopped the top of his finger off. Through some twist of ironic fate, when the nail eventually grew back, it was extraordinarily tough, and could be used as a guitar or bass pick. Handy!

As quickly as he could, Alex extricated himself from the viola and set about badgering his parents for a guitar. His wish came true on Christmas Day 1965, when he unwrapped a "Kent"-branded Japanese import, classical guitar. Meanwhile Gary had borrowed an acoustic from a neighbour, and was starting to pick out chords and play along to the radio. Alex could barely wait for the new semester, the first of 1966, taking his new guitar into school as soon as he was allowed. From this point on, breaks between classes were spent sitting on the low walls outside the school, strumming tunes and picking out new songs, much to the delight of their friends and the disdain of their enemies (though, they conceded, it was rather cool!).

If the name sticks...

It was in Gary's second year at Fisherville that he picked up the name that he'd take for the rest of his days. Gary's friends called him Geddy, from his mother's pronunciation of his name in her strong Polish accent.

Alex and Gary's shared experience may well have led to the discovery of an equally shared determination, a joy in taking up a challenge and meeting it, driven by the work ethic that had been part of the furniture in both their houses. One school friend, Steve Schutt (who later became a national hockey player), recalled later: "You could tell even then, even before they were doing anything, that they were looking for something to pour their energies into." The idea of guitar lessons was floated by both sets of parents but neither boy considered it seriously; "I thought it was all 'Mary-had-a-little-lamb' stuff," said Alex. Catalysed by the guitar, the relationship between the pair developed without ever becoming an imposition.

It wasn't all some idyllic musical adolescence, however. For Gary, 1966 was marred by the death of his father, who had never fully recovered physically from his four years of internment. At the age of 12, Gary found he was the man about the house. It was time to grow up, and fast.

There was no one record that made Alex want to take up the guitar seriously, more a combination of Jimi Hendrix and The Who, his opinions cemented by Led Zeppelin's Jimmy Page. "I loved what he represented," Alex remarked over thirty years later. "I loved the looseness in his playing: it was structured, yet it walked along an edge, I found that so full of life and so exciting." The idea of dancing along the tightrope of structure, matched Alex's world view – fitting in was fine, but he could never resist expressing his individualism. Gary's motivations were different: where Alex saw guitar as a basis for experimentation and discovery, Gary found playing guitar was a way to calm his nervous disposition and helped him build his confidence. As he said: "Music was the thing I always came back to as something I felt I could do." Working in his mother's shop, before long Gary saved enough to afford a guitar of his own, "a cheap acoustic with palm trees painted on the front." Meanwhile Alex wasn't going to let his Kent classical guitar prevent him from following his electric heroes. Ever the improviser, he made repeated modifications, not least he sought to provide amplification by working the needle from his record player into the guitar's body. Eventually (and perhaps unsurprisingly) he broke the guitar, there's only so much Polyfilla even a cheap musical instrument can take.

Gary and Alex might have jammed together at school, but outside, they went their own separate ways. For Alex, this meant teaming up with his closest friend and neighbour, John Rutsey, something he had done since he first unwrapped the Kent. John had gone for the drums, borrowing a set before his parents found him a second-hand kit. Alex and John spent many hours practicing together in John's basement, joking and dreaming about what might be to come, playing the same half dozen songs over and over. Eventually they started to accept invitations to play at basement parties of their friends and neighbours.

It would have been rude not to.

The Third Man

Mostly Armless

Neil was a sucker for getting into scrapes when he was young. As a toddler on Violet Street he fell through one of his basement windows on his trike, breaking the glass. Once on holiday, he ate an entire bar of Ex-Lax. On another occasion he fell out of a tree and cut his arm open to the bone, so it was back to the hospital.

Clearly it did him no permanent damage.

Not seventy miles away, around the shore of Lake Ontario in the town of St Catharines lived a lad called Neil Peart, the latest in a few generations of Pearts. Neil was born on 12 September 1952 in Hamilton hospital, not far north from the family dairy farm near Hagersville, a wide open space in the middle of wide open spaces. Neil's parentage was hard working, farming types, descended from solid Welsh stock. By way of example, Neil would explain, "My Dad gave Mom a choice of a vacation in Bermuda or an automatic dishwasher, and she chose the dishwasher."

When Neil was 3 his mechanically-minded father, Glen, took a job as parts manager at the International Harvester farm machinery dealer Dalziel Equipment[2] in St Catharines. The Pearts moved to a duplex (that's a semi-detached house) on Violet Street in St Catharines, "a big old house" and his mom found work in a restaurant called The Flamingo. Shortly afterwards Neil gained a brother, Danny, and then a sister, Judy; little Nancy came a few years after that. Despite choosing urban life over farming, the Pearts never really lost touch with their roots. "I grew up in the suburbs, but at the same time, most of my relatives had farms," said Neil. "So every summer or holiday I'd be out at the farm."

Neil went to kindergarten at McArthur School and then he went on to Gracefield, a stone's throw from Violet Street. It was a picturebook childhood – of bike riding and apple-scrumping, hiking and swimming, exploration and family trips at the weekends. Neil's musical education also started from an early age: he would go to see Elvis films with Mom, and was fed a constant diet of Big Band Jazz from his father; he even had a foray into piano lessons, but they didn't stick. In 1962 Neil built his own crystal radio set, and a diet of more modern music started to feed his consciousness. His minor epiphany was when he heard a song called 'Chains' by an obscure artist – something about it just clicked. "It was no great classic or anything," he remarked, but it set in train his desire to be an active part of something musical.

Neil was never destined to be the physically strongest or the most co-ordinated kid, but he could hold a beat and he found himself drawn towards the rhythm section. Taking some inspiration from his Uncle Richard, already a drummer in a band, Neil picked up the "hitting things with sticks" bug when watching Sal Mineo playing jazz musician Gene Krupa in a Krupa biopic. "Big Town, here I come! Me and my drums! Me

and this crazy rhythm!" said Gene in the film, and pre-teen Neil wanted to do exactly the same. He was drawn to the exuberance as much as the discipline, and was fascinated how a harmonious relationship could be found between both.

That was it, Neil had found his mojo. He slapped, tapped, bashed and beat his way around the house for the next year or so, playing chopsticks on every available surface and his sister's playpen (no doubt to her utter delight) before his parents gave in to the tortuous tappety-tappings. On his thirteenth birthday, they paid for some drum lessons at the local Peninsula Conservatory of Music and gave him a practice pad and some sticks, drawing the line at a full kit. No parent wants to invite a drum kit though the door unnecessarily, so the aspiring percussionist was told he had to prove himself truly worthy before his parents would buy him one of his own. "I used to arrange magazines across my bed to make fantasy arrays of drums and cymbals, then beat the covers off them!" Neil laughed. From early on his teacher, Don George showed Neil techniques that were way beyond his reach, creating challenges that would continue to drive him long after the lessons had finished.

Though other oldstyle drummers, such as Buddy Rich and Billy Cobham, were also helping define Neil's ambitions, it was Keith Moon, the drummer in his then-favourite band The Who, who continued where Gene Krupa left off. "The Who was the first band that made me wanna play drums and write songs," he recalled later. Perhaps above all, it was the physicality of the drums that inspired Neil. "One of the things that I liked about drums from day one was that you hit them," he said. It wasn't just the sound of the drums, but the look – the kits came in various sparkling shades and Neil was fascinated by the whole visual and aural experience. "It was a physical relationship that I responded to right away."

When another full year of banging, clanging and haranguing had passed, by 1966 Neil's parents relented once more and bought him a Japanese-made Stewart kit, "in red sparkle". One has to feel sorry for the Peart family, not to mention the neighbours at this point – as Neil himself would say, "It's the drummer's curse – all your life no one wants to hear you practice". Not least Violet Street as he honed the technique of playing with the "butt-end" of the sticks, for extra oompf.

A passion for drumming wasn't the only thing Gene and Keith taught the young Canadian: both drummers lived on the edge, and crossed it frequently. With his death, Keith Moon's story in particular was a cautionary tale about the excesses of rock stardom, and where they could lead. Neil may have been a maverick, but he wasn't stupid.

While Neil's home life was a delight, his time at school was anything but. At the age of 12 Neil had gone to Lakeport High School two years early, straight in at Year 9. Immature and somewhat out of it relative to his peers, he was an obvious target for ridicule. The lessons Neil found a bit of a distraction, apart from English that is. "I was always in love with language," he said. Indeed, and not for the last time he would find solace in fiction, absorbing the words from the pages like a sponge.

Neil's own outward demeanour didn't help his case – he would never have been labelled an extrovert. He wasn't so much a loner, more a guy who knew his own way and wasn't going to compromise. "I really wanted to be an only child, I never liked to share," said Neil of the arrival of his siblings, describing a principle that he would apply again and again. He stood out from the crowd and wasn't prepared to muck in for the sake of it (not that he could, if he'd wanted to – at school dances, he was nicknamed "Birdman" due to his rather unconventional moves). Above all, he was in control of his emotions, a coiled spring to be released on his own terms. "When I was a teenager, I recognized that I had a bad temper, and set out consciously to control it and keep it back," he would say. All the same, part of him suffered for his stance. He dared have long hair ("below the ears, that is") and wear vibrant items of clothing, in an age where dulled-down conformity was essential to a quiet life. He didn't fit, and occasionally suffered as a consequence, but that only spurred him on to conform even less. Eventually he conformed only with the "freaks".

There was always the drumming. He pursued his hobby with a passion, over time building his skills and hooking up with others to play. By the age of 15 he played his "first public performance" at the school's annual variety show, as part of a three-piece called the Eternal Triangle. He even threw in a drum solo, and to his surprise and no little, coy delight, for the first time in his life he felt genuinely cool. It was all he needed to determine whether the path was good – if life held any options for him before, now there was only one. To the continued exasperation of his teachers, Neil spent more time thinking about drumming than the subject matter at hand.

Fortunately for Neil, his parents were right behind him. When Neil joined his first real band, Mumblin' Sumpthin', he convinced his dad to underwrite a $750 loan for a full Rogers drum kit. From then on, his leisure time was spent on the roads of Southern Ontario, as he would recall later. "We lived for that weekend gig at the church hall, the high school, the roller rink, and, later, so many late night drives in Econoline vans, sitting on

Too Far from Shore

A major event in Neil's adolescence was when he attempted to swim out to a floating raft a way away from the shore of Lake Ontario. He made it to the raft to find that bullies from another school (ironically where he went to kindergarten) refused to let him hold on… so he turned back. As he approached the shore, he found that he couldn't get there… it nearly killed him. Fortunately, a couple of his real friends were in the vicinity, and they came to his rescue, dragging him out of the water. Whenever things got too much in his later career, he would associate that with a sense of drowning…

Blowing Bubbles

When Neil was fourteen, he decided that working at the Lakeside amusement park on the shore of Lake Ontario was the thing to do, so off he went. He recalls how he used to sit and watch kids on the trampolines when there was nobody approaching his Bubble Game stall. Unfortunately it was Neil's job to get people to approach his stall, so before long he was fired.

the amps all the way home from towns like Mitchell, Seaforth, Elmira, and even as far as Timmins." There was nothing that he wanted to do more in life than this. Soon afterwards Neil packed in the drum lessons, but the discipline was set, and he would practice two hours every day. "It was no sacrifice, it was a pleasure," he said later. "I'd come home every day from school and play along to the radio." As Neil left, teacher Don admitted he was impressed by the lad, commenting that he was one of the few pupils he had seen that had the potential to make it as a pro.

When Mumblin' Sumpthin' slipped apart, Neil tied up with a band called Wayne and The Younger Generation, which changed its name to The Majority shortly after. "All the first bands I played in were blue-eyed soul bands," he said. "All of us grew up playing 'In The Midnight Hour'." After a few attempted break-ups, The Majority came to an end for a final time and Neil was without a band again. One of the best bands in the area was J.R. Flood, and Neil began lobbying the members (apart from the drummer, of course) to convince them that he'd do a better job. Surprisingly to Neil, they tried him out and agreed to go with him. J.R. Flood's music wasn't all standard blues, it included some epic tunes such as the 8-minute 'You Don't Have To Be A Polar Bear To Live In Canada'.

Soon after Neil had joined the band, at the age of 17 Neil talked his parents into letting him call school a day and go into music full-time, ostensibly for a trial period. Free of the shackles of education and drifting ever further from conformism, he learned the character-building effects of travelling on a public bus to band practices with "a frizzy, obligatory Hendrix perm, long black cape and purple shoes."

Making Waves: Neil with J.R. Flood

Neil wrote his first lyrics with J.R. Flood and had his first experience of working in recording studios, not least Terry Brown's Toronto Sound Studios, over on the other side of the lake. At the weekends, Neil helped his father back at Dalziel's Equipment. Neil had made his choices, and would take the consequences until he chose to move on.

He was that kind of kid.

In The Basement Bars

To say there was a great deal going on musically in the late sixties is an understatement in the extreme. In particular, many bands that had forged their reputation on folk blues were now pushing the boundaries of their art. A combination of drawing on new influences (not all of them musical), experimenting with more complex arrangements and exploiting increasingly powerful amplification technologies led to the arrival of day-tripping psychedelia and its more seriously-minded companion, progressive rock. The Beatles and the Beach Boys, The Who and Frank

Zappa's Mothers of Invention, Cream and the Grateful Dead were leading the musical revolution on each side of the Atlantic, and the message was clear: this is not stuff you want your parents to listen to. "The music of the early sixties was safe, the messages were just on the border of rebellion," says Rush's keyboard technician Tony Geranios, who was working the circuit at the time. "Later there were real messages to unite youth into some kind of awareness. You could see a lot of questioning, some violent, some downright criminal." Agrees Toronto-based photographer Bruce Cole, "We all grew up in an era of rebellion."

Old hands like singer-songwriter and Rush collaborator Mendelson Joe felt that musically at least, they had seen it all before. "The sixties were relevant but the seventies were just the commercialization and regurgitation of what made money in the 1960s," he says. In Canada as in the USA, for newcomers this 'regurgitation' meant there was a structure for their non-conformity. This offered an opportunity for angsty youths not to drop out, but to create something on their own terms; any band starting out had a potential road map and an understanding that they might actually become something. It was a tempting vision for any teenager, and the Willowdale boys were not immune.

In the spring of 1968, Gary – sorry, Geddy joined his first band. While he might have started as a rhythm guitarist it wasn't long before fate, or at least the band's original bassist, decided to play his own part in Geddy's destiny: he quit. The new boy was "offered" the bassist's position, and his mother agreed to loan him the money for a Japanese "Conora" brand bass guitar, as long as he paid it off – 35 dollars in all. Despite her outward acceptance, Mom was none too happy at the thought of Geddy becoming a musician, but still, he was young, it could be just a phase. As Geddy moved over to playing bass, he discovered a new set of heroes in the shape of Cream's Jack Bruce and John Entwhistle from The Who, and Jack Cassidy who played with Jefferson Airplane. "What I liked about Jack Bruce was that his sound was distinctive," said Geddy. "It wasn't boring, and it wasn't typical. And he was very busy. He wouldn't keep his place, which I really liked a lot. He was obtrusive, which I like in a bass player." Like many of his peers, Geddy started to grow his hair, rebellion sprouting from the top of his head. "We were very typically suburban," said Geddy later, "what you'd call weekend warriors. I guess we thought that we were kind of cooler than the next guy, but we probably weren't." Confirms Bruce Cole, "They were middle class guys, as opposed to starving musicians – they all had a family fallback position." Indeed – not everyone had parents willing to cough up a loan for an instrument.

Meanwhile, fifteen-year-old Alex had teamed up with neighbour John Rutsey to form a band of sorts, which they called The Projection. "We were horrible," said Alex later, recalling the dozen or so songs they used to play at their friends' parties. "We just kept repeating the songs during the course of the night until everybody would leave!" Alex had his own "Conora" electric guitar, bought for him by his parents back at Christmas a couple of years before. It had to look like Eric Clapton's guitar, "like a Gretsch Country Gentleman," explained Alex. He'd also acquired a Fuzz Face distortion pedal, but he had to borrow an amplifier from friends. "Even before I could really play guitar, I had an effect," he said, setting the scene for his love of gadgetry. For home practice, Alex wired his parents' TV to take his guitar and pedal as input. "That sounded pretty lousy, but with the Fuzz Face, I thought I was hot stuff!"

Geddy and Alex would still play together from time to time, particularly as Geddy's next purchase was an amplifier – a Traynor twin-15 guitar amp with a Bassmaster head unit. Back at Geddy's place after school, they re-created their own British Blues

Invasion. Recalled Geddy, "Alex would pretend he was Eric Clapton, I would pretend I was Jack Bruce, and we'd play 'Spoonful' for twenty minutes." Alex played to an extent that would put even an obsessive to shame. He played every available minute of every single evening, taking breaks only to eat and, if absolutely necessary, to rush his homework. Somehow he also found time for his new girlfriend, Charlene McNichol.

The Projection took its influences from the heavier end of the blues spectrum, such as Jimi Hendrix and Led Zeppelin. By the summer they were joined by Jeff Jones who took on the bass duties and added rudimentary vocals. Jeff was an established player, working with a band called Lactic Acid at the same time as joining the pair of hopefuls.

Nobody liked the name 'The Projection', and the need to find a better one was becoming ever more urgent. "The bass player in my jazz trio was in charge of a drop-in program at a High School in Toronto and part of his responsibilities was to arrange entertainment," explains local man and Rush cover artist Paul Weldon. "Geddy Lee and his friends went to this drop-in centre and when he announced that he had a $50 budget, they said they would like to play. He said okay, but what do you call yourselves? They said they didn't know." So he explained he needed a name for the promo posters, and sent the youngsters on their way. Inspiration came quickly: after several rejected ideas, an off-the-cuff remark from John's older brother Bill Rutsey caught everyone's attention. "Why not 'Rush'?" he suggested. While the fifteen-year-olds might have joked about the drug connotations, they mostly thought it was just a good name.

So Rush it was.

In early September of 1968 the newly named band was offered the opportunity to play a regular slot on Friday nights at a coffee bar for teenagers, in the basement of the local United Church on Kenneth Avenue. The Coff-In, as it was known, charged 25 cents admission to Rush's first date, on 18 September. The band had ten songs in their repertoire, which they repeated throughout the evening to the thirty or so people who had bothered to turn up.

The gig brought in a meagre 10 dollars, but nothing could suppress the feeling of excitement felt by John and Alex. Jeff didn't share the enthusiasm however: he had seen the band as a bit of fun and he was already over-committed to other projects. Indeed, Jeff only ever played that one show at the Coff-In: the following week he failed to turn up, having "gotten himself drunk," according to Geddy, who was called up at 4 o'clock that afternoon. A worried Alex offered (nay, begged) Geddy to play that evening. How could he refuse?

Geddy had two hours with the others before the gig to agree a dozen songs they could all play. Fortunately, Rush's repertoire incorporated the John Mayall and Cream tracks he had been playing already with Alex, together with a few bluesy numbers that he could jam along to. The threesome clicked: by the end of the evening Geddy was invited to join the band, and Jeff was awarded the same level of support that he had given. The changes were not that much of a deal, to either party – it wasn't as if anyone was about to make it big.

As time passed invitations came up to play at high school functions, sometimes for slightly better money, with long-suffering mothers driving the youths to gigs with all the equipment in the trunk. "We wanted to play every chance we got," says Alex. Over time, the band built a relationship with Toronto's parks and recreation department, and picked up gigs that way. The threesome slipped into what could be called a routine, with school during the day and gigs at night, the regular slot at the Coff-in punctuating the frequent journeys out of town. One of the regulars at the Coff-In was a green, yet determined lad of 16 years named Ray Danniels, "a local street-type, hustling kind of a guy," according to Geddy. Only a year older than Alex and Geddy, Ray had quit school and set up an artists agency called Music Shop.

Alex was forever experimenting with instruments, which he would buy, borrow or rent for the purpose. As the gigs continued, he was able to save enough money for his

The line-up with Mitch Bossi

first "real" guitar, which he bought new – a Gibson ES-335 in Tobacco Sunburst, together with a Marshall amp and a few pedals, supplemented on a regular basis by borrowed equipment to support his experimental habits. As 1968 came to a close, Alex asked his friend Nancy Young if he could borrow her brother Lindy's Gibson Firebird guitar. When the band discovered Lindy's talents not only on the guitar, but also keyboards, vocals, drums and harmonica, they quickly invited him in to complete the line-up. Slightly older, he also brought a certain amount of experience to the band.

At the same time, Rush voted for a name change to Hadrian, more suggestive of the loud, solid, hard-rock edge they were delivering live. Ray Danniels offered to book a few gigs for Hadrian, and would leave no stone unturned in promotion of the newly named band – borrowing a motorbike to go and put up posters.

Hadrian's reputation grew quickly. By March the following year the numbers at the Coff-In had grown to the hundreds, and these were people that were coming expressly to see the band. "We built up our own little following," said Geddy. Income had increased accordingly – the wages had been increased to 35 dollars.

If only things could have stayed that simple, but they were teenagers. John, who was undoubtedly the coolest (but also the moodiest) band member, didn't think Geddy fitted with the profile of the band. By May, the drummer convinced Alex that they could do without Geddy, suggesting another friend, Joe Perna in his place. With little aplomb Geddy was kicked out. Unperturbed – well, a little perturbed – Geddy wasted no time in setting up his own band, "with a little more of a blues profile." He named it Ogilvie, but quickly renamed it Judd; by July, Lindy had left Hadrian and joined him because Ray was having more success booking Judd than Hadrian. Joe Perna left as well, and Alex and John were left with little choice but to wind up their own band. There was little opportunity for Geddy to gloat, as Judd wasn't to fare much better. By September 1969, it had broken up too – Lindy was going to college, amongst other reasons.

Forever Young

The Lindy period was not totally without merit. Geddy asked Lindy's sister Nancy for a date, and shortly afterwards they were going out.

Seven years later they would be married.

Sometimes, they all realised, its best to stick with what works. Rush was reformed in its post-Jeff line up, with Alex, John and Geddy. Who needs keyboards anyway – the previously spurned vocalist/bassist was welcomed back with open arms and a sheepish grin.

The trio set out again with renewed vigour and no little determination. "We were brought up to realize that if you want to get anywhere, you're going to have to work for it," Alex once remarked, so knuckle down they did.

Ray Danniels was quick to volunteer his services as Rush manager, an offer that the threesome accepted gladly. All four were competent, ambitious, and unafraid of hard work, and it wasn't hard to see that both sides stood to gain. "Ray and the guys were philosophically aligned," explains DJ Don Shafer, who knew Ray prior to Rush. "Despite the fact he started very young, he always understood what was necessary." Immediately, Ray put his back into finding some bookings for the newly reformed band. His scope was limited – the sixteen-year-olds were not allowed in the bars of Toronto – but he was undaunted. "He was an entrepreneur," says Don. "He figured out the basics of how to book venues and fill halls. There were no schools to go to, you had to be adept at learning the business." From Ray's perspective, he didn't know what else he'd do. "If I didn't succeed with this I didn't even have the education to be a postman," Ray said later. Don recalls the pair of them sitting in the back seat of an old car, talking about the future. "He was focused on putting his heart and soul into it," says Don.

The bookings came, the rehearsals continued, the repertoire grew and gigs started to happen at a gentlemanly pace. Alex and Geddy would get picked up from school, stop off to get John and take off towards a town in the middle distance, to play a set list consisting mostly of covers – "the only way we could get hired," according to Geddy. The band was accompanied to gigs by Ian Grandy, the band's first crew member, who helped with the drums (the rest of the band could cope with the guitars) as well as organising and working the sound and lights during the show.

Over time a routine developed, bringing with it a steady musical progression towards harder rock. Cream was out, Led Zeppelin was in, and Geddy was quick to adapt his singing to match. After experimenting with different vocal styles, he trialled a falsetto that was immediately unique, raunchy, exciting – everything the boys wanted to distinguish themselves from the R'n'B masses. The desire to do something fresh and exciting was greater than that to make money – and if Led Zep could make it on their own terms, why couldn't Rush? The trio even started to write their own songs, all three contributing to what would become the blues number 'Losing Again' and the rockier 'In The Mood', which would be inserted into the set at appropriate intervals. It was a clever strategy – keep it relevant to the newcomers, but give them something unique – and it paid off. Not everything made it to posterity: songs such as 'Child Reborn', 'Keep In Line' and 'Run Willie Run' were all trialled live, never to be recorded.

One thing nobody felt comfortable about was writing the lyrics. These largely fell on John's shoulders, though he never felt anything he wrote was particularly good. Still, the lyrics were good enough to fit the music, and for Geddy and Alex, that was all that mattered.

As the sixties became the seventies, the band had a growing reputation on the teenage coffee house circuit and was playing a significant number of its own songs[3], with additional titles like 'Morning Star', 'Margarite', 'Feel So Good' and 'Garden Road'. The newer tracks offered an opportunity for the band to further distinguish themselves by adding more complexity to the music, which wasn't to the taste of everyone in the audience – the high school crowds would be a trifle baffled by the occasional, experimental piece, incorporating time changes and a variety of dissonant sounds, not all of which were necessarily good. Rush was determined to find its own unique way, and so the band struggled on, in the knowledge that wherever it was going, it was not the same road as the mainstream bands. This did niggle a bit, particularly with John, but he indulged Geddy and Alex. He'd dropped out from school, by this point, and didn't really have anything else he wanted to do.

As Alex was turning 17, suddenly and unexpectedly, things got serious. Really serious in fact, as he found out from his girlfriend Charlene McNichol, that he was to become a father. Alex took this news on the chin and was determined to ensure he did the right thing, moving in with Charlene as soon as they could find a place. Justin Zivojinovich was born in March 1971. For Alex at least, this additional responsibility served only to increase his determination to make it work.

One month before Justin's arrival, the band decided to try out a second guitarist, Mitch Bossi. He lasted three months before going the same way as Jeff Jones, deciding for himself that the others were all taking things too seriously. As he left, those who remained became even more of the opinion that three was the better number.

Still, there were bigger things afoot. About the same time as Mitch was saying his goodbyes, the legal drinking age in Ontario was dropped from 21 to 18. This could not have been better timed for Geddy, Alex and John, who were all having their 18th birthdays at the time – Alex and Geddy's birthdays were in July and August. The potential opportunity was huge – "In Toronto in the early 70s there was probably a club on every other downtown corner that had a trio or a live band," says Bruce Cole. When Ray got onto the case, he found that the bookings didn't come easy, but when they did the money was better, the audiences older and the venues bigger. By the summer, Rush was starting to play in Toronto's many bars, getting their first gig at The Gasworks on Yonge Street in the middle of town. At the time, The Gasworks was the place to be seen, as well as heard[4]. "Everyone played at The Gasworks," says co-founder of the Orbit Room, Tim Notter, who was an early follower of the band and a friend of Alex. "We were thrilled! Alex – when he was nineteen, he was fabulous!"

The eventful times required some big decisions. The band members agreed that they should make a proper go of it, so Geddy and Alex quit school completely to concentrate on their music. Their parents were dubious, but the young men were unrepentant and excited at the new opportunities. "All of a sudden it wasn't just two gigs at weekends, it was six gigs a week, five sets a night!" Geddy's mother in particular had been a little distressed when he said he was going to go with the music thing, rather than going on to college. Alex's folks were a little more understanding, especially given his personal circumstances.

Opportunities were not as frequent as everyone hoped, and

Classic Rock

In 1972, Alex decided to go back on his opinions and take up guitar lessons with another friend of his, Eliot Goldner, under tutor Eli Kassner. The lessons lasted six months, until Eliot had a motorbike accident which took him in and out of hospital for the best part of two years. This made lessons difficult... In the end they just had to give up, but it gave Alex the classical grounding he needed to build on in the future. "When I started the classical, I had to use my baby finger in stretches and pulls. So I developed a lot more strength and agility in the finger: I even have calluses on the end of it. And it's given me the ability to stretch more and add some interesting notes."

the bar audiences were as tough as they ever were, particularly in the north of the state. "They don't care if you do the greatest original material in the world if their ears haven't heard it before," Geddy recalled. "They just want to get drunk and hear their favourite tunes." But, he admitted later, "Our compositions were probably too strange for them." There was also the volume issue – on one occasion, the band were ejected from a club because the barmaids couldn't hear the beer orders! Not without reason, the summer of 1971 was nicknamed "the dead summer" for the band.

Despite Ray's cajoling for the boys to play more popular songs and the clear difficulties they were having in getting a gig, they stuck to their musical guns. Ray was frequently frustrated by their single-mindedness, says Don Shafer, "Ray picked up the band because nobody else would," and the agent didn't always enjoy the experience. "Without a doubt they were the hardest act I had to sell," he remarked. "Sometimes nobody came to see them, sometimes the gyms were packed. And that's what convinced me they were the ones who could happen if anybody could." Ray booked the band in any and every venue that would have them – in his opinion, the most important thing was to get out there and play, helped out by friends and neighbours who would drive them. On one occasion, the band were taken on a 600-kilometer round trip to Sudbury for a 35-dollar gig, though they could earn up to $350 for some gigs – such was their desire to take every opportunity that presented itself. As things developed, Liam Birt was taken on as an additional crew member to assist Ian Grandy.

Finally, at the end of 1971 the band managed to get a regular downtown slot, at the Abbey Road pub in Toronto: it paid $1000 weekly, so the guys had some guarantee of income. Some of the money was put towards an Econoline van to accommodate the ever-increasing piles of gear. While things were working out, this was clearly not going to be an easy ride to the top. Nor did anyone expect it to be – the feet of the band members, as well as the growing support structure, Ray, Liam and Pegi Cecconi, Ray's assistant, were all firmly planted on the ground. "This thing came from the ground up," says Don Shafer. "It was not a formula – it took really talented people to build the brand. The finest enduring qualities of the organisation and band – they were all genuine down-to-earth people who never lost contact with their audience."

On 17 June 1972, Ray scored a gig for the band at the Grande Ballroom in Detroit, playing alongside The Rumor and Spangus Marangus. Back home meanwhile, to make ends meet, Geddy worked in his mother's shop and did some painting work, while Alex helped his father on plumbing jobs and held a job at a gas station. They even wrote a song about it – 'Working Man' chronicled the humdrum existence of the blue collar worker, seen from the perspective of someone who wanted something better[5].

Carnaby Blues

Just as Alex, Geddy and John were settling into some kind of a routine, Neil Peart was doing anything but. J.R. Flood's time in the local limelight was not leading to a record deal, but nobody in the band seemed to mind except Neil. Meanwhile, the influences on the young drummer were growing in complexity and depth. Modern, progressive drummers such as Michael Giles of King Crimson, Phil Collins of Genesis and Bill Bruford of Yes shared one facet with his previous heroes – these were all real musicians, practiced in their art, and they wanted to share their virtuosity any way they could. As he would comment, "it was really the music that mattered and the idea of formulae for making music... was totally alien."

Bad Timing

"When I sat down behind the borrowed drumset, the keyboard player announced, 'this first tune is in seven,' which meant absolutely nothing to me at the time, but I kept quiet and just tried to join in when they started playing. The keyboard player was kind and patient, and said that I seemed to have a good 'feel' for odd times, but they were looking for someone more experienced. I was crestfallen and humbled, but from then on I set out to learn everything about playing in odd times, and followed my own advice, 'Go home and practice.'"

Neil Peart, interview with Zildjian 2003

Neil's ambitions led him to think further afield than his compatriots, and his heart yearned to get closer to the action. By early 1971, as J. R. Flood was coming to an end, Neil realised he was ready to try his luck on the other side of the Atlantic. In July he bought a ticket and flew to the UK, leaving behind a girlfriend and taking only his savings, his drum kit and his record collection. He'd already contacted his childhood friend Brad French, who was a welcome point of contact. London in the early seventies was the place to be, to start bands, to listen to music, to meet and influence people. At least, you would have thought so. For Neil, things didn't quite work out that way.

On arrival, Neil was met by his mate from home, Brad, who offered him a place to crash at his bedsit in New Barnet, North London. Neil spent the first few weeks painstakingly visiting record companies and management agencies, only to be shown the door on each occasion. Undaunted, he started working through the small ads in the music papers. He landed a few auditions, and even picked up some "unglamorous" session work, but it was never really enough to pay the bills. After a month, he started to run out of money and found despondency starting to set in – he found the attitude of many British musos to be snobbish in the extreme, and the frequent rejections took their toll. Some solace was found in books, as Neil would fill his commutes with literature of all descriptions. Not least science fiction, with the futuristic trilogy *'Fall of The Towers'* by Samuel R. Delaney re-igniting a passing interest from childhood. "I grew up in the suburbs and it was all pretty prosaic and dull, so I started getting interested in all those kinds of things just in the belief that there must be a more interesting world out there," he said.

A chance meeting at Piccadilly Circus with another acquaintance from back home (Sheldon Atos) led to Neil landing a job, in a souvenir shop at Carnaby Street[6] called Gear. More importantly than the money (though it helped), this was Neil's first foothold in a social network that fitted with his drumming aspirations. A series of firm friendships were forged working in the trendiest street in Britain, punctuated by initiations into a variety of uncontrolled substances that were available at the time. It was also the first experience, for the small town boy, of having openly gay people as friends (one of whom, Ellis, would become the Hero of 'Nobody's Hero', when he died of AIDS in the late 80s). It was only 20 pounds a week, but it was a job. Finally, Neil's new-found connections resulted in the opportunity to join a band, called English Rose. In October 1971 he quit his job and went on the road.

Despite Neil's previous touring experience, this was not what he had expected at all. One by one, all of Neil's daydreams of glamour, making it or even musical integrity were quashed as the band's story unfolded. Neil learned that all their equipment had been stolen from another band. "Even their van was stolen," he remembered. "I had to play it cool, just nod and say nothing." Using the "borrowed" van, English Rose used to head out of London for gigs in the north of England, with Neil squashed between pieces of equipment for hours at a time. After a month or so, the work dried up and so did the gigs, leaving Neil to rely on the generosity of other people in the band. The equipment manager used to slip him a fiver from time to time, which Neil accepted gratefully even in the knowledge that he used to "do over" petrol stations.

Fortunately, he refused Neil's desperate offer of assistance.

Neil had a short lived gig with "Heaven" ("turned out to be hell…"), went home for Christmas with a ticket paid for by Gran, and had a rethink.

When Neil returned to Britain after the break, he took the offer of a post from Bud, his old boss at Gear. True learning experiences are rarely pleasant, but there were a few good things that came out of Neil's sojourn. Not least a Persian co-worker at the gift shop, Ahmed, introduced him to a piece of music called 'Movements'. This included playing by one of London's most versatile drummers at the time[7], Harold Fisher, whom (without knowing who it was), Neil found to be an utter inspiration. Neil found some solace in revisiting his dad's music, "the big band stuff like Duke Ellington, Count Basie and Frank," buying his own copies of albums from a second-hand shop such as 'Sinatra At The Sands' and listening to them on headphones because the speakers were so poor ("because we were so poor").

Reading offered a continued escape. On his way from work one day, Neil procured a copy of 'The Fountainhead' by Ayn Rand, from a tobacconist in the tube station. Remembering Ayn Rand as a pretentious read from his school days, Neil found the book to be a revelation, as he explained a few years later. "For me it was a confirmation of all the things I'd felt as a teenager," he said. "It is simply impossible to say all men are brothers or that all men are created equal – they are not. Your basic responsibility is to yourself." In Rand's character Howard Roark, himself loosely based on architect Frank Lloyd Wright, Neil found an antihero that he could relate to absolutely, the ambitious individual who had no concept of compromise. The wake-up call coincided with Neil's discovery that the only person he could play in life, and in his drumming, was himself – and not any of his drumming idols. "All I wanted to do was get in a band that would play some Who songs so I could wail like Keith Moon did" he explained. "When I finally got in a band that was playing Who songs, it was all so crazy that it didn't suit my character. My personality demanded structure and organization, and… it wasn't me." One other thing Neil learned from Keith Moon was that drumming needed to be visual as well as aural. As such, he worked on twirling his sticks and flicking them in the air – it was part of the show.

Things were finally stabilising for Neil, not least his finances. In the spring of 1972, he and Brad moved to a larger flat near Wimbledon, and Neil was even able to splash out on a new hi-fi. He continued to look for gigging opportunities, and had varying levels of success: a band called Music came and went, and Neil managed to hook up with the jazz-prog combo Seventh Wave, but nothing he tried ever came to much. Neil found the honesty of such bands refreshing. "Most acts have the attitude that they won't get anywhere anyway, so they might as well do what they want and to hell with it. Groups have nothing to lose from being as crazy as possible, or from being themselves." He also saw his fair share of ego issues, which as a developing individualist, he could live without.

Despite these insights, by the end of 1972, Neil remained disappointed: if pots of gold existed at this end of the rainbow, they had eluded him. If there's one place it's not good to be destitute, thought Neil to himself, it's London. Feeling "sadder and wiser", he once again came home for Christmas, but this time it was for good. "I was searching for fame and fortune. It wasn't there," he said, but he recognised the value of the experience. "It was worth more than success at that time."

Neil's return was accompanied by some big decisions. Drumming as a hobby was fine, he thought, but a career as a professional musician? No thanks: "I decided I would be a semi-pro musician for my own entertainment, would play music that I liked to play, and wouldn't count on it to make my living." In the spring of 1973 Neil took a short-term job back with his father at Dalziel Equipment, and found an apartment of his own. Before long he was also working at the St Catharines' branch of Sam The Record Man, where he worked with colleague and friend John Fillion, as well as Keith and Steve Taylor. Their younger sister Jackie also worked on the tills for a while, and caught his eye.

As a self-proclaimed "adolescent car nut", Neil graduated from building models of cars to owning them, buying first an MGB and a Mercedes ("Neil could never drive a car that was too big," says friend Andrew MacNaughtan). By his early twenties he was sharing a house with the Taylor brothers, in the countryside just near St Catharines. Neil's feet were well and truly back on his home ground, but he couldn't put off playing the drums for long. A couple of members of J. R. Flood had formed a band called Bullrush, but they had no need for a drummer; instead Neil hooked up with a few local musicians to help re-form the semi-pro band Hush[8], with Brian Collins and Paul Lauzon on guitar, Bob Luciani on bass and Bob's brother Gary, on vocals. They played a variety of seventies blues-rock covers, including The Who, Zappa and Genesis.

Then, a Toronto-based manager called Vic Wilson turned up at Dalziel Equipment for a chat, and everything changed again.

If At First...

By the end of 1972 things were coming together for Rush on the live circuit, through stamina and the continued determination of Ray Danniels and his cohorts. The band had a growing following, and were deriving income from up to five sets a night; they had gone from being a me-too covers band with a bit of sparkle, to defining for themselves a heavier, louder, and altogether more original sound. Each band member was able, confident and accomplished enough to consider himself a musician, not just a player. Furthermore, the threesome had enough material, and had nearly saved enough money, to make a record.

Despite the lack of previous experience, everyone involved was well aware of what they wanted to achieve next, and the steps required. The goal was simple – to achieve a recording contract. This was as true for Ray as it was for the band members, thinks Bruce Cole, recruited at the time to capture the essence of the band on film. "Their manager had the vision that they wanted to be a super-band, from the beginning," says Bruce. This vision was as shared as the approach they took to achieving it. "From the time I got involved, the band members treated it as a business. These guys were serious about being musicians from day one. They did the right things in a conscious manner... they just weren't playing in some club and somebody came along and said, wow, you guys are great, I'm gonna sign you up and make you millionaires. Every band that starts has a big vision, but they approached it, not from a rock and roll, 'lets get laid tonight after the set,' point of view. They were going back to their wives, they were musicians."

The one thing they didn't all share was the music itself. John was in many ways as ambitious as Geddy and Alex, but his musical tastes were far more mundane, as were his plans. John wanted to make it onto the Toronto circuit and keep going for as long as possible, but this didn't fit with where Geddy, Alex and Ray wanted to take the music or the band. For now however, it was so all much speculation – for short term at least, the aspirations were the same.

In a makeshift studio known as The Sound Horn at Toronto's Rochdale College, engineer Bill Bryant recorded the band playing an album's worth of two-track demos. Recorded straight after a gig when the band was already warmed up, most of the songs took only a couple of takes to get down on tape. Copies of the resulting demo were sent to record labels, only to be met with universal rejection by the Canadian musical establishment. Unsurprising perhaps, given that tastes in Canadian recorded music were still catching up with what was going on in the local bars, never mind with what was happening on the other side of the pond. The "loud is good" philosophy of heavy rock might have filtered onto FM, but it was still a few tributaries short of the mainstream. Furthermore, however diverse their claimed influences, Rush did take a number of cues from Led Zeppelin. Alex was listening to little else than Jimmy Page at the time, and Geddy's piercing vocals drew inevitable comparisons with Robert Plant. As Geddy might remark at the time, "oooooh, yeeah yeeah!"

There was little for it but to keep plugging away on the live circuit, where things were going from strength to strength. According to Bruce Cole, the band would work on their act like no other band he'd seen. "I used to go in to shoot Rush during rehearsals because it was very difficult shooting them live," says Bruce. "They just got crazy during their rehearsal as if they we actually doing a live show. They would not only practice their music, they would practice their stage presence. I never thought that much about it, that's just the way they did it." They even went as far as the glittering costumes that were de rigeur in bands that had made it, but weren't quite so common in the downtown bars. "We had the whole schmear," recalled Geddy later. "Shiny clothes, big shoes. I see pictures way back then every once in a while and it's pretty embarrassing stuff. We'll write it off to the exuberance of youth." Embarrassing it may be in hindsight, but it worked. According to *Rolling Stone* journalist John Swenson, "Rush built up a reputation as one of the best live bands in the Toronto area, and became a bona fide underground sensation." Agrees Bob Roper, who was about to play his own part in the Rush story, "The band were workaholics and put a lot of energy and professionalism into their performances. They were loud and aggressive and got a huge and enthusiastic response from their audiences most shows."

It was early 1973. To help with the ever-increasing workload of managing Rush's live activities, as well as those of his growing roster of bands[9], Ray joined forces with a former competitor, Vic Wilson. At the time, Vic was running a management agency called Concept 376. Ray and Vic both sold their enterprises to form SRO Productions. SRO stood for Standing Room Only, both a reference to the amount of office space Vic and Ray were juggling with, and an indication of the band and management's approach to "passengers" – there was to be no room for hangers on. At the start, Rush was one of SRO's least successful bands, but it was also the most unique, and as such it had the most potential. Ray and Vic wasted no time in inviting US-side booking agencies to see what the band could do, in the hope of winning support slots with more popular acts. One such was the ebullient, charismatic Ira Blacker of New York-based booking and management agency, American Talent International (ATI). "They were earning 150 bucks in a Toronto bar, doing some pseudo Zeppelin thing," recalls Ira.

Buoyed by the live roster and unperturbed at the failure of the demo, Ray and his new partner Vic convinced the band it was time to put a single together. In the absence of a record deal, SRO formed its own label – Moon Records – for the purpose and borrowed money to finance its first pressing (not least from Geddy's stalwart mother).

It was suggested that a cover song would be safest, rather than one of the band's weirder compositions – the boys agreed to record the Buddy Holly number 'Not Fade Away', with a Rush original, 'You Can't Fight It' on the reverse. The single was recorded at Eastern Sound Studios in Toronto in the spring of 1973, under Englishman David Stock who worked at the time for SRO. David was an established engineer – though admittedly his experience was more in radio jingles than rock songs.

Several hundred copies were pressed, and never-say-die Danniels took it around the record labels and sent it to the radio stations, but to no avail. Despite a distribution deal with London Records, the remaining copies were sold mainly after gigs for the princely sum of 69 cents.

The pressure was starting to show, not least on Rush's drummer. That summer, John took some time out from the band. This was ostensibly through illness – he had suffered from diabetes throughout his childhood – but it wasn't helped by his discomfort at his situation. While John would have been quite happy to continue down the heavy blues line as part of a jobbing band, it was becoming clearer by the week that the others had different, higher aspirations. For Geddy and Alex, it was difficult to make out whether there was writing on the wall, but it was clear that John was hitting it. The pair started to think about whether, and how he could be replaced.

There was too much momentum for anyone to change anything in particular. After a couple of weeks to recover, John came back, but the unease hadn't gone away.

Ray and Vic's efforts nurturing relationships with US promoters were starting to bear fruit, and their second foray outside Canada was to be the biggest gig yet for the boys. In September 1973, the band played a festival at The Brewery in East Lansing, Michigan to 3,000 people. It may have been small in festival terms, but to the threesome it was immense. In the first of many bizarre pairings, on October 27 Rush played to a 1,200 strong Toronto crowd at the Victory Burlesque Theatre, in support of the New York Dolls. These were very exciting times indeed, and there was evidence enough that even if the band hadn't yet made it, it had all the potential to do so.

While the band was making it live, there was still no record deal on the table. Ever in the shadow of the label-heavy US, Canada wasn't the best of places to be starting a new musical movement. Its recording industry consisted of a number of small, independent labels, jostling for space with the subsidiaries of US-based companies who were geared towards promoting US-based rock rather than taking the risk of prowling for new Canadian talent.

As the nights of 1973 started to shorten, Ray decreed

that if the single wouldn't cut the ice with the labels, then he might stand more chance with an album. David Stock was again asked to produce, and they booked five days of studio time at Eastern Sound. Money was tight – the band could not afford to break from the gig schedules, which were an essential source of funding for both studio time and equipment rental[10].

Nobody had been happy with the live lyrics, and John had been working on improved versions for some of the studio versions. At the last minute before the band went into the studio however, he tore them up and threw them away rather than show them to the others. It is unclear whether this was through a loss of confidence, a fit of pique or both but he was later to regret the action. "It was an incredibly selfish, stupid thing to do," he said. For the others, writing new lyrics was just one more thing to fit into the schedules.

During the day, the band would catch up on sleep, rehearse and gig, and when they had finished they would head to the studio for the late night slot, which could be booked at a quarter rate. The band would carry on until the wee hours, recording songs and writing lyrics for the next batch before dismantling the equipment and going home again, ready to do it all again the next day. It might have been gruelling, but it was also "very, very exciting," according to Alex. The first song to be recorded was the cover 'Not Fade Away', which was to open the album. The band worked through 'Need Some Love', 'Take A Friend', 'Here Again', 'What You're Doing', 'In The Mood', 'Before And After' and 'Working Man'. Already recorded for the single, 'You Can't Fight It' was also to be included in the running order.

At the end of the sessions, they listened and found that it was... well, a bit poor really. David's lack of appropriate production experience, coupled with the understandable haste of recording and mixing, resulted in the initial mixes lacking any of the vibrancy of the live performances. The raw edge had been well and truly blunted, and some of the tracks didn't sound like they'd ever be album material. What to do?

Clearly, there was more to engineering than the band and management had imagined. Vic suggested bringing in the "teabag" Englishman Terry Brown, a producer who had cut his teeth on such popular bands of sixties London as Procul Harum and Manfred Mann, and who now part-owned the highly reputed Toronto Sound Studios. "Trained in Britain, he was ahead of the curve of what was going on in Canada," says fellow producer Paul Northfield. "His studio was probably one of the best in Toronto at the time and certainly he would probably be one of the most experienced rock recording guys at the time."

Terry was delighted to help out. "Vic said, we've got these boys, they've been working the graveyard shift over at another studio," says Terry. "They've got this tape and they don't know what the hell to do with it, and we need to cut some more songs, so can I send them over to see you?" Ray and Vic stumped up the extra cash for Terry to rework the mixes for the album. On his advice, the band re-recorded the flaccid 'Need Some Love' and 'Here Again', and replaced the unrepresentative 'Not Fade Away' with 'Finding My Way'. 'You Can't Fight It' was dropped altogether. As the boys started to do their thing, Terry was captivated. "Recording was just a thrill," he says. "Superb would be a stretch, but they were good, and they had so much enthusiasm!" Alex's guitar skills particularly caught Terry's ear. "He doubled his guitar like no one I'd ever heard before, it was phenomenal. He was brilliant at it, totally brilliant. I remember to this day, I had this huge grin on my face!"

Spending a further few thousand dollars on studio time, the band recorded the remaining three songs, then Terry mixed the album in a way that captured the raw energy of the band's sound. "They were great, they played really well, they cut the tunes really quickly," says Terry. "Within three days, I handed Vic this finished, two-track master, and that became *'Rush'*." For a cover, SRO turned to graphic designer (and keyboardist in local band Edward Bear) Paul Weldon, who had also designed the Moon Records logo. "I used the explosion graphic because I felt that it represented the nature of the band," he says. "For a three-piece group they had a lot of power and force in their sound."

'Rush'

Of course it is derivative, like so many debuts. However the solidity of the band's first album is a testament to how much time had been spent rehearsing the music, both live and in the family basements and rehearsal studios. From the opening guitar riffs and a Geddy-sings-Plant *"yeah, ooh, yeah,"* 'Finding My Way' is an indicator of the band's ambitions and its lyrical content a statement, a definitive launch into the world of professional music.

It is pointless to spend too much time on the lyrics however, as they had been hastily thrown together. While John had previously occupied the role, Geddy scrawled the words for the majority of the songs without due consideration so the functional verses were not likely to win any prizes for literature. With *"You're making me crazy, the way you roll them eyes,"* and *"You need a friend, someone on whom you can always depend,"* as Geddy said much later, "The things I write about are real close to my heart – I can only write if I'm personally motivated by something." If this were true at the time it would appear he was largely motivated by girls and feeling good.

Nonetheless, the album is a showcase of youthful musicianship. High-energy songs such as 'What You're Doing' and 'In The Mood' give Alex an opportunity to demonstrate what he was capable of, but there is little to distinguish them from any other heavy blues songs being touted on the Toronto circuit at the time. The quieter, more considered and structurally more complex songs 'Here Again' and 'Before And After' offer more of an indication of the shape of things to come.The final song on the album, 'Working Man' offers a grunge-filled climax, simple and highly effective, a call to arms for the shape of things to come.

There's plenty to suggest this was a three-man team, with Geddy, Alex and John contributing in equal measure, though the latter may have been a more reluctant partner at times. The frenetic drumming that opened 'Take A Friend' was testament to John's own versatility, learned on the live stage from his own heroes.

'Rush' offers a portfolio of music collated by students of the art, starting to put their own mark on their creations, while remaining inside the comfort zone of their personal and musical heritage. In hindsight, this is not such a bad thing.

The finished album was to be released in December 1973, but not even the teenagers' determination was a match for the OPEC oil crisis and its impact on vinyl production. Finally in March 1974, 3,500 copies of the album were pressed and released. *"For best results play at maximum volume,"* said the cover, sealing the fact that this was a rock 'n' roll album in the best tradition. Thanks were awarded to friends and colleagues of the band, not least SRO employee Sheila Posner and the staff at the band's regular joint, the Abbey Road Pub.

The album was a solid debut, acceptable but nothing particularly remarkable: Geddy later characterised it, perhaps a little harshly, as "naïve." Having released an album did put Rush at something of an advantage over other local bands, however. Locally, Rush were well perceived – as much a sign of the times as of the band's prowess. "At the time, things really seemed to be happening in Toronto," says Paul Weldon. "There were all sorts of bands in the Yorkville area playing all the many coffee houses. Many felt that Toronto was going to be the next major source of rock, pop & blues bands." Paul was invited to see the band play Piccadilly Tube in downtown Toronto, a club with a reputation for live music. "I remember that they were LOUD!"

To support the release, the band did a brief, Rush-themed tour with fellow Canadian bands Mahogany Rush (Frank Marino's band, whose name certainly was drugs related) and Bullrush, most of whose members were originally from the St Catharines band J.R. Flood. Then, once again, Ray and Vic began the task of diligently pushing the album at the record labels. Once again however, Rush's wall of sound was met with a wall of silence. The labels were still more interested in the gentler sounds of yore, and they didn't want to risk losing their existing customer base by promoting the raucous new genre that was hard rock. "It started off well locally, but it really wasn't going to go anywhere," says Alex.

The management team had rather more success with FM radio, however. "Everyone listened to the radio," explains long-time tech Tony Geranios. "FM stations played album cuts, and AM was a top-40 listening format." FM played less popular music largely because FM was less popular, and the DJ's were left more to their own devices. The first station to pick up on the band was Toronto-based CHUM-FM, unsurprising as Ray Danniels brought the album in himself. "I remember Ray bringing the album into the control room," recalls DJ Don Shafer, who had the honour of being the first DJ to spin 'Finding My Way' on his daytime show. His colleague David Marsden also played the disc on his evening show, and who happened to have tuned in but Alex himself? "I was thrilled; it was really, really exciting. I just never thought I would ever hear something like that," said Alex, who liked hearing it so much, he called up David Marsden on air and told him so!

Later, the band would often drop by at the offices of CHUM-FM. "The band would come and talk, hang out," says Don Shafer. "The early seventies in Toronto were a great time for radio and a great time for music – it was much more free-form."

With all this good will and effort, sooner or later the band deserved a break. Which, through friends like that, was exactly what they were about to get.

As it happened, some friends of the band shared a house with Bob Roper, at the time working as regional promotion representative for A&M Records. Bob was paid to know people at radio stations, and so it seemed a good idea to pass him a few copies of the album and see what he made of it. "As a record guy, I could see that what they were doing showed huge potential," says Bob. "I offered to help promote it whenever and wherever I could." By no small coincidence, Bob was called by one of his own contacts, the music director for WMMS-FM in Cleveland, who was looking for new

Canadian music for the station's regular import show. Her name was Donna Halper, and Bob willingly sent her a couple of copies, with the message, "this thing deserves airplay."

When the albums arrived, the first track Donna played was 'In The Mood', the intended single. "I'd like to say I was immediately impressed – I wasn't though!" she joked. WMMS was an album oriented rock (AOR) station, so Donna gave a couple of the longer tracks a try. As she listened to 'Working Man', then 'Finding My Way', Donna realized she had something worth playing, and took the disc downstairs to DJ Denny Sanders. Before the end of his show he aired 'Working Man', a track echoing the mundane struggles of the factory workers that counted themselves among the station's listeners. It didn't take long after that for the phones to start ringing.

Before long WMMS had been inundated with calls, with listeners asking where they could get hold of more music from this new band. So – Donna called Bob, and Bob called SRO, and Vic called Donna, and Donna called another contact of hers – Peter Schliewen of "Record Revolution", a Cleveland music store specialising in imports, to arrange a delivery of the albums. Before long the entire first production run had been shipped south and distributed to the eager listeners. "Boxes were coming in and heading straight out of the door," says Donna. Literally thousands of albums were funnelled into the city.

In particular the band regained the attention of Ira Blacker. "Ira was always looking for new bands," explains Donna. "I was thrilled. Ira had a reputation for shaking things up and getting things done, and he was very hard to ignore. When I heard he was interested, I said to myself, now they'll have to take the band seriously." Not least, Ira's company ATI was one of the top agencies in Northern America. When Ira asked who was handling their management in the US: nobody was, so he quickly offered ATI's services and set to work sending out copies of the album to the labels, with notes describing the growing phenomenon. This time however, it was an American agent sending samples to his American network of contacts, missing out the Canadian subsidiaries altogether. In parallel he liaised with the import company Jem, to ensure the figures looked as healthy as possible. Ira was fully aware that this band, like any other, would need all the help they could get.

The ensuing few weeks were fast and furious, and everyone played their part. As Ira contacted labels on one side, other labels were contacting SRO via Donna to find out how they might sign this up-and-coming band. At one point, industry giants Colombia, Polydor and Casablanca Records were all showing an interest. Even A&M Records turned up late to the party! However, in the space of a Monday in early June 1974, it was Mercury Records that got the deal, through an unlikely sequence of events.

Ira Blacker had sent the record to Irwin Steinberger, who was President of Mercury at the time; as usual, Irwin had passed it to his Head of Artist and Repertoire (A&R), Robin McBride, for a listen. On this particular day Robin was on his hols, so his secretary passed the disc on to precocious youngster Cliff Burnstein, who was working as head of album promotion to radio. "So there was a note from his secretary saying there was something that I have to listen to today, there was some urgency about it," says Cliff, whose youthful opinion was often called upon when it came to new signings. As it happened, Cliff confused the band with Mahogany Rush, who he had read about in *Creem* magazine. "I had heard this guy Frank Marino was one hell of a guitar player, the next Jimi Hendrix." His excitement waned when he saw the album, but he gave it a spin. As the opening chords to 'Finding My Way' hit the speakers, Cliff nearly fell off his chair. "It's a cliché, but I was just blown away!" he says. "I wasn't expecting it, I thought this was going to be some second rate piece of shit. I thought, Ohmigod, this is just incredible, now I am flying!"

Of course, as Cliff was an album promoter and Donna worked for an AOR station, the pair were already acquainted. "He was my hero," says Donna. "His selling point was that he always put the band first." Cliff wasted little time calling WMMS, to find that Ira's story checked out. "I said, 'Finding My Way' is unbelievable and an incredible cut," says Cliff. "Donna said, well, 'Working Man' is the one that's driving everyone crazy here, and I said I haven't even got to that one yet!" One listen to 'Working Man' clinched it for Cliff, who went in ears first. "I didn't know if Rush was hot property," says Cliff. "There was nobody except for Donna to tell me people were reacting to 'Working Man', but if there was no 'Working Man' on the album, I felt so strongly about 'Finding My Way' that it wouldn't have mattered. 'Working Man' was the icing on the cake for me."

As Irwin Steinberger was away on the west coast, Cliff called Ira Blacker and set the ball rolling. "By the end of the day we hooked up a conference call with me, Ira Blacker and Irwin Steinberger and a deal was worked out," says Cliff. "At 5pm that evening, we had a deal agreed." "Irwin does due diligence based on airplay and import lists," says Ira, who was able to paint the picture Irwin wanted to see. That was part of the game – but in any case, Ira had Irwin's ear. "Irwin had faith in me," says Ira. "The way I toured bands, I made sure they were all six days per week tours."

Mercury only had one hard rock band on its books, Bachman Turner Overdrive, and was looking to make something of another: the label needed Rush as much as Rush needed Mercury. Says Cliff, "Mercury records was not considered to be the label of choice. People didn't bring stuff to Mercury generally that was highly thought of." So, from his point of view it was an opportunity. "Cliff promised me he would devote large amounts of time and energy to Rush if they signed," said Donna.

And they did. The label granted a contract worth 200,000 US dollars overall, incorporating a $75,000 advance and $25,000 to cover recording costs. The contract was to produce two new albums, with options for several more; furthermore, it gave them complete artistic freedom. "Then a six-year period started of very, very hard work," said Alex.

Mercury's cogs began to turn at an alarming speed, meshing with those of SRO and ATI to synchronise studio, live and outbound activities. For a variety of reasons including the need to shift the band away from the "import" category (which automatically categorised Rush as left field), Mercury decided to re-release their new signing's debut album. This was no more than a Mercury relabelling, unless the change of cover shade from bright red to muddy puce is taken into account – in addition, the band extended a round of thanks to the Toronto and Cleveland booking agents who had been instrumental in their signing, as well as Donna Halper, who they saw as key to the whole thing. Speed was of the essence: "We wanted to take advantage of the fact that it was being played and selling in Cleveland," says Cliff. "We got the album out within five weeks."

To get things moving on the live scene, Ira Blacker sent ATI junior agent Howard Ungerleider to Toronto from New York. Howard's experience was in booking multiple bands for a single night's entertainment ("I booked Savoy Brown, Fleetwood Mac and Deep Purple as a package," he explains). He also had hands-on knowledge of crew work, not least of doing the lights. He got to work quickly, ruffling a few feathers on the existing crew members (Ian Grandy in particular) and getting the show well and truly on the road. To grow the crew he started to bring in a handpicked selection of "reliable people" who he knew from the touring circuit, people who knew the ropes and who wouldn't let anyone down.

Meanwhile, Ira Blacker had been fixing numerous dates for far bigger bands than themselves, including Kiss and ZZ Top, and Rush became the obvious support band. "I toured their asses off," says Ira. Agrees Bob Roper, "The door to American touring opened when Blacker came on board. The band had toured Southern Ontario constantly, to the point where they were playing the same venues over and over. Had they not been given the opportunity to spread their wings, they may have run into the 'over-saturation syndrome'." Canada had failed the band, but the US was coming up trumps. All it had taken was a foothold, south of the border.

Based on his experience of working with major rock bands in the US, Howard had set a number of expectations for what he would find in Toronto. When he arrived however, he quickly found he had to revisit some of his aspirations, not least concerning his own working conditions. It was back to basics, big time – the audacious New Yorker arrived expecting to be put up in expensive hotels, and quickly found that such ideas were way out of Ray and Vic's league. "I asked for Ten G's for expenses, and I ended up sleeping on Vic's couch!" he laughs. He moved on to crashing at Ray's house, where he had to suffer Ray's dogs – a German shepherd, "which used to look at me and growl, it was always pissed off," and a "little, white, fluffy thing, like a snowball, which just jumped up and down," he explains. One day it all got too much – for Howard. "I was in Ray's back yard, the fucking snowdog thing was jumping up, and the German shepherd was biting me..." Of course, when he recounted it to the guys, they thought it was hilarious. "A biter, and the Snow Dog," they laughed. "Sounds like an epic song!"

While Ray and Vic were running to keep up with all that was happening, for the musical threesome it was a time for some big decisions. They were being handed success on a plate, but the question was – should they take it? For Geddy and Alex, the question didn't even come up. For John Rutsey however, this was a watershed moment. He was nervous about his health, and was not in tune with the musical thread that had developed between the other two. John had made it clear he would be happy to fall back to heavy

Fit For Something

Despite his reasons of illness for giving up drumming, John Rutsey went on to be a body builder and fitness instructor at a Toronto gym.

blues, but the art rock bug had already bitten, and there was no going back. "We wanted to make our music more complicated," said Geddy. "John was never really into that." The pressure was not only coming from John: Geddy and Alex also needed John to make up his mind, once and for all. "He just wasn't thinking the way Alex and I were," recalled Geddy. "He decided it would be better for himself and us if he left."

John quit while he was ahead, losing the band a drummer and a competent, if underconfident, lyricist. While the clarity of the decision was welcomed, it didn't change the predicament – by now a fully booked, five-month tour of the US and Canada was looming, organised by Ira who was feeling quite naturally gutted. Nobody wanted to compromise the deal however, and all agreed not to tell Mercury until a replacement had been found. John did the noble thing, agreeing to play a number of the theatre gigs that had been booked as his notice. In June the band returned to the US to play a few dates in support to Kiss and ZZ Top. "Strangely enough, we had the best time we'd ever had playing together," said Alex.

Donna Halper met the band in person for the first time at the end of June, when the three green-looking musicians arrived in Cleveland to play at the Allen Theater in support of ZZ Top. "They were excited about being there, and not at all brash or egocentric," recalls Donna. "They knew that doing well in Cleveland was a big deal, and they meant it when they told me they wouldn't let me down." Already, it was obvious what a pull the band was. "I thought Geddy was wearing high-heeled boots that were way too high and I was afraid he was gonna trip!" says Donna. "But we noticed, Vic and I, that some folks were singing along to 'Working Man'. Geddy noticed that too, and it seemed to give him confidence. I vaguely recall John Rutsey – he was evidently already on the way out – but Alex and Geddy seemed to have fun up there once they got over the initial nervousness."

Meanwhile, Ira was having difficulties of his own. As part of his masterplan Ira had quit ATI and set up his own management company, I-Mouse, which continued to work at booking Rush even though he was in dispute with his old company ATI. Rush and SRO decided to stay with ATI's top dog Jeff Franklin, floating Ira loose and leaving him more than bitter. Nobody won: despite being instrumental in getting Rush's golden ticket, Ira had to take both SRO and ATI to court to get his due.

Night of The Cold Knives

In the rental car, the boys were heading towards Cochran, Ontario for a gig, and the temperature outside the car was a parky minus 40. "Do you have any other clothes?" asked Geddy. "Because, if we had an accident, you would die!" "It can't be that cold," retorted Howard. "Get out of the car for thirty seconds, and take a deep breath," said Alex. "It'll feel like you took two knives and sliced your nose open." "Yeah, sure." So he got out of the car, waited thirty seconds and took a big, deep breath. Sure enough, it felt like he'd taken two knives and sliced his nose open. Not only that, as he tried to get back in the car the sweat on his hands froze onto the door handle, resulting in even more laughter from within.

Bang On

With only a few weeks to go before the next leg of the tour and on the brink of success, Alex and Geddy were stuck with a major predicament. They started auditions for drummers, but they didn't want to compromise their adopted style. A first day of auditions in a warehouse in eastern Toronto produced little, leaving the pair feeling decidedly dubious whether they could recruit someone suitable in the time.

On the second day, a young drummer turned up. After a recommendation from a mutual friend and drummer John Trojan, Vic had been over to visit the farm parts manager Neil Peart. Having watched Neil practice in the back of his Dad's dealership, he was sufficiently impressed to invite him over, so that the boys could take a look as well. When he came... well, Neil was not overly endowed with social skills, and as he hunched into the room and unloaded his small kit of Rogers drums and Ajax cymbals from trash cans, Alex was less than impressed. As a final indictment, if there was one thing the farm boy didn't look, it was cool.

Neil wasn't totally convinced either: he'd already had the low down on this new-fangled outfit Rush from the other members of his own band, Hush. Don't bother, they said, Rush was no more than a "Led Zeppelin clone band." Besides, he'd made his decision to go semi-pro and wanted to stick with it. No wonder then, that he was not selling himself strongly.

Neither was Neil nervous – he displayed a level of confidence that the other two could only wonder at. Neil started from the point of view that he had nothing to lose, so he was uncompromising in what he wanted from the situation. In the subdued atmosphere, Neil set up his well-travelled kit and started to play in the only way he knew how, putting heart and soul into the performance. "He pounded the crap out of them," said Alex. Agreed Geddy, "He knocked our socks off." The pair were bowled over by Neil's passion, not to mention the techniques that he had picked up through the many practice hours and the soul-destroying navigation of the UK club circuit. He even threw in a few stick twirls for good measure.

Despite Neil's weird looks and intense manner, after the threesome jammed together for a while (a session that begat the song 'Anthem'), Alex had to agree that he was the best man for the job. He had brought back from the old country a certain Englishness in his playing, and, said Alex at the time, "He's just too good." When the three talked about subjects from Monty Python to Tolkien, it became clear that their shared interests extended further than music. Following a couple of subdued conversations between the incumbent players, Neil was in – if he wanted to be.

The irony of Neil's arrival on their doorstep was not lost on Geddy and Alex, given their understanding that he'd travelled half the world looking for just such an opportunity. As Neil realised he had to make a decision that went against his thinking, he was forced to admit that his thinking was flawed. There was no way he was going to spend his life as an amateur of anything – it was out of character for one thing, and would leave him with a yearning that he would not be able to fulfil any other way.

Neil joined Rush a week later on Saturday 29 July 1974, which coincidentally was Geddy's 21st birthday. The next day, the trio laughed, hollered and joked their way into Toronto to spend some of the record company advance on new equipment. Recalled Alex, "We went crazy, saying, "I'll take that guitar and those amps. He'll take those drums." It's something you dream about for years and years, and we actually got to do it."

Two weeks later, after an intensive rehearsal period,

Heeping It On

"After the show back in the dressing room there was some young girl sitting there with her shirt mostly open. The story I get is that she had been on the Uriah Heep tour but had jumped off that tour to follow Rush. I thought, I don't have to be too bright to see what is going on here. The groupies are going to know first who is hot before I ever will and if they had gone off Heep and onto Rush, this was a good sign. I know this is going to work. Basically she was my signal that Rush had a great future ahead of them."

Cliff Burnstein

the band went back on tour. They kicked off in front of eleven thousand people at the Pittsburgh Civic Arena, as support for Uriah Heep and Manfred Mann's Earth Band. Joining them on tour were Ian, Liam, Howard and new boy Jimmy "J-J" Johnson, who arrived following a brief period with David Scace as guitar tech.

Having put off the decision, it was with trepidation that Vic Wilson called up Cliff Burnstein to break the news about the new drummer. "He says, I have to tell you something and I don't want you to take this the wrong way, well, John Rutsey is no longer in the band," recalls Cliff. "I said, well, when did this happen. He said, well, two weeks ago... I have got a new drummer... I said why didn't you tell me. He said, well, I was afraid you guys would not want to do the deal." Vic needn't have worried:

Recording a live TV session

Cliff's first meeting with Neil came a few days later, before a gig in St Louis, and he was immediately taken with Neil. "They would have made great music whoever the drummer was but, because it was Neil, it became more cerebral," says Cliff. "Neil was the key in many ways to the direction things would take." Besides, at the time Cliff didn't feel in much of a position to judge. "I didn't know shit," he says. "I was turned 26 and only in the business for a year and didn't know my ass from my elbow. These guys were 20 years old and had never been on the road before and were so earnest about putting on a good show, and ready to play making no mistakes, that kind of thing. It was all very sweet."

Neil's arrival was like a key turning in a lock. Within a very short period of time, Alex, Neil and Geddy realised exactly how deep their shared aspirations went. At least, of all the problems that would beset Rush in the future, the band's line-up was one thing that would not trouble anyone again.

NOTES: 1 Ned and Mellie were from Shovutz and Zraline respectively. **2** This was situated on St Paul Street West, St Catharines, before it closed down. **3** 'Feel So Good', 'Garden Road', 'Love Light', 'Margarite', 'Morning Star' and 'Sing Guitar'. These were later augmented in 1972 by 'Fancy Dancer' and the Larry Williams song 'Bad Boy'. **4** The Gasworks was such a famous bar that Mike Myers used the name in *'Wayne's World'*, as the bar where Wayne meets Cassandra. It closed in 1993. **5** Together with the animal rights song 'Slaughterhouse', 'Working Man' was the band's first song to be published through the Canadian publishing organisation CAPAC. **6** No. 35 Carnaby Street – it is still there. **7** According to Fred de Grussa and Mick Morris, of DrumNet. Movements was arranged and conducted by Johnny Harris. **8** Hush had existed previously. **9** Including Lighthouse, Edward Bear and Beatles covers band, Liverpool. **10** Such as the 12-string Rickenbacker acoustic used on 'Before And After'.

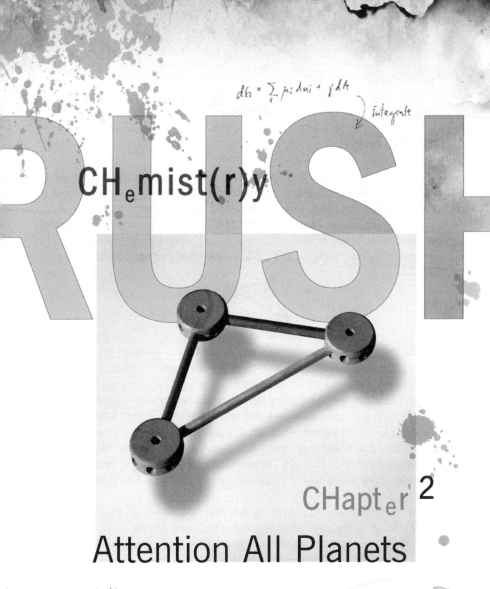

$$dG = \sum_i \mu_i \, dn_i + \gamma \, dA$$

) integrate

CH$_e$mist(r)y

Attention All Planets

$\equiv$ surface concentration c_i

"Wandering the face of the earth..."

$$d\gamma = -\sum_i c_i \, d\mu_i \qquad (3)$$

a binary solution in contact with air

$$G = \sum_i \mu_i n_i + \gamma A \qquad (4)$$

) complete
differential

$$\sum_i \mu_i \, dn_i + \sum_i n_i \, d\mu_i + \gamma \, dA + A \, d\gamma \qquad (6)$$

*"Got my sights on the stars, won't get that far
But I'll try anyway..."*

Write By Night

The date is 14 August 1974, a Wednesday, and the venue is the Civic Arena in Pittsburgh, Pennsylvania. For two young musicians about to walk on stage, there is the adrenalin and excitement of playing live to their largest audience yet. For the third, there is total fear as he steps into the unknown, masked with an accepting determination. And for the eleven thousand or more that fill the hall, there is...

Rush mythology has the figure at 11,642 people, though there may have been up to 18,000.

The first objective when Neil arrived was to get him in place on the drummer's stool. There was just over a week to prepare for the dates that had already been booked, and Neil had a full set of new material to learn. Neil threw himself into the new project like it had been his destiny. Given his devotion to duty, he took it all in his stride – nothing a few hours practice a day with the others couldn't solve. Alex was delighted, but to the introspective bassist, this was just a little scary. "He was very excited and took a very dominant role," said Geddy, who felt a little intimidated by Neil's studious determination. Says Donna Halper, "Geddy thought Neil was more educated and more intellectual – interesting, given that both had dropped out of school!"

Despite such initial worries, everything felt very right. Above all else, Neil had an attitude of making things work, which clicked with Geddy and Alex. However, where with John there had remained an element of 'schoolboys together', Neil's arrival put any such feelings firmly in the past. "We realized that there are a lot of issues contingent to being a musician, a lot of choices to be made," said Neil. "That was when everything became professional." All three players were energised not only by the excitement at having a recording contract and a defined future, but also the abject panic of having to perform together in a week.

Central to Neil's successful integration was that he shared the others' aspirations to push forward with their musicianship. Confirmed Donna, "Geddy and Alex had no intention of being a Toronto bar band. They wanted Neil in the band precisely because of what he had to offer." Agreed Geddy, "Neil was the third piece to the puzzle and he confirmed all the stuff we wanted to do. We started fucking up our music." The unspoken rule was, though hard rock would always be their first love, there would never be any kind of music that was seen as out of bounds to the band. "From our beginnings we decided to remain amorphous," said Neil.

Neil's percussion approach was to let the drums do the talking – a lightness of touch here, a change of rhythm there – which was exactly what Geddy and Alex had been looking for. Not that Neil lacked power, comments early fan and later collaborator Robert Scovill. "The first time I saw Neil play shortly after he joined the band, he was clearly the consummate combination of power and technique. He had all the odd time signature and rudiment chops[1] but presented them with incredible power." To complete the bass section, Geddy's desire to be more than the average bass player fitted with Neil's approach like paper around a stone. Said Neil, much later, "Geddy and I are both much busier than the average bass player and drummer, both individually and together."

Alex, too, was keen to push in new directions, As well as absorbing whatever Jimmy Page could do, he was picking up on still more progressive guitarists – notably Steve Howe of Yes and Steve Hackett of Genesis, both of whom had developed a more textural, layered approach to guitar. Alex applied what he learned to the needs of the power trio, placing suspended chords and arpeggios and finding a middle ground between lead and rhythm guitar. "As a three-piece band it's important for the guitar to fill a wide tonal area... I concentrated on playing suspended chords just to fill in that space," he said.

When the week was up, the band felt ready to face the music. They flew to Pittsburgh for the first date on 14 August 1974, and spent the next four days bouncing from state to state – Pennsylvania, Minnesota, Indiana and Nebraska, in support of ATI stablemates Manfred Mann, Uriah Heep and Kiss. A week after that baptism of fire, the wide-eyed rockers played the Agora Ballroom in Cleveland, and were broadcast live for the first time on Donna Halper's

Neil with Peter Criss, drummer with Kiss

FM station, WMMS. Donna was invited to introduce the gig, much to her delight as she was getting grief from her old station about exactly who had "discovered" the band. "Several of the guys on the staff decided that I was getting too much attention and they tried to put forth the story that they were the ones who really found Rush," says Donna. "When I spoke to Ray and Vic about it, they decided to show everyone who had really done the discovering. When the guys arrived from Toronto, they told my Program Director that they wanted me to introduce the band and as far as they were concerned, the subject was now closed."

The majority of dates were in support of Kiss, unsurprising as Ira Blacker was US tour agent for both. Kiss was, "the only band that's never given us trouble on the road," according to Neil. "Kiss impose reasonable restrictions and we get along really well with them as friends and business-wise." There was another, highly educational benefit of gigging with Kiss, who were not building their off-stage reputation by being wallflowers. Rather, they

Anything to declare?

"We used to drive around in a rental car," says Howard. Once, while in Nova Scotia, the band decided to bring back some lobsters. "We knew they had to be freezing so we loaded up the trunk with ice," he says. "By the time we got back, the lobsters were still cold, but the car was awash!"

You can imagine the smell...

provided an insightful demonstration of how rock stars should behave. Not that our heroes didn't gamely join in with the entertainments… but all three agreed, they were musicians first. Rather than getting too deeply into the sex and the drugs, they settled for the rock and roll. "They weren't into drugs," says Bruce Cole. "This gets back to it being a business rather than it being a lifestyle." Bands such as Uriah Heep and Rory Gallagher taught them that there was plenty of room to be human and friendly, even when you were centre of attention; meanwhile, the others were living examples of how the drink and drugs could get out of hand.

Some support slots were ill-considered in the extreme: on one date, in Baltimore in support to Sha Na Na[2], the band were booed off the stage. "It was like a greaseball dressup masquerade dance and it bordered on horribleness," said Alex. "They didn't like us at all." Perhaps it was more of a mismatch than anything, explains Geddy, "We came out and just blistered their faces."

In general however, the band were more appropriately teamed, and were better received as a result. One of the combo's first national reviews, if not the first ever in the US, appeared in the *Cincinnati Enquirer* on August 31. "It's a more polished sound, complete with the variety you hardly ever find in heavy metal," said journalist Jim Knippenberg. All in all, "a pretty good start," said Jim. "The only weakness has to do with the lyrics, they could use some polish." If only he knew.

Beetle Magazine, just after Neil joined

As the number of dates continued to grow, so did the reviews – each city had its newspaper and its resident rock critic, so the band quickly amassed a comprehensive report card. While some reviews were encouraging, many critics were disappointed to find a new hard rock band jumping on what the reviewers hoped was a bandwagon in the descendant; others just could not get on with the band's idiosyncratic style, led by Geddy's unique vocals.

As time went by, a transition occurred. Songs such as the old Beatles cover 'Bad Boy' were still in the set, and the old Rush style was still prevalent, but the growing confidence of the trio was reflected in the increasingly frequent new arrangements. The threesome started to explore new song ideas, part of a continuing process for Geddy and Alex, who were used to using tour buses and hotel rooms as ersatz writing rooms and demo studios. Indeed, it was becoming clear that a couple of the songs such as 'Fancy Dancer' and 'Garden Road' belonged with the ghost of Rush past, and would not make it onto any future album. Others, such as 'Best I Can' and 'In The End', seemed to have mileage. Neil made his own rhythmic contribution, opening opportunities for the other two to explore new directions and build on the new guy's capabilities, but that was not all.

Sooner or later, the subject of lyrics had to be broached. Neither Geddy nor Alex had ever felt particularly poetic – indeed, explained Geddy, "We hated writing lyrics, we just wanted to write music." Over the weeks, an unexpected aspect of the drummer's personality dawned on them: his head was rarely out of a book. Neil had an "incredible appetite" for reading, according to Geddy, who went on, "He also spoke English better than anyone we knew – in fact, better than anyone we had ever met." It became increasingly evident therefore, that Neil might have a talent for lyrical content.

Impressed by his studious nature (for which he had already earned the nickname 'The Professor'), Geddy and Alex gently persuaded Neil to have a go at the wordsmithing. "I thought, well, I've always been interested in words and reading and so on. I'll give it a shot," he decided. With tangible relief, the Willowdale boys accepted Neil's writings as their own. Said Geddy, "Alex and I just looked at each other – this is the guy to solve all our problems…"

With their more stylised musical compositions, the symbolism in Neil's lyrics was exactly what the others wanted to play to. In the spirit of art rock bands such as Camel, Gentle Giant and King Crimson, the band avoided restraint in either the words or the music. "We had lofty ambitions," said Geddy. "Neil's lyrics dealt with things that appealed to our sensibility – a noble kind of rock 'n' roll." Alex was rarely seen without a guitar to pluck at, and continued to experiment with his style; meanwhile, Geddy was developing his own bass skills, again learning on the job from progressive players, who saw bass guitar as a melodic device as well as part of a rhythm section. Geddy had a strong sense of how to achieve the overall sound, so he focused on ensuring the combined output made sense, working with the others on the arrangements and adding the necessary bass lines and vocal melodies to tie it all together. "I don't like 'metal'. We need a new name for it," said Geddy at the time, rejecting preconceptions and starting as he meant to go on.

New songs started to form, leaving older ones by the wayside if they didn't come up to scratch. The first example of the band's combined output was the song 'Fly By Night', written in October 1974 while the band had a three-day stop over in East Lansing, Michigan. Other songs followed, and by the end of the tour, the band were feeling confident enough to create what was to be their masterwork up to that point – the epic 'By-Tor and The Snow Dog'.

In the course of gigging, travelling and writing together, the relationship

---

Drafting the Dodge

Times were hard. "Look," said Alex to the others on one occasion, as they stood next to a Dodge car dealer in Sasquatch, "A van you can sleep in while its on its road!" "Wow…" said the others, in awed unison. "Imagine that…"

Cheap Shots #2

"The Canadian entry into the 'let's learn three chords and become the new Black Sabbath' derby relied on clichéd riffs throughout its set and only twice did this reporter perceive of anything resembling an imaginative riff."

Marc Shapiro, *Hollywood Daily News*, November 28, 1974

strengthened between the trio but it remained strongest between Geddy and Alex, who would refer to Neil as "the new boy" for many years afterwards. "Alex and I were teenage idiots together, but we didn't know who this strange creature was," said Geddy. Perhaps because he arrived when the tour was already underway, or maybe because of his nature, Neil felt himself to be an outsider, feeling a separation from the other two and a more general discomfort with fame that he would never quite shake off. Explained Neil, "Kids would turn up at the backstage door waiting for Geddy and Alex, and even though they didn't know who I was, nonetheless I felt very strange." Given Alex and Geddy's ability to relax with the fans and press, Neil didn't feel any need to overcome his discomfort. The more existential Geddy took a while to get used to Neil's more introverted approach, but easy-going Alex was sanguine: once he'd made a decision, he was content. Anything for a quiet life.

In parallel with the tour, SRO and Mercury were organising a string of media events on local radio and television. These culminated in the band's first mainstream TV appearance on 10 October 1974, on Don Kirshner's *'Rock Concert'*. It was fortunate that it was pre-recorded, as Neil broke a bass drum and the trio had to re-start its performance. It is probably no coincidence that the debut album reached the *Billboard* charts for the first time two weeks after the showing, on 21 October.

On 6 December they were back on the box, this time for ABC Television's *'In Concert'* Series. As the tour drew to a close, the band managed to pick up a live slot on a New York radio show, recorded directly from the Electric Ladyland studios made famous by Jimi Hendrix.

The tour completed on Christmas Day 1974, back at the Agora Ballroom in Cleveland, and then it was home for some well-earned rest. Though it would be the first of many tours, longevity was not something that entered the band's mind. "On our first tour we collected souvenirs and so on, thinking it might be the last," said Neil. Not that they needed worry – by

Beetle Magazine, just after Neil joined

'Fly By Night'

Neil's arrival changed things, not least it put off the "difficult second album" experience, this release being more of a second debut. As well as filling the gap on the drummer's stool, Neil shared a philosophical, musical and practical ambition with the others and the results are ample testament to this. The opening song, 'Anthem' had come out of the first jam between the three of them, the immediacy of the Ayn Rand inspired lyrics giving Geddy something more solid to sing about than wine and women. "Begging hands and bleeding hearts will only cry out for more..." While idealistic and a touch naïve, the words were altogether more sensitively composed, crossing libertarian with fantasy themes. "Because I was a post-adolescent this reflected my interest and sensibilities at the time," said Neil.

Despite time pressures and the fact that Neil was jumping onto an already-moving train, his influence was significant. A number of older songs, such as 'Garden Road' and 'Fancy Dancer' were skipped as plenty of new material had been written on tour, on the buses and in the hotels, and rehearsed in the front and back of the stage. Indeed, only one straight heavy blues song, 'Best I Can', made it onto the album. Not that all the songs were lengthy epics – the title track 'Fly By Night' is straightforward enough, as is the acoustic number 'Making Memories', but both are indicative of a band drawing from a deeper well of musical styles. Both also share the theme of travel, each offering a whimsical view of life on the road, the first songs of many to recognise the itinerant nature of the newly formed trio.

Drawing heavily on the influences of their progressive rock peers, as well as Neil's own literary ambitions and just a hint of oil of petunia, the band found itself turning to the more fantastic themes of swords and sorcery. 'By-Tor and The Snowdog' is the band's first epic number, loosely based on lighting man Howard Ungerleider's experiences with manager Ray Danniels' dogs, and replete with guitar and electronics in mock battle. Such, more considered songs demanded more considered music, as illustrated by 'Beneath, Between and Behind', Geddy almost chanting the words in this hybrid of blues and prog. Following the constant, epiglottal tension of the majority of songs 'Rivendell' comes as some respite. It offers a gentle, unadulterated homily to Tolkien, but like the Elfin sanctuary of the title the music is a half way house, not a destination.

While the majority of this album remains heavily dependent on outside influences, it closes with 'In The End', an open-hearted expression of the band's own personality. The song starts acoustically but before long the chords are replaced with their electric equivalents; Geddy's vocals are at first tempered, then hollered to bring the band full circle, back to its street corner origins. As if to say, we know where we've come from, we know where we're going, and we know exactly what it will take for us to get there.

the end of the year, *'Rush'* had sold 75,000 copies, making it Mercury's biggest selling début album. Behind the scenes, management, label and agency had been working together closely, and all three agreed a sequel could not come too quickly.

First, there were some songs to finish. 'Anthem' and the Hackettesque 'Rivendell'

were completed last, during some sessions at Beamsville, near St Catharines. As the New Year dawned, the new material was ready enough for the trio to go back to the studio, and to Terry Brown's delight he was invited back. "I was just doing the first album out of enthusiasm, and it worked out really well, but I wasn't really sure how it went down," he says. "We had a ball working together, so it made sense that they'd probably come back." Indeed it did: Terry had got the band out of a hole last time around, and it wasn't a hole they wanted to go back into. So, it was back to Toronto Sound they trooped.

Terry knew that the band had something special, even if it had not come across fully with the first, raw album. "I can remember people would come through the studio, and they would say, 'You're working with Rush, aren't you?'", says Terry. "They would say, 'What are you thinking? They're rubbish!'" Terry had remained undaunted. "There's more to this band than meets the eye, they've got something really happening," he had said to the naysayers.

At least this time, recording sessions could take place without the pressure of fitting them in between live shows, and as before, most of the songs had already been trialled live. However, the band had only two weeks to lay their songs down to tape. "I remember it being a very short experience," says Terry. "We worked every day until two or three in the morning, and just kept at it until we'd finished." There were few pauses for thought, let alone meals, but at least everyone was clear about what they were trying to achieve: less Zep, more feeling, and more of the three of them. "When Neil arrived, I think that sort of cemented everything really," recalls Terry. "It gave the band a lot more depth."

Beetle Magazine, just after Neil joined

Time got shorter and shorter, and so did the nights, until the final 24 hours were worked straight through. There was no slippage time – the day after they finished, the band had a flight booked to play a gig in Winnipeg. *'Fly By Night'*, indeed – the audience in Winnipeg did not know how fortunate they were to see the bedraggled, sleep-deprived performers.

The album was released at the end of January 1975, with a cover painted by

Eraldo Carugati. By mid-February, with barely time to catch breath, Rush were back on the road again. Explains Bruce Cole, "Things were always very organised, prepared in advance… they'd set up their tour dates then everything would back up to that, when they would do their recordings, when they would do their writing. They weren't throwing their weight around, it was a matter of tomorrow they had to be somewhere else, and the day before… Their management team didn't let a day go by that they didn't know where they were. Their golfing days were over!"

For Alex's partner Charlene it was too ironic that the tour started on Valentine's Day, given that the pair were engaged to be married on March 12. Sorry, she was pleased to get married, but not (as she had been asked) to go on honeymoon by herself with the promise that Alex would join her once she was there! At least, Charlene knew what she was getting into, and as it turned out, the week after the wedding was free of musical interruptions.

Cutting Both Ways

'Fly By Night' peaked at 113 in the US charts on 15 March 1975, as if to confirm that Rush were not going to be a 'classic', radio-friendly, mainstream success. These weren't pop songs after all; the sun was setting on the heavy rock acts that Rush had counted as their influences, and the table was already being cleared to make way for disco and punk. AM stations saw nothing they wanted to play, and the band had little more than a foothold on the AOR stations of FM radio, despite Cliff Burnstein's best efforts. "Two thirds or three quarters of the radio stations had never wanted to play Rush at the beginning," says Cliff. "They said this is too jarring, his voice will just turn people off if you play it. I told them how the band was doing and how the following was growing and how various people had success with it, and gradually we started to wear them down."

The only option for a band that wanted its music to reach the ears of the masses, was to tour. So, tour they did. On April 25th they opened for Kiss in front of 4,500 people at the Detroit Michigan Palace, and the tour saw the band play in support of Blue Öyster Cult and Aerosmith. Through the latter, the boys learned how a support band would normally be treated – by a hostile band of prima donnas, together with a hostile crew with the power (and inclination) to deny soundchecks. It was a major learning experience, and left no room for underperformance. "That was kind of an object lesson for us, and also an illustration of how good it is to rise slowly," said Neil. "It's enormously difficult to deal with."

The boys hired a car to get themselves between dates, and clocked up 11,000 miles of self drive in the process. All effort was put into the live act, walking the walk, dressing the dress and talking the talk in an effort to be noticed by the punters. Geddy's approach was to belt it out, as he explained, "The temperament was 'I've got licks to play that I want people to hear.' It was a cocky, strut-your-stuff attitude, and my singing was extreme too, because I had to cut through that."

Read My Lips…
The slide Alex used on 'Making Memories' was an old, metal lipstick container.

For Neil, it was like he'd always been there. The intense experience of tour, write, record, tour, had brought the three together: the drummer was in no doubt he belonged. Neil took a drum solo slot in the middle of 'Working Man', and even started to incorporate a couple of electronic effects into his act.

The tour passed like a whirlwind to the wide-eyed twenty-somethings, as one by one they ticked off the goals they'd set themselves. The number of headline bookings for the band started to outweigh the support slots, with one support act of their own being the esoteric, eccentric folk artist, Mendelson Joe. "I toured with Rush to help promote my records/career because we shared the same pimp," says Joe. "I was lucky to have the opportunity! I guess I did enjoy using Rush's monster amplification and inflicting my music on their acolytes." Not the music however. "Rush has much the same effect on me as opera," he sighs. "I get neither form. Rush's music strikes me more as some sort of amalgam or experience in technique." Not that the Rush fans got Joe, either. "Their fans hated my music!"

The touring strategy paid off: in April, the band discovered to their astonishment and delight that they had won a coveted Canadian Juno award as most promising new band – coveted in Canada, that is, frequently seen as a poison chalice by bands that had subsequently vanished. "It brought us a lot of attention from a lot of people who hadn't heard of us or people who didn't really take us seriously," said Geddy. "But it didn't really help us much anywhere else." This was not strictly true – the first germs of growth were starting to appear across the Atlantic as well. Pete Makowski, a journalist at UK music rag *Sounds* had acquired a copy of *'Fly By Night'*, which he passed to fellow journalist Geoff Barton with the words, "This ain't my cuppa tea but I think you might get a kick out of it."

As Rush developed its own fan base, the fans detected the non-mainstream status and individuality of the band, and reflected it in subtle ways. Indeed, the fans' anti-establishment feelings may have been the contributing factor to the practice of bootlegging: while bootleggers existed long before Rush, they had a disproportionate number of people miking up at their gigs. The different members of the band had differing views on bootlegging: having owned bootlegs of his favourite bands when he was younger, Geddy himself found it difficult to disagree with.

By the end of the tour, Rush were filling halls for up to 4,000 by themselves. On 27 June, as the band played the Massey Hall in Toronto with Max Webster in support, Neil realised how his initial list of objectives had been rather modest. "Ultimately, every city has the place that's the 'in' spot where all the hip local bands play," he said, "I used to think to play at the Massey Hall would be the ultimate. But then you get there and worry about other things." Don Shafer remembers the gig well. "They were so loud, people were pressed up against the wall! Rush were doing what they do now – the paint was peeling off the ceiling. It was very exciting, very electric and very energised!"

As the Massey Hall gig came and went, the thought of what came next filled the hearts and minds of the trio. Writing had continued throughout the tour; when it came to an end on 29 June 1975, the band had already accumulated sufficient material to go back to the studio. There were some songs, but the boys had also decided to go with an ambitious pastiche of musical pieces that together, occupied nearly twenty minutes of music. The sounds they were developing were multi-layered, using all of Alex's textural skills with the guitar, Geddy's melodic capabilities and Neil's percussion as a foundation. The ambition was to be "the world's smallest symphony orchestra," according to Geddy.

Sure, it would be an experiment, but there was nothing wrong with experimenting. Was there?

With barely a pause for breath, the band retreated to a Toronto rehearsal room for a week to complete the tracks for what would become 'Caress of Steel'. By mid-July, they were back at Toronto Sound, having once again recruited Terry Brown (by now, nicknamed "Broon"). Once again, time was tight – only 12 days of studio time had been booked – but the pressure did not dampen the feeling of utter creativity in the studio that everyone felt, the flow of ideas in the control room eased by the occasional smoke.

The second side of the album was devoted to the epic 'The Fountain of Lamneth', a "soul searching quest" according to UK journalist Geoff Barton. Indeed it was for its collaborators, who had underestimated how long it would take to turn the musical compositions into a flowing, coherent whole. Terry and the band worked right up to the wire, and when the twelve days were up, all felt they had gone a long way towards achieving their ambitions. "I was very happy with it when we finished it," confirms Terry. "It was a dark record, the whole concept and depth, it was something you could listen through repeatedly to and get something from, but it needed time to mature." 'Caress of Steel' was the band's alpha and omega, the sum of all three personalities. "We felt at the time that we had achieved something that was really our own sound, and hopefully established ourselves as a definite entity," said Neil.

Towards the end of the studio sessions, the band started putting together some ideas that were too leftfield even for 'Caress of Steel'. Some playing around with recording equipment led to recording Neil (who had already done the voiceovers for 'The Necromancer') saying "Attention all planets of the Solar Federation… We have assumed control…" But they hadn't, not yet. "Even though the ideas had not been cemented there was a seed being planted, the whole sci-fi tech-y thing," says Terry Brown. For now the ideas were noted, ready for whatever was to come next.

Another of SRO's signings, the Ian Thomas Band included a young keyboard player called Hugh Syme. Hugh was a bit of a graphic artist – he'd already volunteered a cover for one of the Ian Thomas albums, which Ray had seen. "He said, would you like to do a Rush cover," says Hugh. "I said, I guess, yes!" The design was planned to be a "very simplistic pencil rendering," but someone at the record company had the bright idea that a metallic surround would be appropriate. "They stomped on an overt sepia tone which I thought was a bit rough, and then they put this cloud of blue around it, it was done at the film stripping stage without my knowledge," says Hugh, who was not the only one to be horrified. "This is probably the very threshold at which time the band became insistent that they control the outcome of their album, both musically and artistically. I think it came as a result of these kinds of surprise attacks, oh won't they love this blue and this lettering form… and we all didn't. We were taken aback by such presumption, a lesson learnt."

For now, it was time to get the album out to a wider public, working through an increasingly dubious record label. "The record company would have liked more editorial say over what the band did," says Cliff Burnstein. "But I always felt that the band was going to do what the band does and they would have a better idea than I ever could so I just said, you signed Rush to be Rush, let them be, they have good instincts and will get a best result by just going with it, don't try to meddle."

Despite Cliff's best efforts Mercury didn't know how to market the album, and they took the option of hardly bothering. Dedicated to *Twilight Zone* originator Rod Serling, the final album was released in September 1975, giving the trio a few weeks off in the summer to recuperate and to contemplate where they were heading.

Down, mostly.

At the start of October the Rush touring machine ground into action again, starting with a number of headline dates. Things started well enough – the core team of Howard, Liam and Ian was joined by Skip Gildersleeve (who the band had met at Michigan Palace on the last tour), to replace Jimmy Johnson. Also, they had a proper bus to sleep in, rather than a hire car. Neil organised the driving rotas for the bus and the truck; everyone, including the band, took their turn to drive.

Breaking the Habit

By-Tor, the bad guy of *'Fly By Night'*, shows his face in 'The Necromancer' as a hero. There is a perfectly rational explanation for this. "I guess he went through rehabilitation!" explained Geddy in an interview. "He had a bad drug and alcohol problem, so he checked into the Betty Ford clinic. By-Tor saw the light. Last I heard, he was living a good life in California. He's a music business lawyer, I think."

The dates in support of the bigger players, Kiss and Mott The Hoople went well enough (after all, they had a captive audience), but the headliners became less and less well attended. Given the complex music and fantastic themes of *'Caress of Steel'*, radio stations had little clue what to do with the album. Whatever people had thought of *'Fly By Night'*, it was nonetheless quite musically straightforward and therefore comprehensible to commercial radio, whereas *'Caress of Steel'* appeared inaccessible, if not downright indulgent.

Unsurprisingly, the album flopped. *'Caress of Steel'* charted at 148th position in the US *Billboard* album charts on 18 October, an even lower position than the first album, *'Rush'*. There was less and less forward play on the radio, which was an essential element of drumming up audiences. As the impact was felt at the box office, the threesome hit their first hurdle – far from continuing to grow, as hoped and even expected, it looked like their popularity was already starting to wane. Indeed, on more than one occasion, Ray had to break the news he couldn't even pay the band's salaries.

There was always just enough to keep things going – not least, the momentum of the tour drove things forward and nobody wanted to be the one to throw in the towel first. Every day, every night Geddy, Neil and Alex were forced to confront the realities

'Caress of Steel'

There are some truly good songs on the much-misunderstood 'Caress of Steel', for Rush the difficult third album that followed their second debut, seen by many as the step too far that nearly broke the band. It is an album of two sides, the first reserved for shorter songs, starting straightforwardly enough with the romp of an opener, 'Bastille Day'. Equally non-contentious is the autobiographical 'Lakeside Park', the lyrics penned by Neil in memory of the sandy beaches and working the stalls at his local stamping ground Port Dalhousie, the music reflective of the balmy evenings and rippling waters.

Even 'I Think I'm Going Bald', an ode to Alex's fears of hair loss which was loosely based on the Kiss song 'Going Blind', could not really be seen as a step too far. It was not a bad piece of whimsy but neither was it one of the band's best. Alex wasn't the only one with hair concerns, remembers Donna Halper.

Summer nights - Lakeside Park, St Catharines

"Sometimes Geddy would worry so much that his hair would fall out in clumps!" The lyrics were a mirror on the feelings of the time: "Seems like only yesterday, we would sit and talk of dreams all night - dreams of youth, and simple truths." Indeed, and now it was time to get serious.

The earnestness of the band's intentions are loudly – always loudly – and clearly articulated in 'The Necromancer', an altogether darker, more complex affair. Broadly derived once again from Moorcock-esque fantasy, the song follows the fortunes of "three travellers, men of Willowdale" as they venture into lands unknown. With Willowdale being a Toronto suburb, the travellers are none other than our three musical heroes, the lands unknown reflective of a voyage still to be charted.

'The Necromancer' was a mere prelude to the second side of the album, the multilayered piece 'The Fountain of Lamneth'. Both gentle and powerful, simple and poetic, the whole side is so clearly a labour of love for the three musicians, delicately nurtured and directed by the band's production maestro and mentor, Terry Brown. 'In The Valley' is followed by 'Didacts and Narpets', the title a reference to didactic teachers and parents ('Narpets' was an anagram) the lyrics a summary of their oppressive nagging. The cry for help of 'No-one at The Bridge' is met by the delicate salve of 'Panacea', the welcome relief expressed on drawing another goblet on 'Bacchus Plateau'. The grand finale is signified by arrival at 'The Fountain' itself, the success of discovery tempered by the exhaustion of the feat. "I'm forever at the start," writes Neil, as not for the last time, the trials overcome in the tale draw parallels with the real experiences of the Willowdale three.

The band may find 'Caress of Steel' in general, and 'The Fountain of Lamneth' in particular, an experience they do not wish to revisit. The shame is that the album offers plenty to be proud of; the unexpected reward is that its poor reception catalysed even better things to come. Above all it signalled the end of an era of post-juvenile experiment, and the dawn of a band in full command of its own destiny.

of the album they had produced – if making it was soul searching, now they were living the consequences on the live stage. "You do your growing up in public," said Neil. As the band were accused of being musically incompetent (which they most certainly weren't) and pretentious (which they... OK, it's a fair cop), it is unsurprising that despondency set in. "It was so close to our hearts, but the public never shared our enthusiasm," remarked Neil. Unfortunately, the band had yet to build up its protective shell against what Geddy described as the "negative and disappointing attitudes every step of the way."

Traipsing from small to smaller venues, the band felt the real fear that all the good work of the previous tour was being undone. With reason, the tour earned the nickname the *'Down The Tubes Tour'*. After a break for Christmas, the last official date of the tour was back at Toronto's Massey Hall, on 10 January 1976. Opening once again was esoteric Mendelson Joe, who understood exactly what the band was going through. "The road is a horrible life," says Joe. "Hard, hard work!" Massey Hall, that symbol of ambition, was this time a symbol of despair. Almost incidentally, the band was getting better in everything it did, and perhaps uniquely, each member was getting better at the same pace.

From feeling despondent, the band started to get cross. *'Caress of Steel'* was in no way a bad album: it wasn't the first of the era to be musically indulgent, neither would it be the last to include a couple of duff songs. However, it was one hundred percent Rush, and there was the rub: it had made absolutely no allowance for commerciality, given the band's relatively new profile. "We thought that music was such an honest form of self-expression," said Neil. "Then we went through the disillusionment of growing up and finding out that it wasn't that way at all – that it was big business and that these musicians were just playing the music they thought would make them the most money and they were writing songs that would appeal to the lowest common denominator."

Which, of course, was the last thing that Rush wanted to do. The band had tasted success and now found itself at a crossroads – having honed its skills, its options were to cave in to commercial pressures, or to take the road less travelled and go head to head with the musical establishment? "We said, Okay, everybody wants us to do nice short songs like we did on the first album. Do we do that, or do we pack it in, or do we say 'Screw you! We'll do whatever we want!'" To Geddy, Alex and Neil, there was only one answer.

In parallel with the soul searching, the band had continued to write. Neil showed the others some lyrical ideas he'd been having, and the irony was, they seemed to fit their own situation only too well. Indeed, said Neil, "We were talking about freedom from tyranny, and meant it!"

It is not too difficult to work out what went wrong with *'Caress of Steel'*. The world wasn't ready for the grand designs being foisted on them by the newcomers, for sure, but also the material was more indulgent than the previous album, and perhaps it was not as finely honed as it could have been. The band wasn't totally ready – they had gone into the third album feeling confident, but they weren't necessarily competent enough to pull off their ambitious plans, and had taken a fall. Finally, the desire to experiment had removed some of the edge from Rush's sound. The band wanted to be a hard rock band, and this was not, in retrospect, a hard rock album. Said Alex in 1992, "We're kinda embarrassed by a couple of the songs. They're tough to listen to now, but they were important at the time."

All the while, and despite the fears of his record label, Cliff Burnstein had been feeling more sanguine. Not least, though the sales of 'Caress of Steel' may have bombed, the overall value of Rush stock (based on back catalogue sales) was up. "I think if the catalogue sales hadn't have been increasing on the first two albums, Mercury might have dumped Rush," says Cliff. Most of all perhaps, he was conscious of the speed of album release. "After number two they were making albums every six months." Not every album had to be as successful as the last: to Cliff, it was just a question of keeping at it, as the band continued to sell its older albums as they toured.

With the benefit of hindsight, the band also came to see 'Caress of Steel' as a turning point rather than a dead end. "For us, it was a very successful album in terms of our own sense of creativity," said Alex five years later. "We tried doing a number of things differently – longer songs, different melodic things – and it was a stepping stone for us." Rush might have over-egged the musical pudding with their third album, but it had all been in a good cause. "Being complicated for the sake of complication, doesn't always make for good music," admitted Geddy, years later. "But you have to be allowed to make mistakes!" Agreed Neil, "In the early days, you want to show off, and if you learn how to do something, you'll stick it in the song, whether it fits there or not. To me, that's cool. That's youthful exuberance, and I don't think that should be criticized in too serious a way."

For the time being, however, the band had to deal with certain realities, not least the lack of money that went with the lack of success. The trio once again found themselves having to look for work to keep the bills paid. "It was very difficult," remembered Alex. "No money and living in a small apartment. Just barely paying rent. I worked in a gas station, played on the weekends, but through the week I pumped gas. And I also did some plumbing. My father had a plumbing business and I worked with him sometimes to make a few bucks." Agreed Geddy, "It was a very difficult time for us."

"It was dangerous from that point, but we know they came through with '2112' right after it and set the record straight," says Terry. As for the epic 'Fountain of Lamneth', the whole experiment was quietly shelved, never really to be played again. It was like something to work through, best left in the past once its purpose was served. A quarter of a century later, a journalist asked Alex about 'Fountain'. "Did we record that? Wow... I honestly do not recall that song ever being played [live]. 'Fountain'... I honestly can't remember that song coming up in an interview."

All Individuals

Back at the office, things were not looking good. Ray, who had mortgaged his house for the third time, had an ulcer and SRO (together with its Moon Records subsidiary) was several hundred thousand dollars in the red; meanwhile another financial crisis was looming: Ira Blacker had threatened a $1.4 million (US) lawsuit[3]. SRO had been busy with a number of new signings, each bringing their own stresses and strains, and the flagship band was sailing off on a course nobody expected. It was not all bad news for Rush – export sales were picking up around the world, especially in Europe and Japan, and *Circus* magazine readers voted the band the second best new group of the year, so they hadn't been doing everything wrong. Even this was a two-edged sword given that Rush had been going for four years already.

At the Mercury ranch, faced with the growing displeasure of his senior executives, Cliff Burnstein remained bullish. "The label started having cold feet because the growth pattern was over, they started to think maybe this is not going to go anywhere," he says. "All I could say was, listen, they are still good! There was nothing wrong with *'Caress of Steel'* it just didn't do as well but the other two albums continue to sell very steadily, so we are getting the numbers up cumulatively on all three albums and that gives us the figure base of people likely to go out and buy the next album, so don't panic!"

In January 1976, following a break it was time to usher the boys back into the studio. Ray met with Terry for lunch as was his habit, but neither knew exactly how things would turn out. "Ray and I would always meet prior to going into the studio," says Terry. "He would always give me a directive about how we needed singles and how we needed to be a bit more commercially oriented, and I would always agree with him. At the same time I had this split allegiance, I wanted to get the best record we could make with the band, so there was always a bit of a tug."

In the minds of Alex, Geddy and Neil, the next album would be exactly what they felt it needed to be. There would be another epic, it was decided, but it would be less musically indulgent and more direct, The music would be more up front, the lyrics would tell a clearer story, it would be better designed and more thoughtfully executed. In addition, the band had reached a comfort zone with its musicality: Geddy, for example, felt he'd defined his style. "I found it difficult to sing and play bass at the same time, so I started making my bass parts more melodic, which gave them something more in common with my singing. This helped make my bass patterns more musical instead of just fundamental roots. It also made my bass playing busier, which I liked." It wasn't just Geddy: all three players felt they now had the grounding they needed to pull off whatever was necessary.

The ideas for *'2112'* started with a set of lyrics Neil had been writing on tour, based on a number of sources but which bore an uncanny resemblance to one book in particular – Ayn Rand's *'Anthem'*, which had already inspired the opener to the album *'Fly By Night'*. Ayn Rand had fled to the United States to escape the totalitarian régimes of thirties Russia, and the theme of the book was very much about individuals against the system; given the context of disinterest, it is understandable that the band chose to make music that followed a similar storyline. "There's a lot of passion there, that's the way we were feeling at the time," said Alex, still smarting some years later. "We knew what we were doing, what was the matter with everybody else? Why were they so worried? We weren't!" Alex and his colleagues weren't the only people to be influenced by Ayn Rand's writings, says Donna Halper. "At High School, the book every self-respecting individualist wanted to read was 'Atlas Shrugged'," comments Donna. "Ayn Rand stood against the mindless conformity and obedience of the fifties and sixties." Perhaps – but as the band were to find out, the messages didn't always translate.

Geddy and Alex developed their music to fit the mood of the lyrics, a significant change from the past. As the band worked with Neil's lyrical ideas, they adopted Ayn Rand as their artistic figurehead. "What caught our eye wasn't her political point of view, but rather the artistic merit of her work," said Geddy. The literary mentor gave

Kimono Days

the three permission to be themselves more than they had ever been before, "not to sell out and to keep doing" – or to really start doing – "our own thing." Terry acted as a conduit meanwhile, and like concerned parents watching their adolescent offspring, Ray and Vic stood on the sidelines and kept as quiet as they could.

Towards the end of the sessions and still conscious of his own experiences with the 'Caress Of Steel' cover, Hugh Syme came over to the studios to discuss the album concepts and share ideas for its packaging. Little did he know that the five-pointed star graphic on the inside cover would be quite so iconic. "The man is the hero of the story. That he is nude is just a classic tradition... the pureness of his person and creativity without the trappings of other elements such as clothing. The red star is the evil red star of the Federation, which was one of Neil's symbols."

Unexpectedly for Hugh, his keyboard skills were brought to bear as Geddy invited him to have a crack at adding some synthesiser to the opening of the title track. "Geddy had an interest in keyboards, so it became interesting for him to have an added texture on the project and I think the band had a degree of trust in checking it out," says Hugh. Not only this, but he added a Mellotron line to Geddy's song 'Tears'. "Whatever was compelling in that song touched me and I was able to respond to it." At the tail end of the sessions, the band found there was room for one more song. Starting a tradition of last minute tracks, they hastily threw together what would become 'Twilight Zone'.

And it was done. The band had managed to stick to their ideals, but these were tempered ideals with a little realism. "'2112' was not commercial in the sense of radio commercial," says Terry, "but it had commercial value, no question about that. I thought it was a pretty good balance, and I know the band did, it seemed to have worked." It was, "like coming back with a vengeance," said Alex. "We came back punching: that album still feels like that to me when I listen to it today - I can feel the

'2112'

What can be left to be said about '2112', the futuristic rock opus that took Rush to another, brighter place, both musically and as a band? This was the stuff of fantasy, borne on a wave of anger and none the less accessible as a result. The second musical piece to be based on Ayn Rand's 'Anthem', this time Neil's lyrics take the theme of an ultra-communistic state and adapt Rand's antiheroic rediscovery of electricity to the unearthing of a guitar. From the synthesised opening bars of the 'Overture' there was to be no compromise, the wealth of musical textures in stark contrast to the screeched introductions from the priests of the 'The Temples of Syrinx'.

This was, in itself, the band's most ambitious statement to date. It doesn't need too much of a leap of the imagination to see the priests as the music industry representatives, enforcing their artistic code on the masses. Across the piece the central character is in turns desperate, then determined, and then his emotions turn back to despair. All this is forgotten in the more upbeat 'Grand Finale', which sees a higher power wrest back control. If only it could be so simple in the world of real life rock music.

Boldly reversing the order of the previous album to put the longest piece first (in one of many "up yours" statements), the second side of the album is back to more "traditional" Rush, little of which could be described as fitting the "progressive" label. 'A Passage to Bangkok' is unashamedly about drugs, the perfumed smoke clouds and midnight oil reminiscent of the control room as much as any eastern fantasy. 'Twilight Zone' was a straightforward nod to one of the band's favourite TV series, and indeed the album was dedicated to its creator, Rod Serling, who had died in 1975 while the album was being made.

Such was the feeling of renewed confidence that Alex wrote the words and music to 'Lessons' on his own, and Geddy did the same for 'Tears'. 'Something for Nothing' was a straightforward, direct and deliberate statement, a last comment on the trio's determination to play the game their own way. Lacking in complexity, the songs nonetheless demonstrate exactly how accomplished the band had become. Three albums in, and the threesome was operating as tightly as any unit could hope. Whatever happened from this point on, it would be Rush and its management alone that pulled the strings.

Making The Cut

"We were cutting vinyl records at the time, not CDs. All the EQ and level moves were made in real time. You wrote these moves down on paper and you recalled them at the proper time in the music. We didn't have computers to store our decisions. This made it an exciting time and if you missed the move you had to start all over from the first song. Sometimes it would take 3 or 4 people to cut one side because you didn't have enough hands to make all the moves at one time. After the side was complete you would do it again because you always had more than one set of lacquers to cut."

George Graves

hostility hanging out."

Terry took the completed album to his friend George Graves, who worked at mastering company JAMF (Just Another Mastering Facility) in Toronto. George was immediately impressed by the boys, who were loath to let go of their new creation. "Rush was a band with members who were down to earth and didn't have an ego problem," he says.

Then, it was over to the powers that be, to see what they thought. First plays of the album at Mercury, now owned by Polygram, did not go well, and as the March release date approached, the company remained dubious about its commerciality, particularly as the band insisted on filling side one with the epic piece rather than the shorter tracks. For once, Cliff agreed with his bosses. "People were a bit freaked out at the company, and I was not one to argue," he says. "I said, it's not commercial in the sense that we pick hit singles off an album, which is the way they were used to selling the records. I said, you know, they have a fine following and it is a very ambitious record, so as long as the following is growing you just go with it."

So, they did, but all parties recognised the huge risk the band was taking. The rebellion was a gamble, and the album had to succeed. "If it hadn't done well, we wouldn't have gone on," said Neil. Released in March 1976, the album included a credit to Ms Rand in the liner notes, not only for her indirect moral support, but also to cover Neil's backside. He thought to himself, "Oh gee, I don't want to be a plagiarist here."

Whatever was the magic formula, this time it worked. By June, '2112' had sold 160,000 copies. The band was delighted, the record company was delighted; the management was relieved. "Just when it was crucially important, we pulled through," said Neil. Then it was back to work.

Cliff Burnstein got on with what he was best at – radio promotion – and this time he found he was pushing against an easier door. "You could feel that there was a ground swell of support for them around the country," says Cliff. "It was very exciting and gradually we got more and more radio stations trying to find Rush. One of the things we would do was to buy advertising time on radio stations that didn't play Rush, and people would hear the advertising and they would go and buy the fucking album, without having heard it before on the radio station. It always had a fantastic effect." With '2112' as well, Cliff found that an increasingly powerful fan base was emerging, that started doing his work for him. "'2112' was an underground album, a total word of mouth thing," he says.

What Rush had attempted with *'Caress of Steel'*, it had achieved with *'2112'*, considered by the band to be the first fully-fledged Rush album. "*'2112'* was the album on which the sound of Rush was born," commented Geddy. "We realized for the first time that we'd won a hard fought battle for our own independence and created a sound that was all of our own." According to UK journalist Geoff Barton, "It marked a turning point in Rush's career." Not that it lit up the world – this was no *'Sgt. Pepper'* – but it did well enough, peaking at 61 in the *Billboard* chart on 4 October 1976. What was more *'2112'* paid for itself, the first time Rush had covered the costs of an album with its sales alone.

Despite all this goodwill, the press was reasonably dismissive. Even rags that were supportive of the band, such as *Circus*, were a long way from fawning. "If Geddy's voice was any higher and raspier," commented the magazine's Dan Nooger, "his audience would consist exclusively of dogs and extraterrestrials. He screams and howls like a man with his joint caught in a thumbscrew." The desire to lead by musicianship led to claims that Rush were serious and distant, much to the band's incomprehension. "We never really were that serious," said Alex later. "You do a couple of things that may seem that way and you're labelled no matter what you do. I don't know, most of the time you couldn't give a fuck, you have a good time and that's it!"

Animate

An edition of Marvel Comics' *Defenders* magazine (Volume 1, Issue 45, March 1976), penned by David Kraft, was dedicated to the band and incorporated quotes from *'2112'*s 'Twilight Zone'. ("Truth is false and logic lost, consult the Rajah at all cost.")

First and foremost a live band, all it took to capitalise on the new-found popularity was to go on tour. The years of live dates had created a fan base that was not automatically swayed by whatever radio was playing; with *'2112'*, the fans found their own anthem, and Rush had found a dispossessed audience that they could relate to. "They got firmly entrenched with their audience, and the audience is always there for them," says Terry Brown. Not least a young Brian Warner, later to take the stage name Marilyn Manson, who claimed *'2112'* was "The scariest album I ever heard."

By this time as well, SRO was running quite a tight touring operation, not least by putting key crew members on retainers. For the first time its stage set incorporated "oil and water" projected visuals, setting the precedent for Rush's future tours. Geddy acquired a doubleneck guitar and bass, largely prompted by the need to play rhythm guitar during 'Passage to Bangkok'.

After a single date in Illinois on 5 March 1976, the tour proper began ten days later, with four consecutive nights at the Starwood venue in Hollywood. As Rush re-established themselves on the live circuit they were frequently having to play support at the start of the tour, so *'2112'* couldn't be played in its entirety, usually missing out 'Oracle' and 'Discovery'. The band played three weeks solid, then took a month off, and finished the tour at a more leisurely pace to growing audiences. The success of the album meant that Rush were headlining the majority of the later events, filling the halls that they had played, half empty, only months before. The band could even afford a transport upgrade: from seeing the Dodge sleeper in a parking lot all those years before, now they could get one of their own. They still took shifts driving, however!

With success came the first controversy. Inevitably, the five pointed star on the *'2112'* cover brought up suggestions of devil worship, and the nod to objectivist Ayn

Rand even led to rumours the band were closet fascists. Unlikely, given Geddy's parentage, but rumours seldom worry about the facts.

To capitalise on the upbeat mood, in August 1976 Ray Danniels proposed that it was time for a live album, a "greatest hits on stage" to serve as an introduction to the band's material. Even before '2112', the plan had been to do "something historical", according to Geddy, which offered the opportunity to offer more polished versions of some songs, than on the original vinyl. "Some of the old songs have developed until they're superior to the originals," said Geddy at the time. "This gives us a chance to bring them up to date."

The double album consisted of material taken from three consecutive dates from the previous tour, 11-13 June at the symbolic Massey Hall in Toronto. During the last night at the Hall, on which the majority of the album was based, the band played even more aggressively than usual, largely because they thought things were messing up. Neil broke a snare drum during 'Temple of Syrinx', and Alex broke a string on 'Working Man': it was that raw anger that the band wanted to capture.

Unexpectedly, the band ended up spending over a month mixing the album, which was more than any previous, studio album. "We were going nuts by the end of it!" laughed Alex. In hindsight the result wasn't that refined, as Geddy acknowledged over a decade later. "It was very raw," he said. "Our sound was like that in those days anyway, and we did very little fixing up or knob twiddling. We were growing so fast that by the time it came out we thought we could have done better."

Many consider 'All The World's A Stage' to be the closing of the first chapter, as the cycle of four albums then a live album would repeat three more times in the band's career. Indeed, said the liner notes, "This album to us, signifies the end of the beginning, a milestone to mark the close of chapter one, in the annals of Rush."

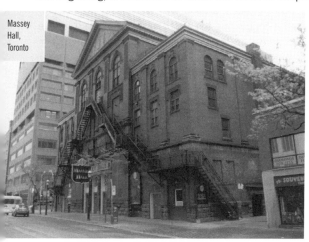

Massey Hall, Toronto

The touring fans were thanked, just as the previous album '2112' had thanked the core team that kept the band on the road. "We felt we had reached a first plateau," said Geddy.

Released on September 29, 'All The World's A Stage' sold extremely well, at Number 40 charting higher than even '2112', and going gold in under two months. It was then that the touring began with a passion. It was incessant, week on week on week, indeed rarely did a seven day period pass that didn't have a Rush gig in it. The US leg of the tour ran from 18 September through to 22 May, a full seven months, and the venues were an order of magnitude larger than the tour before. This tour in particular tipped the balance between Rush acting as a support act and performing their own headlines, not least their first Canadian headline dates outside the Toronto area! The band had to import their live equipment set from the US, and were slapped with a $15,000 fine for the privilege. Welcome back...

Despite the steady progress, one thing that was still not happening enough, was radio play. As an indication of Cliff Burnstein's exasperation he put together a radio sampler, called *'Everything Your Listeners Ever Wanted To Hear By Rush... But You Were Afraid To Play'*. "That was my little contribution," says Cliff. The EP was compiled with what were seen as more radio-friendly songs, namely 'Something for Nothing', 'Making Memories', 'Bacchus Plateau' and an edited version of '2112'. In parallel, an advertising campaign was devised to promote each of the five albums to date.

Rush had only limited success with radio perhaps, but the same could not be said for its relationship with its burgeoning fan base. Perhaps because of the band's pariah status with popular radio stations, the band were becoming role models for disenfranchised teens and twenty-somethings who saw through the mass marketing of the pop charts. The growing numbers of fans had not gone unnoticed by the band, and the players were keen to develop the relationship. "If you look at the very big bands with longetivity, they've grown and progressed and their audiences have grown and progressed with them," said Geddy. "We're not looking for immediate results; we're hoping to be around for years and years."

It wasn't just in the US and Canada that the band was picking up a following. While the band was now focusing on conquering the East Coast, *'2112'* and its live successor had sparked a growing interest on the other side of the pond, through a number of good write-ups in the music press. English journalists on the look-out for the next big thing, were very conscious of the growing phenomenon that was the Canadian band, Rush. In particular *Sounds* journalist Geoff Barton was devoting significant column inches to the cause. "I was saying, this is a band you should pay attention to," says Geoff. "I think that sort of set the ball rolling, people genuinely seemed to be interested in this band. There was no great hidden agenda, it was just finding these weird albums from this Canadian band and being enthusiastic about it!"

In addition Rush caught the attention of UK-based booking agent Neil Warnock, who had a reputation for placing Stateside acts such as Kiss and Aerosmith in Europe and overseas. "I was doing a lot of work with ATI, who were Rush's US agents," he explains. "There was an underground thing already coming through on the band." Neil phoned his contacts and fixed a potential European itinerary, before calling SRO and

> ### Cheap Shots #3
> "Before a multitude of outraged fans run to apply pen to paper and tell me they hope I expire behind my typewriter for such sacrilege, perhaps they should stop to consider the insult laid upon them after parting with $6.50 to gain admission to last night's monstrosity... Lead singer Geddy Lee continues to sound as though he played one football game too many without ample equipment, guitarist Alex Lifeson studies the stage charisma of the great guitarists without ever noticing their craft, and drummer Neil Peart should take a long, hard look at learning computer programming."
>
> Stephen Ford, *The Detroit News*, 11 February 1977

proposing himself as Rush's international agent. "They told me on that first call that I was the first English accent that they had on the phone! They couldn't believe there was any market whatsoever for Rush in the UK, or anywhere else outside of Canada and the US."

Rush's distribution label weren't helping their international interests – while Cliff might have been batting the band's corner, there was little awareness from Mercury's UK office. "The band hadn't even heard from their label and had no idea if they had sold any products," says Neil Warnock. "The first thing I asked Ray to do, was fly around Europe with me and meet all the label heads and to meet the respective promoters who had been involved with the band, because I wanted him to understand the absolute apathy that the label had towards its bands, and I wanted to hear the opinions of the promoters, market by market. He went away quite disillusioned with the attitude of the label, but very, very, encouraged that there was a group of promoters who were absolutely in love with the band and were supportive of the band any time they wanted to come into the tour."

Neil Warnock's arguments were compelling. SRO and the band agreed an eight-day, stripped down tour of the UK's major cities for June of 1977, with one date in Stockholm, Sweden. Neil hit the band just at the right time, he believes. "I was lucky enough to make the first call."

The band was well aware of the growing interest in the UK, to the extent they even had Geoff write the words in the *'2112'* tour book. Not all the feedback from Britain was good, however: it was also in the left-leaning UK music press that the accusations of fascism were growing louder. "There was a remarkable backlash," said Neil Peart. "Collectivism was still in style, especially among [English] journalists." The band remained a goodly distance away however, so were protected… for the time.

Over the summer of 1976, the musicians took some well-earned R&R. Geddy married his long-time girlfriend Nancy Young ("we'd been together on and off for seven years") in a traditional Jewish ceremony that was followed by a couple of weeks in Hawaii.

In the autumn it was back on tour, but this was altogether more comfortable, its peak two sold out nights at the Maple Leaf Gardens bowl in Toronto, playing to over 7,000 punters a night. While the trappings of success were starting to appear, not least in that the band no longer had to do its own driving, the road was still as long as ever: the tour didn't conclude until May the following year, at the Aragon Ballroom in Chicago.

Things were getting big, and Vic and Ray knew it. In preparation for renegotiating a deal with Mercury they decided to reorganise their interests and in May 1977 they created Anthem Records, a new label that could pull together all of their existing artists, make room for new ones and ensure that Rush would not be ripped off by the larger companies. Though their hands had been forced in the early days, SRO had been operating its own label and publishing company independently of the major labels since the start, leaving the majors to do what they were best at – distribution. All three band members were set up as associate directors and local man Tom Berry was brought in as managing director. Mercury were given what would turn out to be a ten year distribution deal, with what amounted to an excellent package: an advance of 250,000 US dollars to cover the recording costs of each new album, and a 16% royalty rate. That's entertainment.

'2112' had shown Neil, Alex and Geddy that they could make the music they wanted, and win. Not least, for future albums the band knew exactly what to do with everyone else's opinions but their own (and perhaps Terry's). As Geddy put it, "Fuck off, leave us alone. We know what we want to do and we are going to do it." While it was time for a bigger sound, the band had rejected the idea of adding any new members to the band. At the same time, they required that they could reproduce their music live. They started to look for ways of expanding their capabilities without compromising either quality.

To continue the journey, Rush found its path drawn inexorably towards its musical roots, across the Atlantic.

Back To Blighty

The band had done its time in Toronto Sound, and was looking for a change. 'All The World's A Stage' had been a chore, and the relentless touring, interviewing and other complications meant any new material was nowhere near complete when the band headed for the Electric Lady studios in New York, a frequent location for past tour-mates Kiss. There was a near-complete, longer song called 'Xanadu' and another shorter track, 'Closer to The Heart' was also studio-ready... but that was it. The time in New York did enable the band to write a number of songs and experiment with some new sounds. Nothing really seemed to gel, however. The US feel of the studio didn't seem quite right for a band that had been steeping itself in the music of UK bands such as Genesis, Van Der Graaf Generator and Yes. Of course, having already decided to tour there, the logical choice would be to go to Britain instead... but would that be taking an idea too far?

Nobody seemed to think so, particularly a band of brothers who were getting quite used to doing what they wanted. "Not my decision, but one I was very happy to go along with," laughs Terry Brown. "The boys felt that it would be a nice change to go somewhere else other than my studio." The plan, hastily formulated, was to do more than recognize the UK-sourced influences of Rush's music, by attending the same studios and using the same engineers as their progressive heroes. Said Geddy at the time, "We've always looked up to the English progressive bands and it's gonna be a good opportunity to go over there and try to capture the same sort of atmosphere." All the same, the trio wanted to retain the hard edge that made Rush unique. Said Neil, "We looked at the roots we had, which was hard rock music, but we decided that there was a lot more we could do with it. We decided that what we wanted to do was a combination of progressive music and hard rock."

At the end of May 1977, following a second live onslaught on the hard-bitten cities of North East America, the band and their entourage climbed aboard a plane at Toronto's Pearson international airport – the one with the YYZ call sign – and headed for Heathrow. On arrival of course, the band had some gigs to play. Journalist Geoff Barton was already looking forward to the tour, having already been over to Toronto to see Rush play, in support of Aerosmith. "I was quite delighted to see Aerosmith, but the thing that swung it for me was the fact Rush were supporting," says Geoff. "It was only a 40-minute set but seeing them live I realised they could reproduce what they were doing on the record, so they weren't beavering away in the studio without actually doing stuff, they were a genuine live band as well."

In all, the band played 8 dates over the first two weeks of June, including a brief foray onto the continent, playing the Gjta Lejon in Stockholm, Sweden. Not least, having risen to the challenge of US audiences, the band found their European counterparts somewhat more respectful. The latent audience having developed through the import catalogue, meant that Rush went straight in to filling reasonable sized concert halls, much to the band's surprise. "We just expected small to average crowds," said Alex. "When we realised how strong the fan level was, we were totally blown away."

Unsurprising they'd no inkling – nor had Mercury UK. The first date at Sheffield's City Hall was attended by Geoff Barton who had called the record company, as a journalist would, for a press pass. "They barely knew Rush were over!" laughs Geoff. "I remember I had to drive up and pay my way in, which was incredibly unusual for the music press, particularly in the seventies, when you're used to having everything laid at your feet." Of course, it was no laughing matter for the band or SRO, who expected more from their label. All of this reinforced the band's "us against the world" position, clearly there was still work to do.

With the mini-tour under its belt, it was time to record. Initially the plan was to use George Martin's AIR studios in London, but they were not available so Terry Brown proposed the residential Rockfield Studios, near Monmouth in South Wales. Remarks Geoff, who stopped by for a visit, "They were definitely awake when I was down there! It was a nice environment, it was perfectly suited to Rush at that point, obviously in the middle of nowhere… I think that at that time Rush were still fairly mystical and the environment where that album was recorded was very suitable to their mood at that time. It's a real snapshot, it's a real moment in time." For Neil perhaps, some of the surroundings were a little too evocative – not least the cow barns, which had that unmistakeable smell of his childhood.

Once at Rockfield, the band slipped quite easily into the routine it had worked out with Terry. "We'd spend a couple of days getting sounds together, and then we'd embark on rehearsing in the studio," explains Terry. The priority was laying down the drum tracks. "We would cut a tune in its entirety, but we wouldn't be trying to get finished guitar and bass sounds. All the pressure was on Neil really, in the first week. Then we'd overdub hundreds of guitars and basses!" However, it was at this time that the band passed a noble law, to ensure that the band was capable of reproducing live, what it had done in the studio recording. Explained Alex, "When I was young, going to concerts and not hearing the solo that I heard on a record, it really bugged me because you loved every note of that solo on the record, and if the guitarist didn't play it, you felt that he was copping out... like he couldn't remember how to play the solo."

As time passed at Rockfield, the foursome settled into a what became a slightly less conventional routine, of working later and later in the day. "We were sleeping outdoors during the day, getting up about three in the afternoon, by five o'clock we were eating this humongous meal," says Terry. "We'd start work about seven, and finish at around seven in the morning!"

Some equipment changes were inevitable. To give 'Xanadu' a fair chance live Alex had picked up a double necked guitar when passing through Nashville – of course this had nothing to do with the fact that Geddy (or indeed, Jimmy Page) already had one. Geddy's latest acquisition was a set of Taurus bass pedals. "I wanted to play double-neck guitar, and I wanted to keep the bass going while I backed up Alex on rhythm guitar," explained Geddy. As well as a Floyd Rose vibrato for his new Strat, Alex picked up a Roland Jazz Chorus amplifier, and his immediate reaction was, "Where has this sound been all my life?"

The new instruments fed the fires of experimentation: everything was good, nothing was left untried. Before long, Alex had picked up his own set of Taurus pedals, and to provide some extra feel, Geddy got hold of a Mini-Moog. "It was so refreshing to add a texture that we could drone behind our sound – we didn't use it blatantly," said Geddy. "That feeling and pulse in the background was really how it started. Then when we went to a very tight three-piece, it didn't feel so dry and empty." Little did anyone know at the time, exactly how much impact the synthesiser would have on Rush's sound. Agrees Terry, "Certainly in the original stages it was just a colour, just sort of messing around with equipment to come up with the sci-fi aspect of the record."

Inevitably, the arrangements for the album were more complex than their predecessor, but just as balanced. "All the songs were approached in much the same way," says Terry. "We'd sit with a pen and paper and figure out how we were going to go about it. With something like 'Xanadu', when you've got large stretches of open air, and solos and all kinds of stuff going on, mapping that out and getting it together is more difficult, as opposed to a four-minute pop song."

Once everything was worked out, the recording came together smoothly, with resident engineer Pat Morin's skills freeing up Terry to start taking more of a producing role than he had previously. "I was co-producing, they were involved in the production as well," he explains. This was very much a two-way process. "We were fine tuning lyrics and melodies, what parts were played and where they were played." The 'Cygnus X-1' spoken part was by Terry, whose position as the fourth member of the band was now confirmed.

How very idyllic it all was. 'A Farewell To Kings' was nominated as the title track, its opening bars played in the studio courtyard to make use of the gentle, natural reverb. 'Xanadu' was laid down in a single take, and birds could be heard singing in the background, as Neil's percussive additions were also recorded outside. Overall, the album took three weeks to record. "It was an excellent experience, the tracks were going really well, and when we left Rockfield we had everything recorded," says Terry.

To mix and complete 'A Farewell To Kings', a fortnight had been booked at Advision Studios in London, an old haunt for Yes amongst other luminaries of the progressive scene. "It was right in the West End of London," says Terry. "A lot of good records had gone through there, and they had an automated console, which was relatively new

'A Farewell To Kings'

If '2112' is a release of angry tension, 'A Farewell To Kings' is a heartfelt soliloquy to Rush's past. As the steadily maturing band sought newer, more contemporary pastures it turned its attentions from matters fantastic to poetic. Opening with the deceptively dulcet sounds of songbirds and a hand-plucked guitar, the pseudo-medieval title track is a final ode to the past, to the ancient fiefdoms and battles far away that had played such a major part of previous albums.

All the same, as this carefully crafted set of compositions was released, nobody could ever accuse the threesome of giving in to mainstream demands. As if to illustrate this, the band opens its new era with 'Xanadu', a virtual transcription of 'Kubla Khan' – Coleridge's finest, opiate-induced hour. Deliberately recorded in a single take, the carefully crafted eleven minutes of ambitious music and virtuoso playing, including a vast array of percussion sounds, showcase a band at the peak of its compositional and musical abilities. In so many ways, and for so many people the song captures every essence of the band, standing out at the time as a direct riposte to the delightedly anarchistic, vulgar and more musically reductive elements of the punk movement that was burgeoning in Britain and abroad.

Again and again, the band was determined to hammer home its disdain for how it had been treated by the mainstream pundits of popular music. The one-man-against-the-system journeyman tale 'Mr. Deeds Goes to Town', originally a film with Gary Cooper, was inspiration for the soulful 'Cinderella Man'. This theme might have been well-trodden by this point but unusually the lyrics were penned by Geddy, demonstrating how closely Neil's anti-establishment sentiments matched his own.

Contrary to its title, 'Kings' concerns voyages of discovery, be they rowing through caves of ice, journeys into the inner sanctum of the human psyche or the weary realisation that home is where the heart is, as pronounced by 'Madrigal'. While both this song and the title track reflect a desire to move away from the heroic, a better title may have been the original name for the album, 'Closer To The Heart', the song itself based on a lyrical one-liner Neil had been given by his friend Peter Talbot. While it worked reasonably on the album, it would be in the live setting that this song really found its feet, with the paced lyrics perfectly suited for audience participation.

The finale of the piece is titled 'Cygnus X-1, Book One – The Voyage'. Based on a piece about black holes that Neil read in Time magazine, the song charts the journey of space ship the Rocinante, itself named after the horse in Cervantes' picaresque classic novel 'Don Quixote'. 'Kings' is the stuff of science fiction, blended with literature and backed with music. A modern classic, indeed.

back then." In all, the band had planned ample time, had had a good time, and were pleased with the results – an altogether more genteel way to make an album than the previous four.

Where '*2112*' had still been an out-and-out rock album despite its grandeur, the new songs were altogether more refined. The band was, indeed, progressing but the output remained unmistakably that of a power trio. Good, old fashioned guitar sounds were still firmly in the mix – from the opening bars of the title track to the long solos of 'Cinderella Man', joyfully accompanied by bass and drums. All was well, a happy marriage of organic and electronic sounds. "'*Kings*' was a step in a different direction for us," said Alex at the time. "We introduced other instruments. Although we weren't very proficient at them, they did what they were supposed to do."

By late June, Rush were back in Toronto to record their first ever video, a "live show" filmed at Seneca College. The video featured 'Xanadu', 'Closer To The Heart' and 'A Farewell To Kings', recorded while the songs were still fresh in the minds of the players. As the album was being mastered, there was time for the players to take a few weeks away from their instruments, before the big wheel started turning again. Geddy liked to keep one eye on the recording during the mastering process, and Neil spent some time with Hugh, who by now had become the band's artist, to finalise the cover art. The role fell to Neil not only because he had more time to spare than the others. "Neil's part as a drummer and lyricist allowed him time in the interim where there was a lot of knob twirling and decision making," says Hugh. "It was not just the path of least resistance, he was truly interested in having the cover depict the contents which are notably the lyrics."

The album cover featured a demolished warehouse from Buffalo, NY in front of a Toronto skyline, which happened to feature Howard Ungerleider's condominium. "It was a total accident," says Howard. "We didn't realise until years later!" The "king" was Josh Anderson, who had been guitar player in the Ian Thomas band. "He really was a rake of a man, really, really thin and he was perfect for the part," says Hugh. "He had a beautifully receding forehead already and all I had to do was go and retouch his mouth, shoulder and knee joints to appear mannequin-like."

It was time to take the show live, a process that had been started back at the management offices while the band were sniffing the Welsh breeze. On the '*2112*' tour, SRO had been developing a crew of the highest order, and with a reputation as demanding as the band. This time, given the array of electronics that had somehow sprung up around the threesome, some additional help was called for. The band had met electronics whiz Tony Geranios through Blue Öyster Cult, whose star was now in the descendant, and he was invited to join the Rush

The Last Horn

In 1978 at a gig at the Nassau coliseum, on Long Island supporting Blue Oyster Cult, a PA speaker broke loose from the rigging and toppled onto Alex's guitar rig, ruining his Gibson doubleneck and damaging the neck of his trusty Gibson ES-335. "That really hurt," he said. "The 335 had been with me for ten years; the neck was worn down just right, the finish was worn down from playing thousands of bars and high school dances, and I was proud of it. After that I said, "This guitar is staying home. I'm not taking any further chances with it.""

Instead, he had a copy made: a custom Gibson with the same cream-colored finish, which became his main guitar.

THRIFTY'S PRESENTS

RUSH

'A Farewell To Kings' - World Tour 1977
with special guests
Max Webster

crew as keyboard technician. Tony set to work interfacing the different pieces of equipment they required for their live show. This was pre-MIDI, but Tony's brother George (also with Blue Öyster Cult) had already managed to connect an Oberheim to interface with a laser light show. "I wanted to develop a system where Geddy could play the bass pedals and trigger other synthesizers," said Tony. He set to work, enabling the lower inputs of the Oberheim to be controlled by the bass pedals, and the other part with his keyboard. "You could have a horn sound on one module, a string sound on another, a wind sound on a third, and you could have different types of decay[4], all mixed into one total sound. It was a white elephant, but it worked, and it was very interesting."

Following a few warm-up dates in August, the tour kicked off on 6 September 1977, in Thunder Bay, Ontario. Days later, the album was released simultaneously on two continents. 'A Farewell To Kings' achieved Top 40 status in both the US and Britain, peaking at 33 in the *Billboard* charts on 24 October. Despite the impending dawn of punk, it had not yet made much of an impact on the charts which were occupied by a wide variety of acts, from the Bee Gees, Elton John and Elvis (following his death), to The Eagles, Wings and Pink Floyd, and there was plenty of room for Rush's far more publicly accessible sound. Indeed, this position was about as mainstream as a self-respecting rock band could get, at least a band that was yet to break through to stadium status.

The band even took the plunge and released a single – 'Closer To The Heart' hit a respectable *Billboard* #76 on 26 November. The boys needn't have worried about the unspoken curse of "best newcomers" – at the end of the year, the band received a Juno gong for Best Group. Cliff Burnstein's instincts were proved correct, as sales of the back catalogue grew nearly as fast as the new release. 'Kings' achieved Gold status in the US at almost the same time as '2112' and 'All The World's A Stage', and the band had accumulated six gold and three platinum discs in Canada.

The tour was an altogether better produced affair, and the crew were more than showing they were up to the additional demands of the arena-sized venues. There was time for good-humoured fun – band and crew delighted in racing radio-controlled model cars during the dead time before sound checks. While not pop stars, the band did have the occasional brush with 'star struck' fans, "… like the one with the kung fu grip in San Diego who stormed the stage and tried to tear out the lead singer's throat," wrote journalist Roy Macgregor, or, "… like the top-heavy girl in Atlanta who come up onto the stage to show the band her instruments."

All the same, it was another 6-month date-stuffed epic and it took its toll – on 7 October, at Salt Lake City, a gig had to be cancelled as Geddy's voice needed a rest. "Drive 'Til You Die" was the tag line for the tour, altogether more satisfying than "Down

The Tubes", but no less stressful. The partying, therefore, was kept in moderation: now the boys had found a stable position, nobody wanted to blow it. "We're not like a group of priests going on the road you know," said Alex, a decade later. "But that's never been what's important to this band. A lot of times for a lot of groups it's a lifestyle and it's an ideal. It's to go out, sex, drugs, rock-and-roll is the ultimate, have a good time for 5 years, then it's over. But for us, we've always been musicians before being a particular rock band." Alex was speaking from experience – they'd seen bands on the way up and on the way down, not least they were now being supported by previous headliners Blue Öyster Cult and UFO.

One support band was Max Webster, a band started by Kim Mitchell and Pye Dubois, the latter contributing lyrics and keeping out of the limelight. Max Webster were managed by Ray, and had just released their first album (produced by Terry Brown) on the label, Taurus Records, that SRO had started in 1975. The musicians became firm friends, not least Geddy and The Websters' keyboard player, Terry Watkinson. Along the way, Geddy spent time learning synth techniques from Terry. "Terry used to sit down with me and explain the fundamentals. He used to draw little charts for me; he was like a tutor I had on the road."

For some fans, Mr Watkinson would have a lot to answer for.

Over the water, *'Kings'* was selected by Mercury's über-label, Phonogram as Rush's launch album in Europe. Previous albums had been available on import, but not as standard sales. *'Kings'* sold by the shedload, and when a 16-date tour of Britain was announced at the end of 1977, tickets sold out almost immediately. This time, and setting a precedent for the future, the band insisted on bringing its entire live show across the Atlantic. The February dates were a resounding success, one of which (at the Hammersmith Odeon in London) was recorded for radio. However, when the band listened back to the tapes, they didn't like what they heard. "Geddy had problems with his voice that night, at least that's the way we remembered it," Alex said later. So the tapes were stuck in a cupboard back at SRO, and left to gather dust.

Success in Europe in general, and in the UK in particular, appeared to Rush like a bolt from the blue. The band were feeling buoyant, and indeed a little ebullient that they had managed to take the system on and win, and they were unfazed about telling people they were now reaping the hard-earned material rewards. At the same time however, the threesome were blithely unaware of the rapidly changing muso-political situation in late seventies Britain. The small-c conservative values of hard work and reaping what is sown being so gleefully described by the three Canadians, were an anathema to music publications such as *NME* and *Melody Maker*, who were more likely to side with the anti-establishment. Punk bands such as the Sex Pistols and the Clash might not have been dominating the charts, but their effect on the British musical consciousness, and by extension the pundits of the music scene, was enormous. Anarchy was in the UK, but nobody had told Rush that it was any big deal.

Unfortunately for Geddy, Alex and Neil, it was a very big deal indeed. The muted charges of fascism finally came to a head in March 1978, when *NME* journalist Barry Miles interviewed the band, at the Marble Arch Holiday Inn, in London. Older, worldly wiser and certainly more socialist Miles was understandably shocked by what he saw as their pro-capitalist stance. "I was just reacting to massive political naïvety more than anything else," says Miles. "They really did think that market forces would provide everything and I do remember that they had no idea about the conditions of the poor in Britain in Victorian times, or in Ireland in the 19th century when there was no state intervention – something they were advocating."

The band were unrepentant in their capitalism. "For us, capitalism is a way of life, it's an economic system built on those who can do, and succeed at it. For us it is a very material way of life. Your material things should give you pleasure." Alex confirmed the sentiment, a little more directly – the band had worked their butts off for five years, and deserved some breaks. "It feels good," he said. "It is our just reward for all the hard work." Indeed, the band had all agreed years before that they would get fancy cars when they made it, and they agreed the moment was now. For Alex it was a Jaguar XJS, for Neil a Mercedes SL and, for Geddy, a Porsche Targa.

Perhaps it was Barry Miles' frustration at the naïvety of their attitudes that goaded him into writing what he did, but few would deny that his reference to the gates of Auschwitz was below the belt. Geddy's parents had spent some of the war under the shadow of that very sign – and its slogan, "Arbeit Macht Frei" – and most of his family had been killed by the Nazis. The singer was understandably distraught, and his co-conspirators were bowled over. "They were calling us 'junior fascists' and 'Hitler lovers'. It was a total shock to me," said Neil. "I'm not a Fascist. I'm not some extremist," he said. "Yes I'm a capitalist and I believe in self-reliance – but not without caring for other people."

Of course, it was all Ayn Rand's fault. Given her objectivist philosophies, it was dubious that Rand was a fascist herself, but she was certainly an anti-communist and these were the polarised seventies. Not that the band members would ever wholeheartedly embrace anyone's philosophies: "I am no one's disciple," as Neil put it. Rush agreed with Ayn Rand's ideals, "only as they pertained to the idea of artistic freedom," said Geddy later. "I always thought those fascist remarks were way off the mark. I found Ayn Rand's work at a certain time in my life to be a great liberator and a great relief because her artistic manifesto was so strong and inspiring. Her views on art and the sanctity of individuals were very inspiring to young musicians in a band, fighting for their own identity." Confirmed Alex, "*'Anthem'* isn't fascist, it's about individuals making the best of their lives. I read the book, but it's not like it was a uniform mind-set for the band. The *NME* got it wrong."

Years later, other UK music rags would seek to distance itself from the remarks, not least Geoff Barton's *Kerrang!* which stated how the *NME* "foolishly labelled" the band. At the time however, the only way was forward and (according to the SRO schedules) there was no time to lose. The closing words labelling 'Cygnus X-1 Part 1' were "To be continued": It was time to return to Toronto and start developing and rehearsing material for a new album.

Back at SRO, Ray and Vic were keen to build on the success of *'Kings'*. In much the same way as *'All The World's A Stage'* after *'2112'*, they agreed with Cliff Burnstein at Mercury to re-release the first three Rush albums as a triple set. The hastily packaged "album" *'Archives'* was released in May 1978, with an accompanying tour supported by Uriah Heep. Band and crew were quick to assure the same level of kindness that the Heepsters had shown to Rush on their first US tour, just four years previous.

The tour was really two sets of dates in March and May – April was kept clear for Neil and Jackie's impending arrival. Daughter Selena was born 22 April 1978, a delight to the parents and a welcome respite to everyone else. Meanwhile, the studio time had already been booked, so it was time to tackle the second episode of the stories, rhythms and moods that inspired *'A Farewell To Kings'*. After only two weeks off at the end of the *'Archives'* tour, the band returned with Terry Brown to Rockfield Studios in Wales, feeling on top of the world despite not really having developed much material. "We were all pretty much of the same mind – that we were going to do another *'A Farewell To Kings'*," says Terry.

What could go wrong.

Powers That Be

Spending several months away on tour was not the best way to prepare for the creative process of making an album, especially as the band no longer really had the time, nor the will to develop anything new on the road. Starting work at a rehearsal room not far from Rockfield, the approach to the music was becoming awfully democratic. The threesome would jam together, see what worked, and try to arrange things into more complete songs and instrumental parts. "We would write fourteen different pieces, or bits, that were in different time signatures and stick them all together to create a concept," explained Geddy. As well as mucking in on the arrangements, Neil was writing lyrics and passing them to Geddy, who would trial them with the evolving music.

Not all the material was necessarily long or complex – the band found time for short and sweet pieces such as 'The Trees', which provided a welcome respite. Based on a cartoon Neil had seen of – er – trees, the lyrics were "a piece of doggerel," that he alleged to have scribbled down in five minutes. "I certainly wouldn't be proud of the writing skill of that. What I would be proud of in that is taking a pure idea and creating an image for it. It's simple rhyming and phrasing, but it illustrates a point so clearly, I wish I could do that all of the time." A better lyrical achievement perhaps, was 'Circumstances', a simple but effective catharsis of Neil's time spent in England.

As the band worked on its new themes, Geddy was finding more and more use for the synthesiser. The unobtrusive addition of keyboards (and in particular, the Oberheim eight-voice he'd been using on tour) provided an additional dimension, a few more tools in the tool chest... at least, that was the theory. "That's when I really started to get keyboard crazy," said Geddy. This was despite the pre-MIDI connection issues that dogged the technologies at the time – in fact, these added to the challenge.

Keyboards could do no wrong. Truth was, Geddy was falling in love.

After a couple of weeks and at the scheduled time, the band went into the studio proper, and each of the foursome had to confront the fact they weren't as prepared as they would have liked. For a start, the technology was starting to exert its own individuality. Geddy had hired a specialist company to build an Oberheim synthesiser rig, but when it was delivered from the US, it wasn't working so a local engineer came and patched it up as best he could. "Rockfield was where Geddy's keyboards were torn apart and rebuilt," says Terry. "The Oberheim, oh my goodness. It was crazy!" Neil and Alex were content with what they had – for Alex, his chorus and other new effects were enough to keep him occupied, and Neil was content with good ol', traditional drums. "I don't feel comfortable with wires and electronic things. It's not a thing for which I have a natural empathy," he said at the time. "It's not that I don't think that they are interesting or that there aren't a lot of possibilities. But, personally I'm satisfied with traditional percussion."

Second on the list of headaches were the arrangements, not least for the instrumental 'La Villa Strangiato'. The ideas might have come to Alex in a dream, but Rockfield was hard reality, particularly as the band tried to make the piece work in one take. "We felt it was a song that needed the feeling of spontaneity to make it work, so we spent over a week learning it before we recorded," said Alex. "After we were finished, none of us thought we'd ever be able to play it again." In total, 'La Villa Strangiato' took more time to record than the whole of *'Fly By Night'*!

At least the title track, 'Hemispheres' was more a collection of parts, each of which could be recorded separately. All the same the constant arranging and re-arranging was taking its toll and dragging out the schedules. Studios do not work on an open-ended basis, and originally six weeks had been booked. This was extended by a further four weeks, at the end of which the pressure was starting to show. "We felt so much like machines," remarked Neil, "and all of us were crippled by that."

It was all quite an eye-opener for journalist Geoff Barton, who was present for some of the final stages of arrranging. "To me it seemed very simple, you stick out an album, you put songs on it and that's fine," says Geoff. "I didn't really realise how much debate would go on about which track should open the album, which track should be half way through... and this debate raged for ages. I was frankly getting very bored! I guess it worked out alright..." For some maybe, but not to Geoff, nor to many fans who were so looking forward to a science fiction continuation to 'Cygnus X-1'.

The one area that nobody had worried too much about was Geddy's vocals, which as usual had been left until last. During the writing sessions, Ged had sung along to the rough tunes and was reasonably confident that he could sing them – he didn't really give it any more thought until the time came to actually do so. When it came to recording his vocal parts, Geddy realised with horror that they were off the top of his usual singing range. By this time, re-recording all the other instruments in a lower key was not an option, so Geddy was faced with no choice but to sing them in anger as they were written. Terry and the others had been slow to realise that this might be a problem. "It was like, what do you mean it's hard to sing!" recalls Terry.

Geddy's first attempts at vocals were understandably poor, and besides time at Rockfield was running out. A slot had been booked at Advision in London for the mixing, so off to London they went, feeling a growing sense of panic. "The night before we left Rockfield, it was not great," says Terry. "We got to Advision and started doing vocals instead of mixing." Geddy was giving his best, but he was working way outside his comfort zone and becoming frustrated as a result, losing his rag on a number of occasions. "Things were said, mugs were thrown," says Terry. "Alex would say, 'I think I'll just go get a cup of coffee, and Neil would say, I think I'll just go get a smoke...'"

Finally, with the vocals more achieved than completed, everyone needed some time out. The boys jumped on a plane and went back to Toronto for a well-earned break, before returning only a few days later for the mixing. The initial mixes were far busier than would normally be acceptable, but Terry was determined not to say die. "I had a cassette tape of rough tracks, and it sounded phenomenal. It just had this vibe to it, so I knew it was going to work," says Terry. "But sometimes it's just hard to translate it into something that you can turn on and everybody gets the story." After trying out the tapes at several studios, he booked two weeks at Trident where he felt he had a chance to pull things together.

Indeed it did, thanks to the doggedness of all involved and to Terry's own tenacity. "If you hear it, you can do it," says Terry. "So I hung in with it, and it did turn out good." Agrees Neil, "I don't think that the result suffered – working under pressure can be really productive. You pay a high toll for it in how badly you feel afterwards. It was so draining and difficult." Following a couple of nights of celebratory high jinks, it was back to the new world for a well-earned break.

Following the relative straightforwardness of *'Kings'* the resulting album, *'Hemispheres'* was more indulgent and complex than had originally been planned, but it worked. Furthermore, some of the songs on the second side were an indication of the shorter, neater shape of things to come. The time in the studio was a learning experience for the whole band, in particular the challenge of complex compositions. "That was all well and good for the time, but in a certain sense, it was really an easy way out," said Geddy later. Surely he didn't mean it was that easy? "Okay, it wasn't easy to play and it wasn't easy to think of, but it was easier than trying to write a great song that's got a lasting melody and a moving feel." Point taken.

The band's – and particularly Neil's – extended absence in the old country had made communications with cover artist Hugh Syme difficult. To fit with the themes of the album, the cover was intended as an elaborate pun, with the 'severe, Magritte business man' Apollo, opposed by the naked Dionysus. "The band told me, 'Go ahead, we'll see it when we get back'," said Hugh, "and all my conversations with them were over the telephone." Inevitably, signals got lost and the resulting cover wasn't anybody's idea of perfect (said Hugh, "Technically, it's an abomination."), but there

'Hemispheres'

It came as some surprise to many fans that the second book of 'Cygnus X-1', introduced on 'A Farewell To Kings', did not continue the story of the Rocinante's final flight (though the ill-fated starship gets a mention towards the end of the piece). The concept for 'Hemispheres' was taken from the book 'Powers of Mind' by George J. W. Goodman (better known by his pseudonym Adam Smith), which compared psychology to religion. As an allegorical framework, Neil chose a mythical dispute of Olympic proportions between the gods Apollo and Dionysus. Where both Apollo's rule of reason and Dionysus' rule of love led to failure by themselves, balance between the two was brought by the shapeless upstart, Cygnus.

With no embarrassment, while 1978's punks were restricting their songs to 2-3 minutes max, 'Cygnus X-1 Book II' occupies the whole of the first side of 'Hemispheres', and while Geddy's vocals were pushing hard at the top of his range, they capture the intensity of the ancient battle. Musically, the five-part morality play acts largely as a backdrop to Ged the Storyteller, and lyrically once again it closes like the waking from a dream. "We can walk our road together if our goals are all the same, we can run alone and free if we pursue a different aim," repeats the unabashed mantra of collective individualism, in thinly disguised defiance of any anti-socialist accusations brought upon the band by the press.

Following the complexity of the first side, 'Circumstances' opens the second with an almost-audible sigh of relief. Lyrically based on Neil's own childhood and his time in London, the song presents a hard-fought world view as a French proverb: *"The more that things change, the more they stay the same."* More overtly political (and again, defiant) is the acousto-electric 'The Trees', which returns to the theme of two sides fighting. This time the battle is for individual rights, the upstart Maples determined not to remain in the shadow of the lofty Oaks. Sadly, no bringer of balance was available on this occasion, instead "they" – the powers that be – impose a draconian, blanket equality on both sides.

Subtitled 'an exercise in self-indulgence', 'La Villa Strangiato' is a hotchpotch of borrowed musical pieces and concepts, rejigged and woven into a complex and powerful, multilayered tapestry. The first part 'Buenos Nochas, Mein Froinds!' is based on the song 'Gute Nacht, Freunde' by the German composer A. Yondrascheck. Elsewhere the piece incorporates some old Warner Brothers cartoon themes (notably the production line section of 'Powerhouse' by Raymond Scott, who was later content to be offered a one-off sum for his contribution). Indulgent and influenced maybe, but packed with inspiration and goodness nonetheless.

was no time and little will to do anything about it.

'Hemispheres' was released in October 1978, coincident with the start of the tour. Once again the band were managing to fill arenas by themselves but financially, things were still not easy: it was well into the tour before the tour debts were paid off and the band started to feel they were making any money – understandable given that the kit itself cost $10,000 per day, and there was a 25-man crew to pay. Howard Ungerleider ensured an even better light show than before, building on the set (and the success) of the 'Kings' live show – but this cost money. Nonetheless Rush turned down the opportunity to play the first annual Canada Jam festival, which would have earned them $200,000 Canadian. Despite all the talk of capitalism, it clearly wasn't all about the money.

The crew incorporated a couple of new faces, not least Larry Allen, who was brought in as drum technician. Another newcomer was Nick Kotos, who did what any good crew member would do – what he was told, otherwise keeping out of the way. Nick was surprised then, to receive a summons from the band. "Having worked with other bands, I assumed that there was a significant problem, why else would they want to speak to me?" says Nick. "When I walked into their dressing room, the three guys asked me, what the problem was and why wasn't I hanging out in their dressing room?" He got the message – this was no ordinary band, they were ordinary people.

By 18 November 'Hemispheres' had charted at Number 47 on the Billboard charts, which was a competent, if not glowing result. The album wasn't to everyone's tastes, not least because some of the band's harder, more populist edge had been smoothed by the additional layers of production. "I went off them when 'Hemispheres' came out," says Geoff Barton. "The thing that disappointed me was that I really wanted this fantastic conclusion to 'Cygnus X-1', which never really happened, and it just went into this Greek god chorus stuff... I was upset about that!" He wasn't the only one, but the album was enough to ensure the growing, gentlemanly popularity of the band. What was more, radio play on the AOR stations was starting to pick up.

In The Mix

It was during the 'Hemispheres' tour that music lover Neil started to put together his "ShowTapes" – the cassettes of music that would be played before a gig. "I started mainly because we had a sound man with questionable taste," he would remark. In the late seventies the tapes included Talking Heads, Ultravox, Japan, Joe Jackson and The Police mixed in with the usual staples. "We were touring in Britain once around that time, and our sound engineer told me that when a song by the Police came over the PA, the English audience actually booed." Little did they know what their band had round the corner.

There was little time to stop and think about this. The boys were playing at least 20 days every month, with only four days for the Holiday season, and were being rewarded with a commensurate level of support wherever they played. Any last traces of the idea of playing two hours then partying until dawn were quashed, as the guys found they had to reserve most of their energy to keep up such a routine. "You have to be in first class shape to be able to do it in the first place, so you can't afford to let your health run down," said Neil. "You do start learning after a while to get a good meal and a good night's sleep."

The continued trappings of success were not without their problems, as a minority of fans started to cross the line into the trio's private lives. When fans discovered where Geddy lived, in the Beaches area of Toronto, they disrupted his day-to-day existence to such an extent, he and his family were forced to move to another, more exclusive suburb. "There's always a fringe which doesn't understand, and will never understand, that an artist's main responsibility is to perform well," said Geddy later.

"And that's where it ends." Support bands were also subject to the fans' collective wrath, as discovered one band, Blondie, on Jan 23, 1979, as they were booed off the stage. "The stage was filled with debris," wrote one report.

The first leg of *'The Tour of The Hemispheres'* came to a welcome close at the Pink Pop festival in Geleen, Holland, on 4 June 1979. The event was more than a little surreal - the band shared the stage with Mick Jagger, The Police and Dire Straits, Alex was nursing a broken finger, and one crew member fell out of the rigging and broke his leg.

By the end of the *'Hemispheres'* tour the band's finances were finally, well and truly sound, but the uphill journey for the Willowdale three had been steep and long. Perhaps, the band said, as they won a second "best band" Juno award, our touring work is done. Not that anyone wanted to stop; all agreed that touring was the ultimate connection between music and audience. However the need to tour incessantly for the sake of promoting the interests of the band – that was different.

From the record label's perspective, the band was playing to the converted, its music was delivered consistently and the albums provided a guarantee of sales with little requirement for marketing. From the child the label wanted to control, the band were now left to their own devices. "Most bands at that time, or especially this time, would not get that kind of latitude," said Geddy. "We were kind of overlooked. It was a small company at the time and they were a little bit disorganized." That was a sword that could cut two ways, but at the time, it was ideal.

The band had found its niche as a highly successful yet non-mainstream band. As one journalist, New Yorker Robert Christgau[5] ceded they were, "the most obnoxious band currently making a killing on the zonked teen circuit." All the same, the band's increasing popularity was taking its toll. Neil in particular was suffering from being under the spotlight: he loved being a successful drummer, but hated being a famous person. "Not only don't I care about superstardom, I hope it never happens," Neil had remarked. "We travel a lot around the country every year and we've pretty much just been able to do our jobs without a hundred people hanging on our every movement. I think that kind of privacy and isolation would be hard to give up."

> **Cheap Shots #4**
> "The day belonged to headliner Rush and blues-rock band Foghat, both of whom performed with a great deal of energy if little subtlety and, in the case of the alternately droning and shrill Rush, even less discernible talent."
>
> Lynn Van Matre, The *Chicago Tribune*, 20 August 1979 – Chicago Jams, with Sha Na Na, Blondie and the Beach Boys

Unfortunately, Neil was finding he had no choice, and was becoming frustrated as a result. "Having famous hands is okay, even though that carries its own set of pressures and insecurities. But having a famous face? That's nothing. I mean, what's your face? I didn't work all this time for my face." Above all perhaps, Neil's solitary nature and ability to observe were being squeezed. "You can't just sit back and soak up the vibes if you're the centre of attention."

Despite the outside pressures, the threesome was happy sticking together. There was no one big personality in the band, so the weight fell on three sets of shoulders. "I don't think we have too much trouble being humble 'cause none of us would let each other get away with any other kind of behaviour," remarked Geddy. "We each have a strong tendency towards normal. I think we were just brought up right." The fellows knew exactly where they stood with each other, which was a better protection than anything. "It's almost beyond family," said Alex. "We've shared so many dreams, and we've shared so many good times and hard times together. And, basically, the chemistry is right between the three of us."

In terms of musicianship, the technical learning curve was levelling off, and it was time to raise the bar in other ways. "We realized that one element often lacking in our music was feel," said Geddy. "We felt like we were just repeating ourselves, and we thought it was time to start experimenting at different ways of writing songs." The world of music was changing as well: in 1979, the brashness of punk was giving way to more polished production values, and a wealth of electronic devices were transforming disco. Said Neil, "When more thoughtful bands like Talking Heads came out and later the new romantics, I embraced it totally. It was an irresistible force at that point, it was just rock music that could call itself new wave."

New wave? Old wave? Whatever.

NOTES: 1 Skills. **2** Sha Na Na played the high school band in the film *'Grease'*, to give some idea of their musical style. **3** A $250,000 out of court settlement was later agreed. **4** As opposed to delay. **5** More recently, Robert was asked if his opinions had changed. "I have tried occasionally, most recently with their utterly forgettable covers album, to reaccess Rush's music, without any success," he says. "Not my kind of band in any way. The opinion stands."

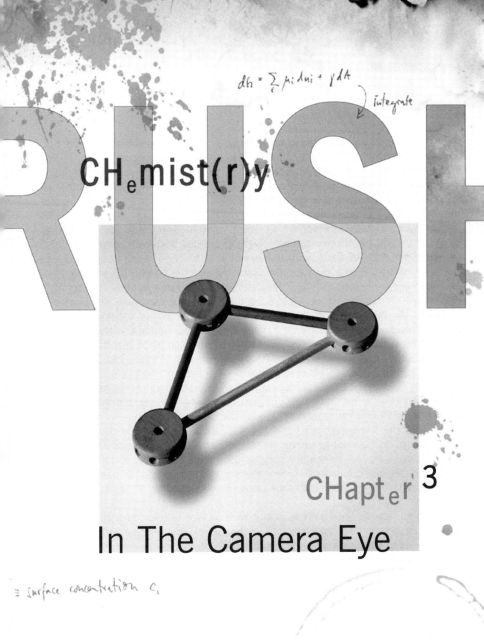

$dh = \sum_i \mu_i \, dn_i + \gamma \, dA$

) integrate

CH$_e$mist(r)y

CHapt$_e$r 3

In The Camera Eye

≡ surface concentration c_i

"Wondering what our dreams might be worth..."

$d\gamma = -\sum_i c_i \, d\mu_i$ (3)

a binary solution in contact with air

$G = \sum_i \mu_i n_i + \gamma A$ (4)

) complete
differential

$\sum_i \mu_i \, dn_i + \sum_i n_i \, d\mu_i + \gamma \, dA + A \, d\gamma$ (6)

"Conform or be cast out"

A New Reality

By the summer of 1979, the entity known as 'Rush' had achieved everything it could have asked for live. If fame was the goal, measured as bums on seats in the forums and arenas, then the boys were famous, whatever the press wanted to have people believe. The back catalogue of albums was selling well and each member of the band had attained a level of competence that other musicians could only strive for. From the outside in, things were on a roll.

Seen from the inside however, things looked very different. *'Hemispheres'* felt like the end of an era: the success achieved with *'2112'* had been built upon by *'Kings'*, and was then done to death with the album that followed. Long songs were, in hindsight, no more than a number of musical segments to be cobbled together in a way that made some sort of sense. "They just became too easy to do, a little boring," said Geddy. "We felt like we were just doing the same song over again, just changing the words. Anything you can do too easily isn't that much of a challenge." The resulting pieces were an indulgence, a musical rag rug for Geddy to stand on, as he preached the word according to Neil. Recent experience suggested that the challenge was becoming more intellectual than musical, while they made the simplest of mistakes, and were losing sight of why they were in the game in the first place. "It's very easy to fall into the trap of producing yourself to death and planning every minute of your life[1]," Geddy had remarked. Rather than being fulfilling, the experience of creating *'Hemispheres'* revealed only how far the band had to go.

Not ironically, the band's faith in its musical abilities catalysed a desire to write simpler songs. "We started to feel more assured as both musicians and songwriters," said Neil. "We were able to look at a song as just a song, and no longer felt compelled to overdress the music in order to hide inadequacies." This realisation marked a point of no return, kicking off a series of experiments that would draw the band ever closer to the mainstream.

First of all, and for the first time in four years, it was time for an extended break. Immediately following the last *'Hemispheres'* tour date at the beginning of June 1978, the travel-worn lads took a six-week vacation. "It was our intention to give ourselves a creative rest," said Neil. "We decided that we owed it to ourselves." The threesome spent time clearing their heads, remembering there was life outside music, and simply enjoying family life. Having spent much of the tour in flight manuals, Alex was gearing himself up for flying lessons and joining Geddy for the occasional game of tennis. After a while for Neil the call of the drums became too great, as he indulged himself in a new, mahogany-effect Tama kit from his favoured outlet, The Percussion Center. "I've always liked a good-looking drumset," he had said, and this time was no exception, deciding on a deep burgundy kit that matched some Chinese Rosewood furniture he had back home. "They experimented with different kinds of inks, magic marker inks of red, blue, and black, trying to get the color," he said. "It was very difficult."

Bless.

When Neil's honeymoon with his kit was over, it was time to start things anew. The boys reconvened to spend a couple of weeks at Lakewoods Farm near Georgian Bay, a two-hour drive north of Toronto, to regroup, decide what to do next, and maybe even develop some material. The farm was a peaceful place, with woods, and, well, a lake; next to the farmhouse was a cottage where Neil could develop his lyrical ideas in solitude. Much of Neil's inspiration started from his notebook, where he scribbled down thoughts derived from the world around him. "Many lyrical ideas come from conversation or TV, some little twist of phrase that I like and write down," said Neil. "By the time I start to write lyrics, I have pages and pages of just little jottings." One such hastily written note was only three words, that he'd picked up from a short story[2]..."roll the bones". Nice phrase, he thought to himself. Might come in handy sometime.

Compared to rushing straight in to a high-overhead, well-staffed, expensive recording studio, the approach that allowed some writing time was more cost-effective, and much less stressful. Ideas began to flow, remarked Neil, "in such a smooth and painless way that it almost seemed too easy!" The very first evening, a jamming session resulted in a piece of music (or, in Neil's words, "a giant hodge podge of instrumental mish-mash") called 'Uncle Tounouse'[3], which was later stripped for parts every time a song was lacking.

It quickly became apparent that the new album wasn't so much about breaking with the past, but more catching up with the present: there had been some major developments in popular music that were too much of a good thing to ignore. Once again many of Rush's driving influences came from across the Atlantic, where a song didn't have to be "pop" or "rock" to work on the radio. The players still wanted to define their own style, and they could not change their heritage – but they could incorporate a little reggae here, a touch of ska there, more through a desire to talk the language of the day than any commercial drive. "We are a sponge and we don't try to hide that," said Neil, whose eclectic tastes had been frequently foisted on the others in the tour bus. "We're perfectly open to new influences all the time and love them, and love being inspired by them."

Got it Taped

Neil's efforts to pump Geddy and Alex with new music had to be put on pause at Lakewoods farm, as the band was using his JVC cassette player to record their ideas.

Within a few days, the boys had laid the foundations for a number of songs, the first of which took direct aim at the inadequacy of the North American airwaves. 'The Spirit of Radio' offered a release of tension for the band, whose attempts to reach a broader listening public still led to a frustratingly small amount of airplay. The title came from the motto of CFNY in Toronto, an FM station that was steadfastly refusing to give in to the big business pressures of what should be played, when. "They were totally free-form, at the time when all these big programmers were coming in, and, you know, consultants were telling all these stations, and all these station managers, how to keep their jobs," said Geddy. As it happened, the programme director at CFNY was the same David Marsden that had played 'Finding My Way' on CHUM-FM all those years ago, to the delight of a young Alex. What goes around, indeed.

The desire to produce simpler, more accessible music drove a need for simpler, more accessible lyrics. "It was time to stop the concept stories," Geddy remarked, "to come out of the fog for a while and put down something concrete." To his initial disappointment, this meant Neil had to shelve a piece called 'Sir Gawain and The Green Knight', but he quickly got over it. "Whether it gets used or not isn't too important to me anymore, really, having done it," he said. "It was really a challenge to me as a lyricist to take something like an eighty-page medieval poem and try to encapsulate it in a reasonably (even for Rush) lengthed song." Its loss was not mourned for long, as the players realised how much more coherent things were becoming. "It was probably our first album that was in touch with reality," Neil would remark. "It was about people dealing with technology instead of people dealing with some futuristic fantasy world or using symbols for people."

Alex wasn't too ruffled about the bigger picture of change: taking on the trends of the day was nothing new, his latest techniques influenced by Allan Holdsworth's use of the whammy bar on his preferred Strat. "I couldn't really say what my style of guitar playing is like," he commented, a fact confirmed ten years later by producer Rupert Hine. "Alex is about the moment, and just letting things go and seeing what happens," says Rupert. The guitarist's free-form playing was naturally juxtaposed to Neil and Geddy's more structured approaches. "I like to take up as much space as I can in the context of this band," he said, but he recognised that there were other ways to create such textures. "We could fill in a lot with synthesizers now, but I still think the guitar chording aspect is important." His remarks were a nod to the new kid on the block, as if to say, "you're welcome to come along, just keep off my patch."

It was not that big an issue, at the time. Such was the relaxed atmosphere at Lakewoods Farm, nothing seemed to be too much trouble. Alex cooked most of the meals (he made a fine lasagne); for entertainment, he spent much of his leisure time building model aeroplanes that had a nasty habit of crashing into large, inanimate objects – such as the ground. Watching Alex's exploits seemed to be sufficient entertainment for everyone else. "Alex would spend hours every day re-assembling the pieces with gallons of epoxy, styrofoam cups, elastic bands, toothpicks and bits of plastic," said Neil, who would watch gleefully with the others as the resulting creations spun a few times in the air before crashing down.

As the musical pieces came together, Neil took advantage of the writing time to rehearse his drum parts, in the knowledge that he would be recorded first. When the fortnight of creativity was up, it was time to get Terry Brown back in the frame. "I would listen to material and just get fired up and say, well, this is great, I can't wait to record it," he says. The omnipresent schedules were calling, however: almost as quickly as they arrived, it was time to take some of the material live.

A four-week tour spanning August and September gave an opportunity to road test a few songs, not least 'The Spirit Of Radio' and 'Freewill', which both still lacked guitar solos; the band spent the soundchecks working on a song called 'Jacob's Ladder'. Witnessing one gig were two staffers at *Modern Drummer* magazine, Karen Larcombe and Cheech Iero, who also caught support act the Pat Travers' band with drummer Tommy Aldridge. "I remember Karen saying she and Cheech were more impressed with Tommy Aldridge's drumming than with Neil's!" comments Scott Fish, who was about to become managing editor at *Modern Drummer*. While Neil might have been winning prizes for his technique, he would have been the first to agree that he still had a way to go if he wanted to reach the bar his own heroes, such as Buddy Rich, had set.

Due to the overwhelming demand last time across the pond, a couple of extra dates were tacked on at the Bingley Hall, Stafford in England on 21-22 September, with a 10,000 capacity sold out crowd both nights. On the last night and to his own delight, Pat Travers joined in with Alex on 'Working Man'.

On returning to Canada the band decamped to Le Studio at Morin Heights, situated in the mountains just north of Montreal. Le Studio was only a short hop away from home rather than the long-haul flight the band had become used to on the previous two albums, and it boasted spectacular views from its glass-fronted recording room. "A wonderful place," enthused Neil. In attendance was resident engineer Paul Northfield (who had cut his teeth at London's Advision and moved to Canada the year before), together with assistant engineer Robbie Whelan. It didn't take long for Terry and the band to settle in with the pair, as Paul's friendly professionalism and Robbie's keen attitude quickly put the band at their ease.

A couple of weeks were spent finalising arrangements, melodies and lyrics, as well as deciding exactly what equipment would be used where – so-called pre-production. Once complete, Neil led the band on his new Tama drums to lay down the basic rhythm track, which was to be used as the foundation for the main instruments, vocals and other embellishments. Just because Neil could play each of his pieces note perfect by the time it came to record, this didn't mean he would be happy with the first take. "We would always record multiple takes of the three of them playing together," explains Paul. "Then we would edit between them and make up composite master takes."

Having fixed this "just-so" approach, Neil was not about to make changes on the fly for 'Different Strings'. Explains Terry, "I suggested in my infinite wisdom that a tempo change in a song was the right way to go, but Neil said to me you've got to be kidding! You've banged it into me over the years about tempo, and now you want me to make a tempo change? And he said, well, I can't do that, it's not going to happen." For better or worse, the routine was set.

Bottoming Out

Geddy makes the thunderclap sound in the middle of 'Natural Science' with his posterior, by sitting on the keyboard. They made them robust, them days.

Owned and operated by Yaël and André Perry, Le Studio offered the perfect antidote to the experiences of the previous album. The 'Hemispheres' sessions had been cold, wet and Welsh, the timescales had overrun and everyone had been pulling their hair out by the end. By contrast this was idyllic and dreamy, the vestiges of summer hanging in the air like notes to be picked, and the food (prepared and brought to the guest house by Parisian chef André Moreau, who had his own, "fabulous" restaurant in local village St Saveur) was far more "haute cuisine" than the country fare of Monmouth. The band and crew wasted no time in co-ordinating some leisure activities – a makeshift volleyball court was constructed, complete with floodlights for night playing in between takes. Meanwhile Alex had his planes, a hobby that Terry joined in with wholeheartedly... and building on the flight theme, keyboard technician Tony Geranios started building rockets. Tony also lent his nickname to some off-the-wall productions by band and crew of 'The Jack Secret Show', cobbled together using the Le Studio video recorder.

Business-wise, having avoided the pitfalls discovered on 'Hemispheres' (not least, to ensure the tunes were sing-able), it took only a few days to capture the essence of most of the tracks on the album. The songs were simpler, but the band wasn't actively trying to be commercial, whatever the management might have preferred. "There was always pressure to have something that could be played, and we usually managed to come up with one song that we could say was 'the single', even if it really wasn't!" laughs Terry. "They were not the kind of band who would like to compromise their art by making an album of pop singles. It's not like they were riding just on record success, they were out there working hard as a working band, and their audience were with them all the way, so, they weren't looking to the Top 10 pop charts."

As the band developed confidence working with Paul Northfield as engineer, Terry continued to take more of the producer's role. "I did all the hands-on stuff, I would recommend we would do this and that, and Terry would add his point of view as well," says Paul. Agrees Terry, "My motivation for not engineering was to bring more expertise to the table and free me up to concentrate on the production side. We were always moving forward and there was positive energy galore, and I think that comes across."

Indeed things moved so fast that the album would have been virtually complete, were it not for the "gaping hole" left by the departure of 'Gawain and The Green Knight'. Once the drum parts were recorded, Neil had been sent into solitary confinement to come up with some lyrics that would fit better with the rest of the album: he emerged triumphant after a few days with the 9-minute 'Natural Science'. To "set the monster to music," the band reverted to the knit and stitch approach of 'Hemispheres', using the remnants of 'Uncle Tounouse' to create the epic. Overdubs on the song took a cue from 'Kings', with many instruments being recorded outside to add to the ambiance. The 'Tide Pool' splashes, for example, were made by Neil and Alex, hitting the waters of the lake with oars. Explained Alex, "We stuck a speaker cabinet outside, and we recorded the natural echo off the mountains in combination with the sounds of splashing water and Geddy's voice."

Hugh Syme, who turned up to discuss cover ideas with Neil and the others, once again ended up contributing to the album – he played Grand Piano on 'Different Strings'. "Being in attendance and spending time with the band often led to, why don't you play on this, why don't you try something like this," explains Hugh. "I would go down the hall and work something out, and if they liked it we would use it." Alex was particularly pleased with his own solo on that song, inspired in part by the relaxed atmosphere. "It reminds me of soldiers sitting around a piano in a smoke-filled pub in England during the war," he said.

For a change the band didn't overrun the alloted studio schedule: there was time, and even material, to spare at the end. One piece of guitar music was left over after the final mix had made it to mastering, "a classical piece", said Alex. It wasn't decided what to do with it at the time, though it was saved to maybe take onto the next album. The final mixes, nips and tucks took place a week later, back at Trident Studios in London and giving some continuity with the previous two studio albums.

The working title of the album had been 'Waveforms', but it quickly became apparent that the name was already taken – several times over. Eventually, and perhaps more appropriately, the band settled on 'Permanent Waves', a direct comment on the pointlessness of musical labels. "This era seems to be pushing New Wave, and this wave, and that wave," said Alex. "The material we're doing is just Permanent Wave – it's just music. It's just a continuation, like a wave coming back in from the ocean."

The cover went through a similar evolution as the name. The initial idea, according to Hugh, was to incorporate electro-cardiogram readings of the three band members, taken during a performance. "We were going to strap them all onto the ECG and have them play," says Hugh. "Then, take a slice of their electro cardiogram from that particular point in time and run that on the cover as three separate colours. Very minimalistic, very all grown up." But as often happens in these things, a throwaway remark at the end of his discussions with Neil, blew the deliberations out of the water. "I jokingly said, why don't we have Donna Reed[4] with her whole permanent Toni hair do, walking a tidal wave, and someone waving in the background," says Hugh. "I was just intent

Second Wind

Unfortunately for weather photographer Flip Schulke, his expertise would come back to bite him, as Hugh Syme discovered. "When I called him, his house had been hit by a tree from a hurricane in Alabama. I talked to his wife and she said, he is just on the roof just trying to get this tree out of our roof!"

'Permanent Waves'

For many bands each album is a reaction to the one before. Where 'Hemispheres' built songs around concepts, 'Permanent Waves' collated the concepts into shorter, more humm-able songs, turning their musical attention to the post-punk New Wave, while retaining the band's hard rock edge. Punk was dead, and the New Wave sounds that now dominated the popular scene, created by altogether more competent musicians such as Talking Heads and The Police, were a powerful source of inspiration. The album kicks off with 'The Spirit of Radio', inspired by its radio station namesake and recounting a nostalgic rant at the ever-shrinking number of stations that were prepared to do their own thing. Ironic in the extreme that it has become one of the band's most played songs on the radio! The album is most of all about relationships, with only one song – the lyrically short ode to stormy weather that is 'Jacob's Ladder' – an uneasy fit with the rest of the album.

Interpersonal relationships are covered, appropriately enough, by a pairing of songs. 'Entre Nous', originally simply called the same in English, 'Between Us' is a love song that only Neil could write from his individualistic, observational standpoint, setting out the boundaries of any lasting relationship. Its message is reinforced by 'Different Strings' – 'We are islands to each other', perhaps, 'but there are times for you and me when all such things agree.' The connection is all the more poignant given that one song was written by Neil, and the other by Geddy, the final time he wrote a complete Rush song by himself. "I got really lazy, because Neil is so prolific," he said at the time, but he never needed to worry whether he would be able to interpret the lyrics.

Self-awareness is a necessary element of any relationship. Continuing the staple theme of self-determination, 'Free Will' bemoans the lives of those who believe they can't change their destiny. As if to prove the point, from a musical perspective it is a song that does not bow to the pressures of simplicity. "I don't think that you have to play in 4/4 to feel comfortable," said Neil at the time. "We work in nearly every [time signature] that I know of that's legitimate. All of the 5's, 7's, 9's, 11's, 13's and combinations thereof."

The band's last ever concept piece concludes the album. 'Natural Science' picks up where 'Different Strings' leaves off, suggesting that relationships between humanity and nature are subject to similar pressures to their interpersonal counterparts. Shorter, less complex and indulgent the three movements see the band inside its comfort zone, stringing together musical sequences to support the central theme. There is a sense of continuity about it all, a suggestion that there is a right way to do things, which strongly coincides with the band's own position at the time. There is no angst here, only understanding.

on rattling their cage with this entirely preposterous notion!"

To Hugh's surprise, after a couple of days of deliberation the band agreed with him. "I thought, no you don't! I really resisted it." Unfortunately he lost – insofar as he discovered how difficult it was to collate an appropriate set of images. Not least for the wave itself: "We finally came across a photo by a man called Flip Shulke," says Hugh. "Flip had been known to strap himself to telephone poles to grab the worst of the weather on the Florida coast and this was one of those images. I was able to work with that as a foundation." The girl was a then-little known model called Paula Turnbull. "The woman on the cover is really a symbol of us," said Neil later, in a hastily considered riposte to any cries of sexism. "The idea is her perfect imperturbability in the face of all this chaos." As for the man waving, well, you'll have to ask Hugh.

The resulting pastiche was subject to a number of copyright issues, or rather, threats from companies that were worried about being misrepresented. Not least from the *Chicago Tribune*, whose "Dewey Beats Truman" headline portrayed on the cover still smarted. "To boot, Coca-Cola asked that we strip out their billboard way off in the background because it was too close to a cotton-clad mons pubis," said Hugh. Some people are so sensitive.

With the album in the bag, the trio went their separate ways for a while. Alex finally started his flying lessons at Toronto's Buttonville municipal airport, and Geddy picked up his first producer's credit, working on the Wireless album *'No Static'*. This was as much a favour as an opportunity – hard rockers Wireless were on the Anthem label, and the band had played support at a number of dates on the *'Tour of The Hemispheres'*. An altogether family affair, the album was recorded and mixed by Paul Northfield at Le Studio, and Terry remixed one track back in Toronto.

'Permanent Waves', released on the first day of the New Year, was grudgingly recognised by the band's Greek chorus (the press), as more modern, more relevant, more in touch. Despite opening with the paradoxically radio-friendly diatribe, 'The Spirit of Radio', the album fitted with the journalistic preconceptions about what popular musicians should be doing. With no hint of irony, despite its anti-corporate undertones, the opening song provided a welcome release for fan-pecked DJs. At last, they thought, we can play some Rush, and get these blasted fans off our backs. Confirmed Neil, "It became that we were so popular in so many cities with touring all the time and people calling them up and saying, hey, play Rush, that radio stations couldn't avoid playing us! They certainly didn't do it voluntarily. For a lot of people airplay brings popularity, but for us it was the other way round."

It was time to tour, once again. Bookings were up an order of magnitude – Rush were selling out (in advance) arenas of up to 18,000 fans (for example the Cleveland Coliseum, still the epicentre of the Rush story) – and band and management were finding themselves far more able to have their say than before. Not least, this enabled Rush to achieve its goal of playing seated venues, a decision catalysed by tragic circumstances the year before. On December 3, 1979, 11 fans of The Who had been crushed to death at a concert in Cincinnati. "It's treating the kids like cattle, which they're not," said Geddy about the tragedy. "It's something we've fought for a long time but nobody listens to you." Suddenly, SRO had the ear of the venue organisers who were suddenly a great deal more interested in writing seating into the touring contracts.

The increased scale offered a huge opportunity to lighting designer Howard Ungerleider, who was delighted

That's the Spirit

In Montreal, the fans took it upon themselves to help the promotion of *'Permanent Waves'* along a little. A rep from the label turned up at Montreal's CHOM-FM to play an advance hearing of 'A Spirit of Radio', then left with the tape. The fans choked up the station's telephones for days afterwards, repeatedly requesting to hear the song again.

to fill the largest auditorium he was given with the widest array of lights and effects. Howard had been doing his homework, listening to the more down to earth feel of the album and tuning his designs accordingly. "I was trying to create a natural atmosphere," he says. "I'd watch the Jacob's Ladders coming through the clouds, or headlights in a forest at night, and I'd think, how can I recreate that?" Expectedly now at the start of the tour, SRO was in debt once again – 300,000 US dollars all told, spent on the ever-increasing tonnage of equipment the band needed for its live show. Requiring four huge trucks to transport it all, the stage equipment was worth 600,000 dollars alone!

All the same the band insisted on playing less profitable locations, both to repay the debt to fans of previous tours and radio stations who had promoted the band in the past, and to grow presence in new territories. Wherever they went they took the full show, a decision that made overseas engagements difficult: in the end they settled for a 19-date circuit of mainland Britain. Neil was pleased to announce he had put his Carnaby Street ghosts to rest. "It's tremendously satisfying to do well in Britain," he said. "It's not the most important market in the world in terms of record sales but we all have a special relationship with this country. I've lived here for a while, we've recorded several albums here and enjoyed doing them tremendously and we've also experienced a lot of loyalty from the fans. You really can't have a better relationship than that."

Today's Louis Lawyer

The soundchecks were used to test out ideas, not least a few keyboard ideas Geddy had been playing with, and some guitar riffs. Neil had worked in some lyrics to the former from Pye Dubois, Max Webster's wordsmith, which had started as a potential Max Webster song, called either 'Louis the Lawyer' or 'Louis the Warrior'.

Geddy would chant over the top of the heavy rhythm. "A modern day warrior, mean, mean, pride…"

All dates were headliners, and the band settled into a routine that drew a line under the past. They'd had their fun and they didn't want to blow the present, a professionalism that rubbed off on the crew. "The band members were not really caught up in the trappings and aura of fame and stardom," says crew member Nick Kotos. "Everybody on the entourage, band and crew alike, enjoyed themselves in a myriad of ways, but at the core of any successful touring entity, band or production staff, is the central theme of providing the best possible show every day."

On 2 February 1980, with the band already having 30 dates of the tour under their belts, the single 'Spirit of Radio' reached an acceptable #51 in the *Billboard* chart. The album hit the charts in a way that no previous Rush album had ever done – it peaked at *Billboard* #4 on 2 February, and reached #3 in the UK album charts. "I guess our time has come," said Neil, though the band's hands-off record label reacted only with bemusement. "We haven't got the time to wonder why," said a spokesman. "We're too busy shipping the albums." To be fair, the sudden popularity was as much of a surprise to the band, who saw the album as evolutionary. "There's nothing radically new or different on it," he said. "It's just another step, like *'Hemispheres'* was to *'A Farewell To Kings'*. And yet, the feedback we're getting on *'Permanent Waves'* is that a lot of people think it's very new, very fresh, and something quite different for us."

Some of the band's sternest critics started to soften their outlook, influenced by the inevitable – the band were appearing on covers of music magazines, and in the UK, Rush was ranked highly in readers polls in both *Sounds* and *Melody Maker*. As *'Permanent Waves'* went from strength to strength, it became harder to dismiss the band as irrelevant. "Are Rush finally winning over the critics who've mercilessly been directing written abuse at them for years," lamented arch-cynic Steve Weitzman, who was finding himself increasingly isolated. "Will there soon be only one writer left unimpressed with Rush?"

Not all the changes were good – as the audiences grew bigger, so did the size of the band's entourage, in particular the amount of security. With reason, perhaps – on January 3rd, 20 police had to be brought in to break up a near-riot among fans, who had been waiting in the freezing cold outside the Detroit box offices and ended up venting frustration (and perhaps warming up a little) by smashing up the booths.

"We became a little over protective of our privacy," remarked Geddy later, noting that Neil had had a harder time than most. Unfortunately, the more introverted Neil had no choice but to cope as best he could. "I'm not any kind of a misanthrope – a person who hates human beings, but I am a private person," explained Neil. "I'm basically shy with people I don't know, especially when I can't meet them on equal terms." In particular, he didn't like the idea of putting on a show after the show, so to speak. "I've projected all I have to project," he said. "All I want to do is go home, and if you walk out after that to a big crowd of screaming people, it's horrible … there's no middle ground to walk there, no way of being natural in a situation like that, there really isn't." Ah – the fans. Not only was the number of me-too 'fans' – the autograph hunters, the screamers and the backslappers – on the increase, so was the number of slightly obsessives. "There are a lot more weirdoes coming out of the woodwork," said Neil, with characteristic bluntness. "We could start a 'Flake of the Week' club."

In the main however, the fans were harmless. On occasion they were exceedingly useful, as Geddy found at the Queens Hall in Leeds, UK, with what he still remembers as his worst nightmare on stage. "I went onstage to sing 'Closer To The Heart' and for the life of me the lyrics would not come into my mind. I just stood there silently waiting for them to come back. I just looked to the audience and the kids are singing it, and they're trying to prod me on." Eventually the words came back, but not before the occasion had been indelibly stamped on his memory.

Every night was a huge test of stamina, and the necessity of playing quite so many dates became a frequent subject of discussion on the bus. "We're getting home every five to seven weeks for five days, and it's not a lot of time," said Alex. "We all have kids – well, Geddy's got one on the way – and we like to spend time with them." The band owed much of its success to past touring, so it was not something anyone wanted to give up completely but perhaps, it had served its purpose. At least, from the band's perspective the scale of success was the final nail in the coffin for any commercial pressure. "For a long time, we had to fight like hell," said Neil, "Now we're at the point where we can say 'Shut up, it's none of your business' to people who would try to tell us how to work."

He's Behind You

Many of the dates were supported by SRO stablemates Max Webster, whose kit would be set up in front of the Rush kit, Neil's drums hidden under a tent of tarpaulin. Unbeknown to the audience, on the last few songs of the Websters' set Neil would quietly sit down at his drums and play along with drummer Gary McCracken, to warm up.

The 96-date tour ran from January through to June 22, ten months on the road. The crew recorded gigs in Scotland and London to be used on a future live album, and the tour marked the first time that the band had achieved any reasonable profit. "We're not out to become millionaires or anything like that," said Alex, more sanguine than ab year or so before. "If we happen to make a lot of money or get material success, all well and good: we're not going to not take it. That stuff is nice, but we're doing what we want to do, playing the music we want to play, and I think audiences pick up on the fact that we're happy with being performers."

Geddy had spent much time on the road on the phone to his wife Nancy (who was expecting); no sooner had the tour finished than he became a father, to Julian. All three band members had the welcome opportunity to take two months with their respective families. When it had just been Alex and Charlene with children, little had changed, but then Neil and Jackie, and now Geddy and Nancy had gone the family way. Having kids was changing everything.

The Art of Noise

Well.

Whatever the band had done, last time round, it had worked. *'Permanent Waves'* had been an altogether more pleasant experience to record than *'Hemispheres'*, and had resulted in a top ten hit album. Nobody was under any illusions – there was no clear formula, no direct way of doing the same again, and anyway, who would want to do that? Besides, there was too much going on "out there" to spend too much time navel gazing about the past. "Rock music was changing dramatically at that point," said Geddy. "With the influence of reggae and white reggae, and more sort of aggressive punk music that was coming out, we very much wanted to be a part of that."

As well as the new artists on the block, a number of older performers were re-inventing themselves. Yes vocalist Trevor Horn had turned producer and was spearheading a technological revolution in music, accompanied by such stalwarts and innovators as Peter Gabriel. New Wave was being replaced by synth-laden pop counterbalanced by a resurgence of heavy rock, the latter characterised by journalist Geoff Barton as the "New Wave Of British Heavy Metal", or NWOBHM. With Rush's credentials and capabilities, it seemed possible for the band to steer a path through both.

The initial plan had been to release a live album based on the gigs recorded on the *'Permanent Waves'* tour, but a number of jams during the sound checks had been generating material that was too good to be left on the shelf. The band were also being badgered by Cliff Burnstein (who had, by this time, gained a reputation for being right), to release another studio album and capitalise on the success of *'Permanent Waves'*. "The creative hiatus provided by a live album was not really necessary," wrote Neil at the time. "It would be more timely and more satisfying to embark on the adventure of a new studio album." For a bit of light relief, the band cut heads with Max Webster to record the song 'Battlescar', one of the Websters' live songs that both bands had been playing during rehearsals.

In the early summer of 1980, taking time out from Geddy's fatherly duties, Rush got together at Stony Lake Farm, Ontario, a musical retreat rented from fellow musician and Canadian rockabilly hero Ronnie Hawkins. While Neil spent his time at the farmhouse working on the lyrics, Geddy and Alex made big sounds in a soundproofed barn. Big sounds indeed: the high-tech yowls of Geddy's Oberheim synthesiser resonated around the barn and were immediately latched upon. Based on powerful, synthesised intros, the pair constructed 'The Camera Eye' and 'Tom Sawyer': the songs were wake up calls, dragging the band physically and philosophically into the eighties.

Synthesisers were proving irresistible, but only to add the occasional, dramatic swathe of colour. "Some of the first really interesting polyphonic synthesiser keyboards were being made," says Paul Northfield, who was to be engineer on the album. "The polyphonic Oberheim and the Prophets, they were texturally very interesting sounds because we had not heard those before. At that time it was a level of orchestration that had never existed." All in the band were "for" the use of keyboards – and all were happy that it was Geddy in charge of the keys.

In his room, Neil noticed an evolution in his lyric writing, adopting a more observational approach. Indeed, Neil would later say that his writing came of age with this album. The philosophy was hidden beneath the surface of more reality-based songs, such as 'Red Barchetta' and 'Witchhunt'. "We looked at all those songs as little films, I think," he said. "We were trying to make the stories that we were telling affecting, and having some kind of emotional impact." The approach set the scene for the album, a series of short cuts that quickly earned the title *'Moving Pictures'*.

Musically the tracks were shorter, echoing with the simpler song structures of the band's New Wave contemporaries. Alex was to be particularly disparaging of the lengthy arrangements of the past. "You can take five different key signatures and go through them all in one song - big deal!" said Alex. "We tried putting something together in 4/4 time for four minutes, that had all the elements of something we once would have done in ten minutes. It's a little different... it's a little tougher."

At end of August 1980 the band decamped to Phase One studios in Toronto and hooked up with Terry Brown and Paul Northfield, to lay demo versions of the songs to tape. A month of dates followed, supported by Saxon, which gave the band an opportunity to trial 'Tom Sawyer' and 'Limelight', the other songs being rehearsed during sound checks. On October 3, after a single day off it was back to Morin Heights, the guys still buzzing from the tour. "They arrived at the studio fully rehearsed," says Paul. "Neil had absolutely everything, every drum fill, everything rehearsed in detail, and it would not change." With this in mind, it didn't take long to get things going. "I remember it being Friday night, we loaded in, and we started getting drum sounds," recalls Terry. "By the end of the night, we had this phenomenal drum sound, and we went, that's it! We came in the following day, and we cut 'Tom Sawyer', and it was stunning. Absolutely stunning."

Some new recording tricks were tried, particularly with the drums as Neil continued what had become a bit of a bugbear – "I've never heard my drums recorded the way I hear them," he

Morin Nights

"I dived behind the couch, with a scotch in one hand and a loaded banana in the other hand, and the scotch glass found its way into my head. So I was talking to Alex, and Alex is standing right in front of me talking, and he goes, Broon, is there a reason why you have blood running all down your face? So I went to the bathroom, and I was like, completely covered in blood! So, they whisked me off, Alex was driving, and we went to the hospital. I got checked in and they stapled my head together, right under the hairline. It was one of those crazy nights, they checked me in under some false name, my wife's name was some crazy Italian name they'd made up, the whole thing was just a hoot!"

Terry Brown

said. Paul Northfield suggested recording the drums through a PZM microphone[5] taped to Neil's chest: it wasn't quite there, but it helped. "It added to it and it helped apply that special dynamic that I hear," said Neil. Another recording change was with Alex's guitars. Traditionally Alex recorded as he would play live, with the guitar plugged into an amp, which was miked through to the mixing desk and thence to tape. As Alex spent more time in the control room listening to the result, he realised he might as well record from guitar straight into the desk.

The mild autumn slipped deceptively into the closed off, wintry atmosphere, as Geddy described it, "of a prison in a home which is snowed-in." The encroaching isolation worked in the band's favour: cut off from the real world, they were able to focus exclusively on what they were recording. The team had the routine worked out – Neil and the others would record to a click, then Geddy would spend a few days recording his bass and a few pieces of keyboard. Alex was up next, and Geddy would finish off with the vocals. Simple.

Not everything responded well to this approach, but this was more down to the arrangements than the principle. "'YYZ' was an incredibly difficult piece to cut," says Terry. Indeed, Alex had a particularly hard time with his parts. "He worked really hard, and there were times when we didn't really know where we were going to go. We didn't stop until we were absolutely sure we'd got the magic take on everything."

It wasn't all so intense – there was time for laughs over meals, and for occasional days off at the local ski resort, where Neil – for better or worse – was learning to snowboard. Some frivolity even crept into the recording process itself, not least with 'Witch Hunt'. The song required an "angry mob" sound effect, so band and crew trooped outside Le Studio where a couple of microphones

> ### Attention Daily Planet
>
> 'The Camera Eye' included a snippet of dialogue ("Let us through") piece from the first 'Superman' film. Explained Neil, "We were looking for an urban sound effect, and we ended up using a part of 'Superman', when Clark Kent is arriving at the offices of the Daily Planet amid the traffic and bustle of 'Metropolis'."

had been set up in the mid-December snow. What started serious, ended hilarious, explained Alex: "It was so cold, it was really cold! We started... rauw, raew, wrow... ranting and raving." Someone had the bright idea of cracking a bottle of Scotch to keep the blood flowing. "As the contents of the bottle became less and less, the ranting and raving took on a different flavor... we were in the control room after we had laid down about twelve tracks of mob – in hysterics. Every once in a while you'd hear somebody say something really stupid."

From starting the album with an innocuous, Oberheim-driven wail, the new technologies remained mostly a framework for the other instruments. "Geddy only played the big Oberheim, playing just a single string note that would just gloss over the top, bass pedals or the occasional Mini-Moog piece, which would be like a simple melodic," says Paul Northfield. Designer Hugh Syme added a bit of keyboard as well, to 'Witchhunt'.

Like 'Gawain' before it, left behind at the end of the sessions was a lyrical piece based on Thomas Hardy's 'Wessex Tales'. The literary work was squeezed out by 'Vital Signs', a song of the digital age based on a sonically synthesised backbone, as if to say: this was the way of the future. "'Vital Signs' was a pivotal point in Rush's career," said Neil. "It was the first time we tried a new style, which worked." Its lyrics were to prove almost prophetic, however – 'Signals get lost, and the balance distorted' – nobody would have thought the words could ever apply to the band. Perhaps as a cautionary tale of relying on too much technology however, various failures of equipment, not least the digital mixing desk, set the schedules back two weeks.

When the album was done, Broon and the band realised they had achieved exactly what they were aiming for. They had deliberately aimed at something more accessible and commercial, continuing in the vein of the previous album. "I was convinced that we were going to be very successful with *'Moving Pictures'*," says Terry. "It had a commercial edge to it, and we seemed to fine tune it just a little bit more. The boys were always pushing themselves to play that much better, better than they were really capable of doing, they worked so hard to get there, and they pulled it off. I thought it was the best thing since sliced toast!"

There is more to music than the recording alone: once the album itself was finished, the band could turn its attention to the cover art and the impending tour. Neil worked with Hugh Syme once again on the cover for *'Moving Pictures'*, which lent itself to all kinds of puns. "I knew immediately I wanted to do something that was simple, a Fellini-esque interpretation of moving pictures," says Hugh. "We had a couple of ideas, one was to have a faded place on a wall where a picture had been and there was still a nail and a string hanging there, like the picture had been there and had been moved. Simply that, but it was a bit dry and retiring and we decided it would be more interesting to do something a bit more cinematic." The final cover was taken in front of the Ontario seat of provincial government, at Queens Park in Toronto. It included pictures being moved, and pictures that move, with people taking moving pictures of them. Geddit? For extras, Hugh borrowed friends, neighbours and even his hairdresser's parents – "I had to call in a lot of favours," he says. Given the number of extras, equipment costs and other overheads, the cover was extremely costly to make, so expensive in fact that the band had to foot $9,500 of the bill themselves.

Meanwhile, Geddy and Howard Underleider went to town on the live show. There were practical reasons why the visual effects needed to be taken to the next level: the high kicking had been relegated to the past and the players were ever more tied to the equipment they played, leading to a genuine fear that the audiences would not have enough to watch. "Geddy was looking for some really cool animation to accent the tour," says Norm Stangl, at the time working at Nelvana productions in Toronto: he set to work on the first of a series of animated pieces that could complement the overall musical and visual experience.

The visuals were not the only things due for an overhaul: there were just too many new songs the band wanted to take live, and some older material was sounding stale in comparison. "There comes a day when we have to say, we have nothing to say with this song anymore. We can't play it with conviction," said Neil. So, songs such as 'Fly By Night' and even 'Working Man' were out – for the time. In were the new, keyboard-laden tracks – which led to questions about how (and indeed, whether) the songs could be reproduced live. 'Witch Hunt' was considered impossible, but there was a precedent of studio-only songs, such as 'Different Strings', 'Madrigal' and 'Tears'. So that was OK – 'Witch Hunt' would be left out of the set.

To deal with the newer songs there were a number of options – play "live versions" with new arrangements or get someone else in to join the live show. Neither felt particularly in the spirit of "Rush", so stage right engineer Tony Geranios suggested creating a setup to enable keyboard parts to be triggered remotely. "When I saw

'Moving Pictures'

From the bassy, synthesised growl of the opening song, it is clear that this is going to be no traditionalist's Rush album. 'Moving Pictures' is of the present, continuing the drive with 'Permanent Waves' to bring the band's thematic and musical roots bang up to date. There is no messing – 'Tom Sawyer' hits the listener between the ears, Pye Dubois' lyrical input leaving the trio to concentrate on writing a solid rock song.

'Moving Pictures' can be considered a relaunch, a reinvention of the band, its technical skills and slick songwriting turning its attention to the now. Thematically the album is decidedly autobiographical, its focus on how the band was finding themselves having to respond to mass popularity. 'Living on a lighted stage approaches the unreal,' states 'Limelight', the upbeat nature of its opening riffs belying the difficulties coping with the increasingly intrusive public. "It's about the alienation that fans try to force on us," explained Neil. "They force us to check into hotels under false names. They force us to have security guards to keep people away from us."

The rant repeats later in 'Vital Signs', which tries to explain the contradiction between wanting to perform, and being seen as a performer. Lyrically the song is almost apologetic – "The impulse is pure; sometimes our circuits get shorted, by external interference," they say. Neil reserved his worst criticism for England, "You can't even open the curtains in your hotel room," he said. "If you open your curtains, there'll be people staring in at you – shamelessly staring into your life." While still a rock song, the reggae beats of 'Vital Signs' demonstrate just how far the band was prepared to go musically, with no thought of compromise to meet the demands of past fans.

For Neil in a number of songs, group behaviour is the enemy, illustrated and enacted by the actions of the many, taken to extremes by the few. 'The Camera Eye' contemplates what a city – be it New York or London – must think of it all. With its Hammer Horror chordings and mob scene mayhem, 'Witch Hunt' takes this one stage further, itself one facet of a broader picture, treating the influence of fear on everyday lives. Neil had sketched out three "theaters of fear as I saw them: how fear works inside us ('The Enemy Within'), how fear is used against us ('The Weapon'), and how fear feeds the mob mentality ('Witch Hunt')." The original running order was reversed for practical reasons, as 'Witch Hunt' was the easiest for Neil to clarify at the time. One wonders why, but given his growing inability to cope with fame, not for long.

There is room for some older subjects to be reiterated, not least travel and society, both of which are distilled into 'Red Barchetta'. Based on Richard Foster's short story 'A Nice Morning Drive', the tale of a Ferrari's near-final altercation with newer, "safer" vehicles, the song places Ayn Rand's 'Anthem' in a contemporary, high-speed setting. Musically rich and diverse, 'Moving Pictures' continues a musical journey into the well-charted waters of the mainstream, without losing touch with the core values of the band – moments of instrumental indulgence like 'YYZ' offering the listener some respite to the well-structured songs. With its opening beats based on the call sign of Toronto's international airport, the instrumental piece was designed to evoke the leaving and homecoming emotions an airport could bring. For the travellers from Willowdale this album is indeed a homecoming, and the world welcomed its prodigal sons back with open arms.

what the band was doing, and the willingness to do everything themselves, I put forward the idea," says Tony, who (and this was prior to MIDI) had been watching his brother's experiments in triggering synth modules from a snare drum. All agreed, it was worth a try.

With a final reference to "our computerized companions: Albert, Huey, Dewey, and Louie," *'Moving Pictures'* was released on 7 February 1981. Ten days after the album was released, off they went, band and crew, the tour schedule a checklist of the major venues in the US and Canada.

It was like someone had knocked over a fire hydrant. "As the record went out I started getting phone calls from people saying, Wow, this is an incredible record!" says Paul Northfield. As a precursor to its own chart success, three weeks after the release of *'Moving Pictures'*, *'2112'* went platinum, the first Rush album to do so. On March 4, so did its live follow-up, *'All The World's A Stage'*. By March 13, a week after *'Moving Pictures'* had achieved Rush's highest ever chart position at Number 3, it went gold, and stayed in the charts a further two weeks, tipping platinum status. After some debate at SRO (as to which ones) a couple of singles were released – 'Limelight' reached *Billboard* #55 on 14 March; in August, 'Tom Sawyer' reached #44. 'YYZ' was nominated for a Best Rock Instrumental Grammy, and the band had never been so popular: the real world was a good place to be. "It really cemented our career," said Geddy. Not least, it allowed the band to renegotiate its record contract with Mercury. Over in the UK and Europe things were looking good as well – catalysed by the growing NWOBHM movement, the band also reached Number 3 in the UK charts.

Things were going far, far better than anyone had expected, often with amusing results – not least when Geddy won Most Promising Keyboard Player of The Year, in *Keyboard* magazine. "We used to laugh about that," says Paul. "It was hilarious, he had only just graduated from playing one note to playing chords!" Hilarious perhaps, but while Geddy and Neil were becoming regular recipients of awards, Alex had yet to pick up a gong. As others were quick to note, he was always coming second to Eddie Van Halen, which grated more than a little.

As the tour proceeded, the band realised they were being treated as fully-fledged rock stars, for better or worse. "We'd see all these people at our shows who had no idea why they were there or what we were doing," said Neil. "For some reason we were in that year. That record and that tour did twice the business we did before or since." Backstage there were accumulations of hangers-on; stage front was packed with people who dearly, dearly wanted to achieve some sense of proximity with their heroes. The band did the best they could: Nick Kotos, who was tour manager by this time, watched the band's valiant efforts. "I never saw any big gap between the band and their fans," says Nick. "To the contrary, the guys in Rush would always stop and talk to their fans, regardless of my attempts to get them into the gig to start their sound

Picture Perfekt

Most of the pictures to be moved were decided by the band, with Hugh Syme requesting a Joan of Arc pic to represent 'Witch Hunt', largely because he played on it! He was to pay for his attention – "it ended up being a bit of a nightmare because I couldn't find any archival pictures or paintings which were suitable. So I ended up getting some burlap, and a pine post, two sticks and a bottle of scotch. Deborah Samuel, the photographer who I used on that session, got wrapped up in burlap so she could make her cameo appearance. We just lit lighter fluid in pie plates in the foreground. It was basically a half hour session because we had no other alterative but to do it ourselves."

check." Fair enough – those very people formed the backbone of the best audiences the band had ever entertained.

All the same, outgoing Geddy and Alex started to feel the strain. "We had to get a little more insular," said Geddy. "We had, I guess, a midlife crisis." As for Neil, he coped – just. "Things were kind of overwhelming, I had a sense of just treading water, trying to keep afloat in all of what people were expecting me to do," he said. "The more fame we got, the more uncomfortable I became, until I had to overreact and refuse to have pictures taken or anything to do with the machinery because it was taking over."

Cracks even started to appear between the band and their long-standing, loyal crew. "Exposure gaps became inevitable," says Nick Kotos. "As the production grew, the crew would start working at 7:00am and finish around 1:30am, Tour Management had more demands for financial reporting, the band had more demands on what little personal time they had, and we all got a little bit older."

Almost inevitably perhaps, the success story was not without its casualties. In April 1981, co-manager Vic Wilson decided to throw in the towel and follow his other interests, selling his share of SRO to Ray. "He had other things that he wanted to do with his life and he wanted to get out," says agent Neil Warnock. "He was tired with the business and I don't think he got any satisfaction out it." Also in April and without warning, Kim Mitchell (support band Max Webster's vocalist), packed his bags and left the tour. Later he explained that his decision was in part due to feeling that the Websters hadn't been promoted as well as they could be by SRO – a consequence of Rush's runaway popularity. On the upside, FM stepped in to replace Max Webster, the band including esoteric instrument player Ben Mink.

There were plenty of highs. Geddy, Alex and Neil had the opportunity to jam around in sound checks just like in the old days, the output of which (recorded for posterity by soundman Jon Erickson) was the starting point for the aptly named 'Chemistry'; another song captured was 'Tough Break', which had started as a jam between Neil, Tony Geranios and fellow crewman Skip Gildersleeve. On occasion the band showed that it did know how to party – "Once or twice in the course of every tour, there is a night of blessed excess," said Neil as he described one such event, at the Italian Village in Chicago. "All around, there is ceaseless laughter, and the constant roar of shouted conversations. People are at the tables, on the tables, and under the tables!"

Neil wrote a daily diary on the tour, with the intention to release it one day. "If I could complete one good short story, I'd feel like a real writer," he said. "But to do a novel or a series of short stories takes a 100% commitment, and I don't want to compromise what I'm doing as a musician by any means."

Red Alert

On April 10, a day off, the band took a jaunt to the Kennedy Space Center to watch the maiden flight of the Space Shuttle Columbia, invited by NASA director Gerry Griffin. Due to computer problems the launch had to be postponed until two days later, when the band was playing Fort Worth in Texas, but nothing was going to prevent the threesome from attending. "It was an amazing thing, an amazing sight to witness," said Alex, who watched with the others from the viewing area called Red Sector A. "I've never heard anything so loud in my life. Your pants are flapping, you could feel the ground vibrating and this was three miles away. That's the closest you could get." "Truly a once-in-a-lifetime experience," said Neil. As a token of their appreciation, the band planned on the spot to write a song about the experience. They made it to the Texas gig – just!

As the tour closed on 5 July 1981 it was finally deemed the moment to put a live album together, to capitalise on the moment as much as anything. After sifting through tons of reels of tape, the band agreed to a double album based on the Glasgow and Canadian dates of the *'Permanent Waves'* and *'Moving Pictures'* tours respectively. Recording a live performance is not as simple as it sounds – the knowledge that every false move will be captured for posterity can be a great way to freeze up what would otherwise be a fluid performance. All the same, "They were not panicking when they played," says live recording engineer Guy Charbonneau, who had seen much worse.

Terry Brown got on with most of the production at Le Studio and the boys came to add some overdubs – re-recording any bum notes and missed cues. For a bizarre reason all agreed to minimise the input from the crowd. "We were trying to keep every hair in place," said Geddy. "We were being naïve and missed the point." As Terry did his thing, the players started to hunt around for other things to do. Neil found a set of thin-shelled Hayman drums in the basement of Le Studio (which initiated conversations with Tama about releasing a thin-shelled model of their own kit), and the threesome started to play with more ideas for the next album in the smaller studio room, developing what would become 'Subdivisions'. The song claimed the dubious distinction of being the first song Geddy had written completely on keyboard.

Pegi Cecconi, who had taken over a number of Vic's publishing roles, got to work with Hugh on the live cover, a collage of the band's previous output. The theatre scene was captured at Toronto's Winter Garden Theatre, which had been closed since 1928 and had fallen into disrepair[6]. The plan was to use the original people from previous album covers, which caused no end of problems. "We discovered the perils of having people waiting," says Hugh; worse, some had unexpected expectations. "Paula Turnbull became a noted model in Europe – enough that when I brought her back, she was appalled to know that I didn't have a trailer for her." Josh Anderson, the original "king" on *'A Farewell To Kings'* couldn't get there at all: his plane was delayed due to the weather.

With a final, composite image incorporating a stage shot taken on tour in Buffalo, *'Exit... Stage Left'*[7] was released October 1981. As a humorous aside, the cover was intended to include the tail of cartoon character Snagglepuss – that's it, just the tail. Clearly it was a cat's whisker too many. "Forget it!" said Neil. "They wanted all kinds of legal hassles and tons of money."

Unexpectedly, a few months before the release of *'Exit... Stage Left'*, Mercury's German office issued a single greatest hits album – *'Rush Through Time'*. The band and SRO were not best pleased, and it resulted in another black mark against the label's European operations. Remarked Neil, "It certainly contains nothing of any interest – not even the cover and certainly not that title. Have you noticed that everyone puns with our name except us?"

Of course, having released the album (or even, both of them), it was necessary to tour. Ho hum – at least it offered an opportunity to road-test 'Subdivisions'. Off they went for the last two months of 1981, starting back at Stafford's Bingley Hall in the UK. The fans continued to stamp their mark: the trio needed a police escort when they landed to play at the Royal Highland Exhibition Centre in Scotland, and on November 28 at the Hollywood Sportarium in Florida, Neil learned the lesson of being late to a gig. Following the unfortunately named support act Riot, the fans started a riot of their own when the band failed to come on stage on time. It would have to be Neil, who was travelling back from a visit to the Virgin Islands.

More feeling "trapped by" than "the trappings of" fame, the drummer found himself fighting ever harder for his right to be normal. He wrote a heartfelt riposte to an article in the *Daily Texan* newspaper in which, based on a lecture entitled 'No-one gets out of here alive', Rush was a named example of a band of "satanic rockers". Ouch. "I can certainly assure you that my lyrics contain no 'demonic' secret messages or cleverly concealed mystical commercials," he wrote. "It is not only absurd and pathetic, but it is also totally incompatible with my philosophy, my work and my beliefs."

Incorporating the acoustic piece 'Broons Bane', *'Exit... Stage Left'* sold better than anyone had expected, reaching #10 and #6 in the *Billboard* and UK charts respectively. Together, the live album and *'Moving Pictures'* achieved two out of the four Juno nominations for 1981, in the Best Album category. Neither won, but nobody was too disappointed – there was no shortage of new gongs on SRO's shelves. After the tour, life went on: Neil accepted a post on the advisory board of *Modern Drummer*, and Alex was building a studio in his house with a 24-track analogue desk.

Onward and upward.

The Joy of Touring

"Consider a typical artist's schedule. Arrive at a hotel (Somewhere, USA) at 3 or 4 in the morning, stumble into a room, and go to sleep, wake up in an anonymous room in an anonymous hotel in an anonymous town. Do a couple of telephone interviews (be brilliant and funny and entertaining). Try to have a normal life, maybe talk to your wife or friends not on the road, see a movie, read a book, shop, eat, do laundry. Drive to the gig, Soundcheck, eat "what is this supposed to be?" Dinner, "Meet and Greet" Record Company, Radio Station, Record Store, Press and Fans, deal with crew and production and business issues. Then compose and prepare yourself to perform the "best show of your life" in front of thousands of fans for a couple of hours. After the Show, more meet and greets, and then climb onto the bus and go to another hotel in another city in the middle of the night. Oh yeah, you do this regardless of how healthy or sick you are, how tired you are, whatever personal issues you might have, and by the way, you've got to start working on the next album.

THAT IS THE TOURING MUSIC BUSINESS."

Nick Kotos, Tour Manager

Signals Get Lost

The experiments started with *'Permanent Waves'* culminated in *'Moving Pictures'*, as commented Geddy, "these two albums have an equal meaning in the history of Rush." However, the last thing Rush wanted to do was to repeat the exercise a third time. Confident they could move in whichever direction they wanted, it was almost an obligation to do something completely different. Geddy predicted a dark album; as things turned out, he was right – but not for reasons anyone expected.

Of all the influences the band had been absorbing, one in particular had grown in stature. First introduced by Hugh Syme on *'2112'*, synthesisers had offered Geddy a few additional textures on *'Hemispheres'*, innocuously biding their time. Their lure proved irresistible, for Rush as for many other bands of the time. For Geddy in particular, keyboards were about to take centre stage.

From ground level, as the band broke up for Christmas, things did not seem so complicated. We're just going to be making another album, right?

In the spirit of experimentation, the threesome went their separate ways for a few weeks to play with ideas. "We stayed in our little rooms, and did our own work," said Geddy, for whom the obvious thing was to sit down at the keyboards. "To me it was a new toy, a new texture," he said. He was not alone: keyboards offered a constantly evolving source of inspiration for many musicians, at the time. "The most exciting things that were happening in sound were coming from keyboards," says Paul Northfield. "With every new keyboard that came out, it was like, wow, this one is great, and we had to get this newest one because it gave you such a creative texture to work with." Geddy's fruitful experiments provided the starting points for 'The Weapon' and 'Analog Kid'; at the time he wasn't even sure if his outputs would be right for Rush, and was quite prepared to shelve them for a potential solo effort.

Alex was no less prolific, or experimental for that matter, there were plenty of new styles to try, and untapped ways to manipulate guitar sounds. As Alex was coming up with the theme for 'Losing It', Neil was still happy to stick with "real" drums, buoyed by the real-world experience of *'Moving Pictures'*. This time he would throw in ska, a little jazz-fusion and more than a hint of reggae. When Rush got back together at The Grange, a writing studio at Muskoka Lakes, Ontario, they found they had more material than they knew what to do with. "We had so much stuff it was ridiculous," said Geddy. A melting pot approach ensued, the trio testing ideas out on each other, trying out new stylistic and lyrical combinations to see what worked.

As Geddy spent more time writing and arranging on the keyboards, so he was less focused on the bass lines. This had the unexpected effect of Alex spending more time with Neil, as a surrogate bass player. "Alex and I developed a relationship as a rhythm section, which guitar players and drummers do not do," said Neil. "We developed an understanding of each other's approach, and of playing sympathetically to each other, which we still use. The knowledge, and the relationship between us, was gained forever."

The dynamics were shifting, but there was clearly no harm in that. Furthermore the schedules were calling, as usual, the momentum carrying the band along. At the beginning of April the band went on tour for a couple of weeks: 'The Tour of The Nadars' was an opportunity to give the first outings to 'The Analog Kid' and 'Subdivisions'. 'Digital Man' and 'The Weapon' were played in soundchecks, and 'Chemistry' was already in the bag. Everything was looking good - after the fortnight was over, it was time to head back to Morin Heights, to complete and record their efforts.

By the time Terry Brown was getting involved, demos of all the songs had been worked out. "That album was ready to rock," says Terry. "I had input, but not as much as I would have had on previous albums." As usual, the first period at the studio was to get the sounds and finalise arrangements, so the now-pat recording process could take place. All three recorded the rough tracks and Neil laid down his drums, then came bass, then the more textural layers – the keyboards and guitars. "We wanted the guitar to become part of the rhythm," said Alex.

Oh, dear.

It was a simple enough error, if it could even be called that. As Geddy and Alex stepped up to the plate, the keys were always just a little better prepared than the guitar parts. "The mistake we made was not in getting into keyboards that heavily; the mistake was doing them first," said Geddy. "Alex would have temporary parts worked out by the time we went in to record the keyboards. He wasn't prepared enough, early on." By the time Alex had worked out the problem, it was already too late. "Somewhere along the line we lost it," said Alex. "I have to blame myself for it, but we were trying something new at the time."

By filling the textural spaces with keyboards, Geddy was unknowingly tampering with a major part of Alex's *raison d'être* within the context of Rush. On the surface, things continued much as on any other album, but the underlying frustrations were tangible. Alex was, according to Paul, "battling through a wall of keyboards." In Geddy's terms, "The guitar and keyboards were sharing the same range too much, and it was a struggle. They were each fighting for their fair share of sound." The normally easy going Alex felt more and more frustrated, but his desire to go with the flow overwhelmed any other feelings.

If anyone was to watch the threesome goofing around outside the studio, they would have been surprised to learn that anything was wrong at all. There was plenty of fun to be had during leisure time, for example when band and crew challenged the female bar staff at 'The Commons' hotel in Morin Heights to a softball match (a return request by the male staff was politely declined!)... such occasions were as deeply enjoyed and memorable as ever. Within the walls of Le Studio however, not everything was well.

As time dragged on, band and producer alike felt less and less able to understand the issues bubbling up, let alone resolve them. "We were confused as to what our direction should be," said Geddy. "You get so locked into it, it's tunnel vision," agreed Alex, whose usually jovial demeanour was being steadily undermined. "You get used to hearing it a certain way day after day after day, month after month after month. After a while it seems normal to you, seems the way it should be." The tunnel vision was affecting Terry as well. "It was all becoming very electronic," says Terry. "I had arrived at the point where I couldn't contribute more if that was the direction we were going in, it just wasn't my *forté*. The keyboard thing was becoming overtly the band sound, which I

Platform Soul

A photo shoot by Deborah Samuels for Tama drums involved setting up Neil's kit in the middle of the lake. "The boys took the drums out on the rowboats and set them up on this little swim platform," says Terry. "The stool was literally right at the back, and I know it freaked him out – it scared the crap out of him!" Back on shore, Paul and Terry were working with Alex when they heard this astounding drum sound reverberate across the water. Quickly, the pair rushed out with a pair of mikes to capture the effect. "His drums sounded amazing, amazing! Thunderous, and the delay and the reverb was all natural, it was phenomenal," says Terry. "You could probably hear it from miles!" Sadly, the final recordings couldn't be used, not least as they were interrupted by a helicopter flying past.

didn't think was cool either."

On 'Countdown' the keyboards even encroached on Alex's last bastion, the solo slot: even Geddy admitted it was a step too far. "I don't think I'll ever do that again," he said. For 'Losing It', the band agreed to get in Geddy's friend Ben Mink to add a solo on electric violin. "We worked him hard, squeezed him dry, and threw him away!" laughed Neil. "He just stood there in front of the console taking it and giving it." Ben did a great job, but it seemed that Alex was being pushed even closer towards the door.

In such uncharted territory, the one thing lacking more than anything else was an outsider's view. "Perhaps we had too many producers in the studio, all vying for their own little thing," said Alex; unfortunately, having developed a routine with the others over seven years, Terry was no more likely to add perspective and take control than anybody else. "We really needed Terry to sort of give us that direction at that point, like a proper producer," said Alex. "Our relationship was too familiar, too easy, and it lacked." Says Terry, "There wasn't a big incident, but I think the writing was on the wall. There were some edgy moments, which was very unusual with us."

The one attribute uniting both players and producer, was a dogged determination to bring things to a successful conclusion. As the project neared an end, the foursome rose to the challenge of 'Digital Man', a song that did nothing at all for Terry. "I wasn't crazy about it, it had that sort of Police thing going and it didn't really sound like Rush," he says. "But, you know, it was a tune, I had to make it work, let's get on with it, let's do it as well as we could. I think we made a good job of it, but it was, a little odd." "We refused to give in," said Neil. "We wore away at him inch by inch, until he got tired of hearing about it, offered a few half-hearted suggestions, and relented."

The last track to be written, codenamed Project 3.57 as it had to come in under 4 minutes, was 'New World Man'. And with that in the bag, it was over.

'Signals' turned out to be a dark album indeed. As the final cut went to be mastered, a month late on 15 July 1982, the band confessed to being under-impressed. "We felt it was kind of a failure in getting the right balance between synthesizer technology and hard rock," said Geddy, using 'Subdivisions' as an example. "We leaned too heavily into keyboards and ignored the guitar aspect of it." Duh. For many years, Alex still felt a little too close to the experience but over time he managed to develop a certain level of stoicism. "We tried things that I listen to now and know weren't right, but we learned from it," he said. "At least we're trying something different."

At the time however, everyone was glad that the recording was out of the way, and the desire to move on was tangible. "The big keyboard thing was a change up, and we were going to go somewhere else next time around," Terry says, a touch wistfully. "Little did I know at the time, there wouldn't be a next time around."

The cover design for the new album was tricky, given Hugh's limited remit – he was given no more than the word "signals". "It was such a broad concept that it was baffling for all of us," he says. It took a number of months to come up with a cover concept everyone was happy with, as Hugh trialled everything from Marconi and the RKO tower, to the ECG idea again (lucky they didn't use this – The Police came up with a similar idea for *'Synchronicity'* soon after). "We went through every permutation we could," says Hugh. Using Canadian logic of a kind that Bob and Doug

'Signals'

'Moving Pictures' might have finished with the message that 'signals get lost', but the upbeat synthesisers that open 'Subdivisions' suggest they've been rediscovered – though to many observers, this intensely autobiographical song about the self-imposed structures of society was a step too far into the contemporary. Not least Alex himself, whose guitars are no more than one of many electrical signals, each vying for a share of the bandwidth in this opening song. Geddy's bass is also noticeably absent, but that is through his own choice.

'Signals' is mostly about the music, the band's determination to take their influences centre stage resulting in a decidedly comprehensive overview of what was happening stylistically at the time. 'New World Man' is an almost-direct homage to that other power trio, The Police, and songs like 'Digital Man' are a patchwork of musical ideas, according to Neil, "We ended up with three pieces of one song held together by Crazy Glue!" There might have been a danger that the album would have resulted as a musical gloop but, despite the internal tensions that were part and parcel of the production, the result is surprisingly good. Following the ill-fated opener there are guitars a-plenty, for example the backbone to 'The Analog Kid' presents a frenetic play-off between axe and sticks.

Where there is a central concept to the album it comes across as one man's trial. 'Digital Man' is similar in many ways to 'Tom Sawyer', continuing the journey into the digital age as the analog kid becomes a man and does his best to get ahead. The second part of the Fear trilogy is 'The Weapon', reminiscent of 'Room 101' in '1984' as our ordinary Joe faces his demons. We meet him again in the next song, 'New World Man' as he sets out on the path of life, "old enough to know what's right, but young enough not to choose it." Finally, it is an older, sadder Joe we see in 'Losing It'. Side-glances to a despairing Hemingway and a fictional ballet dancer capture the moment when even the most creative and artistic find that the spark has gone.

Not the happiest of themes but to the band at the time, the soul searching was very real. The final song, 'Countdown' doesn't really fit with the rest of the album but it was too big an opportunity to miss, documenting the band's experiences of the Space Shuttle launch through a mixture of real radio footage, paced vocals and multiple layers of music. A good song nonetheless, the fade-out leaves us hanging in mid-flight, as if to remind us that what goes up, must come down.

would be proud, in the end he went for the most primitive of messages. "I said why don't we have a Dalmatian, a dog sniffing a fire hydrant. I don't get it, they said. Well, think about it." Once they'd got it, they liked it – particularly as the hydrant fitted with both the suburban undertones of 'Subdivisions' and certain meanings of 'Chemistry'. The back cover incorporated a mock-up local map, showing imaginary subdivisions (that's housing estates, for anyone in the UK) and buildings based on the band's nicknames[8].

Whatever had happened behind the closed doors of Le Studio, the wider public was none the wiser. 'Signals' was released in September 1982 to a generally receptive audience (though clearly, a hard core of '2112' fans found little to change their minds that Rush had sold out commercially). At the same time as the release, a specially produced laser show went live at Laserium installations in cities on both sides of the

What a Hoser

Geddy performed on *'Take Off'* with Bob and Doug McKenzie, in fact old school friends Dave Thomas and Rick Moranis in their guise as Canadian hicks. Recalled Geddy, "I went in to record and they were in character, and it was really a hoot! Thus my life in comedy started." This appeared on the album *'Great White North'*, which was released on the Anthem label. It made the US top ten and went triple platinum within a few months. "It was strictly a fun thing to do with some pals," he said. "Nobody had any idea it would get as big as it did."

Atlantic. Externally at least, the band put a positive spin on how the album had turned out – but Geddy was the main spokesman. "*'Signals'* is definitely the direction that we've wanted to go in for a long time," he remarked at the time – but he had been driving it, and the keyboard-laden 'Subdivisions' was one of his favourite tracks.

Everyone felt able to look forward – not least to the tour. Howard and his crew had been configuring what was the band's biggest set yet – doubling the number of lights and upgrading the sound system. Bigger wasn't necessarily more technically complex, but it did mean more stuff. "The only real issue, if it really could be considered an issue, was finding enough space in the trucks," says tour manager Nick Kotos. The visuals were extended as well, a deliberate tactic as the band became ever more fixed to its kit. This time, the plan was to integrate film clips with the live performance. "It's a very expensive medium to get involved with so we had to budget ourselves carefully, and try to get the most out of 30 seconds of film that we could," said Alex. Despite their growing popularity the boys were still refusing to play festival-sized events, as they didn't want to compromise their stage show.

The tour started 3 September, each opening night with the *'Three Stooges'* theme tune – an indication (if any was needed) that the band weren't taking themselves too seriously. There was plenty of *'Signals'* in the set, so it can't have been all bad, but the band declined to play 'Losing It' live in the absence of Ben Mink. Taking his usual stage right position, Alex favoured short hair, sharp suits and narrow ties, spurning heavy rock garb for pop togs. "You can only wear satin pants and boots for so long," he said. The third night of the tour, and with no particular fanfare, the proceeds were given to UNICEF.

In chart terms the band were as big as they'd ever been. The afterthought track 'New World Man' reached *Billboard* #21 in October 1982; despite Neil's opinion that

> ### Intro Music #1
>
> "A selection of lesser known songs from that era, by New Musik, Simple Minds, King Crimson, U2, Ultravox, Max Webster, Joe Jackson, Japan, Thinkman (sic), Go, XTC, Talking Heads, Jimmy Cliff... Pete Townshend... Bill Bruford and... Orchestral Manoeuvres In The Dark."

the reality audio of 'Countdown' didn't quite work, it was put out as a single in any case, with a video of the space shuttle launch provided by the band's NASA contacts. "They've been very cooperative and quite friendly," said Alex. You betcha.

'Signals' gave the band its first ever Number One – in the newly created *Billboard* album rock chart at least, a position it held for two weeks. Video play of 'Countdown' via MTV played its part in the album's success, despite the band's mixed feelings about the channel. "MTV has the same flaws that radio has, in terms of being too programmed and too easy to try and find a formula for," Neil had remarked: unsurprisingly, the band turned down an opportunity to participate in an MTV contest.

Neil was starting to work through his own demons of fame, not least by taking a bicycle on tour for the first time and discovering the art of pedal powered obscurity. "I'm just another guy on the road," he commented. "I'll always choose a little farming community and go into the local diner and just sit there and listen. The incognito aspect of it is really nice but also you're seeing real people in their real, everyday lives." Neil found that by mixing with the ordinary, he was able keep in touch with normality, even when on tour. "I have acquired a whole new affection for America," he said.

The *'Signals'* tour came to a close just before the holiday season, and the first couple of months of the New Year had been allocated to non-Rush activities. As well as quitting smoking, Geddy produced an album for the Howard Ungerleider-managed synth-pop band Boy's Brigade, who had been the support band from the tour. Geddy also played bass on a couple of tracks for Marie Lynn Hammond, on her album *'Vignettes'*.

Most importantly, the self-imposed break provided a much-needed opportunity to think about what on earth it was all for. Nobody was suggesting a split, but all recognised that things could not go on as they were. The possibility of dispensing with electronics was less than remote – they were part of the musical fabric of the time. One by one, the various options for change took one step back, leaving one poor soldier still standing, oblivious, in the front line. The producer.

As Rush had gone on tour they had expressed their continued satisfaction with Terry Brown, but the months of tour bus discussion and introspection had given cause to re-evaluate this perspective. By the beginning of 1983, the band's feelings about their "fourth member" were clearly in turmoil, as indicated in an interview with Geddy by the UK music mag, *Melody Maker*. "One day we might decide to go for a change, but if we did it wouldn't be through any lack of respect for Terry," said Geddy. "It would be merely a case of time and change, but I really don't know if that'll ever happen."

Oh yes it would, and indeed did. Not only was it deemed necessary to involve someone more up to speed with electronica, but also the band felt that an outsider's view on the recording process – a so-called "objective ear" – would help avoid the in-too-deep situations of the last album.

Terry hadn't created the situation on *'Signals'*, indeed, nobody had. Neither was he able to resolve it, no more than any of the three band members. "We were so close to Terry, he was in the band almost, and he wasn't objective anymore," said Geddy. "We could anticipate his input and structure our music around that." Says Paul Northfield, "I think they reached a point where they knew what Terry was going to say before he said it."

While the trio recognised the fact that Terry wasn't the main cause of the problems, they saw his departure as an opportunity for resolving them. "It was really a necessary thing, not out of any disrespect or any problem in communicating with each other, but a matter of our band falling into a dangerous rut," said Geddy at one point. "We wanted to put ourselves in a kind of shock treatment." By projecting the situation onto the hapless producer, they could avoid having to look too hard at themselves. "I think it was a smart move," says Terry philosophically. "It was either that or a band member change, and that wasn't on the cards."

The person who had been so vital to Rush in the early days, who had snatched *'Hemispheres'* from the jaws of defeat, and who had such a huge influence on *'Permanent Waves'* and *'Moving Pictures'*, was to be given his cards. Just before the band went back on the road, they went to Terry and told him what the plan was – in the manner of, we'll still be friends. "They basically said that, you know, we're just going to have a sabbatical, and we'll get back together again," says Terry. "It never happened, unfortunately, which was rather a shame." Despite all that, the band were still proud of what they had achieved with Terry as co-pilot. "I think there will always be that recognizable chemistry that happened back then with Terry," said Alex. "Terry will always have a soft spot in our group."

And then, for the band, it was time to move on.

In truth, it wasn't just Alex who thought the technological balance was lacking. Geddy's live performances were complicated by having to juggle between the different instruments, and his bass playing – his first love – was suffering. Dangerously, he and the others started to wonder – why?

It was like the band had eaten from the tree of artistic knowledge – once they'd asked themselves why they were doing what they did, it became difficult to carry on with any zest. "I found myself going on stage thinking about baseball rather than the night's show," said Geddy. There was too much momentum for any existential thoughts to change anything, however – SRO had just taken on a new general manager in the shape of Val Azzoli, the band had just picked up top group and top live band awards at the Labatts' Music Express awards, studio schedules for the next album were already being defined and besides, there were all these dates to play.

On a stormy night in Phoenix at the end of February, the novelty of the technology became all too apparent. "Before the show there was a big voltage surge that blew out all of the keyboards and all of the sequencers," explained Geddy, who managed to salvage a Mini-Moog from the mess. "We just said, Fuck it, let's just go on." Snatching victory from the jaws of defeat, the band took heart in doing what they did best – getting out there and playing their hearts out. Effused Alex, "The night ended up being fantastic! It didn't sound quite the way it was supposed to sound, but after a while we got comfortable with it and were able to forget it, and we played our hearts out! The audience was really behind us, and it was a great feeling to be up against a real serious problem and finish it off, coming together and being positive."

> **Dom Jolly**
>
> Concerning the *'Signals'* tour rider, Alex remarked. "It just happens that we got a deal on Dom (Perignon – very expensive champagne) and we bought Dom. Everybody is very budget conscious this tour and rather than going through promoters or in-house caterers, we stock our own and eliminate it from the rider."
>
> Budget conscious???

The tour continued into Europe in May – and, as had become the norm, the band brought its entire set across the Atlantic. "The shipping bills are enormous," said Nick Kotos, "but we do make a profit." While on the UK leg of the tour, Rush took the opportunity to approach a number of producers, including such luminaries of the eighties pop scene as Rupert Hine, Trevor Horn, Peter Collins and Steve Lillywhite. "They went traipsing around England," says Paul. "They loved Frankie Goes to Hollywood, and they were very interested in a lot of what was going on in England so I think they pretty much exclusively looked to England at that time." Trevor and Rupert declined the power trio's approaches: "I didn't really understand what I could do for them," says Rupert. "I too quickly thought of them as being a heavy rock band." Not that they lived like one – the boys were spending their pre-show time in Berlitz French lessons, with a different tutor in each city. "Of all the bands that I have represented, I have never walked into a back stage area where it had 'quiet please lessons in progress'," says Neil Warnock.

Rock and roll.

By the last date of the tour, a level of agreement had been reached for the next album – not to dispense with electronics, but to ensure that guitars had their fair share of the mix. The usually mild-mannered Alex was not entirely mollified – he started remarking he should get out more, take up a hobby or find a solo project; however, the forced march the band had undertaken for almost ten years, left little room for manoeuvre. "There's not enough time," he would complain – quietly.

As the recording schedules started to loom once more, Rush still didn't have a producer. "We talked to so many people who were looking for that magical person with all the answers who simply didn't exist," said Geddy. "Working with Terry spoiled us because he was a very honest and responsible person and we were running into all these people who were horrible." "They interviewed a lot of people," said Paul Northfield, who was given the opportunity to set out his stall. "I got a phone call from them saying look, we have interviewed 20 people and 15 of them don't know as much as you do." He flew to Toronto, but his arrival served only to remind the band they needed a fresher pair of ears. "Alex said, 'I love you, but I want to work with somebody I don't know'," says Paul, stoically. "It was a little tough, but I understood his reasons."

Finally the band settled on Steve Lillywhite, whose track record with U2, the Psychedelic Furs and Simple Minds fitted exactly with the band's aspirations. He was able, willing and most importantly available, so the band could stop worrying about that aspect. It was time for another album, and as far Alex was concerned it was going to have guitars.

Lots of guitars.

Under Pressure

For continuity's sake, the band decided to stay local – to work on new material at the Horseshoe Valley rehearsal studios in Southern Ontario, before heading to the now-familiar Le Studio. Early in the writing sessions it became clear that the album wasn't going to be about bluebirds and posies. "We went for more of an aggressive sound," said Alex, who had more than a little tension to get out of his system.

For Neil, any implied tension was more of a reaction to what he saw around him. "The mid-80s were difficult times, economically, and people were losing jobs, having trouble getting work, having relationship problems and all that," he said. Every morning at breakfast, Neil would read the Toronto daily papers he spent time on the lyrics. "The world looked dark," he said, so a dark album it became, with dark lyrics and as importantly, dark music. Uncertainty about the future was a global phenomenon, somehow reflecting the mid-life situation Rush found itself in – the issues of the day became an opportunity for transference, with Neil's conceptual lyrics reflecting what he saw as well as externalising the band's own fears about the future.

Musically speaking, the only direction the band knew to take was in reaction to 'Signals', balancing new with old. Things had moved on in the 18 months since they'd last been in the studio however, not least in the domain of the keyboard. "We went into the studio with a whole different arsenal of studio equipment," said Neil. "The synthesizers that they have now that can take any sound in the world, synthesize it and modulate it for you, and it's just... ridiculous!" Ridiculously tempting for Geddy, who continued to seek inspiration from the ivories. "Of all the instruments that I play at home, I end up playing keyboards more than anything because it's such a challenge," he said. "It's also more satisfying than playing bass on my own. A bass is a lonely instrument on its own, but with synthesizers, you can put up a sound and bathe yourself in it. Who needs anyone else?"

The result was that Geddy was writing far more on keyboards than with guitar, transposing what he had written for the stringed instruments. Or not – Geddy and the others weren't going to restrict access to the keys. "At times their role is to enhance a fundamental three-piece sound, but at other times they come to the forefront – theirs must be the primary sound," he explained. "I don't think any of us are content to be a guitar-oriented band any more; not with all the music that's going on now and with all the refreshing sounds that are being made." Geddy took one lesson from the last tour – to write in a way that could be played live. "Almost every time I had a right-hand keyboard part, I would write a bass pattern for the left hand, even if it was basic, just to get into the habit of doing it," said Geddy. "That way I could set up different bass sounds too."

Neil was also trying out a few electronic items, not least a Simmons drum kit, but he wasn't convinced it could replace a "real" set. "You want to know about the new technology, what it can do, if it can do anything for you, and at least know either way," he said of electronic drums. "There just isn't near the satisfaction or the involvement with them. I feel like I'm hitting them, but I don't feel like I'm with them the way I do with my real drums."

Before going into the studio proper, at the end of September 1983 Rush played a series of high profile gigs at New York's Radio City Music Hall. "We figured we'd take a big chance," remarked Neil. "We hadn't played live at that time for about three months through all the writing and holidays and so on, and we were going to go right out of that period onto one of the biggest, most prestigious stages in the world." As well as debuting some new material (with Alex improvising solos on the fly), the band also attempted a number of new equipment setups. "It was fairly risky, but I think it worked out very well. I think that we were all kind of dizzy when we got out of it." Not so well for UK band Marillion who were playing support – they hadn't before experienced the zeal of Rush fans.

Following the gigs and buoyed up by the live experience, the band returned to Horseshoe Valley to complete pre-production. Two weeks before the band decamped to Morin Heights to start recording however, calamity struck. Steve Lillywhite called and said he wasn't comfortable working with Rush after all. With little time left before the allotted studio time at Morin

Anyone For Tennis

Keen players Alex and Geddy had been playing together since touring in 1979. They took the time out to join in a Celebrity Tennis Jam with John McEnroe, Vitas Gerulatis, Buddy Guy, and Clarence Clemmons (Bruce Springsteen's sax player).

Heights, the band and SRO worked on filling the gap, jokingly borrowing an action figure (named "Roger Kneebend") from Geddy's son Julian, and adopting him as surrogate producer.

After almost 50 interviews, the band happened upon Peter Henderson, a UK-based producer/engineer who had cut his teeth working with Paul McCartney and Supertramp. Time was running short when Peter was invited over to see whether he gelled with the guys. "We spent three days together at a rehearsal complex," says Peter. "A day was spent talking and chatting, and a couple of days playing tennis!" Peter was highly competent, amicable and congenial, and most of all he was available – so he got the call. "We really hadn't found what we were looking for, but we couldn't wait any longer and had to get on with the record," Geddy remarked.

When Peter arrived, the band had already created demo versions of 'The Enemy Within' and 'Distant Early Warning'[9]: there was just time for a final week in pre-production before the ensemble headed off to Morin Heights. "Everything was written," says Peter, who found the whole situation a little alien. "It was a strange juxtaposition. Rush came from working with one guy, I came from working with one band – I wasn't that confident, and it took a bit of time to get the band's trust." For Peter it was like jumping onto a moving train – inevitably he took time to get up to speed.

The Price of a Hentor

Peter quickly gained the nickname "Hentor," explained Alex. "When he wrote his name out to leave us his number, it looked like Peter Hentor instead of Peter Henderson, so we nicknamed him Hentor The Barbarian. I got some Letraset and put it on this white Strat that I had. It has a Shark neck - these are unlabeled replacement necks - so I threw 'Hentor Sportscaster' on there. Amazing all the mail we used to get over that - 'Where can I buy a Hentor? How much does a Hentor cost?'"

Peter saw that he had little choice but fit in with the band's chosen approach. Not that the band made him unwelcome, far from it – in their own way of course. "Alex was immediately outgoing, warm, incredibly funny, easy to get on with," says Peter. "Geddy was a lot more retiring – harder to please, but as you get to know him he's incredibly nice. Neil was the hardest one to know, it took a lot of time before I bonded with him." In watching how they dealt with others, Peter really understood how things were. "They treated everybody so respectfully – the fans, the technical crew," he says. "I'd never seen that before – fans would call up and they'd be on the phone for an hour!"

On arrival at Le Studio, the four fellows were greeted by resident engineer Paul Northfield, together with assistants Frank Opolko and Robert Di Gioia. "I remember hearing those demos and thinking, why are they re-recording?" says Frank, who was experiencing the band's attention to detail for the first time. It quickly became clear to Frank that this was not going to be a picnic – he would have to earn his place. "Alex could be sullen and hard to talk to," says Frank. Geddy also was quiet: "although he said little in the studio his presence was great – you did your best."

And so, to business. First the band played as a threesome to a click track, to get the drum tracks down. "Neil did his drum parts fairly quickly and efficiently. Almost machine-like – like the man himself!" says Frank. "There was not one wasted drum pass – always solidly locked to Geddy's amazing snakey bass lines. It was very hypnotic to follow these two." Nothing was foregone in pursuit of perfection. "Neil would play up to ten takes then we'd splice the two inch tape together," explains Peter. "Neil's view was that Alex and Geddy could have as many goes as they wanted to get the best take so why couldn't he."

Then, it was time for the bass proper, the demo-standard licks replaced by near-perfection. "Geddy would spend a day on one song, doing it over and over again," says Peter. "The first take would be fantastic, 95% correct, there was a degree of obsessiveness to get everything perfect. Sometimes I couldn't hear the difference." Every note was carefully placed, "It was like he had the whole picture of the music in his head and produced bits of this musical puzzle only at the appropriate time," says Frank. "Understated repeated notes would take on a life only after weeks of overdubbing other parts."

Peter found it difficult to see what he could add to such a highly tuned environment – the idea of telling the band to do things different was beyond his ken. Comparisons were inevitable with his previous experiences. "With Supertramp, there were five musicians, and we were trying to get the freshest, most energetic take, and then you'd patch it," he explains. Rush's approach was totally different – Geddy and Neil at least, appeared methodical to the point of clinicality. Over time Peter found it difficult to avoid adopting more of an engineering role – not just because it was a comfort zone, but also because the band's demands on the engineers were great.

Once Geddy's bass parts had been done it was time to work on guitars and keyboards, and this time, Alex was given first bite of the cherry. Only the keyboard pads – short musical segments – were done first. Alex flew into his parts with joyous gusto. "With Alex we kept a lot of what he had done on the basic tracks," says Peter. "He was very quick and would really perform every take. He always had a fantastic sound."

As Alex worked on his parts and Geddy oversaw the production process, Neil was spending his spare time cross country skiing or working on the artwork with Hugh. As was by now a tradition, when Hugh came over to meet with Neil and the others, he played with a few ideas with the band – this time adding a synthesised intro to 'Distant Early Warning', which would become the first song on the final cut. Together with the cover, the band had to decide a title, and they settled on *'Grace Under Pressure'* first and foremost because of the subject matter. The title fitted both the general mood of the album, and the atmosphere in the studio.

It was becoming apparent however, that the title was equally apt for the descending fog of tension in the studio. Geddy's personality led him to adopt more of a producer's role than the other two, resulting in a situation Alex found a little too overbearing. "Geddy was always directing things – he wanted what was right for the song," says Peter. "Alex would try different things, sometimes Geddy wouldn't like the direction and Alex would get frustrated at that." At one point, things degenerated to the point that Alex and Geddy stopped speaking altogether, but still they struggled on. "I found their way of dealing with each other fascinating," says Frank. "Instead of confronting each other directly – they would write things down on bits of paper (which I would find the day after) and gradually the tension lifted..." All the same, Peter noticed, the band still worked hard to maintain themselves as a unit. "With other bands, there was always so much back-biting," says Peter. "I never heard them talking badly about one another. They're all so different, but they were always very supportive of each other."

Jim Burgess (from the aptly named 'Saved by Technology') came in to help set up Geddy's new PPG synthesiser and assist with a bit of programming, as did Le Studio resident Paul Northfield. Finally the vocals were laid on top of everything else. The recording process was complete but there remained the mixing – which was always a challenge, particularly for Geddy, who by this stage was virtually burned out. "I'm so close to everything," he explained. "I know every part of every instrument so intimately, and yet I have to act as if I've never heard those parts before." The process became unnecessarily drawn out as the tracks were remixed and rearranged on the SSL mixing desks, a couple of tracks taking up to 5 days as the band and producer tried to achieve a consensus on what worked. "Almost every sound and musical phrase was discussed – argued over and repeated and repeated," says Frank. "I know this because I would have to keep track of all the analog 2" tapes - and there were over 40!"

For Peter, the mixing process remains his one regret. "I wasn't satisfied with the final sound," he says. "I had been used to recording with Neve's warmer sound and it was my first experience of working on an SSL. The album is musically great, but the mix is too thin, the drums are too quiet." It was difficult to tell at the time however – by that stage, everyone was shot. "We had cabin fever by the end," said Geddy. "You get to a dangerous state, you want to finish the record because you want to get out of there."

"Even during the end of our 5 months I thought that very little had changed," says then-rookie Frank, who found Alex lightened up a bit once it was all over. "He and I drank vodka on the last day of the session. I still think he tried to kill me by getting me to keep up – although they tell me I had a good time." Geddy went to assist Bob Ludwig in mastering, and rejected two test pressings before he was satisfied enough to move on. "I don't think I could have liked it given the circumstances," said Geddy. "As soon as the record was done, I wanted to get away from it – and I've rarely listened to it since, because it's attached to too many difficult memories."

Lost for Words

"Um, grace is the heroic quality, really, that's uh, it's very difficult to define. It's like the quality of, uh, well, of quality. Everyone thinks they know what quality is, but it's very difficult to put in words, and grace under pressure is a quality like that, too."

Neil Peart

While Peter had the technical skills for the job, as things turned out, he wasn't to be the man who could drag the band from its doldrums. "Peter worked really hard and gave 150 percent, but at the end we were left feeling cheated," said Geddy. "We went through this wrenching experience and felt that we still hadn't found what we were looking for." "Perhaps they needed someone with more experience, who had worked with lots of different people," says Peter. "I think the band was going through a growing up period where they had to take charge of all the details, musically and otherwise," says Frank. "They were never rude about it – just insistent. I thought that Peter was great and his quiet manner sometimes was off-putting for the band. They were used to guys who had 'great' ideas... Peter was a great engineer – but the 'BIG' production idea just wasn't in his bag of tricks. In any event, had anybody suggested big changes, they would have been kicked out of the room!"

If there was one thing the band took away from the experience, it was the need for a producer who could stand up to them. "I don't think we could ever produce ourselves," commented Geddy.

Perhaps Rush didn't need a producer, they needed a therapist.

'Grace Under Pressure' was released April 12, 1984, an appropriately dark year for such an album. The title was autobiographical, but there was little grace about the process, or the result. "It was kind of like childbirth, but instead of 20 hours, it was six months of non-stop labor," said Alex. Unfortunately, it didn't click with the buying public. Neil surmised it thus: "People do not want to hear about sadness when the world is so gloomy."

Neil, who had not been quite so affected by the gestation as the two schoolmates,

'Grace Under Pressure'

In one word, bleak. A desolate, empty landscape with the occasional, shattered stump overlooking a pool of black water, the air thick with noxious gases, this is the world conjured by *'Grace Under Pressure'*. It is deliberately unclear whether it is a return to past battlegrounds or a post-apocalyptic vision, and indeed the image it conjures of the dark side of human nature is applicable to both.

Not least in the album's centrepiece, 'Red Sector A', its title innocuously enough based on the band's vantage point for the Space Shuttle launch reported on the previous album. On the surface Neil wanted to capture an abstract view of some futuristic prison, but the song was more fundamentally based on a direct description of wartime concentration camps Auschwitz, Belsen and the like. "Are we the last ones left alive," sings Geddy, echoing the feelings of his mother Manya at the liberation of her own camp, her disbelief that there could be anything left outside the wire, and perhaps his disbelief that he could ever be accused of fascism, given his family history. The band were feeling introspective and prepared to reveal more of themselves, not least the singer who had discussed with the others the horrors of the camps and their impact on his parents.

Almost as a deliberate decision to break continuity with its more derived predecessors, the music on *'Grace Under Pressure'* is downcast, appropriate for the theme but in contrast to the band's New Wave influences. The opening bars of the environmental call to arms 'Distant Early Warning' return us to Alex at his dissonant best, backed with reverberating drums and keyboards. The guitarist is well and truly back at the centre of things, as illustrated by 'Kid Gloves': ostensibly about keeping up appearances, but the line *'Anger play the fool'* could have been written for the guitar player. "I'm not giving up on implausible dreams," went part 3 of the 'Fear' trilogy 'The Enemy Within', the reggae-backed words echoing the band's determination to press forward despite the difficulties it was facing inside the ranks. Indeed, the cry for help that was 'The Body Electric' might well have been just as much from the band members as from a distressed android.

Some songs don't try quite so hard to hide their subjects. 'Afterimage' for example, was written for Le Studio engineer Robbie Whelan, who would do anything for anyone, and who had been killed in a car accident only months before. And where no amount of clever drumming could bash life into 'Red Lenses', all can be forgiven with the brilliance of 'Between The Wheels', a heartfelt diatribe about our inability to react to the bigger events we face. *'Bright images flashing by, like windshields towards a fly...'* even as the song quashes our dreams, its very existence, drawn from the ashes of despair by a band struggling to keep afloat, offers some hope for the future.

Introspective, indeed.

thought of the album as a major watershed, like *'2112'* and *'Moving Pictures'* before it. "Neil thinks that *'Grace Under Pressure'* is another solidification point, but I don't agree with him," said Geddy. "I think we're still on the way to some other place." Not least, the balance between technology and the organic three-piece was yet to be struck.

Accomplished video director David Mallet was brought in to direct a video for 'Distant Early Warning', filmed at the swanky new Limehouse Docks studios in London UK. "It was not a good time in London," says Hugh, who was also working on the videos. "It was probably notable that the Libyan Embassy being under siege and the death of the police woman[10] had taken place that week." The Kubrickesque video was the band's first real effort to produce something that would be suitable for MTV. "David shot the thing and made it believable," said Geddy. "We saw it as being this big production. He would say look guys, leave it to me, it may not be realistic, but I can promise you it will be surrealistic." The video featured Geddy's son Julian. "I don't remember too much, except sitting on this rocket thing as if I was riding it for a really long time," Julian recalled. "Neil let me play his drums, but I had to be REALLY careful!"

"David Mallet was a treat to work with," says Hugh, who was not quite so happy with the quality of the final result, it being recorded entirely on video and not film. "I am almost reticent to say that I had much to do with the video of 'Distant Early Warning' but I did," he says. This being the video generation, a number of other videos were made at later dates: Tim Pope directed 'Afterimage', and Rocky Morton and Annabel Jankel of Cucumber Productions, who had done some animations for live shows prior to *'Grace Under Pressure'*, also directed 'The Body Electric' and 'The Enemy Within'. The "little piece of science fiction frippery" that was the video for 'The Body Electric'[11] was loosely based (once again) on Ayn Rand's *'Anthem'*.

Rush released 'Distant Early Warning' as a single, to a generally receptive audience: it reached Number 3 in the *Billboard* album rock chart on 28 April. The pull-through onto previous albums was tangible: on October 12, *'Moving Pictures'* went double platinum. Six months later, it had doubled that figure.

Thankfully, rehearsals for the inevitable tour were less traumatic than for *'Signals'* – the band was better prepared, the songs were more tour-friendly and the technology was more reliable. One older song to benefit was 'Witch Hunt'. "We felt that we could never reproduce it live so we never played it," said Geddy. "Then just on a whim, we tried it in rehearsal and it sounded fine. We'd grown so much since writing it and had acquired all these new keyboards that it works now." Incorporating all manner of triggers, Neil's new Simmons kit took much of the strain. "Neil has just gotten into things you plug in as opposed to things you just set up and hit," said technician Tony Geranios.

Following a dress rehearsal on May 7, Rush were off again. David Mallet was along for the ride, directing the footage for a planned live video. The tour machine carried the fellows forward by momentum rather than the euphoria of success, and not for the first time, the idea of a split was discussed. As always however, the chemistry on stage and the social time on and off the buses reinforced the trio, and nobody had the heart to buck the routine and call it a day; besides, they hadn't been brought up to be quitters. The schedule was more relaxed than previously – the band only played up to five nights in a week, and took a week off out of every four on the road so there was time to stretch out a little, for each of the players to re-establish why exactly they were doing it at all.

It wasn't just Geddy and Alex – Neil was also equating his own playing with the law of diminishing returns. "It was easy

Thatcher Rights

"In the middle of a take with no regard to our production schedule, the huge loading bay doors opened and an entourage of 12 people with brief cases, clipboard, two glaring halogen light rigs, a camera in the middle and Mrs T looking more like a Madame Tussauds effigy than the woman herself, walked towards what felt like me. I thought, I will move aside and have them go properly to Geddy or someone. I moved to the left and they moved to the left. I moved again, they moved again, so I stopped and she walked up and said 'hello' and we had a conversation which lasted 10 unnerving minutes. That was really quite interesting. 'Do you create the video concert prior to the music or do you more often than not create the music prior to the creation of the visuals.' I thought, well, probably it would be better to ask one of the band members, so I gestured to Geddy to come into the light and he wouldn't. He let me hang in there."

Hugh Syme, on Margaret Thatcher's impromptu visit to the set of 'Distant Early Warning' when we first got together - we weren't that good and I wasn't that good, so it was easy for us to improve, and we improved by leaps and bounds," he said. "Where I used to have five or six new rhythmic areas that I would explore during the tour, now I might have one or two."

On the tour, the band finally caved and agreed to play a couple of festival dates, at the Dallas and Houston Texas Jam festivals. "The band were huge in Texas," says Bruce Cole. Rush played to 60,000 people, something the band had never wanted – but higher powers work in mysterious ways. The band had classed itself as a hockey team rather than a baseball team, but the world hadn't listened.

Following the last date of the North American leg of the tour, on November 9, a jet plane took the players off to a four-night stint in Japan and a couple more dates in Hawaii. To make the most of the trip, Neil headed off to North East China for three weeks on his bike – from cruising small town America at 15 miles an hour, Neil was going international. It was an opportunity to meet new people (not least, other cyclists), to cut himself off from the environment he'd grown to despise, and more – as well as visiting the Great Wall, Neil found lyrical inspiration as he mounted the staircase of the Buddhist holy mountain Tai Shan, jotting down a song in its honour when he reached the top. Neil came back to Canada all excited about some temple blocks and small cymbals he had seen, and sent his tech Larry Allen off to try to source them.

Back home once again, it was time for some hard decisions. Frustrations within the band were at an all-time peak and none of the three players were in any position to take the lead: that just wouldn't be Rush. Having eliminated all other options, once again the band came to the conclusion that the "right" producer (whatever that meant) could be the answer. At the very least, for the sake of the band's own sanity it was not worth trying to go back into the studio without having somebody new at the helm. Over and over, the phrase "objective ear" came up: it would not be enough to have somebody who was stylistically tuned to the band's musical direction; the players also needed somebody with the courage of their convictions, and the necessary detachment, to steer the show back on track when necessary.

Many of the dates of the *'Grace Under Pressure'* tour had been played with Gary Moore second on the billing: when he heard of the band's predicament, the blues player took the opportunity to introduce the band to his own producer, Peter Collins. "I remember Gary raving about how good Peter was, but he hadn't done anything vaguely resembling our music," said Geddy. All the same, Peter was clearly a crossover producer, not least in giving a commercial edge to Gary Moore himself.

Perhaps, just perhaps, he could be the right man for the job.

NOTES: 1 Such as setting the correct vocal key for the 'Hemispheres' epic. **2** *'Gonna Roll The Bones'* by Fritz Leiber, a short story that appeared in the *'Dangerous Visions'* anthology, published in 1967. **3** Uncle Tonouse (note correct spelling) was an eccentric character (played by Hans Conried) from the *'Danny Thomas Show'*, a family-friendly sitcom which ran from 1953 to 1965 on ABC and CBS. **4** Donna Reed starred alongside James Stewart in *'It's A Wonderful Life'*. **5** A Pressure Zone microphone, which responds to changes of pressure rather than picking up sound waves. **6** The theatre was bought shortly after, by the Ontario Heritage Foundation. It was re-opened in 1989. **7** The title refers to the cartoon *'Snagglepuss'*. **8** The school was named after Warren Cromartie, at the time a baseball player for the Montreal Expos. **9** The Distant Early Warning line (DEWLine) is a line of radar stations stretching from Alaska to Greenland. **10** Yvonne Fletcher. **11** 'The Body Electric' was named after an episode of *'The Twilight Zone'*, itself based on Walt Whitman's 'I Sing The Body Electric'. For the ego theorists, the number 1001001 equates to the ASCII character 'I'. The video was released in November 1985.

$$dh = \sum_i \mu_i \, dn_i + \gamma \, dA$$

integrate

RUSH

CH$_e$mist(r)y

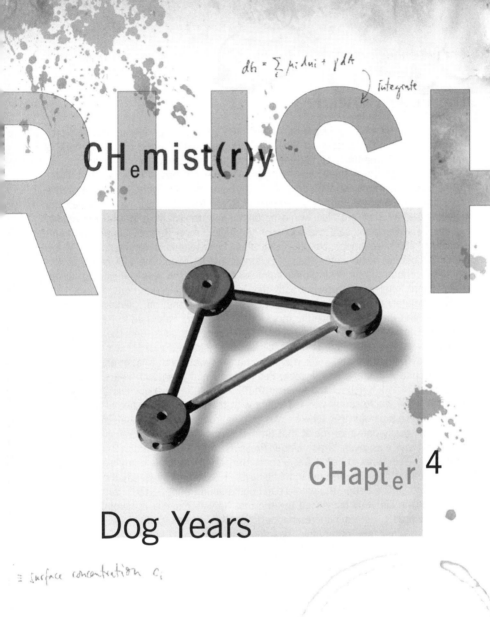

CHapt$_e$r 4

Dog Years

= surface concentration c_i

"Learning that we're only immortal for a limited time"

$$d\gamma = - \sum_i c_i \, d\mu_i \qquad (3)$$

a binary solution in contact with air

$$G = \sum_i \mu_i n_i + \gamma A \qquad (4)$$

complete
differential

$$\sum_i \mu_i \, dn_i + \sum_i n_i \, d\mu_i + \gamma \, dA + A \, d\gamma \qquad (6)$$

"I'm old enough not to care too much about what you think of me"

The Peter Principle

If the secret of working in the music business could be summed up in one word, it would be "timing". Success, or indeed failure, can result from a chance remark, a whim, or indeed whether a certain individual happens to switch on the radio.

Nobody could have predicted, for example, that UK-based pop producer Peter Collins would be in LA, working on a single for heavy blues player Gary Moore, at the same time as Gary was touring in support of Rush. Nobody could have planned the fact that Geddy, Alex and Neil would be bemoaning their failure to find a producer, even as Gary was being sent two copies of his single 'Empty Rooms' – one before, and one after Peter's treatment. No-one, least of all Peter, would have imagined that the highly successful rock band Rush was struggling to adopt the influences of the eighties, without compromising their quintessential sound. It was coincidental in the extreme that Peter was to prove exactly the right man to help them out.

Appropriately enough, it was in Providence, Rhode Island, on 7 November 1984, that Peter and the boys arranged to meet for the first time. Peter had low expectations to say the least. "I had barely even heard of Rush," he says, and the plucky pop producer was enthralled by his first experiences of stadium rock. "I was completely blown away!" All the same, Peter was in no hurry to work with this, or any other rock band. Despite a heritage in folk rock, Peter's *forté* had been with chart-friendly UK artists such as Nik Kershaw and Musical Youth, hardly the most obvious CV for a rock producer. "The whole sound was exploding with that Trevor Horn style of production, which was the area of music where I was coming from," he says. "The simple organic sounds had really dated for me at that time, they were just uninteresting."

When Peter was given *'Grace Under Pressure'* for a listen, he didn't hold back in his critique – why should he? "I was a cocky British pop producer doing extremely well in my career at that time in England," he says. "I believe I told Geddy that his vocals could sound 100% better, the whole band could sound a lot better." Perhaps he was right – and he certainly convinced the trio that he was capable of helping out. From having adopted a determined resistance to outside direction, the band found itself enthused by what this "diminutive, bearded, cigar-smoking Englishman" could bring. With his first comments, Peter Collins was already taking control.

It was all going to be alright.

While Rush felt uncertain about their future, they knew they still wanted to play rock music. "We were really feeling isolated through the 80s," Geddy said later. "We were one of the only rock bands out there playing real instruments and playing rock songs in front of rock audiences." With Peter, everyone thought, the band could improve the balance between old and new, without compromising what it meant to be "Rush". It was going to be an experiment, for sure, but that was as good an incentive as any.

As the band members parted for a month's break after the tour, each recognised his own challenges. While Geddy was struggling with technology and Alex was fighting for room, Neil was wondering whether he'd taken his technique a step too far.

In March 1985, one event in particular caused him to start rethinking this perspective. Neil had been invited to San Francisco by jazz bassist Jeff Berlin, to add a few back beats to Jeff's record *'Champions'*[1]. Neil was understandably nervous, particularly as he was to share drumming duties with Journey's Steve Smith, who had a solid background in jazz. "It was a major milestone for me to walk into a situation like that with no rehearsal," said Neil, for whom things panned out as well as he could have hoped. "The satisfaction level was enormous!"

Geddy and Alex also had their invitations. Geddy worked on Ken Ramm's *'Euphoria'* project, and sang a line on the charity record 'Tears Are Not Enough'. Meanwhile, Alex added a couple of guitar solos to a Platinum Blonde album, *'Alien Shores'*. For Alex it was a refreshing change – the only person telling him what to play, was himself.

By the time the threesome got back together, at the Elora Sound studios in Southern Ontario, the fires of creativity had been lighted once more – not least because everyone loved the writing stage, brought in after the challenge of *'Hemispheres'*. "It has really shifted our focus, spending more time doing sketches before the final painting," said Geddy. Indeed, the step had become Neil's favourite activity. "It's just us," he said. "We just go away together and work very closely and tightly – and live and breathe new things, new songs and new ideas and possible directions."

Jimbo Barton and Peter Collins

The mood was upbeat, and this was reflected in the styles of the songs. The first songs to come together – 'Middletown Dreams', 'Big Money', 'Emotion Detector' and 'Mystic Rhythms' – were balanced affairs with no instrument having the upper hand; indeed, Alex showed he had learned the lesson of the past by preparing appropriate guitar solos in advance, particularly for 'Emotion Detector' and 'Middletown Dreams', rather than relying on spontaneous inspiration when his moment came in the studio. There were some electronic expedients – a "guitar riff" that opened 'Big Money' was to be a sample played by Geddy on the synth, but all in all things were balancing out.

Over time the unifying theme evolved of 'power', the first time the band had developed a single concept to link all the songs on an album. *'Power Windows'* was the antithesis to *'Grace Under Pressure'*, suggesting hope where the former album had been about despair, but with a healthy dose of reality. "It's perhaps a cynical view of people while remaining idealistic about life," said Neil.

A few dates in Florida mid-March gave the opportunity to try out the new material in sound checks. Peter had proposed engineer Jim "Jimbo" Barton, his insistence overruling Geddy's desire to stick with Paul Northfield. "I was very stuck in my thing at that time," says Peter. Jimbo saw the band perform for the first time at the Lee County Arena in Ft. Meyers. "I had no idea who they were, I burst out laughing!" he says. "I'd just come off Blancmange, I was shocked that this sort of thing still happened." Like Peter, Jimbo was direct in expressing

Open and Shut

"I remember being amazed by Neil's bicycle flight case that he used to take everywhere on the road with him. They stayed in the Tower Hotel and he used to cycle every morning to the studio. It wasn't totally bicycle shaped but a big rectangular thing."

Dave Meegan

Writers' Cramp

Neil and Alex sometimes communicated using what they termed "moronese" – written phonetically and with the wrong hand.

what he thought. "That's where confidence of ignorance came in!"

Jimbo at the studio

Accompanied by the new producer and engineer, when the week was out Rush went back to Elora to record demos, and to start work on arrangements and pre-production. Neil was dabbling with electronics once again, experimenting with how he could make best use of his Simmons pads. There was one clear benefit – through sampling, Neil could make room for many more sounds than in the past. "I can have access to every percussion sound ever played (and some beyond), and still be able to reach them all! Paint cans, big sheets of metal, industrial sounds, pipes being struck – you name it!" As well as these, more esoteric noises, Neil took samples of a whole range of ethnic drums from Africa and elsewhere. "I rented a whole pile – some big giant ones covered with some strange kind of skin, some Indian tabla drums, and all different things," said Neil.

Neil's dabblings came at a cost, not least as he struggled over the manuals to understand how to burn the samples onto E-PROM chips. "I do not have a natural empathy with technological things – they often give me a headache," he said, acknowledging that hard reality of "hitting things with sticks" could never be replaced by a set of pads. "It's not going to come even close to replacing my acoustic drums," he said. Even if Neil wanted to, Peter wouldn't have let him move too far from real drums. "He's become very jaded about the Simmons sound," said Neil. "He didn't really want to hear it."

Once pre-production was complete it was time to head over to England – another recommendation from Peter. The chosen location was Richard Branson's Manor Studios, one of Peter's favourite haunts, and a very different proposition to the rainy outback of South Wales. "You arrive with two Irish Wolfhounds to greet you," says Peter. "It is just a fantastic sort of medieval atmosphere. Serving wenches, a big banqueting table and everything in excess!" The Manor offered a sure-fire way of creating a relaxed atmosphere, thinks Jimbo. "It was a very homely existence," he says. "Richard Branson used to drop by to say hi!"

Astutely, Peter recognised that each player needed a kick start. "I looked at each one of them and thought, what can we do here, to change this up," says Peter, who gave little thought to the past or what the fans might think. "I didn't have a great respect for the tradition of Rush, it didn't mean very much to me." Peter's suggestions came fast and frequent, and the band were delighted to have someone telling them what to do. "I don't touch the decks," says Peter. "I sit there in the old tradition of producer and consider the arrangements and the performances and how the record is going to sound in the end." As such the band could get on with what they were best at – the music – and they loved it. "The band did not show any tension at all," says Peter. "It was fun from the outset."

One of Peter's first changes was to add a stage into the recording process. The traditional approach (of the threesome playing to a click track) wasn't ideal: Geddy and Alex found the click a distraction, wanting to play before or after the beat as the mood took them, while pace-setting Neil found his buddies to be the distraction. Peter proposed that Alex and Geddy laid down rough, regimented guitar and bass using the click; Neil could then play to this recording to capture his drums. This was ideal for single-minded Neil, who could focus on his own performance. The other advantage was for the engineer, explains Paul Northfield, who experienced the process on later albums. "You could punch in the drums," says Paul. "If Neil is happy with the first half of the song but not happy with his overall performance, you can just spin the tape back and press play, he can play along, you hit the punch in button and then record."

As another change, Neil's drum parts were recorded in the Stone Room at the Manor, acoustically different from anywhere he had recorded before. He didn't let this phase him: having developed his rehearsal technique over the previous two albums, by the time Neil arrived in the studio every one of his performances was rehearsed to near-perfection. "There were no Neil overdubs ever," says Jimbo. "As he would say, 'unrewarding' – he'd arrive, pass through the control room, sit down and you would hit 'record'. Maybe there were 3 songs he did two takes at. We were sitting looking at him, saying to each other, what just happened?"

Once Neil had his parts down, it was time to build up the layers. Inevitably, there were some technical teething problems – Jack Secret managed to blow up Geddy's keyboards by overlooking the voltage differences ("We didn't get off to an auspicious start with the keys," says Peter), and some issues with Geddy's bass strings caused a bit of tension, but these were quickly overcome.

The band was spurred on by some early successes, notably with 'Marathon', which had proved difficult in the writing stages. "We thought, this song is going to be like pulling teeth once we get in the studio," said Alex. "Of course, we get into the studio and it's a breeze."

> ### Neurotica
>
> "I can be extremely neurotic in the studio. I get very into what I am doing, I get very passionate about it and I want it to be as good as I can make it. Its kind of a curse really, I drive myself crazy!"
>
> Geddy Lee

Having put Neil in the Stone Room, Peter set about changing some of the fundamentals for the others. "With Alex I took away his pedal board to a large extent," he says – initially dubious, Alex decided to go with it. "Peter suggested things that opened up directions that we wouldn't normally pursue," said Alex. "It was really an eye-opening experience to work with him." Peter also suggested Geddy tried his own Wal bass, which had a built in battery preamp. "It was a very exciting bass in England at that time," says Peter. "Nick Kershaw had used my Wal, it had a very distinctive sound, and I thought that would be quite a leap from the Ricky and the Fender." Geddy already knew of Wal as Percy Jones used one – Percy played in one of Geddy's favourite bands at the time, Brand X[2].

Rhythmic keys and guitars were added, and any discomfort Alex might have had about his guitar sound were quickly laid to rest as Jimbo got to work. "He can very quickly translate a guitar sound you have in your mind to the console, so that you can actually hear it," said Alex. "The sounds that we got were great and quite different for me – much cleaner, crisper sounds than I've ever had before."

The atmosphere was relaxed, lots of fun was had, and for Geddy and Alex, the pair might as well have been back at school. Geddy's quick wits were matched with Alex's often maniacal ideas in displays of humour that Peter found hard to keep up with. "It is really, really incredible, wonderful, fast repartee," says Peter. "Characters and language, the Rush language is something that will stay with me." As things progressed, the band realised what they had found with Peter – the elusive "objective ear". "Peter was very clear about what he liked and he didn't mince words," says Paul Northfield. "He didn't come in and tell them the parts to play, he just would be very clear about whether he liked it, and whether he thought they were going in a good direction or not." Whatever combination of qualities a producer needed, said Geddy, "I think we found him in Peter Collins."

The posse moved from the Manor to Sarm East studios, back in central London, for the vocals and overdubs. Dave Meegan, then a junior engineer at Sarm, spent a day or so at the Manor to ensure no time would be wasted during the transition. "In Peter's sessions, you couldn't say to him when he walked in, oh, we'll just be a half hour while we do this, you'd get the look of Satan!" he laughs. "That was the good thing, you knew you'd get decent hours with him, but you had to be ship shape." Dave thought what he heard was great. "I remember hearing the tape when we came from Manor and it just sounded so really good, so energetic, I loved it."

Peter coaxed a number of changes to the vocals, not least bringing them down a key or two. For the first time, Geddy also took the challenge of overdubbing some of his vocals, for added texture. All of these things needed careful handling – but Peter was the consummate people manager. Neil helped as well, ensuring the lyrics fitted the mood. "I'm very empathetic toward Geddy, who's a real sounding board for my ideas," said Neil at the time. "If there's a line he just can't get behind as a singer, I put it away."

In the meantime, to fill the gaps, Alex tried out oil painting.

Once the basic tracks were recorded, Peter proposed the addition of certain "specialists". There was ex-Strawbs keymeister Andy Richards for example, who'd worked with Frankie Goes To Hollywood and Grace Jones, brought in to provide the intro for 'Big Money'. "It seemed to me that Geddy was more of a bass player than a keyboard player, by his own admission," says Peter. Indeed, Geddy went along with it – and then some. "I remember Geddy putting a cape on him, a Rick Wakeman style cape, and Andy entered into the spirit of it all and got an incredible result." Jimbo Barton recalls what it was like to work with Andy. "Spaces were left in the music for him," says Jimbo. "He was amazingly talented, a great ideas guy – we'd open up tracks, hit record and let Andy go."

Ant and Czek off on a date

The band had a lot of fun going touring Peter Collins's favourite haunts from two decades in the business. Peter recommended strings for 'Manhattan Project' and 'Marathon', recorded at Abbey Road with a 30-piece orchestra (some of whom were jobbing musicians from the London Symphony Orchestra) and a 25-piece choir.

Once the London sessions were finished, George Martin's efficiently run studios on the island paradise of Montserrat had been selected, to complete the guitars. Why Montserrat – well indeed, why ever not? "It might have been a reaction to *'Grace Under Pressure'*, but they just wanted to have fun and really enjoy making the record," said Peter, who was happy to comply. There were no budget restrictions, so the most important thing was to ensure everyone got the most out of the studio time.

Alex used a Telecaster on most songs, having trialled the guitar on *'Grace Under Pressure'*, and despite the pressure to trim down the effects he used, he wasn't prepared to give them up entirely. "I'm using effects a little less than I have in the past," he conceded. "I'm starting to lean more towards a cleaner guitar sound."

The trip was welcomed by everyone, but it wasn't without some unexpected problems: not least Alex's skin started reacting to the climate. "His hands swelled up so it was so painful for him to play," says Peter. This wasn't the only issue – as the sessions continued, the truth dawned that once again, the guitars had been left until last. All those gleeful overdubs, fun as they were, had left little room for Alex's trademark sounds. "We just loaded that record with keyboards," remembered Alex. "When it came time to do guitars, I really had a tough time trying to fit pieces in."

If there was one issue Peter couldn't resolve entirely, it was between Alex and his guitar. Alex the relaxed, Alex the outgoing was becoming Alex the fearful when it came to doing what he did best. "Alex seemed really, really confident as a person, but at times he was quite nervous about his guitar playing, bordering on being just a little bit edgy," says Dave Meegan. "He was just a touch nervous of not impressing everyone in the room. Peter used to get him settled down each time, pretty sharpish." All the same, the growing need for approval led to Alex's solos becoming more democratically constructed than necessary. "Everybody sort of dives in," explained Alex. "Geddy likes to really get into doing that. He and the engineer sit down, and Neil makes some suggestions. Of course, the producer is there, too, and they piece together a solo. I come back in after a couple of hours when they have something assembled, and if I like it, then we either stick with it or we keep that as a starting point and go for another whirl over some of the older tracks." Not that he saw that anything was particularly wrong. "I'm concentrating so hard on what I'm doing that I can't possibly be objective," he explained. "I'm better off if I go crazy on eight tracks, take a break from it, and then come in and listen to what they've assembled."

Ultimately, it just wasn't healthy. "I have a tendency to be a little bossy," admitted Geddy, who was the polar opposite of Alex, in his own words, "The type of person that takes a back seat a lot of times." All three were perfectionists, and all three were highly analytical about how they were doing, but Alex was just that little bit more susceptible to criticism than the others. Things nearly came unstuck with Alex's prepared solo for 'Emotion Detector', as Neil blamed the solo for failing to give the song the right "feel".

> **Farewell to Work**
>
> "The studio took us out to a beach to do a barbecue. There was a cavalcade of cars, as studio staff and various people and the band and crew headed off to the beach. We had this wonderful barbecue on the beach, and then on the way back Alex, who had had a fair amount to drink, decided that he would be King Lerxst on the return trip. He wore a crown and cape, and sat on a chair on the back of a flat bed truck. As we were heading back to the studio he would be bestowing favours on the locals, the natives with goats at the side of the road, and he would be saying, 'I am King Lerxst and I have proclaimed that tomorrow you shall be free of work.'
>
> "The guy looked up to him and said, 'But… I don't have a job!'"
>
> Peter Collins

"That was tough," said Alex. "It was so hard to divorce what had been in my head as a solo for three months and come up with something that was a totally different feel." But the whole song was at fault, not just Alex's parts. "We did our best but didn't achieve what we wanted," remarked Neil. Agreed Alex, "I'm still not really sold on that song. It never ended up sounding the way I had hoped it would."

Despite feeling the squeeze, the experience with a hands-on, objective producer was very different and Alex was more comfortable going with the flow in the knowledge that he was being taken seriously. "For me, it's always been very important to be a cohesive part of the band," he said. "With *'Power Windows'*, I finally achieved that. With the way the songs were written and arranged, I felt much more tied in with the whole band, instead of being a single musical unit."

A month of mixing took place back in Blighty: for Peter, it was the first time he had spent over three days on a single song, as was the case with 'Big Money'. "It was definitely a difficult process, the mixing process," says Peter, who was unused to what had become an over-democratised decision making process. "It's all those little things that everybody gets fired up about," says Alex. "Moments that go by that don't really do anything for the song, but if you listen to it on headphones or in your car, suddenly you notice them." There were very few arguments, however – not least, to defuse any tension there was the daily cigar challenge to contend with. "I always associate mixing that record with the cigar testing time," says Peter. "Geddy was staying near a cigar shop, we had a chart and he was bringing new cigars every day." To compete, Dave Meegan was sent out on errands to come back with bigger and better cigars. "Pete wouldn't have let it get into an argument anyway I don't think," says Dave. "He would have defused it, sorted it out."

And it was done. Six months was the longest time Peter had spent on an album, but he'd loved every minute. "Enormous fun," he says. "My experience of pop music was, no loyalty to anybody: you get in and out fairly quickly, hope for a hit and move on. This was the first time I had ever worked with guys that had been together for a long time, that truly loved each other and had a team of people that had been with them a long time as their crew." Dave Meegan was also impressed by the chemistry. "It was definitely a total, total unit where everybody was as powerful as any other part," says Dave. "They all seemed very focused towards one thing. I don't know what that one thing was, but they were all doing something and they were all 100% committed to it!"

Overall, the "overproduced-like-crazy" (according to Neil) *'Power Windows'* cost $325,000 to record, with $80,000 being spent on the trips to the UK and Montserrat. Like so many before, the album was mastered by Bob Ludwig in New York, supported by Geddy to ensure the quality of the results, extending his overseeing role to the most final of final mixes. It was a busy album but a good one, as Neil re-discovered ten years later. "I found it dizzying," he said. "There was so much stuff coming at you all the time. Which was great for the record and it works, and I still really like that album."

Consumate professionals

'Power Windows'

About power perhaps, but *'Power Windows'* maintains what have become staple themes in the band's repertoire – people and places, and the relationships they share. We have the power of big business in 'The Big Money', inspired once again by the writings of US author John Dos Passos – in this case, "the J.P. Morgan loans and the economic causes of World War I". Despite best intentions Neil found it hard to talk in absolutes, as he grudgingly recognised the good works bequeathed by foundations of the rich. Even when he turned his attentions to the first atomic bomb with 'Manhattan Project', steeping himself in the histories of the time, he was forced to acknowledge that the scientists were ordinary people too. "They weren't heartless crazy monsters, just regular, patriotic people caught up in the momentum of events," he conceded.

Musically, and far more than the two previous albums, it is clear that a level of negotiated agreement has been achieved between the performers. Nowhere is this more obvious than with 'Marathon'. This running song seems to establish a rhythmic groove more than a rut, with Peter Collins' production hooks bringing each instrument to the fore as and when it is needed. This continues through both 'Territories' and 'Middletown Dreams', travellers' tales which are based respectively on Neil's experiences cycling through China and through towns closer to home. "I was looking at these places and kind of looking at the people in them – fantasizing, perhaps romanticizing, a little about their lives," he said. The characters were a composite of people like writer Sherwood Anderson[3], artist Paul Gaugin, and no small amount of Neil. "They dropped out of their jobs in insurance and banking, deserted their families, and took off to pursue a dream." Or perhaps, they gave up a job at a farm equipment reseller.

Power plays between people are rife on the album. 'Grand Designs' suggests a return to Ayn Rand in the shape of the sociopathic architect Howard Roark, or perhaps the latter's own inspiration, Frank Lloyd Wright. Power plays in relationships are briefly explored in 'Emotion Detector', before the album's grand finale – 'Mystic Rhythms'. This is Neil's song – this time as a drummer, more than a lyricist, building layers of tempo around a solid back beat and drawing on samples from every size and style of drum he could find. Alex's contributions add texture, Geddy's bass punctuates the vocal message – that there are powers we can only glimpse, which are bigger than all of us. Far from rendering our existence pointless, it stimulates and excites us – "We suspend our disbelief, and we are entertained."

So perhaps, we are.

The cover concept was down to Hugh Syme once again, who planned a painted project. "My father had just passed away and I really felt like digging into a painting, which is always very personal and very consuming," says Hugh. The original concept was thought-provokingly uncluttered and simple – just a boy (modelled by an off-duty junior stockbroker) with a TV remote control, aimed out of a window – the TV itself was added through Geddy's insistence. Hugh later realised Geddy was right, for two reasons. "From a commercial standpoint, the icons of those old televisions were lovely, recognisable," he says. "It also had a Marshall McLuhan[4] nod to the power window that television is, so it all made sense." The cover still required location shots – this was no imaginary room. "Dimo Safari and I tirelessly searched locations to find the right window and cedar floorboards," says Hugh. "We 'auditioned' several vintage televisions from several collectors that Dimo had been acquainted with[5]."

In September, a video of 'Big Money' was released, directed by Robert Quartly and produced by Geddy's brother Allan. Neil had to play live – it's difficult to fake hitting things with sticks. Afterwards Neil went off to cycle from Munich to Venice with some friends, via the Alps. When he came back, it was straight back into the tour rehearsals, interspersed with another video – this time for 'Mystic Rhythms', directed by Gerald Casale. "He found some weird toys in this shop in London," according to Geddy. "Everything he said it was going to be, it ended up being which very rarely happens."

'Power Windows' was released on October 26 1985, "brought to you by the letter M" as many of the songs started with the letter. Thanked on the cover was Jim Burgess, who had supported Geddy throughout his keyboard initiation. 'Big Money' was released as a single on both sides of the Atlantic, reaching Billboard Number 45 on 9 November 1985, and 'Power Windows' peaked in the album charts at Number 4. By December 18 the album had gone gold, selling 500,000 copies; a month later, 27 January 1986, it had gone platinum at a million copies sold worldwide. Not a bad result. Once again, MTV offered Rush the opportunity to participate in a contest; once again, the offer was politely declined. They wouldn't be asked again.

Not only could they go anywhere they liked, they decided, but neither did they have to go anywhere they didn't, fixing an itinerary of the North American continent only. The band required a couple of extra months to prepare, given the additional

Neil prepares to release some tension

complexity of the songs, many of which could only be played with the support of samplers and sequencers. Jim Burgess organised an Emulator keyboard to call up specific samples at specific times. "Things got so complicated that I thought it would be impossible to remember everything," said Geddy, who worked with Jim developing colour charts to choreograph the samples. "We assigned different colors to each block of the KX76, so when we did, say, 'Big Money', I'd flip the chart. It turns out to be a lot easier to memorize than I thought it would be. If you can memorize a thousand notes in a song, it isn't too hard to memorize four different colors."

This was also a time for major transitions in the lighting technology. Howard having

> ## Toss Up
> "For me, to toss a stick up in the air is a really dangerous thing. Who knows where it's going to come down? So it adds a certain amount of risk to the performance, and a certain amount of excitement. And I like to toss them high, so it's a challenge. It's not something you can take for granted; it's a little moment of tension for me."
>
> Neil Peart

quite deliberately, wanted to "exhaust all the possibilities of the moving light world," he took the plunge into a brave new world of electronics-based lighting. "It was like moving from vinyl to CD," he says, "a revelation."

Eventually the tour started in Maine on December 4. It lasted until May, the band playing a sedate ten days a month. Support band Marillion had been invited back on some of the tour dates, despite the reception from fans last time around. "They came back and said, please do it," recalls Marillion keyboardist Mark Kelly. "On the opening night there was a bottle of champagne in our dressing room, saying welcome to the tour, hope you enjoy it!"

Every night of the tour Tony Geranios was constantly on his toes, loading samples from 5" disks into the sequencers for the different songs. Technology, and its tendency to cause human error, got the better of the band on more than one occasion. Fan Michael Ordaz[6] remembers the gig in Austin, Texas on January 18. "Midway through 'Middletown Dreams', Geddy was late triggering the sequencers, thus throwing everybody off and bringing the song almost to a stop! I am sure that Neil was upset. I was in total shock!"

On at least one occasion, Tony remembers having to play a sample himself, because the trigger failed or some other error crept in. "He used to be sat at the back of stage in a pit behind some black curtains, with a shitload of keyboards, loads of Emulator 3's and stuff," says Mark Kelly. "He claimed all he ever had to do was put disks in drives and set up programs. I know he played some stuff, because if you were listening very carefully, you could hear keyboards playing and Geddy was nowhere near them!" It was all quite understandable, according to Mark, "It wasn't anything like a big deal, I didn't think – a-haa!! – it was just the way he was so adamant that he never did anything. I suppose that was all part of the thing, it was important that it felt for them, they stayed a three-piece. They succeeded 99% of the time, and they got a huge sound for a three-piece, whichever way you look at it!"

It was true – it might have been a compromise, all the same it sounded awesome. "The band was trying to get the maximum, both musically and lyrically, out of their tunes, an experiment in expanding the textures and music," says Tony Geranios. While his guitar was losing prominence on a number of the new songs, Alex frequently found himself picking up bass duties.

> **Smokin'**
>
> "We watched them quite a bit on that tour. In one of the songs, on the line *'smoking guns'*, these huge pyro's would go off, huge big explosions... One night I was watching from the side of the stage, stupidly I didn't realize, but the crew all knew I was standing on top of one of these things pretty much, and they all were just watching, waiting, hoping I'd stay there, I mean I wasn't on top of it but I was fucking close! And this thing just went KABAMM! and nearly took me off my feet! I was absolutely half deaf in one ear for a while, but there was no permanent damage!"
>
> Mark Kelly

Despite these inconveniences, the tour was a lot of fun, helped along by "entertainment director" Andrew MacNaughtan who ensured a constant flow of silliness. Not that this meant overdoing it. "We did have a bowling for bimbos night," says Mark Kelly. "There were no bimbos... it was more bowling and drinking." It was all a far cry from the hedonistic earlier days – but they'd tried that and didn't particularly want to do it for ever. Having tried out oil painting in the duller times at the studio, Alex planned to try watercolours on the road – in the end though, he settled for tennis with Geddy. "Geddy and I like to get up early and play racquetball or tennis," said Alex. "Exercise wakes you up and makes you feel a little healthier."

Neil had also found his own way to avoid his touring demons. Not least he kept up his cycling, frequently choosing to bike the final hundred miles to the tour hotel rather than travel on the tour bus. In March 1986, he held his first ever drum clinic on the band's second LA date – he really had relaxed sufficiently to parade himself in public.

Indeed, through his relationship with *Modern Drummer*, he was opening up considerably. He had written columns, personally answered letters he was sent, and was good friends with a number of the staff. Taking a step further he held an essay contest in the magazine, the main prize being his Tama kit. He laughed, "The only trouble was that I had to read 4,625 essays!"

The three musicians were building relationships that would stand them in good stead for the future. While on tour, Neil got to know Rod Morgenstein, drummer with the support act the Steve Morse Band, and jazz bassist Jeff Berlin came to visit the band one night. Jeff unconsciously gave Geddy some lessons as he was backstage, not to mention a reminder of where his musical heart lay. "I had the opportunity to watch him goofing around with a bass, and was just amazed at his knowledge of bass chords," says Geddy. "That's something I had never really exploited in my playing, so he inspired me to play around more with it. He probably doesn't know it, and would be embarrassed to hear it."

After the tour, Neil biked through Switzerland with his brother, Dan. Meanwhile Alex moved house, and took the opportunity to build a more soundproof studio, "a fully floating room built within a room." Alex's own solo prospects were drawing inexorably closer.

And Then There Were Three

'*Power Windows*' had been a success, and this was in no small part down to Peter Collins and his cohort, Jimbo Barton. "We enjoyed working with Peter - we feel he is good for our music," said Neil. So, they decided to do it all again.

The gang - with Jimbo Barton and Peter Collins

Writing started at the end of September 1986, back at Elora Sound, this time with Peter in attendance from the start. A concept quickly evolved – this time introspective, focusing on the creative process itself. "It relates to the burning desire to do something and how important it is to keep your fire lit, regardless of circumstances," explained Geddy. "It's important to hold yourself together or stick to your guns."

Indeed, not least with respect to technology, which was now encroaching on how songs were written. "I think it's just a handy tool," said Geddy of his new Apple Macintosh, on which he was running Composer software. "You can put a Mac in the hands of five people, and not everybody's going to write a good song." Even Neil tried using a Mac for lyric writing, delighting in shifting phrases around without writing the whole thing out again. The first time he did this, Geddy wasn't quite so impressed. "I'm so used to his little hand-written lyric sheets that he gives me, 'cause they're always so cool and he draws these

Giving In The Past #1

As the writing was to start Neil returned to his favourite drum shack, the Percussion Center in Fort Wayne, to test out some new drums. Six kits were set up at a farmhouse nearby, from Tama, Yamaha, Premier, Ludwig, Sonor and Tempus.

Then the testing began. "I would have been happy to record or tour with any of these drums, but I was looking for something special – that extra bit of tonality and 'snap'." To Neil's surprise, he eventually settled on the Ludwigs over the Tamas. "The overall excitement of the Ludwig sound was just fractionally better. So...I ordered a set!" Look was important. "As much as I loved the Candy Apple Red finish of my Tamas, I just couldn't have the same color again! Neal and I discussed a few possibilities, and he did me up a sample with a mix consisting of an opalescent white base, with just a hint of pink in it, and a few metallic flecks to highlight the opalescence."

Neil also took the time to add to his growing arsenal of electronics, picking up an Akai digital sampling unit chained into a Yamaha midi controller, as well as a KAT keyboard percussion synthesizer (like an electronic marimba). To test out all of his new equipment, Neil also realised his ambition to create a piece of stand-alone percussion music, entitled 'Pieces of Eight' "because of all the different time signatures it ended up meandering through."

little pictures on the top of them and stuff," he said.

Symbolically perhaps, Neil's lyrical printouts were finally freed from the symbolism and allegory that had been his trademark. "I've grown out of such a style as both a person and as a writer," he remarked, finding inspiration instead from non-fiction writings. "I'm much more into history and sociology, geography and the world around me," he was to say. Across the album, Neil returned to the theme of, as he put it, "trying to recognise idealism with clear-sighted reality."

Computers or no computers, it all came together smoothly enough. The final song to be written, 'Force Ten' was an experiment in the same, genre-crossing mould as 'Digital Man', squeezed into the last couple of days of writing time. Peter had suggested that a rock song would balance the album, and Neil had just been sent a piece of lyrical material by his friend Pye Dubois – the two ideas seemed to fit. "Neil played with it a bit until he was happy with the result and showed it to us," said Geddy. "We brainstormed for about 2 or 3 hours, and we had 'Force 10'." Writing came to a close 14 December, just in time for the holidays.

After the break, recording started back at the Manor on 5 January 1987, followed by Ridge Farm studios, near Horsham. The process with Peter was by now off pat, with just the right balance between schedule and creativity. Neil had perfected the art of rehearsal, trying to perform his parts in a single take and making good use of his new equipment, to flick between sound samples. "In one of the new songs, I play an African drum setup for the verses, and then 'click' to a setup of my acoustic Tama drums, sampled from 'Grand Designs', for the choruses," said Neil.

"Fantastic! I love it!"

Once again a number of collaborators were brought in. For 'Time Stand Still', in the writing stage the band took the step of bringing a female into what had previously been a men-only club. Geddy put it succinctly: "Hell, let's get a girl in here!" Having approached both Chrissie Hynde and Cyndi Lauper (who turned the boys down), someone at SRO sent down a copy of a 'Til Tuesday album, fronted by Aimee Mann. "I don't know if she'd heard of us," said Neil, "But we were impressed by her great range – between the angelic quality, and that emotional contralto she has." Aimee's voice was also "used" at the end of 'Tai Shan', played backwards to give "an eerie, pseudo-Chinese sound."

> ### Brain Teaser
>
> Peter Henderson hadn't seen Geddy, Alex and Neil since the end of the *'Grace Under Pressure'* sessions back in 1984. Three years later he was recording at Metropolis studios in London. At a restaurant one evening he was passed a note: "Ann Uumellmahaye and Dr Hfuhruhurr[8] would like to buy you a drink."
>
> He kindly accepted, of course.

Peter was making even wilder suggestions for the arrangements. "I was pushing the envelope with them," says Peter. In particular, he suggested a brass section on 'Mission'. "I had them try a colliery band on that song – sort of the 'Hovis'[7] sound. It was a little too much for them," he says. "I remember thinking, perhaps I have gone a little too far this time, but at least they tried it! That was what was always so fantastic about them, if I had a strong idea they would always try it even if they didn't use it." Peter went to enormous lengths to find what he wanted – eventually settling on the William Faery brass band, recorded in Oldham in the North of England.

New Yorker Steve Margoshes and Englishman Andrew Jackman also helped with a number of the arrangements, then it was off to Montserrat again for three weeks to record the guitars. Just as with the last album, Alex's parts were recorded after the others, but at least this time the others remembered to leave some gaps.

When at Montserrat, the band met recording engineer Ken Blair. "What I found remarkable about those Rush sessions was the truly organised, methodical and business like way the band worked," says Ken. "A whole range of amps and speaker combinations had been set up in the studio area and an extra long guitar lead routed from the control room through to the amps so that Alex could sit in the control room and play. When Alex recorded a part the speakers were cranked up loud to get a good vibe going. However, once a part had been recorded the speakers were turned way down for the playback. They were working with the knowledge that it was pretty easy to make things sound impressive if you listened loud but it was important to them that the parts also sounded good and impressive even at low replay level."

Aw, come on! Geddy behind the desk

While Geddy, Peter, Jimbo and Ken worked with Alex on the sound, Neil kept out of the way – he was planning another cycle trip, and he always had his reading. Once a track was done, Neil would join the others in democratic discussion. "Neil brought a fresh pair of ears to the situation, gave his opinion and any issues were discussed between the band," says Ken. "If anything needed to be redone it was; otherwise they moved on and Neil left them to it again for a while. It was an extremely effective and efficient way of working but also never lacked a sense of doing good creative work, never clinical or mechanised." Effective perhaps – but just slightly oppressive for the unconfident Alex. "In the control room he was very sensitive," says Peter. "What does Geddy think, what does the producer think. You are very aware of their vibe and facial expression even if they don't say anything. You are picking up a vibe that if you have done something that is not quite right it can be very discouraging to keep doing it over and over again and not knowing exactly what one is going for."

With guitars and final vocals done, in May 1987 the team trooped off to the Guillaume Tell Studio in Paris to do the mixes. Each studio offered a change of scenery and had its own strengths, and besides, it kept everyone happy to move around. "I think it kept giving us a new outlook on the album," said Geddy – and why not?

'Hold Your Fire'

Burning bright... The concept behind 'Hold Your Fire' centred on the creative process itself, according to Geddy. "It relates to the burning desire to do something and how important it is to keep your fire lit, regardless of circumstances," he explained. Trouble is, for the band the contextual circumstances couldn't be better, as indicated by this slickly produced album released by a band at the peak of their popularity, during a period of poppy, highly produced music. Look no further than the opening track: if "tough times demand tough songs," this isn't one of them. Neither is 'Lock and Key' – '*I don't want to face the killer instinct*', says Geddy in 'Lock and Key' – but when exactly would he have to, given this level of comfort? The concepts are well-considered, but become less believable against such a background of gloss.

Most songs work better than these, not least 'Second Nature', 'Open Secrets' and 'Time Stand Still' which say little but say it well, the latter with choruses supported by fellow Canadian Aimee Mann. The music is straightforward, the hooks are catchy and everything works. There are also opportunities to be technical – Geddy's busy bass on 'Turn The Page', for example, supporting a cacophonic layering of guitars that somehow works.

Contrary to public opinion, Neil was not writing about himself on the album. "If I chose to write them from the perspective of the 'first person singular' then it was because that was the most effective way of transmitting my thoughts," he commented. Despite this, there was room for allegorical parallels with the band. "Who you are and what you're going through is very much a part of the record," said Geddy, and 'Mission' in particular, was unashamedly autobiographical. "It grew out of a conversation Neil and I had about the kind of people we consider ourselves to be, people who always knew what they wanted to do in their lives and always had this ambition and desire," said Geddy.

The last two songs are more concerned with the environmental – first 'Tai Shan', returning to the peaceful serenity Neil discovered on the holy mountain during his cycling visit to China. Then 'High Water', again a travelling song. So many Rush songs are journeys, and the band journeyed far to come to this point but on arrival, it finds the destination somewhat lacking. All the same every choice is now available – when they start out again, the route may lie in a different direction but the long walk is over.

"I could either mix at home or I can mix in this cheap studio around the corner; or I can go to Paris, spend a few extra dollars and have a wonderful new experience mixing, so I vote for the latter, you know? Let's have some fun."

All in all, *'Hold Your Fire'* had been a rather pleasant recording experience, and everyone was happy with the results. "[What] we've been striving to achieve over the last three or four records has finally come to rest in *'Hold Your Fire'*," said Geddy. All the same, while there was a feeling that *'Hold Your Fire'* had been more focused, clearly there was more work – or less work – to be done. "We climbed up a hill and now we've gotten to the top and we have to decide where we go from here," he said.

Who Needs Computers?

"The final photographic components (the juggler, the 3 fireballs, the boy in the window with the binoculars, the Dalmatian, his fire hydrant and the shot of the miniature road cases in the loading bay) were sent out to the lab for what was then called emulsion stripping, where the film for all these separate elements is literally cut to create one composite transparency. This was then exposed to separate full scale film sheets that were each impregnated with ink. These were then each laid onto the paper to create the final dye transfer print. I would then, using bleach and dye, retouch the print to create a (hopefully) seamless sense that the final shot was taken all 'in camera' as a believable study in 'improbable reality'.

"This is why I often say (and have t-shirt bearing) the words 'Command-Z means never having to say you're sorry!'"

Hugh Syme

The cover of *'Hold Your Fire'* was art-directed by Hugh Syme as a pun-filled street scene. To tie up a city street and wet it down for a shoot was considered extortionate, so Hugh, living in Los Angeles at the time, decided to go small, engaging photographer Glen Wexler and three miniaturists, Patrick Johnson, Scott Alexander and Olivia Ramirez to help bring the dark, wet street to life. "We all descended on North Highland Avenue for the better part of a month, where Glen lent his studio, his legendarily critical eye, and his creativity to yet another collaboration, proving to be the consummate host, all the while," says Hugh Syme.

"The main building was built at 1/12 scale, as were the Jackson alley buildings," explains Scott. "The diner and other details to the right side of the main building were done at 1/24 scale, as forced perspective elements." Apart from working with Scott in the painting and finishing of the set, including the neon sign on the Chinese diner, and a cat in the alley that Hugh cut out of some black paper, fraying the edges to catch the light, Hugh and Glen worked for several days to light the finished set. The 'water' on the street was paint thinner, continually having to be reapplied as it kept evaporating, and the juggler's fireballs were basketballs, coated with highly flammable rubber cement. "I combined several individual photographic images by re-exposing them on 8x10 film in my darkroom," says Glen Wexler.

One part of the set – the "Jackson Alley" – was left over from a Michael Jackson shoot. "Glen still had the buildings, so we used them to create an alley to the left of the foreground building," says Scott. For characters, the original plan was to use actor Dennis Hopper as the juggler but a schedule conflict prevented this. "We ended up casting Stanley Brock, best known for his role in the movie *'Tin Men'*," says Glen. The boy in the window with his binoculars was the same Toronto stockbroker as Hugh had sit for his painting for *'Power Windows'*, flown down to LA for the shoot.

Perplexing as it was for management to comprehend (who were approving the budget for this street scene extravaganza), Hugh decided to retire the street scene to the inner sleeve, replacing it with an outer cover that was shocking in its simplicity. In these pre-digital days, however, even this was not simple to produce. "The 'Rush' type was vacuum formed and inset into a 4 by 8 feet plastic surface that was then painted by an auto body shop," explains Glen. "The red balls are a repetition of a suspended billiard ball." There was plenty that could be read into symbolism of the three balls, caught in a mutual, perpetual orbit. "Sure, you can look at it as three people, three balls, but it's all that and more," said Geddy.

Following mastering, over the summer the band took the time to make a couple of videos, bringing Aimee Mann back in for 'Time Stand Still', directed by Zbigniew Rybczynski. As the production process neared its end, Alex managed to squeeze in a session with his friend Rik Emmett of the band Triumph, on 'Beyond Borders'. It gave him the opportunity to try out new directions that he felt wouldn't have suited Rush. "When I got involved with this project, everything was just about finished," he explained. "That enabled me to sit back and put my feet up and play whatever I wanted[9]."

'Hold Your Fire' was released on September 8, 1987, and as it was being released, Neil took off to climb Mount Kilimanjaro. 'Time Stand Still' was released as a single, reaching Number 3 in the *Billboard* single rock charts. When Neil returned it was time to get the tour together, ready for kick-off at the end of October.

This time, the band had agreed to make a proper go of touring, not least going to Europe for the first time since *'Signals'*. Somehow, it was hoped, the songs would translate to the ever-expanding live show. A few songs, like 'Time Stand Still', required a click track to ensure the band stayed in sync with the visuals (not to mention with Aimee Mann's recorded voice). "We're using so much electronics, sometimes it's easy to go overboard and just play the tapes," said Geddy. "We're trying to avoid doing that and feel that if we have hands-on control it's still part of the performance." The idea of a fourth player was brought up once again – and rejected. Even though there was a number of talented players in their close entourage, not least Hugh Syme, nobody wanted to change the central dynamic of the band. "Every year I get closer and closer to saying yes to that," said Geddy, "At this stage, we believe we can pull it off. If we fail, maybe next time around you'll see another guy banging on the keyboards." Like the others, Neil was determined to ensure the band could play multiple parts without a fourth member. "We take a lot of pride in being able to do it all ourselves."

Red Riders

Coca Cola was to be included on the tour rider, "only if bottled the old-fashioned way."

Once again, Tony Geranios took the brunt of the technical strain. After his *'Power Windows'* experiences, Tony worked hard on ensuring nothing would go wrong. "I built in lots of redundancy," he says. "If something were to go wrong, we had a backup." All the same, he says, "It became very stressful at times!" Geddy learned certain tricks to minimise the margin for error, such as assigning the same sample to three adjacent notes on the keyboard, a necessary trick when he found himself running across the stage to hit a trigger.

The technologies themselves were improving all the time, not least for Neil's rig, his KAT MIDI mallet controller meeting his live needs nicely. "All of the keyboard percussion stuff that I had been trying to fit in physically and also get reproduced in a live setting, I was finally able to do," he said. However, it was perhaps inevitable that the synthesisers would lose their shine given the demands they imposed. Geddy had been content to forgo a bit of bass to make way for keyboards, but he wasn't happy with the thought of them taking over completely. "When we're recording, a lot of times I know I won't be able to play bass in certain parts of songs because I'll be playing the keyboards," he said. "I'm very reluctant to put a bass part on the record that I won't be able to play live. So it's a battle."

Keyboards had grown to fill the space allocated and then some, first to Alex's chagrin and then to Geddy and Neil's. "It's like the little thing that grew," said Geddy. "We became addicted to the idea of having an extra member in the band without having an extra member. Now almost every limb I have is connected to something." Perhaps most of all however, and despite taking up piano lessons ("It's really boring, but it's already helping me."), Geddy realised that he would never be a master of the keyboards, in the same way as he was of the bass. This was not a battle anyone could "win", and trying more was just making things harder still.

Perhaps, trying harder was not the answer.

The Birmingham, UK dates in April 1988 were considered the most appropriate to record a live video and a live album. As director Larry Jordan came on the road to prepare for the recordings, he immediately saw the main difficulty with capturing Rush live. "They don't do anything," he says. "For them, it's all about the musicianship. Documenting their performance was my challenge. I had to make it interesting visually, and gain their trust that I'm not going to mess with their image." To achieve a sufficiently dynamic result, Larry chose to work with multiple cameras, being careful not to put off the musicians, particularly Neil. "You don't want to cut away from the punch line," says Larry. "In a ten minute drum solo, you've got to change angles."

Still, he got what he wanted, and by working with the individual operators and careful editing, he ensured there appeared to be plenty of activity. "Geddy said we look like twenty years younger!" he laughs.

The following night, it was Guy Charbonneau's turn to record an audio performance. In the absence of cameras, the boys relaxed visibly. "It almost felt like nothing was happening," said Geddy. "Everybody gave a very loose performance in relief that there was no camera pointed at us."

The band had the offer to play a festival gig at Castle Donnington in the UK, but didn't fancy it, particularly given the feedback of Howard Ungerleider, who had worked Donnington with Metallica. "It was everything they hated, in terms of the integrity of the show," says Howard. "It would compromise everything they worked

Mike Positioning

"Something which will always bug me... Geddy's playing electric bass, wireless, and I remember that wireless drifts from time to time. I hear a little drifting, when I listen to the bass, by itself. We try to work on the bass, to move the transmitter, to see if we can clean it up. With Geddy, I say, 'Listen, your bass is drifting,' Geddy is, like, 'uuuuhhhh!' If we put in a cable – nice sounding bass, but his performance cannot go all over the stage, will suffer. You have to remember these guys are on tour for 2, 3 months at a time, and if you change things, you might mess up more than you're going to gain.

"So we ask, are we capturing performance, are we capturing vibe, or to get the best bass possible, and they decide to go for performance. Now, they go to the studio, the sound engineer mixing the project, says, 'Oh, now you've got to fix that bass.' Poor Geddy, he calls Val Azzoli, Val calls me, says, 'the bass sounds bad,' I say 'yes,' and I feel very bad because I want them happy.

"I see them 6, 7 months after and I ask Geddy, does he feel bad, and he says, 'no, we're not,' but I never did record with them again, that's why it really bugs me!"

Guy Charbonneau

for. The kids were throwing mud and shit at the stage, I couldn't see them dealing with that!" Indeed, said Neil, "Why put yourself through that."

Indeed, why put themselves through touring at all? The last day of the tour was May 5, 1988, supported by Wishbone Ash in Stuttgart, Germany. At the end of the six months the band felt tired and bemused. Alex had flu, and Geddy had voice problems. The band had played up to 250 dates a year and they were, unsurprisingly, burned out. There was plenty to feel good about, but it was clear that shorter tours in less countries were the better model. "We still enjoy touring so long as it's not too crazy as it has been at times in the past," said Alex. "We prefer to work a little less than we used to and spend a little more time at home with our families."

Of the threesome, it was perhaps Geddy who suffered the most. "That tour was a very difficult tour for me personally," said Geddy. "I was getting ill a lot on the road and I wasn't very healthy and the tour seemed to go on forever. Following that I think we had kind of a dark period." Things were working out in the studio, but there wasn't quite enough to give anyone a solid feeling that it was worth doing it all again – not yet. "I don't know if we ever talked about splitting up but individually we all thought about it," said Geddy. "It's never actually came out of our mouths."

The live album, to be called 'A Show of Hands', freed the band from any last obligations to its record label Mercury/Phonogram, and nobody was too bothered about renewing the contract. Mercury's pre-'2112' panic had been replaced by a conspicuous lack of attention. Initially this had been to the band's advantage; after 'Moving Pictures' there was a flurry of support, but this had died back again, as management changes at the label pushed Rush back into a pigeonhole. Neither was there anyone batting their corner, particularly – Cliff Burnstein had left the label years before. "Rush has out-lived, it would seem, countless hierarchies of management at the label," said Geddy. "We didn't have any feel for who was at our old company anymore and I kind of objected to being inherited and transferred from one president to another." The band felt like a cash cow, with minimal effort required from the label to generate the requisite amount of sales. Said Neil, "We felt that the whole machinery rested on us – that if we stopped doing interviews, if we stopped touring for any reason, nobody else would be doing anything," said Neil.

Old ally Donna Halper, who had worked at Mercury for a year as East Coast A&R Director, saw things from the inside. "There reached a point where it became obvious that Mercury was a small label without a lot of clout," says Donna. "They lacked the leverage to get Rush into places that perhaps an Atlantic or another major label could." To indicate they'd had enough, Rush insisted that 'A Show of Hands' be released as a single CD even though it had to be a double vinyl album. "Everybody was freakin' out about that," said Val Azzoli, working at SRO at the time. "They wanted two CDs so they could charge $40 instead of $20. They were just being greedy. That would have been pure profit for the record company and the retailers, profit which we wouldn't have seen, but we won that battle."

Leaving the label gave everybody pause for thought. The band took a six-month sojourn to spend time with their families, hold their own fire and contemplate the future. "We found ourselves free of deadlines and obligations – for the first time in fifteen years – so we decided to make the most of that," said Neil. "We took some time off, got to know ourselves and our families once again, and generally just backed away from the infectious machinery of Rash – I mean Rush."

The boys needed a break, and while the question hung in the air about carrying on at all, the reality was far more complex. "The reason for this break," said Geddy, "is one of those little awareness-moments where you realize you're burning out on being ambitious, that you're burning out on the treadmill of accomplishment. You're living one life and visiting another and trying to teach yourself to assimilate instantly – you get home and you try to meld yourself into that person that you left... So we're finally taking time to fully live a settled life."

If time was the great healer, it was time to take some.

Time Stand Still

Seven Months.

When grown men start getting big on DIY, it can mean one of three things. First, they've always been a bit homey and they know where their slippers are. Second, they are under duress from their partners. Or third, they've lost some of the perspective on what they are doing, and they need a period of procrastination to give their subconscious time to breathe.

Geddy bought a cottage in this period, and was doing the décor.

Never one to miss a good break, Neil was delighted to have time for the things he'd been dabbling in – cycling in general, and writing about it in particular. He'd cycled from Munich to Venice, from Barcelona to Bordeaux, and latterly from Calgary to Vancouver. "A cyclist is obviously a harmless eccentric," he'd said, a role he felt he fitted perfectly. Neil had kept notes as he went, writing them up as a series of books that were shown only to his family and friends, with titles such as 'The Golden Lion' (in 1987), followed by 'Raindance Over The Rockies'. "The nice thing about travel writing is that it encompasses anything you damn well want to throw in there," he'd said. His books had always been self-published, and distributed to friends and colleagues – there was little interest from mainstream publishers, and besides, he didn't feel his writing was quite ready for a wider audience.

In November 1988 Neil went to Cameroon with specialist "holiday" company Cycle Africa. Drumming was part of the culture in some places he visited, and Neil just couldn't resist joining in. "I've had some situations where the whole village just gets dancing and laughing and pointing and screaming and just can't believe what they're seeing, but at the same time still having a great time with it." He documented his experiences in a new book he had called 'The Masked Rider'. "That one, strangely enough for me, represented the turning point," said Neil, "the only one I could look at a year later and still like."

While Neil's horizons were opening, Alex still lacked just a little distance. Back home, SRO general manager Val Azzoli sensed Alex needed a return to his roots, so he proposed that the guitarist produce and mix a five-track EP for SRO signing, Clean Slate. "I wanted him to get back to, hey listen, we got eight dollars to make this

Rhythmic Mystics

"The drum master gestured to me to try and play a rhythm. So we began playing together, and he started smiling because he could tell I had a rhythm – maybe not his rhythm, but a rhythm of some kind. We were playing and playing, building the intensity, and little kids started coming in, laughing at the white man playing drums. Then a few women came into the room, and everybody began dancing to our beat! The master and I even started trading fours. It wasn't a spoken thing, but he could tell that I would lay out and listen to what he was doing for a certain amount of time, and then he would do the same. It was just a magical moment." When they finished, a confused and startled missionary ran up to Peart and asked, "How can you do that?" Chuckling to himself, Neil politely responded, "I'm in the business."

Neil Peart, finding his feet in the Gambia

record," said Val. "We can't record in Montserrat and Paris and Istanbul. We got a dingy little studio at 40 dollars an hour. Ya got three weeks. You're not gonna sleep... Remember this? By doing that he realizes all he's got is a guitar, an amp and a lotta coffee, just like the old days in between tours. He's now in the mood of, 'Hey I got an idea, fuck the outboard gear, I'm back to guitar and fingers!'"

Once the six month period was over, the trio met up at Neil's place to find out what conclusions each had drawn. "There was no sense of compulsion about it – it was simply a question of what we wanted to do," recalled Neil. "We decided what we wanted to do was make another record... without any obligations on us, we found we were still excited about making music together, and truly wanted to make something new."

The decision was – let's rock. "As much as we like to get heady or pseudointellectual, the reason we play in a band is because we like to play rock," said Geddy. "We like to play hard rock. I think that's the one thing you'd get the three of us to agree on: we don't want to be wimpy. So I guess whenever we feel like we're getting too old for it, something in us rebels and wants to kick some butt!" There was a battle to fight, the kid gloves were off: the enemy was the bland, MTV-ised music that plagued the airwaves. "We're in this homogenous zone of the most boring fucking music I've heard in my life," said Val Azzoli. "Radio is not listening to the kids, which is a fundamental mistake society is making as well."

Faced with whether they were getting too old for it, they were philosophical. "I think the age barrier in rock 'n' roll has gone," said Geddy. "I think the bottom line is whether or not you sell records." Speaking of which, the live album 'A Show of Hands' was released in January 1989, and Larry had got the shots he wanted for the live video. "When I delivered the Rush cut, there were not that many changes," he says. The video was finally released in October 1989, with a preview night held at a number of selected cinemas. Geddy thoroughly enjoyed the experience of what the band looked like. "I never get to see us," he said. "There are effects and magical moments I'd never known were happening."

Message Received

Geddy contributed a line to the Climb Japan-only release of 'Take A Chance'. Climb's drummer was Warren Cromartie, who played baseball for the Montreal Expos and who famously lent his name to the school on the back cover of 'Signals'.

The bigger business beckoned for Val Azzoli, who left his post at SRO to go work for Atlantic Records as General Manager. Shortly after this, SRO started negotiating a new record deal – with Atlantic Records. While Val may have helped the process, there were many other reasons for the decision – not least the refreshing attitude of the label's founder, Ahmet Ertegun. "We got to get you playing jazz," said Ahmet. "We are NOT a typical band," said Geddy. "We're regarded as difficult because we have low-key lifestyles. We went to Atlantic because they are more music orientated. We just needed a fresh start!"

There was the inevitable litigation between Phonogram and Atlantic for the rights of previous recordings, but that was for the management to deal with – the boys had music to make.

It was 1989, and as the decade came to a close much had been happening with music, with post-rock, post-goth and post-hair-metal bands such as U2, The Cult and Guns 'n' Roses all demonstrating (in their own ways) that it was time for things to come down to earth. "Suddenly nobody cared anymore about any new keyboard, the whole music industry suddenly moved back to raw guitars, live drums," says Paul Northfield. "Guns 'n' Roses came back in to fashion and we moved back to a whole sensitivity of raw-energy playing."

Inevitably, some of this was rubbing off on the trio that now found themselves a decade and a half into their careers. As Alex started preparations at his home studio, he happily decided less was more, meaning no keyboards and minimal effects. "I made a rule that I'm not gonna plug into a single synthesizer or keyboard, though I use a Roland G-10 for drum patterns," he said. "The stuff that I've been doing just on my own has been really raw, no chorus on guitars, no echoes." It wasn't just about keyboards, but to get away from effects in general, as he put it, his "10-year dependency on chorus" that had first started with *A Farewell To Kings*'.

Geddy was also stripping things back, and the starting point was his bass. "Keyboards can be quite a passive writing tool, and we wanted something more forceful and less pastoral," said Geddy. "I wrote a lot more on bass, which reminded me of the old days when there was nothing more to write on." This was a genuine rebellion, and not just a whim: "I was getting sick and tired of working with computers and synthesizers," said Geddy, who set out a similar agenda for the vocals. "I wanted to focus on writing very strong vocal melodies first," he explained. "In my mind there was a lot of emphasis on what the melody would be and how to layer the harmonies and I really experimented in that area."

While Alex and Geddy were getting fired up however, Neil was becoming a little introspective. Not least, following his extensive travels, he feared for his ability to perform at the expected levels. He needn't have worried: "After so many years of playing, and especially so many years of touring, the muscle memory is intense," said Neil. "All I really had to do was get some calluses back on my hands. It was nowhere near as difficult as I thought it was going to be."

Having erased any doubts about whether he could play, his mind turned to how he was playing: increasingly he had been finding that his consummate capabilities were starting to feel more like a constraint. "I spent 20 years on technique and on learning the finer points of keeping good time, developing tempo and shadings of rhythmic feel, and keeping my mind open to other ethnic music and other drummers," he said. "When I finally became confident in my playing, all of these things finally came together. I had to step back from that 20-year quest for knowledge and ask myself, do I really enjoy using all this stuff?" As with Neil's Jeff Berlin experiences, it helped to work outside his normal framework. "I have a friend who writes TV and film music, for instance. He was writing a lot of slide guitar stuff with old blues patterns, and he called me to play on it," he said. "I had to play a lot of brushes, and all I did was what he told me. It was great. There was no weight on my shoulders, no responsibility, easy."

Following the time at home, the trio headed off to Chalet Studio, in the countryside northeast of Toronto, to work out some ideas and to tune back into each others' thought processes. Run by David Chester, Chalet was an old, white, board-clad farm house, surrounded by farmland. The main studio was in a converted barn, big and glassy like Le Studio, with beautiful views that were offset only slightly by the nuclear reactors on the skyline.

The band quickly settled into its favourite phase – writing together – this time using the guitar as the starting point rather than the keys. "On past albums we tended to write a lot with keyboards and then apply the other instruments afterwards," said Neil. "We thought it would be more interesting to be a bit more linear and do the writing around the guitar framework, and thinking of it as an ensemble as guitar, bass, and drums. Not be reactionary – we don't omit keyboards as a point of principle. To the contrary, we will probably use keyboards as much as ever, but the focus will be different."

For Alex, for now, this was enough of a step. "I think we've ended the development of keyboards and texture," said Alex. "We needed to try it. We were quite happy with it, but now it's time to move on to something else, and what we needed to do was take a step back and re-examine what the core of the band was, and what's always fired us along." Bass, drums and guitar – sounds good, and they weren't the only ones to think so.

When it came to fixing a producer, the boys were reluctant to give up Peter Collins, but they didn't have to make the decision – Peter made it for them. "He told us that he felt his own career needed more variety and scope, and reluctantly bowed out," said Neil. That was a bit of a fib, from Peter's perspective anyway, as he wasn't sure he'd been that good for the band. 'Hold Your Fire' had been moderately successful, but had not done as well as previous albums and Peter blamed himself. "I felt badly for

them at that point, that I had somehow let them down," says Peter. "Geddy did call me, and I said maybe it would be better for them if they went with somebody else."

Disappointedly, the hunt for a producer began again. At this time they started with a shortlist, and near the top was Rupert Hine, who they'd approached a couple of albums before; Neil also had a taste for Rupert's own albums. Rupert was a natural fit, thinks Paul Northfield. "He would have fitted sonically and ideas-wise in a very good way if they had ever wanted a fourth member of the band." All the same Rupert had turned down the opportunity previously, and this time he still wasn't sure what he could bring to this hard rock band. "A couple of people that represented them at the time, thwarted me on that argument by saying, well, I produced Saga," says Rupert.

Finally, the producer took a listen to their more recent output. "I realised there was nothing actually very obviously heavy rock about them at all," he says. Indeed, relative to his expectations of what they should sound like, as well as what was happening in music at the time, he was aghast. "All I seemed to be listening to, was keyboards, keyboards, keyboards, keyboards, bass and drums, and I suppose there must have been some guitar in there. It was beginning to be a bit dated." From a keyboard player himself, this was saying something.

Still, as Rupert realised he had more in common with Rush than he had expected, he thought it might be worth a crack, agreeing to meet the guys at the rehearsal studio. As he listened to the rough cuts, Rupert started to laugh, recalled Neil, "We looked at each other, eyebrows raised as if to say: He thinks our songs are funny? Evidently it was a laugh of pleasure; he stayed 'til the end." As far as the musicianship was concerned, Rupert was astounded, in particular with Neil's capabilities. "When we first played the tape, he thought I overdubbed the whole thing," said Neil. Not likely!

Like his predecessor Peter, Rupert was both a conceptual producer and a forthright

Rupert Hine:
A wildest
wish to fly

individual, and he needed to say certain things before he committed to the project. First there were Geddy's vocals. "I had a thing about those up on the ceiling, heavy metal, squeaky voices," he says. "They set my teeth on edge." He sat down with Geddy and they talked it through. "Quite shockingly and tremendously invitingly, Geddy said, so, what are you saying, what would you do to change that? And he said, after missing a beat, apart from firing the singer!" Half jokingly, Rupert suggested singing the songs a whole octave down. "You wouldn't even have to change the key!" Both Rupert and Geddy were well aware of the potential dangers of changing style. "It was a dangerous thing to discuss," says Rupert. "I knew they might lose legions of fans, who only bought the records because Geddy was up there in the Robert Plant range and that's what they loved. It wouldn't sound like Geddy Lee anymore." Geddy, again very bravely, said, "Well, why don't we experiment, it'll be something new."

Second there was that keyboard thing. "I said, given that you were probably last doing power trio stuff when you were much heavier, it might be really cool to hear the kind of thing you've been doing in recent years, but stripped back to being guitar, bass and drums." This was an easy one for the band to agree – then it was the band's turn to state its position. "Neil said, we don't talk about singles, and we don't talk about radio," says Rupert. "That's pretty empowering to a producer." The band also wanted to meet Rupert's engineer, Stephen Tayler, flying him in for the purpose.

Having agreed the approach and settling on a production team, the decision was made. "We were united in our rebellion," said Geddy.

In the confinement of his room, Neil worked out the lyrics to 'Presto' – an appropriately allegorical title for the fresh new style the band was planning to pull out of the hat – as well as 'The Pass' and 'Red Tide'. Meanwhile, Geddy and Alex used a drum machine as a surrogate, sometimes with little consideration for how a drummer might play the piece. Not least for 'Scars': "They put all kinds of percussion on the track, including congas, timbales, and bongos," said Neil. "We talked about bringing in a

Whirlwind Tour

"I was driven out to this tiny little residential studio, this was deep winter, very snowy. I had dinner with them and then I think I stayed the night, which meant getting two or three hours sleep, being woken at 3 in the morning to be driven back to the airport to fly to Montreal. I think it was probably Simon Pressey met me in a car, drove me the 50 miles to Morin Heights to look around, I was there for half an hour, then he drove me back to the airport and I flew back, within 24 hours. It was terribly exciting; it made me feel very special. I think it was part of their whole philosophy, wanting to get the chemistry right."

Stephen Tayler

The idyllic location that was Le Studio

percussionist to play in addition to the drum pattern I might play." Geddy and Alex suggested he tried playing it himself, using his pads: ever one for a challenge, he did. "I was playing eight different pads with my hands in a pattern, while I played snare and bass drum parts with my feet," he said. "I was using paradiddles[10] with my hands to get the accents in the right place and on the right pads. Then I had to organize the different sounds on the pads correctly so they would fall in the order I wanted them to. Then I had to arrange all of that into a series of rhythmic patterns, not just one. It was more than a day's work before I even played a note."

A week before the band decamped to the studio proper, it was time to get Rupert Hine and Stephen Tayler involved. Rupert couldn't believe the lengthy timescales. "I have never spent more than three months making an album in my entire life," says Rupert, who strongly suggested the band reduce the amount of studio time they had booked. "Blimey, gee, we can't do that!" they said, or words to that effect – finally they agreed to book no longer than six months. Following a week finishing off pre-production work, it was time to return to Le Studio at Morin Heights. The winter was already setting in, recalls Rupert, "The famous lake behind the studio was frozen over, although I never quite fancied going and testing it!"

Stephen Tayler's first job was to deal with the sonic setups, in particular for the drums. "Being such a word master, Neil was really into describing what he wanted to hear in a very powerful way," says Stephen. "Some musicians, particularly ones who are very hands on, might come up and say, well do you know I really think

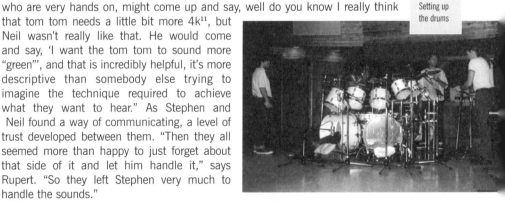
Setting up the drums

that tom tom needs a little bit more 4k[11], but Neil wasn't really like that. He would come and say, 'I want the tom tom to sound more "green"', and that is incredibly helpful, it's more descriptive than somebody else trying to imagine the technique required to achieve what they want to hear." As Stephen and Neil found a way of communicating, a level of trust developed between them. "Then they all seemed more than happy to just forget about that side of it and let him handle it," says Rupert. "So they left Stephen very much to handle the sounds."

The band stuck with Peter Collins's method of recording each instrument separately. Musical arrangements were kept simple, encouraged by the shorter timescales and helped by Rupert's coaxing for the boys to let go. "When we record we tend to go after perfect performances," explained Geddy. "We get so perfectly tight in synch that when we fall short, it hits our ear like an error." But, he admitted, few others could hear the difference. Gently but determinedly, Rupert prised them out of

Alex with his acoustic

the detail and into the groove. "Rupert's sensibility as to when a performance is feeling in a groove and when one is a little too stiff, was the most helpful," remarked Geddy, who adopted the phrase, "Perfect is the enemy of good." "They were very, very impressed by the way backing track sessions came together sonically," says Rupert. "They got visibly very excited about that, it was quite noticeable."

In parallel, Rupert had noticed how Geddy and Neil had democratised Alex's performances. "There's a very Virgoan side to both Geddy and Neil, sort of fastidious," says Rupert. "Alex is an intuitive player, much better left blundering around on his own; he'd naturally like to keep the comedy of errors, the happy accidents. The amount of control they showed, felt like it was holding Alex down. What had started being supportive had grown to being slightly invasive – Alex was almost being provoked into having to substantiate any of his ideas verbally, and in advance of actually doing them."

Neil and Geddy brought out the best and the worst of Alex. By pushing him forward, they were also playing on his open character, his desire to please those around him. "Alex has got a huge, very open heart, and it was as if, as soon as he had played, any criticism would be immediately taken on board," says Rupert. "He'd try to deal with it, as if he was totally unaware that it might be filling in the things that he might just fill in for himself." Alex didn't want to rock the boat, "I'm a little bit lazy and I like ... I like things to be smooth," he would remark. Rupert moved to reorganise things, ensuring at least that Alex had the space he needed to express himself.

At the same time, Rupert and Geddy worked on the vocal approach. "We wanted it to be more of a singer's album," said Geddy. "It was very helpful to have someone who was so versed in songwriting." Geddy tried the lower range, and found it was good. "When you're in the conversational range, you're much more easily able to express yourself," says Rupert. "He did appreciate that, once he got over the slight awkwardness. He was feeling a bit odd, I think he felt too exposed." In the end Geddy did not lower his voice on every track, but he did on a number of tracks.

Geddy gives Alex a lesson in guitar

There were few of the trickier times of previous albums – the dynamic between band members wasn't perfect, but it was perfectly acceptable. Resident engineer Simon Pressey remembers the studio sessions as a constant stream of good times. "Working with Rush isn't really work, it's an opportunity to do what you love, and do it as well as you can," says Simon. "We had many great laughs, meals, jokes, excellent moments, generous spirit and lasting memories. Be it building a scale model of Iraq out of snow with Alex, during the first Gulf invasion, learning the power of self-discipline by example from Neil or being treated as an equal by Geddy and the ensuing rush of confidence that allowed me to rise to the occasion. With Rush, I learned to laugh at myself and make the most of the moment." It helped that there seemed to be a constant flow of birthday parties. "Rupert's and my birthdays are not far apart, not the same year, so we kept on having birthday celebrations!" says Stephen.

As the album progressed, some of the hard-fought principles began to waver. There were a number of gaps, empty spaces that seemed to be crying out to be filled – by keyboards. "In the end, we couldn't resist using them for colour," said Geddy. Even Alex's resistance waned. "When we'd start working we'd go along, and I'd go along with things. Even if I wasn't quite sure that I was feeling right about a particular decision or not, quite often I'd just go along with it." This created textures which Alex took as competition, which perhaps explains some of the very clean, bright guitar sounds he used. "We were peaking on our keyboard explorations at that time, so I gravitated to a sound that was a little more biting to get through that." Additional keys were played by Jason Sniderman, an old friend of Geddy's.

The end often justifies the means, and the whole band was very pleased with the resulting album (despite there being no instrumental, to Neil's chagrin). All felt 'The Pass' was one of the best songs they'd ever written – Neil's lyrics, Geddy's arrangements and Alex's

Omega Concerned

Alex invented a bookstand for Neil, "so he could read while he ate breakfast," which he made out of drum parts. He also made a rear-lit lyric stand for Geddy. The mainstay invention was a guitar stand, as seen supporting his acoustic guitar when he plays live. "The design has been in production for a few years now; it sells at low cost through mail order."

Alex's company to sell it is the Omega Concern. Another device (tongue in cheek, according to Neil) is the 'Omega-Album-Order-Deciding-Device'. This enables song orders to be changed around.

guitars all came together to show where the band could go from here. "'Presto' is kind of a renewal to me," said Geddy. "It's a renewal of energy and a positive

Alex demonstrates his favourite type of keyboards

outlook, in musical terms and in personal terms, both in my place in the band and my feeling about recording."

Having booked six months in the studio, the album was completed in four. "All the studio time put together didn't exceed three months," says Rupert. "They thought it was a miracle!" The band were delighted but Rupert, who had refrained from being too hands-on, felt slightly bemused. "I had to proclaim, I'm not sure I have really been worth the money..." Neil's response was pointed. "Yeah, but you were there when we had questions. It's not a question of quantity, it's about being there at the right time."

Mixing time had been booked at The Farmyard, a UK studio that was co-owned by Rupert. "We heard part way through the recording that his partner had sold the studio and that it was not going to be available," says Stephen. "This was a bit of a blow, Rupert and I had done all our projects for about the previous 8 years in this one place, it was like home, and Rupert had really sold the concept of coming over to England." Quickly the pair had to find somewhere else to mix, and they opted for the Metropolis, in London. "It literally had just opened, and on paper and judging by phone calls it sounded great," says Stephen. "That was a bit of a risk, us going into a place we didn't know. Actually it turned out really, really, well. We were very happy."

Following the mixing sessions in September 1989, Neil popped back to Togo,

'Presto'

In the words of Spike Milligan, "What are we going to do now?"

Competent enough, 'Presto' is an album delivered from a band in transition. There's some good songs here, some good sounds as well, but the band is girding its loins to go to another place – or places – and it shows. Looking on the bright side, the power trio is unmistakeably back: right from the outset, drums, guitar and bass are all that can be heard. "This album was a real reaction against technology in a sense," said Geddy. Rupert Hine's production brings a level of clarity and resharpens the edge that had been wearing off over the past couple of albums. By the second song, 'Chain Lightning', the synthesizers are back, but only to support everything else.

The musical evolution from this album's predecessors is more obvious than any significant change of lyrical style, as the band seeks to distance itself from the sharply dressed, synth pop era and re-establish its rock band credentials. There are some standard rockers which one feels Rush could have written in its sleep, such as 'War Paint' but the majority of songs are more accomplished compositions – not least 'The Pass', 'Scars' and 'Available Light', all of which see the three players balancing their skills to support an earnest, heartfelt lyric. Not everything quite works – 'Presto' doesn't quite get there for example, more heat than light indeed.

Not that the band wasn't drawing on outside influences – just that there was a broader pond to be dipped. The Peart-patented musical sponge took inspiration once again from his travels, this time adding a West African pop beat to 'Superconductor'. Like 'Limelight' before it, 'Superconductor' was a comment on the nature of fame. "I've been involved, of course, in that world for a long time, and watching other people affected by the nature of fame and the nature of that kind of deification," said Neil. "And it really isn't healthy for them either, so I started thinking, 'Well maybe this idea of modern, 20th century western world heroism really isn't so good'."

Based on the kids game 'Scissors, Paper, Stone', the innocuous 'Hand Over Fist' is suggestive of continuity and repetition and not just in the lyrics – the music for the chorus would work well as a round. 'Presto' is a perfectly competent album of songs, and it is just a shame that they don't all quite gel together. For all that it was treading water, the album served its purpose – it kept both the record company and the fans at bay, and offered a precursor for what was to come.

Ghana and the Ivory Coast for another cycling jaunt while Atlantic set about making the most of their new signing. 'Presto' was released on 18 November to reasonable if not overwhelming success in both the US and the UK charts, reaching #20 and #27 respectively. All the same the release by this newly invigorated band, indicated how important the music still was to Rush, despite selling over a million albums a year and, it was claimed, earning $10 million just by sitting still.

The boys gave themselves a few weeks off for Christmas, and after the break they were even looking forward to going on tour! However, despite best efforts and the three-piece approach to writing, the band was still unsure it could reproduce its newer sounds on stage. "We weren't sure that we could pull off all the vocal and keyboard parts," explained Geddy, "In the end we figured our fans would rather see us struggle with technology than get another guy in." The determination to preserve the integrity of the three-piece went way beyond the bounds of duty – many other, equally competent bands, such as Genesis, had no such qualms – but the same factor that had kept the threesome together was unable to contemplate the use of outsiders. "We

A day out with the crew

didn't want to disrupt our chemistry," said Alex, who had his own fair share of triggered samples.

Following the New Year, preparations for the tour began in earnest. By now the band was playing mainly arenas, and the sets had to be created and co-ordinated accordingly. As Howard, Nick, Robert and the rest of the crew put together the sets and co-ordinated the equipment rosters, so Alex, Geddy and Neil rehearsed the new material until it was up to performance standard.

Off they went on 15 February 1990, this time with 70 dates booked; with them for the first time was photographer Andrew MacNaughtan, acting as their personal assistant. "It was the chance of a lifetime, to go on the road with a rock and roll band," he says. The reality quickly replaced any fantasy, however. "I can unequivocally state that they are the most boring band on the road," says Andrew. "We would leave the concert, get on the bus, eat hotdogs, watch a movie and go to bed. They're 3 boring guys, there isn't chicks, there isn't parties, it's not them!"

When the 'Presto' tour came to a close at the end of June 1990, the band had earned $16 million, a quarter of which was made on merchandise sales. The band celebrated with the crew by going – bowling. "We've learned that touring can still be fun if it's done properly and you have the right attitude about it," explained Alex.

At the close of the tour, for a change, the band were gagging to get back into the studio: so much so, the threesome arranged to reunite before the official end of the break. The less meticulous approach, a combination of the band's reaction to the past, Rupert's intervention and a reflection of the musical trends of the times, was indication enough that the band found its groove. "I think part of it was because we're finally comfortable with the notion that Rush is all we need to satisfy ourselves musically," remarked Neil. "I think it was something we always knew, but nobody ever dared to verbalize it until Geddy expressed it to me when we were writing the album."

With all this said, the band felt they could do better. The efficiency of 'Presto' had been an insight into what the band could achieve, and they were convinced they could do better next time.

They hadn't seen nothin'.

Wind and Fire

In 1989 Rush donated a track to George Martin, ex-producer of the Beatles, for his compilation album 'After The Hurricane – Songs for Montserrat'. The band had of course recorded parts of 'Power Windows' and 'Hold Your Fire' at George's studio, which was flattened during the hurricane. Neil Peart wrote about the fragility of Montserrat in the 'Hold Your Fire' tour book, in particular mentioning the volcanic nature which would cause untold damage on the island five years later.

Burning for You

At the end of 1990 Neil was approached by Cathy Rich, the late drummer's daughter, to participate in the Buddy Rich Memorial Concert. "One of his final requests had been for her to try to keep his band working somehow, to keep the music alive, and to 'give something back' to American music," he explained. Despite it interrupting the *'Roll The Bones'* schedules, he reluctantly agreed. "I vacillated a lot about accepting it," said Neil. "I realized that year that I had been playing drums for twenty-five years, so I felt I should do it for myself to mark the occasion." Feeling locked into his own style, he realized what an opportunity it was. "I tried to learn what Buddy played on the songs I was going to be performing, exactly as he played them," he said. "I felt safe, in a way, following his example into what were unknown musical waters for me. It was such a challenge because I had to try and get into his mind."

Neil chose three songs, Count Basie's 'One O'Clock Jump', Duke Ellington's 'Cottontail', and 'Mexicali Nose' by Harry Betts. It was a good job Neil researched his role so intensively before he arrived in New York to practice with the others, because he didn't get the chance to do so when he got there. "I was the last drummer to rehearse with the band on the rehearsal day, and since it was late in the day a few of the guys in the band had to leave to play gigs," he recalls. "The pianist had to leave early, so that was a drag. The Basie and Ellington songs I performed were both founded on piano/bass/drums trio, and to not be able to fully rehearse with the piano made it difficult."

Things weren't much better organized on the day of the concert, 8 April 1991. "I was far away from the band, and it was very tough for me to hear them," he recalls. "The performance came off okay, but I just didn't enjoy it." All the same, for Neil it kick-started his dormant love of big band music. "Since then, it's not only been a course of study, to learn about doing it, but I've gone back through all the CD collections of Count Basie and Duke Ellington, and I have a whole new appreciation of that," remarked Neil.

Road To Redemption

Neil had already been actively pursuing lyrical concepts and themes for the album, using his tried and trusted technique of hunting though his stack of lyric notebooks. "You have to save up your little inspirations," he had said, and one phrase in particular caught his eye. "Yes! Roll the bones, perfect!" Chance, and how it could work for good or ill, seemed a highly appropriate starting point. "The image of the wild card prompted all kinds of thoughts – that a lot of what happens to us is out of our control," said Neil.

At the end of 1990, the three reunited at a nondescript recording studio in downtown Toronto to get some songs together. Neil turned up with his handful of lyrics, and Geddy and Alex were keen to build on the musical ideas of *'Presto'*. Once again, it was planned to move further away from the computer-generated writing approach of the period up to *'Hold Your Fire'*. "We used the keyboards and synthesisers as an orchestration device rather than as a writing tool," explained Geddy.

The vocals continued in the same vein. "I remember the lower register voice stuff

Geddy
gets a
new friend

was working very well and as if to prove it, a lot of the songs already turned up absolutely in that mould," says Rupert, who was to be welcomed back as producer. "His sense of groove is very important to us," commented Geddy. "He's helped us come up with looser and more exciting performances."

After a while the band decamped to Chalet Studios to commence the writing proper. Alex was into lifting weights every morning, and Geddy was a morning person so he naturally led the arranging process. The computer technologies had moved forward, sort of: Geddy was running C-Lab Notator on an Atari, "a pain in the ass" compared to a Mac. "Our next writing session will be digital," he added. Neil found that his own electronic exploits were coming to an end. "I had all kinds of plans for how I was going to update my set-up for new electronic use and all that, but I just didn't need it: they weren't those kind of songs," he said. To force himself into new directions, Neil picked up a double pedal and dispensed with one of his bass drums. "I liked it a lot – the notes were cleaner and more even," he said.

Studio slots had been booked at Le Studio in Morin Heights and McClear Place in Toronto, followed by Nomis in London for the mix. The band had learned not to get the producer in too early, to preserve the distinction between "band" and "objective ear". Ten weeks after writing had initially started, the band reunited with Rupert and Stephen in early 1991, and the team – Geddy, Neil and Alex, Rupert and Stephen, and crew members JJ, Jack Secret and Larry, made their way to Morin Heights.

Given the time taken on the previous album, Rupert suggested only three months of studio time, and following a brief negotiation they settled on no more than five. Rupert's desire to speed things up was not just to save time. "It's quality, not speed or efficiency that makes a good album," he explains. "Energy in the studio, high energy is one of the most creative mental conditions. One idea, when it goes well, leads very quickly to another. The creative juices get a real chance to flow and things get done just incredibly fast." As he arrived, Rupert stressed what was important: capturing the vibe, and not losing it to musicality.

Picture in
picture

Stephen was quick to configure the drums ready for Neil to record his tracks, but then disaster struck. "We had a technical problem with the tape machine, which I think was a Mitsubishi 32-track digital," says Stephen. Of course, Morin Heights was a long way from the nearest Mitsubishi 32-track dealer, and days were lost that should have been spent on the drums. This was extremely frustrating, particularly for Neil who was psyched up and ready to go. He vented his frustration on his kit, rehearsing his pieces way beyond the point of necessity. So much so that, by the time the tape machine had been fixed, he was beat perfect. "Neil put down the drum tracks in a day and half," says Stephen. "It not only brought us back up to schedule, it actually put us way ahead of schedule."

Despite this, Neil still managed to inject some spontaneity into his drumming. "I know that I have a tendency to be too organized, too architectural about my parts," he said. "In spite of all the rehearsal I did before we recorded, I left areas that I refused to work out. Right down to the day that I recorded, I didn't know what I was going to play in that particular part of the song, so that something special might happen."

Lines In The Sand

The song 'Dreamline' is a nod to author Kevin Anderson, who had written a book (*'Resurrection, Inc.'*) inspired by *'Grace Under Pressure'*. It had tickled Neil's fancy – "He complimented me most highly on it," said Kevin at the time. Kevin sent Neil a couple of other novels, *'Lifeline'* and *'The Trinity Paradox'*, which was originally to be called *'Timeline'*.

The bass layer came together smoothly and calmly, and also came in ahead of schedule. "Suddenly we actually ended up with spare time," says Stephen. There was time to mess around and try out new things, not least to play with a section of rap Neil had been working on. As he admitted, "It struck me that it must be a lot of fun to do that!" When Neil had presented the rap to the others, it was the source of some amusement; Rupert latched onto it immediately, and endeavoured to get it onto the record but Geddy had second thoughts. "Geddy felt very self-conscious about it," says Paul. The team tried it in different voicings and suggested different actors: plans included using a newsreader, or even Robbie Robertson or John Cleese. "We didn't want to tip the balance for it to become a novelty track," says Rupert. "In the end, it actually seemed more fun to try it with Geddy." So Geddy's voice it was, pitched down using a voice processor.

For Alex, the extra time meant he cold spend however long he needed on his guitar parts. Based on Geddy and Neil's recorded inputs, Rupert had some rough mixes put together, and he packed Alex off to his room with an eight-track Tascam portable recorder. "Alex was able to work unhurriedly in his own time, while the other two were getting down to doing the tracks," says Stephen.

The family table at Le Studio

The plan was for Alex to work out his solos in advance so there would be less picking apart (however well-meant), but things didn't work out that way. Explains Rupert, "I just said, Alex, why would you be doing this again and be really contrived? You've just done this fresh and flamboyantly, in your own private place, and now we're hearing it, and it's fucking great. You know, it's really brilliant," and Neil would go, "What you mean, it's a dodgy Tascam eight-track!" And I said, well, nobody is going to be going, I'm sure there's a bit of tape hiss in there somewhere!" And so, certain of Alex's solos were used directly on the album, straight from the Tascam. "Rupert and I had always the confidence that we can take any recording and somehow manage to get it back in its right place," says Stephen. "Flying it in is what we used to call it." One example was 'Ghost of A Chance', which came directly from the original demo. "I did it just to fill the space, but it had great spontaneity and emotion," remarked Alex.

Another of Alex's bedroom solos was to appear on the song 'Bravado'. "I think it was a first take," said Alex. "The solo has a particular character and personality that's uncommon for me. If I'd erased that and gone with something else, then it would have been just another solo I put together in the studio, rather than something that happened at a special moment." Rather than expressing concern, the other two were highly complimentary. "'Bravado' has one of my favourite solos Alex has ever played – that was a magic solo," Neil would remark. He wasn't the only person to excel on the song – concerning Neil's own delivery, Geddy commented, "There's an example of limb independence that rivals any drummer, anywhere. The fact that he nailed that in one take blows my mind." Agrees Rupert, "I actually had to get out of the control room and walk into the studio, stand in front of him and watch to work out how on earth he was doing it."

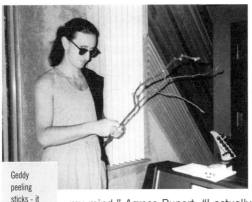

Geddy peeling sticks - it focuses the mind. Apparently.

As the weeks passed, spring gave way to summer. Extra-curricular activities centred around volleyball, which became a regular fixture of the balmy, beery evenings. "Rupert and I had never ever played volleyball in our lives," says Stephen, who gained "rookie of the year" status. Unfortunately, with the warmth, the water and the floodlights came the inevitable mosquitos. "It turned into this ferocious, competitive thing that happened, usually at midnight," says Rupert. "We would finish the session, have a few beers and then put on long sleeved shirts, gloves, hats, sometimes scarves, long trousers tucked into your socks and smother ourselves with this mosquito repellent. We would go out and absolutely murder ourselves late at night." Injuries were rife – fortunately Geddy damaged his hand just after the bass overdubs were finished. "We really used to dive and crash in," says Stephen. "He really did hurt himself!"

The power trio focus meant that Geddy could concentrate more on his singing, even better more established in the lower register. "It seems to be where I feel we have the most musical range, is in that natural singing/talking range," he said. "It's an intentional thing and I think it's helped the melodic character of the band tremendously, because it's opened up just so much scope." He was amply supported by Rupert. "Rupert is an accomplished vocalist and keyboard player and possesses a musical point of view that many producers cannot fathom," said Neil. "In fact, he was particularly helpful with the arranging of vocal harmonies." Indeed, Rupert

Ready Steady Rock

"Cooking analogies for making music are phenomenal. I use them all the time. I say, look, stir fry your album. Put your ingredients in fast, keep them fresh. Get it on the plate and eaten, while its all just alive and fantastic. How many times, look, from every kind of meal that benefits from being marinaded, there are a hundred that just turn to brown stew."

Rupert Hine

'Roll The Bones'

This is a veritable pot-boiler of songs, as Rush the band re-emerges from its doldrum and continues on its way, older and wiser this time, but rejuvenated and ready for whatever the world may throw at the Willowdale three. "We are young, wandering the face of the world," goes the chorus to the opening song 'Dreamline', and indeed the band sets out to demonstrate it plans to make the most of its allotted time.

'Roll The Bones' is the convergence of two factors – a renewed interest in the abilities of each band member, and a shared view on how things should feel and sound, resulting in a more mature, composed style that is woven like a thread through every song. Not without irony, there is a sense of the band trying its luck, setting itself up as a renewed entity. This mostly works – spearheaded by songs like 'Bravado', which with its uber-complex drum beats, confirms the sentiment that life is not to be frittered away. "If the music stops, there's only the sound of the rain," sings Geddy, who has no intention of hanging up his microphone just yet.

Thematically of course, Lady Luck plays a big part in the proceedings, not least her role in human relationships and self-determination as songs like 'Ghost of A Chance' (with its stunning guitar solo), 'You Bet Your Life' and 'Neurotica' clearly demonstrate. Slightly out of place is 'Heresy', which was written as a polemical statement against the wasted years prior to the fall of the Iron Curtain. While the sentiment may have been pure it may have been best kept as a statement, not a song – it does stick with the theme of circumstances, the accident of birth that dictates the regime one has to live by. Neil had based the drum part on a pattern he had heard while he was cycling in Togo. "I was laying on a rooftop one night and heard two drummers playing in the next valley, and the rhythm stuck in my head," he said.

Not a band to baulk at experimentation, Rush even brought a voice-distorted, pseudo-rap piece to the proceedings in the shape of the title track. It sits well with the rest of the song, and indeed the album. There's room for the drive time instrumental 'Where's My Thing', the rock and roll romp that is 'Face Up', and a couple of other musical gems besides.

Lyrically the gambling theme has been well and truly covered by the end. Is there any such thing as luck? 'Roll The Bones' is proof of this, made after fifteen years by a rejuvenated band that can finally look back and see the fruits of its labours. The harder they worked, the luckier they had become.

even sang on some of the tracks, and played keyboards on a couple.

What of the keyboards? "We added the keys at the end to embellish," explained Geddy. "That was the only reason the keys were there – or maybe to help me express myself when I was painted into a musical corner." All the same, this time Geddy had been very careful not to fill gaps unnecessarily. "I think that once you become reliant on a lot of other instruments, like keyboards and so forth, and you develop an ear for orchestration, then every time you hear a space, you want to fill it," said Geddy. "It's a style of recording and writing and arranging that can seem very enjoyable for a certain time period, but then it almost becomes a trap." For once, however, he managed to resist the temptation.

In total, the time in Le Studio lasted eight weeks spread over three months – no mean feat. The recording process itself took no more than a fortnight, leaving time unused at the end of the booked period. "We actually shaved off a couple of months recording it," said Alex, who recorded his guitars in 8 days, rather than the four weeks they were used to. "It was a very positive writing session, and an optimistic recording session," said Geddy, and this positivity manifested itself in the upbeat, even groovy nature of a number of the songs. Geddy explained some of the funkiness was due to his use of Wal bass guitars. "They have a kind of – it's difficult to explain – fruity bottom," he explained.

Once the music was mostly complete, it was off to McClear Place for vocal overdubs, and to finish the guitar before mixing took place at Nomis Studios. By the end of the production process Alex was feeling very firmly back in the centre of things, with the band feeling close, united and confident in the direction it was taking. "We got a really great groove going in terms of writing," remarked Geddy. To Alex's obvious delight as well, after its extended absence since 'Moving Pictures', the guitar was back where it was supposed to be. "There's so much emotion in

The listening room at Le Studio

that instrument and you play off that, everybody plays off that, and it really has to be in that role," he said. "We've even got a little blues," he remarked about his favourite song from the album, 'Ghost of A Chance'.

There was still room for progress: as the final mixes were played back before mastering, a couple of songs lacked the dynamism they'd had in the studio. "We felt, 'you know, you know... we thought we had more here than we really have'," said Geddy. "Maybe there's an aspect of our sound that we're not capturing the way we used to capture it." While it was too late to do anything about it, it gave something to think about for the future.

With a cover incorporating a number of icons in the Dutch 'Vanitas' style, 'Roll The Bones'[12] was released on September 3, 1991, seventeen years to the day after Geddy, Alex and John had released Rush's first album. The band's fourteenth studio album was to prove extremely successful – it went straight into the charts at Billboard Number 3. The band's own favourite, 'Dreamline' was released as a single, followed by the rather unusual choice of the instrumental, 'Where's My Thing'. "I was really proud of our record company," said Neil. "It was just a very creative thing for a record company to do." The instrumental single was nominated for a Grammy, and the album was awarded Juno awards for Best Hard Rock Album and Best Cover. Not bad at all for a few weeks work, up in the mountains near Montréal.

Back in Europe of course, the success of the album was tempered by the fact that

the band were in decline: the band had matched a
dubious amount of marketing from either Mercury or
Atlantic's European operations, with a lack of will
to tour the countries concerned. This time however,
Rush did decide to cross the pond, much to the
consternation of the band's UK representatives, East
West Productions. Said Geddy, "When we came across
to the UK for the *'Bones'* tour we contacted them to get
some information, and they didn't even know that we
were on their books!"

Still, nothing could dampen the band's reinvigorated
spirits. According to journalist Jane Scott, "The trio was
so eager to tour it gave up its holidays for bookings."
Howard Ungerleider wasn't available as he was
working with Metallica and Queensrÿche at the time, so
Shawn Richardson was brought in as tour manager. As
usual, Geddy got heavily involved with animator Norm
Stangl and his team to put together the multimedia
aspects of the live show. "I'm pretty proud of the kinds

Getting On

"We did an interview not too
long ago for a guy from a
magazine, and at the end of the
interview he asked if we wouldn't
mind signing some records. We
said, 'Yeah, sure,' and he brought
out some album jackets that he
had: *'Hemispheres'* and some
older stuff. And I asked him, 'Who
is it for? Who shall I make it out
for?' and he said, 'Oh, it's for my
father. He's one of your biggest
fans.' And I thought, 'Oh, no,
his father!' You know, it's been
a long time."

Alex Lifeson, *'Roll The Bones'*
radio special

of animation we've put together over the last few years," said Geddy. "We've used
some very talented artists in town here and I think we've achieved some really unique
pieces of work." The bunnies were used again in the live performance, but this time
one of the rabbits shot the other, with the "bullet" traversing the video screen. "People
were really upset with us," confessed Geddy, uncontritely.

As the tour commenced in Hamilton, Ontario, the band felt at a musical peak. "On
this tour, we've reached a level of consistency that we never have before," said Neil,

who based his opinions on
the tapes recorded from
the mixing desks. "In
previous years, it would be
a cringing thing of hearing
the flaws and wanting to
correct them and feeling
down about how far from
perfect it was. This tour,
it is more of a pleasure.
I hear little corrections I
want to make from the
drumming point of view,
but at the same time I hear

Going out
for dinner
was never
like this

how well the band is playing on a night-to-night basis and that becomes its
own gratification, too." A lot of fun was had, not least through Alex's growing
reputation for his interlude of spontaneous, verbal gobbledegook, while the
other members of the band looked on, following as best they could and smiling all the
while. All was well.

When Primus joined the tour at the start of 1992, they injected a healthy dose of
musicality of their own. Neil would quite often warm up with Herb Alexander, the
Primus drummer, and before long the jamming session that ensued had become a
regular part of the schedules. "Members of their band and our band would drift in and
join us in making some impromptu music," said Neil. "For the most part people would

be using instruments that they don't normally play. Someone would pick up an accordion, and someone else would pick up a flute – that was *primo!*" On some occasions, instruments were replaced by other items – a bicycle frame, some garbage cans... not least when the band reached Berlin. "We set up in this little shed and both bands were just jamming on 'found percussion' and a few other instruments, flutes and clarinets picked up from pawn shops," said Neil. "It was a great escape from the day, and a good musical exploration." Confirmed Alex, "We had so much fun just trying to make music that it planted a seed."

Not everything was quite so funny – in Sacramento for example, Geddy was hit in the face with a shoe thrown from the crowd, which then triggered a sample on his synth. All the same, in the main the band remained appreciative of their fans. "We've been fortunate to be able to do what we want to do," said Alex. "And for having an audience that allowed us that freedom by buying our records."

By day a famous rock star, and by night...

The tour came to a close, once again, in the last days of June, and Neil proposed a dance party to finish things off. "I helped organise it," says Andrew MacNaughtan. "He's no great dancer but he loves to dance!" As the trio danced their way into their now-standard summer recess, rejuvenated as they were, more than ever they knew what they had to do next. After many years in what, in hindsight, they saw as a musical wilderness, the band knew that it could be itself again.

Of course, Rush didn't have a sense of humour, not to outsiders, anyway. "I don't know how we got this image," said Geddy, "Maybe we wore too many robes in the 70s." Finally somebody recognised the goofiness that was intrinsic to the trio – no less than the Harvard Lampoon which inducted them in May 1993. "They're very literate – one of the few bands that actually puts some humor into its lyrics and tries to make jokes once in a while," said Steve Lookner, a selection board member. "When there's a band that tries to be funny in an industry which doesn't have a lot of humor in it, we respect that."

Respect – all Geddy, Alex and Neil ever really wanted from their audiences, who'd followed them through thick and thin. Arguably the band had now gone through its thinnest patch, despite achieving a great deal of critical acclaim for its endeavours the trio had never been entirely comfortable with the eighties. Now however, musical trends were heading back towards a heartland of guitar, bass and drums, and the band was responding in kind. This time the influences were coming from a southerly direction. "The shift of more interesting hard rock was coming from America, bands like Soundgarden, even the Chilli Peppers, to a certain degree," said Geddy.

From a drumming perspective, Neil could only agree. "In the 80s, just from a drumming point of view, it was getting kind of worrisome, because everything you heard on the radio was programmed drums," he said. "And then suddenly in the 90s all these bands were coming out. Matt Cameron from Soundgarden was suddenly here, and Dave Krusen[13] from Pearl Jam, and this band Live from the States, a drummer called Chad Gracy, again playing great drums."

Not only this, but the new kids were citing Rush as one of their major influences. "All the cynical critics have been forced to accept us because a lot of the musicians in the alternative bands grew up listening to us," said Neil. "That was such an affirmation. Just such a spark of 'Yay, we're not alone' and there's no generational or age factor there now because we're both bands, making records and doing tours in all of these cases, so there isn't really a divide. We've been doing it longer, yes, but we do have the same values."

Indeed, and then some – watching the younger bands was a much needed affirmation of exactly those values. "We started thinking about what we were all about, what was the core of the band, how much we enjoyed the three of us, just being a three-piece together," said Alex. "Geddy and I facing Neil and playing, that's what we got off on when we were a lot younger." Now they were able to do it again, and it felt good.

NOTES: 1 *'Champions'* was produced by guitarist Ronny Montrose, who had toured with Rush in the past. 2 Brand X also featured Phil Collins on drums. 3 Sherwood Anderson left his small town existence and walked down the railroad to Chicago, to make his name as a writer. 4 Sixties media guru, who made famous the saying "The medium is the message". 5 Notably the Art Deco store, The Red Indian, in Toronto. 6 R.I.P. 2004. 7 A very traditional UK brand of wholemeal bread. 8 Characters from the Steve Martin film *'The Man With Two Brains'*. 9 The finished article appeared as a flexidisc on the July edition of *Guitar Player* magazine. 10 Rudimentary drum patterns. 11 One of the sliders on the mixing deck. 12 The boy in the 'Roll The Bones' video and on the cover of the album was Michel van der Veldt. 13 Later replaced by Dave Abbruzzese.

$dh = \sum_i \mu_i \, dn_i + \gamma \, dA$

) integrate

CH$_e$mist(r)y

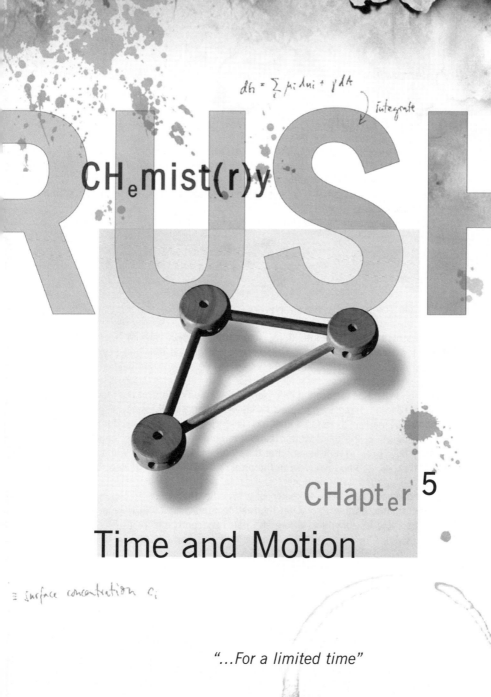

CHapt$_e$r 5

Time and Motion

= surface concentration c_i

"...For a limited time"

$d\gamma = -\sum_i c_i \, d\mu_i$ (3)

a binary solution in contact with air

$G = \sum_i \mu_i n_i + \gamma A$ (4)

) complete
differential

$\sum_i \mu_i \, dn_i + \sum_i n_i \, d\mu_i + \gamma \, dA + A \, d\gamma$ (6)

"Just variations on a theme, islands in a much larger stream"

Too Much English

The Scene: A rehearsal room, somewhere in downtown Toronto. Alex Lifeson is already present, setting up equipment. Geddy Lee walks in with a keyboard under his arm, to be faced with the steely gaze of the guitarist.

Geddy sees the look on Alex's face, glances down at what he is carrying, and looks back up.

GEDDY: "What's your problem!?"

Let's rock. The plan was that simple.

Despite the band's best intentions, the stripped down musical movement was progressing faster than they were. The descent into grunge that had been started by bands such as Soundgarden and Mudhoney in Seattle a few years before, was rapidly becoming a global charge downhill, energised by the global success of Nirvana's *'Nevermind'*. Rush had succeeded in loosening their own collars on the previous couple of albums, but compared to the angst-filled, raw energy of their newer peers Rush's production was starting to sound a little too slick, the music too tidy and rehearsed. Far from being daunted, the band were excited – reminded of the kind of band they used to be, they felt driven to rediscover what they were capable of. "We wanted to be that energetic three-piece band we were in the past," said Alex. "We decided to strip down our approach and bring up my guitar."

First, however, everyone was ready for a few months' break. In October of 1992, Geddy, his mother, brother and sister returned to Starachowice in Poland, so Geddy's Mom could show her offspring where she had been born and bred. Meanwhile Neil went on a Cycle Africa tour of Mali, Senegal and The Gambia. Now a qualified pilot, Alex wangled a day in a CF-5A fighter jet, with Canada's 419 Fighter Squadron. Dispatches report that Alex described the experience as "like sex, only not as messy!" He even got to keep his flight suit, which had been labelled "Captain Lerxst"!

As a warm-up before the studio, Neil and Geddy accepted invitations to guest on albums by The Rheostatics and Mendelson Joe, respectively. Having been a Rush fan in his youth, Rheostatics guitarist David Bidini couldn't believe his luck. "As Neil commanded his kit, he painted my adolescence before me," said Dave.

Rehearsals didn't start as well as they could in March 1993, particularly as Geddy arrived at the farm with an 'old friend'. Geddy had already stated that it was time to move on from the keyboard sound, and had recently stopped taking piano lessons. "My life was too busy and I started losing the ability to practice the way I wanted to," he had said, but he still wanted to use a synthesiser during the writing sessions. "Alex must have said 10,000 times that he didn't want any keyboards on the album, so when I brought my keyboards into the studio there was an immediate atmosphere," said Geddy. "He kept looking at them like they were really threatening. Alex was making assumptions that I wanted keyboards all over the place. It was a very volatile situation."

It wasn't just about the keyboards, but everything that they had come to represent. "There was a lot of stuff bubbling under the surface," said Geddy, and it was clear that it was time for such things to come out. A heart to heart settled things, and Alex agreed to allow the keys over the threshold. Even as the keyboards were being set up however, Geddy realised that his heart wasn't into using them. "Alex and I were sitting there at an eight-track computer machine getting ready to write and watching everybody set up the keyboards," said Geddy. "When they were done, there was this bank of keyboards with all these computer screens. We looked at all these television screens, and nowhere could you get a ballgame. So we just went, 'Pass.'" It is not hard to imagine the grin of relief on Alex's face.

Writing started slowly between Geddy and Alex, as much because of the break as anything. "For the first few days it was hard to get rolling, and that's when you worry because if things don't get rolling naturally, there's no way to force it," said Neil. "But after those few days, suddenly it was like a bomb went off." Once things got going, they really got going, recalled Neil, "Alex and Geddy would run into my room pleading for the lyrics and screaming, 'We're coffee achievers!' There's a genuine childlike excitement to the whole process." This is not to say that things were forever smooth – it sometimes proved difficult to get the genie back into the bottle. "All we wanted to do was fight," said Geddy. "We had some pretty darn good fights, and I felt much better. Mondays Alex and I would threaten to murder each other."

While Geddy and Alex were working (or duking) out their relationship, with a drum machine as a surrogate Neil, the wordsmith himself was struggling with a pot boiler of concepts – about relationships. "I was thinking certainly about gender differences, and I've been reading Jung so I was interested in the anima, the female spirit within the male, etc," he said. "I'd been thinking a lot about the nature of heroism and what was good and what was bad about it, and the idea of a role model, and people I'd known in my own life who were important to me as influences but weren't important to the rest of the world." There – put that lot together. "Duality became the only unifying theme," said Neil, who focused in particular on gender. "I ransacked everything from *Scientific American* to what the great thinkers of the world have had to say about it," he said.

Before long, the collective knew, they had to find a producer again – preferably someone from the US this time. "We listened to some of the records that have been made in America over the last few years, and they had a bigger, bolder, more exciting sound," said Geddy. "At the same time we didn't want to work with a producer who wasn't a song person." Nobody really seemed to fit the bill, so they called up old friend Peter Collins: as it happened he'd moved to the US to record with a number of heavier, stateside bands, such as Queensrÿche. "My taste had moved away from British pop music quite significantly," says Peter.

Chrétien Values

In November 1993, Neil wore his political views on his sleeve when he conducted a TV interview with liberal presidential candidate Jean Chrétien.

Peter's new sensibilities offered an intriguing prospect for the band, who quickly decided he was the man for the job. "It was kind of like an instant, 'Let's do this record together'," said Geddy. "He agreed with the vision of what we saw; and his comments, criticizing the last couple of records, sonically anyway, were very much in line with the direction we wanted to go." Peter was delighted, particularly as his experience with heavier bands had led him to have a better appreciation of the older Rush. "We had done the more high tech sound, and it was now the time to combine some of those things and get back to a more organic, analogue sort of sound," he says.

Peter picked up where Rupert left off, once again proving he was appropriate as much for his role as mediator. "If we are not sure about a part or about a performance, we can bounce that off him," said Alex. "He's an extremely responsible person in the studio. It's great to have that; you don't have to worry about anything because you know Peter's there for it."

More of a challenge was finding an engineer, as Peter's old cohort Jimbo Barton was now a producer in his own right. "We listened to literally dozens of engineers, knowing that we had to find the right guys," said Neil. In the end, Peter suggested Kevin 'Caveman' Shirley, renowned for his somewhat direct approach. "He was very cocky on the phone, which was a somewhat endearing quality for me, because I like people with strong opinions around," says Peter. When Caveman was invited to Toronto for an interview, he didn't hold back in his critiquing. "We played some stuff that I had done and Rupert had done and he was just brutally critical," says Peter. "He was extremely opinionated, so we hired him!"

Recording started in April, and the new team got to work. Kevin was true to form, his minimalist attitude and infectious energy pervading everything he did. "We were after bold and organic sounds, and he was the man for the job," said Geddy. "He has brilliant miking technique and a great ear for natural recording." Not only that, but he refused to take anything for granted. "Why do you do it this way?" he would ask, challenging any linkage with the past. "He's a kind of character that had very little respect for a lot of music that's been made," said Geddy.

First to be configured were the drums, which Kevin had guaranteed to have up and running in 20 minutes. "Caveman's opinion of drums was that they should not be all separated out, but sound like one instrument, and Neil kind of bought into that idea," says Peter. "I believe Kevin got the sound pretty much together within half an hour." Neil was delighted with the results – he wanted drums to sound like drums, and they did. "I didn't want the engineer to process them into something else," said Neil, but there wasn't much danger of that – rather than trying to pin down the sound by moving the knobs on the mixing desk, Kev spent time on the studio floor, shifting microphones.

> ## Dream Lines
>
> Geddy started to get into baseball when it was one of the few things he could pick up consistently on the hotel TV in the afternoons, which was generally when the tour bus would arrive at the next city. 'Tom Sawyer' became a favourite song at major league baseball games, and the relationship culminated in Geddy singing 'Oh Canada' at an all-star game at Camden Yards, on 13 July 1993. "It was so nerve wracking, I don't know if it was the lady who told me that 80 million people were watching was the reason..."

Having dealt with Neil, and having watched a trifle incredulous as Geddy's complex rig was configured, the Caveman turned his attentions to the bass. Kevin had spotted a defunct, tube-based Ampeg bass head, in the basement, apparently dumped by a previous occupant of the studio. He tested it and found it was old, and cranky, and raw – in other words, perfect. "He plugged it into some Trace Elliot cabinets I had, and went out there and insisted on EQ-ing the amp himself, he cranked the shit out of it and miked the cabinets in a way only he knows," said Geddy. "He plugged it in to all these speakers, and he turned it up to like, 15... I thought it was going to explode. So, we used a combination: my regular DI setup, my regular setup, and this exploding amp setup. It sounded great, I had a tremendous amount of energy, and all the explosion sounds of it kind of disappeared in the track, so you're not really aware of the fact that it's an amplifier on the verge of death." Caveman also twisted Geddy's arm to go retro with the guitar. "He had me use my early-70s Fender Jazz Bass, which I hadn't played in years," Geddy said.

Finally, there was Alex. Kevin's advice was simple, and profound: if you want to get back to basics, you've got to get out of the control room. "His theory was that the sound from the speakers goes into the pick ups of a guitar and creates a different sound," explains Peter. "It is not the same sound you get when you run a cable from the guitar out of the control room into the amp in the studio." Great theory, but the guitarist hated the idea – the control room had been his home since *'Moving Pictures'*. "In the control room you have a sense of control," said Alex. "There's immediate communication; if you want the monitors down they can go down, if you want them up they can go up." The other concern was that it might affect his signature sound. "I have been very resistant to this kind of an approach to recording the guitar," he said. "I always thought that we could get power and size and tonal depth in a number of other ways." Perhaps – but in the end he relented.

While there had been many changes in the set-up, the Peter Collins-patented process of production was much the same as it had been since *'Power Windows'*. Neil did his bit first, then Geddy, and all the while (having learned the trick from Rupert) Alex would hide himself away with his Alesis 8-track to come up with something special for the solos. "I tend to be a perfectionist, but I've come to realize my best work is spontaneous," he said. "An unrehearsed solo may not be particularly in time or in tune, but it can possess an emotional quality that's very difficult to recapture. I'd rather live with some technical imperfections."

The key for everyone, not just Alex, was to work on the spontaneity. Once again, Neil left gaps in his performances, to force himself to make something up on the spur of the moment. Not that he was under-rehearsed, particularly as some technical problems in the writing stages had once again reduced his recording window. "Neil was under the gun to get his parts together," said Geddy. "He went through a massive rehearsal period; he works tremendously hard and it's incredible to witness." Peter helped with both speed and spontaneity, rarely letting Neil go back and do something again if it had "worked". "The risk factor does transmit itself through the music, so Peter would sometimes try and grab the second run-through before I think it's even a take," said Neil. "When I'm just running it down for the engineer, he'll say, 'Okay, that's it'. 'But... wait a minute!'"

Geddy was also fighting his desire for technical perfectionism, letting his gift for simple melody take control whenever it could. "There are still the same number of notes per bar, but there is less of a variety of notes per bar," he said. "I felt like I was learning something all over again, and I was able to use things I already knew but applied in a different way." Most of all, he wanted a bass section that had groove, and he worked with Neil to deliver it. "We've been trying to make music that has a little soul to it," he said. "I view my role as smoothing out any rhythmic things that are uncomfortable – to make the rhythm section sound more fluid and glued-together."

Shock, Rattle and Roll

In 1993 Neil got a letter from his regular correspondent, Californian author Kevin J. Anderson, asking if he could use excerpts from Neil's African experiences as the basis for a horror short story. Called *'Drumbeats'*, the story told of "a rock drummer bicycling through Africa between concert tours, and some weird stuff that happens to him." Neil agreed, and the result was published in the anthology *'Shock Rock 2'*, edited by Jeff Gelb.

Some of Kev's suggestions were discomfiting to say the least, not least that he refused point blank to add any reverb to the raw cuts. "He wanted a purity of real sound, which was a unique way of working for us," said Neil. This was tricky: reverb was a handy tool, not least to smooth off any rough edges in the performances. "Holding back on the reverb made this record a bit more difficult because the flaws were so apparent. If there was a 'bark' on the snare drum or a 'grunch' in a guitar note, it was obvious." Any errors were kept in right until the end – and when rough mixes were made, they sounded exactly that – rough.

The band was mostly delighted with what Kevin was bringing to the table. All the same, while nobody stated it outright, people started to wonder whether Kevin was just a little too raw. At least it wasn't put in those terms – all agreed that there was a core "Rush sound" that wasn't to be tampered with. "It's not a total retromovement, you know, we don't want to throw away – you don't cut off your nose to spite your face," said Geddy, referring to Kev's clean slate approach. "But having someone that challenges you to make sure you're doing things the way you should be doing them is great." One thing they did accept, was to leave spaces in the songs without trying to fill them with music: "dry and empty" was good.

The uncertainty came to a head when Alex returned from his bedroom, armed with a fistful of solos. As he plugged in right next to his amp, without the clarity of the control room to help him, his inability to hear himself play was discomfiting in the extreme. This didn't last however, as he realized he could feel his way, rather than hear it. "As long as I could hear the snare and kick drums loud enough, I knew where I was," he said. "I could feel the guitar vibrating against my body, and it was easy to pick up feedback. The amps were really singing." His smile broadened still further as he realised another, unexpected benefit – his guitar was not the only thing he couldn't hear. "I was the only one out there," said Alex, who found himself unencumbered by the well-meant criticisms of his colleagues. "It was just me and my amps humming happily in the corner." That was that – for Alex, everything clicked. "God, I felt young! I really felt energetic. I had a ball, I had a great time."

Alex used his new-found freedom to immediate effect – constructing a quite deliberately "ugly" riff for 'Stick It Out', adding Celtic and Eastern influences to 'Leave That Thing Alone', and going back to a straight clean Telecaster sound for 'Cold Fire'. The latter song was mostly written when it came to Alex's turn, but Peter was able to prise it open again and make room for Alex to do his magic. All the same, he confessed a certain boredom with solos. "Soloing is fun, but I'd rather hear 60 or 70 percent less soloing on this record than is on it. To me it's a dated kind of thing," he'd said. The other members of the band didn't agree – particularly while he was doing so well.

In Sequence

"Alex made this most magnificent artistic creation, this board, and he lists every title. It's like on a magnetic board where every title can be moved around, so you can play around with the sequencing. On each of these little boards is a fantastic drawing representing the essence of the song as Alex sees it, which is convincing us more than ever that he's a sick human being. We played around with so many different combinations and it was really tough, so this is the one order that I think just seemed, when you're listening to an hour's worth of music, and considering how much aggressive music was in there, we felt it was kind of a nice way to ease you out of the record."

Geddy Lee

The whole process was fast, dirty and not always pleasant for the players. "It was a quicker record than I had ever made with them before," says Peter. "Caveman was not a detailed kind of person, he just wanted to catch a vibe and move on." Alex was increasingly finding his voice, in more ways than one – the arguments continued with

'Counterparts'

The idea that this album was about relationships came rather late in its development process. A number of songs fit the bill – 'Alien Shore' and 'Cold Fire', as well as the slightly dubious 'The Speed of Love' all look at the interpersonal, but there are none of the political or geographical references that were a staple of previous albums. Neil is quite prepared to stick his neck out – not least with 'Animate', a song disparagingly in touch with its feminine side. "That became such a cliché certainly through the 80s, of the modern sensitive man," said Neil. "It became a bit of an act of men pretending to be more sensitive than they actually were, and sometimes women pretending to be more aggressive than they actually were."

If this album is about anything however, it is the stripped down, updated sound. Against a musical backdrop which was seeing the death of hair metal and a return to a more analogue recording approach, we see Geddy getting his funk back, a more confident Alex and a timely reminder from Neil that drumming is, first and foremost, about hitting things with sticks. With engineer Kevin 'Caveman' Shirley turning the amps up to eleven, the band confidently bangs through the first three songs on the album, each a vibrant, power-trio mix. There's room for fun and room for anger, the latter working far better here in the raw, than on the more highly polished works of a few albums before.

Songs like 'Nobody's Hero' and 'Between Sun and Moon' offer some respite, returning to a more earnest Rush. The former was written about people Neil knew, who had died without the great send-offs one associates with the famous. Ellis, a friend of Neil's during his time in London, had died of AIDS in the late eighties; another character was involved in a terrible crime in Canada. For once, Alex and Geddy wrote the music to fit the lyrics as there was little they felt like changing. Speaking of which, Neil was happy to tweak the words to 'Between Sun and Moon', which was based on a poem by Neil's old buddy Pye Dubois. "I'm always concerned with Pye, 'Do you think I'm wrecking up your work?' because theoretically when he finishes it, he thinks it's done," said Neil. "But he seems comfortable with it too, so it's just like he said, it's just turning out a good tune that counts."

Overall the album is in turn funky and furrowed, silly and serious. While there is room for humour (Geddy called 'Double Agent' "one of the goofiest songs I think we've ever written"), there is perhaps a hint of indecision, revealing that songs were written as individual entities rather than having a coherent theme, either stylistic or lyrical. While 'Counterparts' does stand up in its own right it is maybe indicative that the band was still finding its feet in this brave new, stripped down world. The closer, 'Everyday Glory' is a sad, but good, song, suggesting continued hope for the future.

Geddy, who felt he had to make too many compromises. Many of these had been brought in by the Caveman – most of all perhaps, he'd not been afraid to challenge the boys, and their beliefs, head on.

As the mixing stages approached, Kevin had to be informed that he was to be replaced with a fresh pair of ears. "They were insecure about having Caveman mix it because they didn't want to go quite that far into the analogue world," says Peter, who proposed Australian engineer Michael Letho. "He brought a certain amount of refinement to the proceedings," said Neil. "If we had just used Michael, the record might have been too refined. Had we just used the Caveman, it would have been too raw. So we had the best combination of influences."

As in the past, Peter was keen to get other "specialists" involved, though in a lower key way to fit with the album. John Webster of Suicidal Tendencies added some keys and Michael Kamen, who had worked on Pink Floyd's *The Wall*', arranged and conducted the orchestral pieces for 'Nobody's Hero'. "John Webster was still fairly minimal," says Peter. "He was like the North American equivalent of Andy Richards to me."

As things drew to a close, the last thing refusing to play was the title. "I started free-associating through the lyrics and I pulled the word 'counterpart' out of the song 'Animate'," said Neil. "When I looked it up in the dictionary and saw how complex its meaning was, that it meant both an opposite and a duplicate, I thought, A-ha! That's what I'm writing about here, that's racism, culturalism, men and women, gays and straights, all of us, we're counterparts because we're the same but we're different." With the word 'counterparts', Neil had also stumbled on the idea of what it meant to be Rush, as illustrated by the very process of putting the album together. "It is a metaphor for the three of us," said Geddy. For better, for worse.

The album was finally released on 19 October 1993, with the cover incorporating a variety of juxtaposed images, not least the band's alter egos, the Three Stooges. Singles 'Stick It Out' and 'Nobody's Hero' were released for radio promo in North America, for what it was worth.

Whatever they'd done, it had worked in the eyes of the wider public. *'Counterparts'* reached Number 2 on *Billboard*, making it the most successful album they'd ever made. If the band's intentions had been to get with the times, with the help of Peter, Kevin and Michael they'd succeeded: according to Geddy, *'Counterparts'* was "a very drastic change in the band's sound, resulting in one of the best-sounding Rush albums in a long time."

Anyone who thought any problems had been put in the past however, would be wrong.

What was it all for anyway? What is anything for?

To Alex, and despite his initial reluctance to break with his own habits, *'Counterparts'* didn't go far enough. "Just about every song could have been better than it was," he remarked. Having started to fight his own battles, Alex had begun to realise that there were some things he would never be able to achieve with the rest of the band, where compromise was essential. Now that the keyboards were largely out of the equation, if Alex was still not happy there was little else to change.

For Geddy meanwhile, he'd just had enough. *'Counterparts'* had been a string of compromises, a huge

Bandana Run

Some fans took the extended absence, coupled with Neil's penchant for bandanas, a trifle seriously. On 24 August 1993, a radio station in Cleveland announced that Neil was dying of colon cancer, forcing him to speak out. "I almost hate to dignify rumors by addressing them," he said, "but it was just a whole bunch of bullshit people dreamed up. People were phoning my parents and asking, 'Is it true he's dying of cancer?' What if it were true? It gets so uncivilized when you think about the realities of it. People always forget that there are real people involved."

The bandanas didn't help of course. "Even my daughter said I looked like a chemotherapy patient! But those bandanas did an excellent job keeping the sweat out of my eyes."

strain; he'd given all he could, and had nothing left to offer. Geddy was feeling "a little fried" by the whole band thing. "I was fed up to here with it," he said. "I needed to get away from Rush, I needed to get away from music period, and just re-examine my life and make sure I was living the kind of life I wanted to live, and enjoying all the domestic things that a lot of people take for granted every day," he said. Geddy needed something else to think about for a while, and the imminent prospect of becoming a father again, gave him a perfectly appropriate reason to act. "When I found out that another child was coming, I was adamant that I would be around more for that whole experience, for the sake of my child, for the sake of myself."

Geddy agreed with the others to play a shorter tour, to ensure he could be there for the birth. In addition, he stated that he wanted to spend some time with his family – initially three months. This was ostensibly to be around for the new baby, but everyone knew there was more to it than that. While Geddy needed his break and Neil would always grab the opportunity to take on other challenges, Alex was thinking of calling it a day altogether. "I don't think that it really mattered to us; we were taking the time off regardless," said Alex. "If it meant that it was over, then so be it. We needed to take a break after 20 years of this continuous touring. We needed to touch base, get a little more anchored, and have the opportunity to experience other things in our lives." Of any of the relationships, the one between Geddy and Alex was the most intense, and also the most claustrophobic. With Neil, this was far less an issue. "With Neil it's a little different," explained Alex. "The tour ends, and I might get a fax from Neil on my birthday, and then that's about it for a year."

When Geddy made his declaration, Alex's mind immediately filled with one thing: Solo Project! "It was time for me to do something like that for myself," said Alex.

With all this going on, it took quite an effort to focus back on the impending tour. Contrary to rumour, Neil wanted the tours to continue, but it was never an easy decision. "Ultimately my subconscious makes up my mind for me, and one morning I wake up and realize, Kid, you've got to do it," he said. Neil saw touring as a necessary evil, and a triumph of discipline over desire. "I always tend to push for continuing to tour because I think it's so important a part of a vital band," he said. "I think for the risk-taking aspect, for the discipline of playing at 100 percent night after night, playing live takes you to a level that you would never willingly drive yourself to."

Of course they had to tour – preparations had been underway for months. Howard, who was now back on the lighting, had been basing his visual set on the snippets of information he'd picked up when he visited the band at the studio. During rehearsals the band sent live tapes to Howard, who was configuring his own setups at a separate venue. "I book ten days for programming," says Howard. "It's about choreography, my job is to make the lights fit the lyrics and music."

With decisions made and a yawning hiatus to follow, the rehearsals themselves became rather relaxed – like working a notice period, which was pretty much what was happening. Geddy's memories were of, "a few fun-filled weeks, vibing together in a lovely suburban warehouse motif, hidden in a scenic stretch of strip malls in East Toronto!!" Everything was up for grabs, and the band felt comfortable enough to mess with arrangements, rather than sticking too closely to the album versions. In addition, Neil was planning a drum solo that stood up in its own right. "I wanted a free standing piece of music with its own dynamic structure," he explained.

Following a couple of days of dress rehearsals, the tour started on 22 January 1994. Although Rush had been in the game for nigh on twenty years, they still felt they owed something to newer bands that needed the exposure. "If we hadn't been able to open shows for four years without radio and without press support, we would have nothing, no avenue of exposure," said Neil. On tour once again were Primus, and supporting one date was the band I Mother Earth, with vocalist Edwin. Alex liked the singer and filed his name away – never know when he might come in useful.

As the synth stacks came back out again, even Alex started to feel a little nostalgic, playing a keyboard piece on 'Time Stand Still'. "It's kind of fun to have the keyboard standing there, for that, little moment," he said. Geddy was thoroughly fed up with the whole thing however. "Trigger that, step on this, play this here... it's ridiculous!"

It was so much like old times, not just because the trio were kicking out: the usual number of dates were being squeezed into two months, leaving fewer rest days. There were no dates outside North America at all – indeed, only two dates in the home country, including a nightmare gig on the last night in Toronto, according to Alex. "It's insane, you get ticket requests, you know from people you haven't seen in 20 years." It was exhausting – the band weren't used to such an intensive tour, and they weren't as young as they had once been. It didn't help that there were bugs going round, resulting in the cancellation of one date, at Hampton. "50 guys living together all the time, it's very easy for these sort of things to go through everybody like wildfire," said Alex. "We were playing in Washington to 15,000 people and Geddy's voice was cracking up after the third song, and that's pretty tough for him, it's frustrating, it's embarrassing."

As the tour ended, everyone was just a little unsure of whether there was something to celebrate. It had been twenty years, and despite the intention to do something special, the band knew they wanted to do something apart. "We can't think of another group which has survived for so long with the same individuals, and since those individuals

Gong Fishin'

In 1994 Rush was inducted into the Canadian Music Hall of Fame, by virtue of having received so many Juno's. Aside from international awards and Oscars, there weren't any more gongs for the trio to pick up. Geddy had achieved the *Guitar Player* Hall of Fame for having picked up the Best Rock Bass award more than five times, in 1993 he picked up *Bass Player* magazine's Best Rock Bass Player award, Alex had (finally) arrived in the *Guitar for The Practicing Musician* Hall of Fame in 1991, and Neil had picked up a good two dozen awards for his drumming and percussion. Been there, done that.

are us, we think the occasion deserves some tribute," said Neil. "We are thinking about the possibility of retrospective shows, live recordings, and videos. Later in the year we will have a clearer idea of what, exactly, we're going to do. But we're going to do something – at least have cake!"

Perhaps – but apart from the cake perhaps, all that would have to wait.

Little Victories

With impeccable timing, Nancy and Geddy's daughter Kyla Lee Weinrib was born a week after the tour ended, on May 15, 1994 at 4:45 am and weighing 7 pounds, 9 ounces.

Almost as quickly as the threesome declared their timeout, they agreed to extend it as they realised they wanted more than a quick break. For Geddy, first and foremost, it meant leaving his music behind altogether. "When I leave the band, I'm gone, I can leave the rock world pretty easily," he explained. "I don't want to bring that life into my household, there's a different thing going on there." Alex had a gentle start to the break, collaborating with Tom Cochrane on *'Ragged Ass Road'*; meanwhile, Neil's multiple hobbies gave him plenty to get on with.

Surprising then, that Neil's first thought was to his drumming. He'd already declared he was finding himself in a bit of a rut, and he wanted to do something about it; unlike the other two, nobody had thought to criticize the "perfectionist" Professor in the studio, so he was having to work it out for himself. His conclusion, he surmised, was that he was trying too hard for his own good. "I was getting perfect metronomic time and was able to play along with click-tracks and sequencers and all that, but I was getting more and more rigid," he said. The rigidity wasn't just affecting his playing, but he felt the results were also suffering. "It all got really stiff and linear, and as a listener, too, I didn't like the way it sounded. It sounded stiff and uncomfortable."

As it happened, Neil had been building up to putting together a big band drumming video, an idea he'd had following his rather stressful live performance in New York, at the Buddy Rich memorial gig. "I'm getting a lot of the pre-eminent drummers in the world in to play an arrangement of one of Buddy Rich's pieces," said Neil. "That's the kind of thing I would like to do just for personal satisfaction, because I think it deserves to be done and I'd rather have me do it than someone else!" While the video was a tribute to the great Buddy Rich, Neil wasn't being totally altruistic – he was doing it because he loved the music. "Big Band music is what I'd like to play on the side," he explained. "It's like playing Rush music. It's conceived archi-tecturally but with lots of room for fooling around in the middle."

The recording of *'Burning for Buddy'* took place at The Power Station in New York, engineered by Rush regulars Paul Northfield and assistant Simon Pressey. For Neil, the whole experience was more than he could have imagined – he'd never seen, or heard, so many drummers in one place. A total of 21 drummers were used, including Buddy's nine-year-old son Nick, as well as Rod Morgenstein (from the Steve Morse band, which had supported Rush in 1986) and Steve Smith, who Neil had met via Jeff Berlin a few years before. "Nearly all of these great drummers were also great human beings," Neil said. "Some of them I will feel close to all my life, even if we never see each other again."

While playing with Steve Smith, Neil sensed something new in Steve's drumming. "Always a great drummer, he had suddenly become a monster, so musical and with such beautiful technique," recalled Neil, who asked Steve what had happened. "Freddie," Steve had replied. Steve explained how he had been working with drum teacher and mentor, Freddie Gruber, a jazz player of the old school who had worked with luminaries such as Charlie Parker, Miles Davis and indeed, the great Buddy Rich himself. "He just knows how to teach drummers," comments Neil's current drum tech, Lorne Wheaton. "He deals with so many amazing things that nobody even sees."

When Freddie popped by at The Power Station, he and Neil got talking. "I mentioned to him that I was fighting the 'war of the grips' – unable to get the power I wanted from traditional grip, or the finesse I wanted from matched grip," explained Neil, who had spent most of his career playing matched[1]. "Freddie said, yeah, I noticed that. I could fix that in half an hour." What an opportunity – Neil fixed a week with Freddie for later in the year. "I knew I needed 'something', I just didn't know what. There was no way of knowing if Freddie was that something, but it seemed better to find out than to wonder about it." When the week came, it was more revelation than discovery as Freddie gently picked Neil apart and put him back together.

The pieces of advice were simple, but profound – for example, that what the sticks did in between hitting the drums, was more important than how Neil did the hitting. He also suggested Neil went over to traditional grip – this might sound trivial, but you might as well be asking a jockey to ride side saddle. Freddie packed Neil off with some new exercises, a renewed sense of determination and something new to be obsessive about – it was perfect. By the time the *'Burning for Buddy'* album was released, on 4 October, 1994, Neil was already well into the routine.

"I spent the last two years in my basement basically playing for the spiders," Neil said a few years later. "That did me more good musically than two years of touring would ever have."

Alex was in no hurry to give up on his playing either, but he needed something to light his fires once again. "I was at a point when I felt lazy and unmotivated," said Alex, for whom the year off posed a conundrum. Alex was not what is called in the trade a 'Completer/Finisher' – his house was littered with half-made projects. "I'm by nature a bit of a lazy person," he remarked. "I can get very excited and enthusiastic about something, and after a short period of time, I lose interest and I don't see it through." However, he thought to himself, he had no more excuses. "I couldn't see myself sitting around for a year and a half not doing anything more constructive than working on my golf game," he said. The solo project was calling him, and given this one opportunity, it would be folly not to take it. At the end of 1994, Alex got off his backside and started work.

For the first time in many years Alex was having to write his own lyrics, and following his initial nervousness he let his imagination run riot. As a theme emerged, it became quickly clear that it was going to be quite a dark record, covering some of the less pleasant sides of love, obsession and retribution. One song, 'Victor' was based on a W. H. Auden poem, the mood of which fitted so closely with his own thoughts he decided to make it the title track. "It really caught the essence of what the record was

Alex jamming at the Orbit Room with Bernie LaBarge, Lou Pomanti and Peter Cardinali.

Big Bad Al

November 1994, Alex got together with his old buddy Tim Notter to open the Orbit Room[2], bringing in house band 'The Dexters' to give the place a 60s blues and soul feel. Explains keyboardist Lou Pomanti, "When they started the club, and Alex was the investor, Tim said, you know, it's going to be key to the success of this club, that you be there, right, a bit, sometimes show up and have a drink, play with the Dexters."

The band was called The Dexters after saxophonist Dexter Gordon. Singer Bernie LaBarge came up with the name. "He also wanted to call it Louie and The Wingmen, and the third option was the Mod Quad," says Lou. The Dexters all took the name of the band, so Lou became Lou Dexter, Bernie became Bernie and so on. "I just kind of, off-the-cuff, started to introduce the guys in the band like that," says Lou. "I portrayed us as brothers, even though all you had to do was look at the four of us in 1994, I mean, there couldn't be four guys looking less like brothers than us! Sure enough, people will believe what ever they tell you, and you know, every night, people would come up and say, that's strange, you don't even look like brothers! It's fucking amazing, absolutely mindboggling."

Entrance to the Orbit Room and inside with Tim Notter

about," said Alex. Some of the lyrics were deeply personal, in particular referencing the 25 tumultuous years he had spent with his wife Charlene.

To lighten things up a bit, Alex put together 'Shut Up Shuttin' Up', involving Charlene and her best friend Esther ("who's a real character"). "I got them in to do this little bit of nagging about the funny little habits that some of us have, and the silly little things that we argue about that end up becoming big things in the overall picture," he said. "We had them in there for about seven hours going through so many different things, and they were well lubricated with a couple of bottles of wine. By the end of it, of course, we couldn't get them to shut up." It was an altogether family affair – Alex's 18-year-old son Adrian co-wrote and participated on two tracks on the album, 'At The End' and 'The Big Dance'. Other songs were co-written with Bill Bell, who Alex had met when working with Tom Cochrane – not least 'Strip and Go Naked', named after a cocktail Bill had invented. "After you've had a couple, that basically is what happens," said Alex. "On the other side, we thought that was kind of what the song was about. We stripped the whole song down to very basic elements."

Just Testing

Having done his drumming in June 1995 Neil went travelling around Canada. As he was riding towards Yellowknife, he saw a structure of giant boulders on the hill above the town. The structure was an Inuit inukshuk, which literally means "in the likeness of a man." Neil bought a postcard of this echo of humanity, and stowed it in his saddlebag for safekeeping. Likeness of man, thought Neil, testing for an echo of humanity. Interesting.

When Alex came to play, Bernie gave him the nick "Big Al Dexter". Playing with The Dexters was a real confidence boost for Alex, though he had to be coached in what it meant to play outside a power trio. "He was in this band since he was a kid, and so he was so used to this three-man structure," says Lou. "I said, I hope you don't mind me saying... the band plays these tunes as a quartet, and it's a full sound, it's done. You're sitting in with us as number five... you don't have to work nearly as hard, you can sit there for eight bars and do nothing, or you can play a little tiny thing, or you can play a lot if you feel like it, or you can be laid-back." Lou was unsure how Alex might take it, but the guitarist was delighted. "I think it shows that the guy doesn't have a huge ego," says Lou. "There are some people who have achieved his level of success, that you just couldn't say that to!"

Alex was careful to avoid over-emphasising his skills as a guitarist. "I don't feel that I need to showcase my abilities," he said. "I've been playing for a long time and I have a pretty good track record – lots of records where I've had a chance to let loose – and I didn't want to do that with this record."

As the material came together for the album, Alex called a few of his friends – bass player Les Claypool from Primus, drummer Blake Manning and local friend and fellow Dexter, bassist Peter Cardinali; he also roped in his son Adrian. For vocalist, Alex decided against using himself. "I'm not a singer," he said. "I didn't feel that I had to really sing on this record all over the place to satisfy something in my ego." Having trialled Sebastian Bach from Skid Row on a number of songs, Alex settled on Edwin from I Mother Earth. "He just has a certain quality and a menace in his voice," said Alex. "I called him up, and he said that he'd love to give it a whirl." Despite Edwin having to work evenings at Alex's home studio (as he was recording an IME album at the time, 'Scenery and Fish', coincidentally being produced by Paul Northfield), Alex was very pleased with the results. "I think he's done just a fabulous job on it," he said. Alex also included Canadian female singer Dalbello on the song 'Start Today', though he claimed not to notice any similarity with early Geddy. "Well, you know, it didn't occur to me when she did it, because I was sitting there in the control room staring at her in the studio doing it," he said.

It quickly became apparent that the schedules for *'Victor'* would exceed the time originally allotted. Fortunately, Neil's own projects added an extra six months to the available timescales. With Neil needing more practice time, and Alex ensconced in his own project, the gap became ever bigger. "It was just a chain of circumstances" commented Neil. "I got all fired up about that and wanted to let all that new information mature in my head." So, the year became eighteen months, and Alex was grateful for the extension. "I realize now it would've been impossible until I had a length of time like I did to work on it," he said.

Over the months, Alex had been involved in just about everything – "I wrote the material, I played guitar, I played bass, I played some keyboards, I did some programming, I worked on the cover, I paid for the thing!" The result was, at the end of the production, that he felt more confident about his own capabilities than he ever had before. "I pushed myself much harder than I think I've ever done before," he said. "I've come out of it with a new sense of who I am and what I want to accomplish, and a whole new work ethic. I love work now, and I can't get enough of it."

The album was released at the beginning of 1996, and true to form, Alex decided not to put his own name on the cover. "I didn't want to call it 'The Alex Lifeson Project' or the 'Big Shot, Big Deal Project'," he said. The album wasn't a world beating success, but it achieved respectable sales; for Alex, it was enough. "It was something I did for myself, and if no one had bought a copy or heard it, it wouldn't have bothered me," he said. "It threw me into an arena where it was like a question of survival - if I didn't finish this, I would never finish anything and I would lose so much self-respect, and I got through it and that's what mattered to me. But I was mostly really moved by the number of good reviews that it got, and that was a wonderful thing."

The feedback included the views of his compatriots in the band. Geddy and Neil were, "very positive and very supportive, and I love them for that." However it wasn't totally to his colleagues' tastes, as Geddy remarked, generously, "I like a few things on it." After all, he confessed, "I can't be objective."

At the end of the project, Alex said that he wouldn't be writing any more lyrics for Rush. "I don't think so... that was enough for me!"

Shooting the Breeze

"They all hate photo shoots. There's a comfort level with me doing them, because they know if they just show up, and if I have only an hour with them, I get 3 completely different setups, which is key to the record company getting publicity, a variety of shots. I can get a lot of variety really quickly with the guys. Neil's always going, 'hurry up, hurry up, I'm not enjoying this, hurry up...' It's like pulling teeth, 'I look exactly the same, why do we need more pictures?'"

Andrew MacNaughtan

Back at SRO's offices, there had been a stroke of luck with the discovery of some old concert tapes, found during a move round. "We'd forgotten about them," said Alex, who took as much delight as his compatriots at listening to the recordings from February 1978, which had been stored for a potential live release. "We took the tapes to the studio for a listen and thought that there was really something there!" Despite the past form of having four studio albums then a live one, a new live album was not inevitable. "We weren't sure we wanted to release another live record," remarked Alex.

"In the past we'd done it to cap those periods in the band's development, but we wondered really how relevant that was, this time." However, the tapes started to push things in the right direction.

With the band being so quiet – as a unit, anyway – the fans took it upon themselves to fill the gap. The idea of a tribute album was put forward for genuine reasons – there were plenty of bands out there who were seeing Rush as a major influence, and they wanted to show their appreciation. The message got garbled along the way, however: SRO made some enquiries about what was going on, and the band weren't sure they liked what they heard. "It came to us that the label was in the quote-unquote business of doing tribute records. That felt a little fishy to me," said Geddy. So, the management made some more enquiries, more signals were crossed, and indeed the balance was distorted. As Geddy explained, "I believe our legal people and our management, misrepresented us a little bit in that situation in an overprotective way."

As the situation got out of hand, some fans became incensed, and the band was left wondering what on earth had happened. "Our only concern was the exploitation of Rush fans by this thing," said Alex, but that's not what came across. Continued Geddy, "Somehow, by virtue of us questioning the legitimacy of the record company's motives involved with that project, that translated into some disrespect for the musicians involved." It got worse – the increasingly powerful World Wide Web played its part at spreading unfounded rumours about injunctions and other litigation. Even producer Terry Brown became inadvertently tangled up in the whole thing. Having agreed to mix the album (and why not – it seemed like a good idea at the time), he ended up part of what was seen as a problem.

Even as the *'Working Man'* tribute album was released, on 2 August 1996, it seemed that nobody ever stopped to ask whether the band wanted to be fêted in such a way. "It's very flattering," admitted Alex. "A tribute is great for people who are no longer around, bands that have broken up that have been an influence. But we're still an active band that plans on continuing for some time longer." Agreed Neil, "It's not a tribute album at all, as far as I'm concerned." Despite his devotion to the cause of Buddy Rich, at least he had the decency to wait until the guy was no longer around. "Just imagine if there was someone going around doing impersonations of you in front of people. I mean, it is a tribute in the true sense of the word, and bless their hearts and all that, but I would never want to hear it."

Of course, none of it would have happened without the Web. That marvellous technological creation, that global interconnection of wires and fibres, sending packets of information flying across the planet at the speed of light, was seriously pissing Neil off. "For the most part, it's the worldwide wank," he remarked. The tribute experience (and the fallout from it) was just one in a series of events that Neil saw as reducing, rather than enhancing his ability to communicate. Not least, word had spread that Neil generally responded to letters he received via *Modern Drummer* magazine. Given the power of the Web, this message had spread and Neil was being bombarded with letters. "Although it might be flattering to consider this just a reflection of my ever-growing popularity, I know that's not the case," said Neil, with a growing sense of unease. Eventually, in the August 1996 issue of *Modern Drummer*, he felt obliged to send an open letter to his supporters, calling an official halt to the whole thing. "By now the total of those responses would number in the thousands," he said.

> ### Cheap Shots #9
> "This is not progress, this is bad taste with staying power. His music obviously works for 15-year-old boys hiding from homework with the headphones on. It has worked in that way for a long time now, and perhaps there's value in that (there's certainly money in it). But others encountering Rush will likely find themselves in a rush to turn the stereo off."
>
> Tom Long, *The Detroit News*, 24 October 1996

Despite Neil's vitriol (and the backlash to it – "I've become the Salman Rushdie of the Internet for daring to poke fun at it," he remarked, "I can't believe the acid that had poured through the ether!"), by 1996 Rush prided themselves in having one of the biggest websites on the net. What don't kill you makes you stronger, perhaps. All was not totally lost for the letter writing, as Neil continued to write to people whose work he admired, such as author Leslie Choyce, who had written a book called 'The Republic Of Nothing'. As it happened Leslie owned his own publishing house, The Pottersfield Press, and he asked Neil if he'd ever thought about publishing anything.

Neil sent him some samples, including the previously self-published version of 'The Masked Rider' and within a matter of months Neil found he could add "published author" to his CV.

It had been quite a year.

By the late summer of 1996, the hiatus was coming to an end and Geddy for one was gagging to get back to work. "I started feeling like there was this hole in my life, and that was the need for me to express myself musically," he said. Nothing was a given however – nobody wanted to make another album just because they could, continuing because they didn't have the nouse to think of anything better. As Geddy put it, "to remain a member of Rush just to be a member of Rush," this was clearly not an option.

All the same, the trio decided that they did want to try to do whatever it was they did. With some trepidation they made their way back to a rehearsal studio to write, and to see what developed. "We kind of left it at, 'Let's see how the first couple of weeks go and if it's not there we won't do it,'" said Alex. This time, it was Geddy who was worried about being up to speed, so much so that he'd taken his bass with him on holiday to Florida, a few weeks before. "I had to take an hour a day, sit in a room and make sure I wasn't losing a step," he said. As Geddy polished away the rust from his strings and redeveloped the calluses on his fingers, he discovered an undesirable side-effect. "I hate the fact that I've proven to myself that practice makes you better 'cause now I'm fucked."

Let It Snow

It was four years since the last writing sessions, but the environment at Chalet Studios was all too familiar. Less familiar perhaps, or at least less easy to define was the musical landscape, which had exploded over the four years into a wealth of variety. Some said grunge had died with Kurt Cobain, but the reality was it had pervaded a much wider variety of music; bands such as Green Day, Nine Inch Nails and the Red Hot Chili Peppers were keen to show how a hard rock edge could combine as comfortably with punk, as funk. While the threesome were well aware of the changing fashions and were keen to explore the pervading production techniques, there was no rush to follow the musical crowd. As for watching across the Atlantic, the

Cooler Stories

"Geddy told me an interesting thing the other day – that when he was doing a small Q&A session for *Rolling Stone*, the writer let slip that we are their readers' number one most requested group for them to do a full story on. But they won't because of who they are and who we are. That's a trip, if you ask me. We're just not cool enough for them. But that's okay, because they're not cool enough for us."

Neil Peart

burgeoning Brit-pop movement spearheaded by Oasis, Blur and the like was of no interest at all, hard edge or not.

Only two weeks after Alex had finally put *'Victor'* to bed, the band reunited with a new zest, and furthermore, a whole new respect for each other. "Everybody was glad to be back there and just finding a new chemistry," said Neil, who was keen to discover how well his new techniques would translate in the context of his band. As for Alex and Geddy, they might have been going for lunch or playing tennis on a regular basis, but the musical wavelength had lain largely idle. As a result, the pair knew each other as friends far more than they did as musicians. "I think I'm a lot closer to Ged now than I have been in years," said Alex. "I think we missed each other."

The three players sat in the sun outside the converted farmhouse, drank coffee and talked. At first, this was worrisome – they weren't talking about music. However, they did touch on how their roles related to each other. Alex really, really didn't want to take a back seat on this album, and he knew to make his case before old habits set in. He wanted back in the control room – but to talk about the others, not just himself. "Having been in the chair behind the console directing it all, it shed a whole new light on what Rush do," said Alex. "I'm a little more definite in what I'm doing and the way I hear things."

> **Out of Orbit**
>
> "Alex and his buddy Jake did this musical comedy night thing at the Orbit Room. Alex dressed as a very big, fat lady [shrieks] and spoke in a voice like this [shrieks]. It was very Monty Python-esque, they sang funny little songs and they just had this whole thing where they stayed in character for an hour. They planned it and they made invites, it was very odd, very odd. The picture is up in the Orbit Room in a photo case."
>
> Lou Pomanti

While Alex was being quite forthright in his views from the outset, Geddy, on the other hand, was anything but his traditional, bossy self. "I was feeling very laid-back, and very enthusiastic, and really eager to write, so I was being, yeah, sure, whatever, let's go!" he said. Geddy came to understand that Alex wanted less of a back seat role in production, and was relaxed enough to see that it was good. "I think it was a slight maturing on my part," said Geddy. "I was happy just to be working."

The first night was washed down with a couple of shandies – bonding, you understand. "The following day I was a bit the worse for wear," said Neil. As he nursed his coffee and flicked through the *New York Times*, one column in particular drew his attention. "The columnist was riffing on about things and she said she's getting tired of living in dog years, where every seven years seem to go by like one and I thought it was a beautiful little image." So, "muzzy headed" Neil set about trying to turn it into a song. "I thought, 'Gee, I don't think I'm going to get much done today, but I'm a professional, I'd better try.'" The result was 'Dog Years', inspired by Neil comparing his state of mind with the actions of his own dog Nick, a seven-year-old, big husky, and how his brain functioned. "What's going through his brain? And I would think, 'Just a low-level zzzzz static.' 'Food.' 'Walk.' The basic elemental things. When I look at my dog that's how I see his brainwaves moving."

The other two appreciated the light relief of 'Dog Years', a welcome respite compared to the uneasy undercurrents that pervaded their conversations. "I really wondered about the future," said Alex, as he and Geddy set about rediscovering each other. "It was a bit weird," agreed Geddy. "We kind of were circling each other like cats in a new territory."

Neil was troubled as well, but mostly about his own writing capabilities. His usual "slightly lost" outward appearance was this time based largely on the fact that he was, indeed, slightly lost. "I did worry about it," said Neil. "I'd been away during the intervening time doing so many different things that I truly wondered – especially from a lyric-writing point of view – whether I'd be able to sit down at the desk and distill all of the thoughts and experiences into rock lyrics." He was less worried about his drumming, and he practiced his new skills every day as a break from the wordsmithing. "Usually, in the past, I've struggled to find new ways of challenging myself," he said. "This time, it was the opposite. I came in with so much, I had to edit myself. I have to say, it was a good position to be in."

After a few days of discussion, Alex and Geddy found some common ground – in particular, that guitars would lead the album. "From that moment on everything went smoothly," said Geddy. "We got to work with an amazing amount of energy." Agreed Alex, "Once I exorcised those ghosts, the following week we wrote five songs. We dove into it, and it was very, very positive from then on." It wasn't all Alex's show, as Geddy discovered when he turned up with the musical basis for what would become 'Driven'. "I brought it to Alex and said, here's the song; I did three tracks of bass but I just did it to fill in for the guitar," said Geddy. "He said, let's keep it with the three basses. So I said, 'I love you'. I mean, who lets a guy do that in this day and age?" 'Half The World' also came out of these sessions, "One of our finest moments as songwriters as far as writing a concise song without being wimpy or syrupy," according to Geddy.

Alex and Geddy were cooking, but trouble was, nobody had told Neil, who had to content himself with writing lyrics and keeping out of the way. Every now and then, Geddy would cross the building to Neil's wing, check some lyrics with him and vanish off again, leaving the "new boy" none the wiser. It was quite deliberate – the musical ideas were coming so fast, nothing ever seemed complete enough to play to the drummer. Geddy and Alex were unperturbed. "We were very confident and we felt really strong about the music, we wanted to complete it," said Geddy. After a couple of weeks however, Neil was becoming more than a little frustrated, not to mention a tad anxious for the others. "I wasn't hearing any of the words being sung to know if they worked or not as lyrics and I wasn't hearing any music to know what I was going to be putting drum parts to," said Neil.

It was quite a relief when Neil was finally invited to hear the Lee/Lifeson output and he found – that it was good! "Before we know it, boom – we were back to writing, ideas were just coming, and everything was fresh and exciting," says Neil. The jokes started, and all three knew it was all going to be OK. Over time, the band developed a new process of slow improvisation, that was very different from past methods of jamming together and seeing what developed. "We're responding to what each other is doing, trying to put forward our own ideas, and trying also to create something larger musically than any of those elements," said Neil. "Instead of happening spontaneously in the moment, it's happening over a slow period." It might have seemed slower at the outset, but it was more efficient overall. "We seem to be getting all our results much quicker than we have in the past, and the results seem to be much more definite," said Alex.

It was time to get the producer in, the choice needed no debate.

Peter Collins – producer, mentor, friend – joined the band at Chalet studios in late autumn of 1996, as soon as there was enough material for rough demos. His strength, as ever, was his objectivity – the ability to distance himself from the material, but retain the right for radical suggestion. "I think Peter is the last of a dying breed: producers who

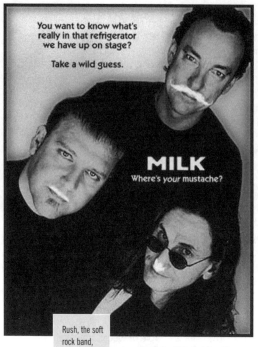

You want to know what's really in that refrigerator we have up on stage?

Take a wild guess.

MILK

Where's your mustache?

Rush, the soft rock band, getting their calcium

are interested in nothing but producing songs," said Geddy. "If something sounds great he doesn't feel he has to change it. No ego involved. There may be only three or four songs on the album that he kind of tears apart totally, but it's a much better record for that." Peter had an ear for what worked and what didn't, and made "bold suggestions" to correct them. Added Neil, "Perhaps Peter's greatest contribution is his instinct for pointing us in the right direction."

This time, writing and recording really was all digital, using Cubase Audio – which was still not quite there. "It drove us crazy! It's a brilliant idea, but it wasn't quite ready," said Alex. "The great thing about it was that we were able to put down ideas and then move the arrangement around. We could add another chorus or take a line out of the chorus, and hear it back instantly." The walls of the studio were decorated with "goofy" slogans to lighten the atmosphere, such as "Being geniuses together", "Individually we are a ass, together we are a genius", "If you want something done right, just forget it." and "I'll shut up when you fuck off", goofy perhaps but serving to bring the trio even closer together.

Alex's new-found self belief was overriding anybody else's potential for pickiness – he just didn't care. "You sit in the studio and someone says, 'That note's a little flat,' or, 'You really didn't hit the beat there.' But I've finally come to realize, who cares? It's all about feeling," he said. Good call – and he wasn't afraid to challenge the others when he felt he had a good idea. There was the mandola on 'Half The World', for example. "I just wanted to try it," he said. "So I just futzed around to get a feel for it, and it changed the whole personality of the song. I remember Ged, when he first heard it was like, 'Whoa, I don't know about that.' It was so unusual for a Rush song to have that kind of texture."

On 1 November a blizzard struck, the claustrophobic, slightly oppressive atmosphere setting the tone for much of the album. Against this snowy background a number of songs came together, such as 'Test For Echo', "the quintessential Rush song," according to Geddy, and a reflection on the band's own concerns. Said Geddy, "We were not certain that anyone listened to our music anymore... so this song is a kind of question: 'Is there anyone out there?'"

Having got the songs to the demo stage, the band took a break for Christmas. They reconvened at the beginning of January and back in the snow, this time over the border in New York State, at Bearsville Studios[3], at Woodstock, in the Catskill Mountains. The decision to record at Bearsville was driven by Peter Collins, who badgered the players until they agreed. "Bearsville was my favourite studio for the drums," says Peter. "I knew that they would like it, a bit hippy-ish but it was just a fun place to be. I don't think they had ever recorded tracks in America, I just love the room at Bearsville and persuaded them that's where we should at least record Neil's drums." Despite Neil's reticence (Le Studio was a stone's throw from Neil's place by the lake, after all), it worked out. "I think Neil loved it there," says Peter. "It was a fabulous room, very big, all wood." Agreed Alex, "It's like a hangar, it's about three stories high – Neil's drums sounded particularly amazing."

In addition, the studio boasted a Neve desk, taken from The Who's Ramport studios in London. "I know that the band were huge Who fans, I thought it would give them a kick," says Peter. Geddy was delighted – initially. "I'm like, It's the one they did 'Quadrophenia' on, cool!" he says. "It was cool until all the knobs started breaking and everything started buzzing!"

The day they arrived at Bearsville, the blizzards started once again. Really. "It was simply unbelievable," said Neil. "There we were right in the middle of the 'Blizzard of '96'."

Having oriented himself to the studio room, Neil settled down to record his parts – it took him three days this time. "He's still very uptight about being able to recreate everything live that he does on record," said Geddy. "Alex and I have loosened up about that stuff, maybe because we're overdubs, anyway!" And overdub they did, Geddy painstakingly laying his bass on top of Neil's hi-tech click track, having decided he quite liked Bearsville too.

It snowed all the time at Bearsville, and was still snowing as the posse arrived at their next port of call: Reaction Studios, back in Toronto, for the guitars and vocals. "What we wanted was somewhere private," said Alex. "There aren't too many studios anymore that are like that, who could accommodate us, with the kind of sounds we wanted and the size of the room." Bass was finished off, then guitars and vocals overdubbed, with the (very) occasional use of a bass pedal or keyboard, for texture. Nobody was about to complain about that.

It was still snowing, just, as they went for the final mix at Toronto's McClear Pathé[4] studios. Accompanying Peter and the band was engineer Andy Wallace, known for his experience with grunge-ier bands such as Nirvana and Rage Against The Machine[5]. "It was my decision to bring Andy in," says Peter. "I was fully committed to the much drier organic sound, no one can do it better than him. I felt also at a personal level the band would really like Andy, and they did. They got on extremely well."

> **Wine Ot**
> One person who came to see them at Reaction was Lou Pomanti of The Dexters. "We were seeing a lot of Alex during that period," says Lou. "I'll never forget going to visit them, I had a piece of Alex's gear or something. When I went to drop it off at the studio, just as Alex came to the door a truck pulled up with a shipment of numerous cases of wine, for Geddy – he's quite the wine buff. I thought, man, I'm in the wrong band!"

As things turned out, Andy was just the man for the job. Andy's skill was to take the finessed elements of Rush's sound, and set them into the context of the late nineties. "When we heard his mix of a song for the first time, invariably we'd say something like, Wow, I never thought of it like that before!" said Neil. In particular, Andy was skilled in knowing what to leave in, and what to leave out. "He was terrific to work with, great to watch, very fast, very knowledgeable, very bright guy," said Alex. "Nothing was in the mix just because it was there, it had to have a purpose and a place."

As the final album was sent to be mastered, for the band anyway, the outcome could be judged as much by what it had achieved for the band, as its musical content. "There's a new level of respect that we have for each other," said Alex, who was so thoroughly comfortable with his position, he wanted to do it all again! "This whole new level of maturity that we've reached is really going to show on this next Rush record." Geddy wasn't so effusive, but then, maybe he couldn't be. "When we do finish an album, I'm really high on it to a certain degree," he said. "I'm also really pissed off at it because it didn't go exactly where I heard it go in my head sometimes."

Snow. Now you should understand the album art.

It's only a model - the Innakshuk in more mundane surroundings.

Following discussions with Neil, Hugh Syme constructed an Inuit effigy – an Innakshuk – out of rocks, but his was less than 18 inches high. As well as being a cry in the wilderness, the snowy cover for *'Test For Echo'* was a direct reference to the weather conditions. "It paid homage to the fact that it was one of the worst winters in the Woodstock area where they were recording," says Hugh. "It was also a lot to do with sending out some kind of a beacon." The band needn't have worried if there was going to be an echo – on release in September 1996, the album hit the *Billboard* chart at Number 5. The title track achieved the most played rock track status on the radio within a couple of weeks, beating even those whippersnappers, Soundgarden.

It was time, once again, to turn the attention to the tour, that Hobson's choice they faced after every album – the fact that it was nearly two years since they'd last played together was incidental. "After 22 years, it's really boring," remarked Alex. "It's exciting to get up on stage and play, but the other 22 hours that you have to deal with can be really tough at times. The buses have gotten a little bit bigger, but the ride's pretty much the same!" Geddy, in particular, hated the wrench from his "normal" life at home; as did Neil, though he was quick to see the upsides. "I think it's something that's hard to step away from, because it is such a monumental challenge," said Neil of touring. "It almost seems like cheating to leave out the hardest part." All the same, the European fans would be the poor cousins once again. "I'm afraid that we haven't paid enough attention to Europe," said Geddy. "Every four or five years we go over and do a token tour. But if you don't go over there like everybody else and tour every album, you're going to fall out of public consciousness – I think that's what's happened to us."

For the first time ever, the band decided to tour without an opening act – not a decision to be taken lightly but there was so much material that was crying out to be played. Neil had always said that '2112', for example, would never get played again. "You can't go back," he had said, but he was overruled, not least because it had never been played in its entirety. "We were still opening a lot of shows back then; we were playing 40 minutes a night and we couldn't really give 20 minutes of that to one piece," said Alex. "Having more time gave us the scope to do things like that, plus give a really nice sampling of the new album." Nothing was ruled out, explained Neil. "The three of us were sending faxes back and forth with potential lists. Some were intended to be ridiculous

> **A Rush Primer**
>
> "If somebody really wanted to figure us out, they must pick up *'2112'*, *'Moving Pictures'*, *'Power Windows'* and probably this album. I think that's our best work, really. But no guarantee that they're going to like it."
>
> Geddy Lee

'Test For Echo'

The spaces in between. so much had happened in the period between 'Counterparts' and this album, it was time to find out if there was anyone still out there. The album opens with the title track, a frenetic, reverb-laden attempt to generate a response from the void. While there remains a solid coherence between the trio, there are understandable symptoms of gaps appearing between the main characters.

The threesome returned to the studio through choice, but conceding there was insufficient reason for any one band member to break off with the other two, and it shows. Some musical parts don't fit quite as well together, the lyrics sometimes have to stretch to fit the music. The traditional themes are there – the itinerant warriors are revisited in 'Driven', this traveller's tale suggesting a never-ending journey, being continued because of a lack of other options.

Neil's anti-Internet diatribe 'Virtuality' harks back to both 'Grace Under Pressure' and 'Counterparts', asking how relationships are going to pan out in this global, virtual village, and 'Half the World' returns to the theme of group behaviour.

The literature of psychology is revisited with 'Totem', a cleverly crafted cornucopia of musical textures based on a book Neil found on the Chalet Studio bookracks, 'Totem and Taboo' by Sigmund Freud. "I had been kind of rediscovering Freud by way of Jung and getting to understand the really deep stuff he was dealing with, as opposed to some of the pop psychology that we were fed growing up," he remarked. 'Resist' was originally to be called 'Taboo', following on from Freud's themes. "I wanted to have the two little set pieces of what we fear," said Neil. Parts 4 and 5, perhaps... there is no such literary inspiration for 'Dog Years' however, for better or worse, but it does have humour, as does the mostly instrumental 'Limbo', which was written towards the end of the sessions as a collection of musical snippets, and borrowed words from the Bobby Pickett and The Crypt Kickers hit, 'Monster Mash'.

Musically the album is harsh and impenetrable, an edge of burnished metal honed by wilderness rock. Overall it is thrusting, in your face, a barrage of sounds and textures that has been carefully designed to make your ears bleed. All the same it allows space for some more traditional riffing, as we discover with songs such as 'The Color of Night'. 'Carve Away The Stone' offers a final respite, slowing the pace all the while keeping up the intensity. Got an echo? You bet your life.

suggestions, but even some of those worked out. Somebody else would take it seriously and say, 'Well, wait a minute. What if we did this? It could really work'."

As they practiced the material for 'An Evening With...', Geddy didn't know how he'd cope with some of the older material, not least '2112'. "It's very idealistic, and here we are almost 20 years hence and, God, can I put myself in the frame of mind to act out this mini-drama? I couldn't help myself from chuckling from time to time." It was also the first time out for 'Natural Science' since the 'Moving Pictures' tour. "Getting 'Natural Science' together so that it flowed was dodgy in rehearsals," said Alex, "but by the time we got on the road, it had become my favourite song to play." The band planned to add a few jams into the show, and also added to its visual effects, with Howard once again

Transylvanian Twist

The original 'Monster Mash' single, sampled for 'Limbo', made it to *Billboard* #1 on Halloween 1962, however it was banned by the BBC because it was deemed to be offensive. It reached Number 3 in the UK charts on its re-release ten years later, in 1973. The Crypt-Kickers included a number of famous names of the time, including Leon Russell, Johnny MacCrae (Ronny and The Daytonas), Rickie Page (the Bermudas) and Gary "Alley Oop" Paxton (Hollywood Argyles).

It was co-written by Bobby Pickett and Leonard Capizzi.

Believe it or not, the guys made a whole album of the stuff.

planning a groundbreaking combination of video and light. "It's probably the most theatrical tour we've ever done," said Geddy.

Before the tour, there was time for a couple of weeks off (Neil and Jackie went for a break to Polynesia), then it was time to get on the buses. And bikes: Neil took his motorbike rather than his pushbike, having convinced his mate Brutus to come along as a biking companion. In the end the pair spent more time in the saddle than in the tour bus, covering almost 40,000 miles. In New Hampshire in June 1997, Andrew MacNaughton took pictures of Neil and Phil from a helicopter, the pictures planned for a "scooter trash" book for which Neil took prolific notes whenever he had the chance.

Taking Orders

On 26 February 1997, the trio were made Officers of the Order of Canada, the first time for three decades (when the award was conceived) that it had been bestowed on a group of people. "I didn't realize the importance until it was released to the press and I started getting calls from people and noticed how freaked out they were," said Alex. Added Geddy, "It kind of touches you in a place that none of these other things do touch you. Something about our home country has kept us here and moments like this make you feel like you've made the right decision."

The order exists to recognize "significant achievement in important fields of human endeavor," and Rush were awarded not only for their contribution to music, but also for their service to the community, having raised several million dollars for charity over the years. As they had been when they gave the proceeds of gigs to local good causes, the players were typically understated about the whole affair. "I'm just going to wear it all the time and see if it gets me better tables at restaurants!" laughed Geddy. Added Alex, "I think I'll wear it to bed. Maybe I'll get more respect that way."

Neil's change of style had a major impact on the live show, at least acoustically. "The dynamics in his playing went through some profound changes, and it changed the tonality of his drums," says Robert Scovill, who was behind the desk for the tour. "Early in the tour I sensed him struggling with some of the older songs that were obviously performed with the matched grip. At some point he began implementing both styles of grip depending on what era the songs came from. The whole thing just sprung back to life and in the end added great breadth and depth to his presentation."

The planned outbursts didn't quite work however – after a while they fell into patterns that repeated show after show. "We fall into patterns in our jams and after a couple months they stop being spontaneous," remarked Geddy. "It's like we cannot exist in a spontaneous world when we're onstage," said Geddy. Old pal Mendelson Joe sees this as an asset for a band such as Rush. "These people sweat, they give all in their own realm of music," he says. "Ever ask an opera singer to jam? Rush's music is very organized stuff. Disciplined."

Engineer Robert Scovill was recording shows for a prospective live album, which had been on the cards ever since 'Counterparts'. Rather than pressure individual performances as had happened with 'A Show of Hands', the band chose to record every single show and cherry pick the best performances. Great theory – but the practice of using DAT for the recordings wasn't so simple. "It was a relatively new format of digital recording and it gave me a great deal of technical headaches," says Robert Scovill. "We had an extremely high failure rate of the recording medium; in retrospect, we are pretty lucky to have captured the amount of shows that we did."

To the band however, everything was just fine. More than fine – the players were getting on better than they had ever, ever done, and they had played together as well as they ever had. Even '2112' had worked – "It was really a lot more fun to play live than I ever thought it would be," said Geddy. Neil was particularly pleased with how things turned out on tour. "I certainly consider that tour to be the zenith of my career, and of my life," he said later, effusive praise despite the tendon problems he had suffered in his elbow towards the end. "After so many years of apprenticeship, I believe we're finally starting to get somewhere. Together."

For A Limited Time

The band played the last date of the *'Test For Echo'* tour on 4 July 1997 at the Corel Centre in Ottawa, and as they walked off stage, the mood was – excellent.

Indeed, the whole *'Test For Echo'* experience had been highly positive. "On this record more than any in the past, I feel like we've arrived as a band," said Alex. "Funnily enough, if this record's about anything, it's communication. We've always been very close, but on this record, we all got so much closer." Finally, Rush had managed to get back to what it saw as its core values – guitar, drums and bass – the process was harder than anyone had anticipated, but the results made it all worthwhile. The break before *'Test For Echo'*, the resulting album, and the success of the tour, all added to the comfort factor.

Whatever works – the external projects embarked upon by both Alex and Neil had only added to the mix, and everyone including Geddy could see the benefits. This was a path that took the band to a new place – one in which work and life could be balanced, and other things could be tried without compromising what it meant to be Rush. Neil had his big band projects (*'Burning for Buddy II'* had been recorded between album and tour), and was finally embarking on an instructional video; meanwhile, Geddy was keen to get into coaching new bands, and Alex had a growing reputation as a producer.

As far as Rush was concerned, nobody was going to be idle. SRO/Anthem had negotiated the remasters of the band's first seven albums, and Geddy in particular wanted to get his teeth into updating them. "We wanted to put the music back in its original form with a fresher sound, something which is long overdue," said Geddy. It also offered an opportunity to fix a few minor errors – such as including Neil on the *'Moving Pictures'* cover. "I mean, you know, we're not a duo."

The first priority was to get started on the live album, incorporating older and newer material as a retrospective overview of the decades. "There was no real sense of immediacy in getting started," says Robert Scovill. "The concept from the get-go was one of archival purposes for a possible future release." In addition, there were tentative plans to produce a CD-ROM. "We actually have people working in the basement of the office, digging up videos and bits of information and all kinds of trivia being put into

Led to Believe

Alex got his opportunity to meet Jimmy Page, when he and Robert Plant played Toronto the summer after the *'Test For Echo'* tour. "You always think of a million things you wanna ask him, things you wanna say, but when we sat down to talk to each other, I kept thinking 'how do I tell this guy I was in love with him?'" Everyone has their heroes – and thirty years after first being inspired to pick up a guitar, Alex had met his.

Cheap Shots #483

"The big nuts and bolts onstage were more like a symbol of how stupid arena rock always has been and how stupid it stays. Rush has always flown a banner of intelligentsia amidst the rest of the rock 'n' roll blockheads; but the fact that drummer/wordsmith Neil Peart borrows every lyric he writes from someone else's book only proves that he's got a library card, not a high I.Q."

Michael Eck, *The Albany Times Union*, 4 May 1994

it," said Neil. "We really want to make it a compendium. So, we're taking our time about that of course, because it is going to take a lot of work."

Nothing needed to happen too fast. With sound finances, a devoted fan base and a re-ignited optimism, there was all the time in the world.

A month after the end of the tour, everything changed. On a rainy night on 10 August, 1997, a policeman came to Neil and Jackie's door with the information that their only daughter, Selena had been fatally injured in a motor accident. Nobody else was involved: according to the *Toronto Sun*, "She died when the Jeep she was driving left the westbound lane of Highway 401, and crashed near Brighton, Ontario."

Immediately of course, Neil turned to supporting Jackie, who had been inseparable from her daughter: Jackie was hit particularly hard by the news and her health started to deteriorate. Over the year that followed Jackie became increasingly more ill, and as best he could Neil stayed by her side, first in London then in the Bahamas, then back to Toronto for the final two months as Jackie slowly but surely let her life spirit escape. "The doctors called it cancer, but of course it was a broken heart," said Neil. A year after Selena's tragic demise, on 20 June 1998, Neil lost Jackie as well. Before she died, Neil asked Jackie what he would do without her. "Oh, you'll just go travelling on your motorcycle," she said.

For Neil, who had been so strong for Jackie for so long, the effect was a shock so great it was a while before he could talk to anyone at all. Neil had lost absolutely everything that was dear. The other members of Rush were devastated at Neil's loss, and could do nothing but stand by, to be there for him as he suffered, as any friends of twenty-five years would do. Of course, the idea of the band continuing was the last thing in anybody's mind.

As Geddy put it: "Rush was all just very quietly 'put away'."

Drummer's Progress

In 1997 Neil released '*A Work In Progress*', a set of instructional videos, recorded back at Bearsville Studios in May of that year. He'd been approached 12 years before by Rob Wallis and Paul Siegel, but he'd always postponed the decision; with the additional benefit of Freddie Gruber's coaching, the moment seemed right. "We'd never done something quite so extensive, with that level of production," says Rob. "It was fantastic working with Neil — he's a great guy, a total pro and when he tackles a project he goes all the way. We're really proud of how things turned out."

NOTES: 1 Traditional grip is where one stick is "cradled" in the left hand; in matched grip, both sticks are held in the same way. **2** Located at 580A College Street, Toronto. **3** Bearsville Studios were owned by Sally Grossman, Albert Grossman's widow — Albert was manager of Bob Dylan and Janis Joplin. Sally Grossman sold the studios in 2002. **4** Originally called McClear Place, the studio was renamed McClear Pathé in 1990. **5** Andy Wallace had also worked on the Run-DMC/Aerosmith collaboration 'Walk This Way'.

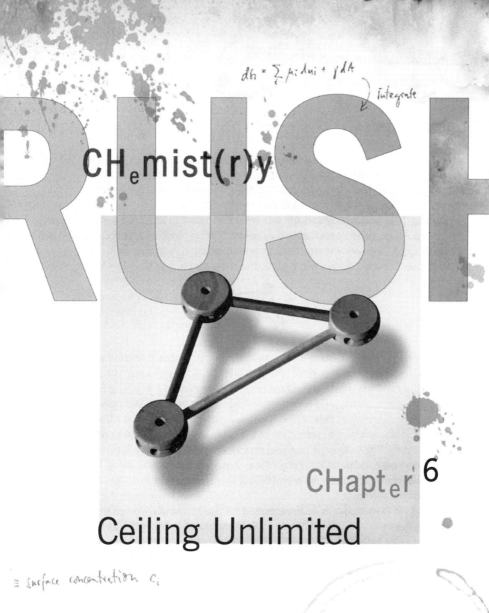

$dh = \sum_i \mu_i \, dn_i + \gamma \, dA$

$\searrow$ integrate

CH$_e$mist(r)y

CHapt$_e$r 6

Ceiling Unlimited

$\equiv$ surface concentration c_i

"Hope is like an endless river, the time is now again..."

$d\gamma = -\sum_i c_i \, d\mu_i$ \qquad (3)

a binary solution in contact with air

$G = \sum_i \mu_i n_i + \gamma A$ \qquad (4)

$\searrow$ complete differential

$\sum_i \mu_i \, dn_i + \sum_i n_i \, d\mu_i + \gamma \, dA + A \, d\gamma$ \qquad (6)

*"Shadows on the road behind, shadows on the road ahead...
nothing can stop you now..."*

Early Stages

As Neil withdrew into his protective, isolating cocoon, Geddy and Alex were left on their own, in limbo. While the pair wanted to do anything that might help, they knew that nothing at all could. "It was heartbreaking to have to watch him suffer to that degree," said Geddy. "I just wanted to be there as a friend."

The last thing on anybody's minds was what this meant to Rush, least of all whether the trio would, or indeed could, ever play again. "For us music is a celebration and all of that left us," said Alex. "It was hard to get interested in music again."

Somehow however, and in some form, the show had to go on.

It couldn't be the end, some might have remarked, as the four-album, live-album cycle that had been kept up since *'All The World's A Stage'* wasn't complete. Trite perhaps, but even the most distant fans also felt they needed something to believe in. With heavy hearts, Geddy and Alex decided to continue with the live project. It was a brave decision. Geddy was determined to make absolutely the best live album he could, a tribute to his friends and a celebration of the band, at the same time as offering some kind of closure. "The landscape changed considerably," says Robert Scovill, who found his work had been given new priority. "Now those live tapes were being looked at as the very real possibility that they were the last representation of Rush live that existed, and that might ever exist."

Back at his own studio in Arizona, Robert had painstakingly worked through every one of the hundred shows from the *'Test For Echo'* tour, collating the best versions of each song onto individual DAT tapes. The process was still dogged by the complications of using the relatively unstable medium of ADAT. "Given the fragility of the masters, we even lost some performances during this process," says Robert. "From the technical end of things, I pray I never have to go through that kind of process again." Analogue specialist Guy Charbonneau wonders why they bothered with the whole digital thing. "A load of machines to save money," says Guy, "and probably at the end it didn't!"

Once the tapes had been created, Robert listened to versions of each song in turn, whittling the list down to the top two or three performances which were then sent on to Geddy and Alex. Some shows emerged with more of a vibe than others, in particular a single performance in Chicago from which the majority of songs could be taken. When Robert had drawn up a final roll call of live cuts, he handed the reins to Paul Northfield, who was to work with Geddy and Alex to mix the album. This was as much for continuity as skill: Paul had been involved with the others in previous live records.

However, while Geddy threw himself into it, Alex found his interest leaking away.

"I kind of lost the heart for it," he said. Alex was quite happy to hand over the artistic control, after all he had just produced an album of his own, and now it was Geddy's turn. "I just thought that if he was willing to get into it, it would really be a good experience for him," commented Alex. In the end Geddy and Paul spent over 18 months working on the material. Only minimal overdubs were required, with whole songs being replaced where necessary to get the best performances. Most of the songs were from the *'Test For Echo'* tour, while a handful, including 'Bravado', 'Analog Kid' and 'Show Don't Tell' were surgically removed from the previous *'Counterparts'* tour and carefully inserted by Paul.

Meanwhile, out came the tapes of the Hammersmith Odeon gig of 1978, which offered a perfect counterpoint to the more up-to-date material. "You get a sense of where the band was back then, how young and spirited we were, the level of energy," said Alex. Listening to the Hammersmith gig brought a feeling of nostalgia to Alex and Geddy alike, causing them to dig out some of the old albums, not least *'Hemispheres'*. "I hadn't heard that in, oh boy, 15 years," said Alex. "It was really cool and a lot of fun. I heard things I hadn't heard us do in a while, like some of the harmonic ideas. Sometimes it's by going back that we replenish the future."

The bassist took Neil's traditional role in the artwork with Hugh Syme, using kids' building blocks to symbolise the three players, joined and yet apart. The final result, *'Different Stages'* was released in November 1998, with the '78 Hammersmith Odeon gig included as a bonus CD.

Publicly at least, Alex's initial reaction had been to keep the Rush flame alive. He talked about the live album buying time for the band, but as the months passed both he and Geddy resigned themselves to the fact that Rush was over. "We felt [it was] unlikely that things would get back together... and, yes, I think we were OK with it," said Alex. "It was definitely a feeling of sadness. I think that there wasn't a sense of closure with the band, that it was a long history that we had, we'd accomplished a lot of things and if that's the way it was going to end, then so be it."

While Geddy and Alex didn't rule out the possibility of working as a pair, one thing was clear – without Neil, there could be no Rush. "I wouldn't do it," said Alex. However, neither could they turn their backs on their own driving force, not to mention their own livelihood. Perhaps, it was time to move on, to do something rather than nothing.

After the work on *'Different Stages'* was complete, both Geddy and Alex started to get itchy fingers. "Time was ticking away, and I needed to sink my teeth into something healthy," remarked Geddy. "For me that's always been music." Neither Geddy nor Alex (nor Neil, for that matter) had ever been particularly good at doing nothing. "We needed to move on and that was part of closure of that period," agreed Alex.

Neil did not have the option to move on, but he could get moving. In February of 1998 he had returned from the UK and gone "home", whatever that meant – he found

Not Forgotten

'Tom Sawyer' was featured on three separate movie soundtracks in 1998: *'Whatever', 'Small Soldiers'* (as the '90s Beatmaster' version, with DJ Z-Trip.) and *'The Waterboy'* with Adam Sandler.

only a houseful of memories providing a tenuous, yet tangible connection to the past. With nothing to keep him there, and while his collaborators, colleagues and indeed his close family were keeping out of the way, Neil got on his bike. On 20 August he packed his saddlebags, made a couple of phone calls and headed on his way, on his red BMW R1100 GS. Where he was going, nobody knew least of all himself – his only focus was to protect the spark of humanity he felt inside himself. "I took my baby soul for a ride," he said.

With music off the agenda for the journey, Neil's writing habits gave him some kind of continuity. As he stopped at viewpoints and hotels, as ever booking in under assumed names for fear of being recognised, he took his notepad with him. Even at his lowest ebb he still felt compelled to write; as the days extended to weeks, then months, he started to feel some glimmer of contact, reflected in and aided by his prose. Like emotional nerves growing, reconnecting and starting to transfer the most basic of signals, Neil developed the ability to deal with his immediate surroundings, which grew to encompass a wider context, day by day.

By the end of September, in some determined effort by the gods to ensure that Neil was absolutely at rock bottom, his white Samoyed dog Nicky passed away. "If I could have felt sadder, I would have done," he said, not knowing that by October his best mate Brutus would be incarcerated in a US jail for drugs possession. That was it. Neil headed on down to Mexico, all the time documenting the depths of his despair, in notes and letters to his friends and family. "My survival remains an act of pure will," he wrote. Only the sentiment that "something will come up" drove him on.

Geddy and Alex had no shortage of projects to keep them occupied. Geddy worked with I Mother Earth, and co-wrote a song for Ken Ramm's *'Euphoria'* project, called 'The Road', released 13 July, 1999. Geddy also produced (and sang on) the debut album from his nephew Rob Higgins' band, *'Rocket Science'*. Meanwhile, as the time passed Alex participated on the album *'Passenger'* by (Bill Bell's wife) Tara MacLean, he produced and mixed a few tracks for the Mississippian band 3 Doors Down, and he composed 'March of The High Guard', the theme for Gene Roddenberry's series *'Andromeda'*.

While there might have been scope for Geddy and Alex to work together in some way, the only opportunity for collaboration was to record a version of 'O Canada' for the film *'South Park: Bigger, Longer and Uncut'*[1]. This was recorded at Alex's home studio and according to Alex, the pair were "standing at attention during the entire recording process."

In their different ways, everyone was moving on.

Living in The Present

Despite Geddy's past interest in playing with new musical ideas at his Rosedale home, he had not seen them as anything more than experimentation, and he certainly didn't intend to put out his own recordings. "I am not really driven by the kind of ambition to feature myself on a solo album," he had said, what seemed like an age before.

Against his temperament Geddy couldn't resist the urge to develop a few lyrics with his friend Kent Bendinck, understandably feeling himself in the shadow of, in his words, "the great lyric writer." He'd also been talking to Ben Mink; indeed, when Geddy had visited Ben back in 1997, when the 'Test For Echo' tour stopped in Vancouver, they'd had a jam and agreed that it would be good to write together one day. "We were hoping it would be awful, so we would never have to talk about it," explained Geddy. But it wasn't. "That's when all the trouble began..." Neither envisioned that the opportunity would arise to do so, not so quickly and certainly not in the circumstances.

Late in the same year, Ben came over to Geddy's home studio for a week to try out some writing. Even as the material formed itself into songs, Geddy was reluctant to consider releasing an album: it felt just a little disrespectful. Eventually however, the songs themselves refused to be silenced. "I liked the songs too much to leave them languishing on the shelf," said Geddy. "It seemed unfair to the music." With a final push from Atlantic exec Val Azzoli, Geddy decided that he owed it to himself, and to the future, to go ahead with what would become his first ever solo project.

No stranger to tragedy, Geddy felt well aware of what Neil was going through. "In my life I've had events like this, ever since I was 12 years old and my dad passed away," he remarked. "And both my parents were Holocaust survivors." Geddy put these feelings in a number of songs on the album, comparing Neil's experiences with what his own family had been through. "When this bad time happened, of course it was a revisiting of all those feelings," said Geddy. "So you work through it, try to make sense of it."

In particular there was 'Present Tense', primarily about existential angst but also about making the most of the moment. Geddy was aware of his own existential weakness, as he commented, "I have it, and I am sure there are other people out there who have it. We can't run from it. That is a healthy part of self-awareness." More directly still, 'Grace To Grace' was largely about his mother, who had been through the horrors of the Second World War and come out of the other side, glad to be alive and still prepared to make a life. The album wasn't all quite so soul-searching – the title track 'My Favorite Headache' summed up Geddy's perspectives on making music. "It describes the creative process to a 'T' – something you love to do but it makes you crazy to do it!" he remarked. To understand why it could make him crazy, look no further than 'Working At Perfekt': "It is the story of my life!"

As the music developed, so did the relationship between Geddy and Ben as they moved between each other's homes, Factory Studios in Vancouver and Reaction Studios in Toronto. One song in particular, which became 'Slipping', cemented the relationship and acted as the catalyst for the rest of the album. "There was something about it that felt too good to ignore," agreed the pair. With both Ben and Geddy involved in both guitars and programming, Geddy managed to avoid any issues of space and priority. The original idea was to use David Gilmour for the guitar solos on the album, but the idea was dropped when the pair realised "there was no soloing" – ironically, that was exactly what Alex had hankered for on 'Counterparts'. Geddy spent more time on the melodies, something which he had a "particular love" for, using overdubs where necessary to strengthen the vocal lines. Handily, he found that this love was shared by Ben. "We both would arrive at the same place very naturally," said Geddy. "That was a bit startling at the time!"

At Ben's recommendation, Geddy brought in producer, David Leonard, who had worked with Prince, Santana and The Barenaked Ladies. David proved to be a good counterbalance for both Geddy and Ben's perfectionism, making sure that an original idea was not thrown away in the desire to achieve perfection. "I found Geddy to be one of the nicest people on the planet," says David. "He'd come in the session every morning with coffee and muffins for everybody and his little dog[2], it was just really nice."

As the writing drew to a close, Geddy and Ben knew they had to bring in a real drummer to replace the black box, and Geddy suggested Matt Cameron of Pearl Jam. Time was short: Matt was going on tour, so the pair flew to Seattle's Studio X, where Matt was already set up. The original plan was to have Matt play on a handful of songs, but he worked through the whole set!

Only one song didn't make it to the album, through no fault of Matt's – Geddy decided to ditch the whole thing, leaving room for another. Over Geddy's birthday weekend, he and Ben wrote the quirky 'Home On The Strange'; on the Monday they called in local lad Jeremy Taggart[3] who added drums to the song, sharpish.

The album was complete, much to Geddy's relief. In the past, Geddy had looked to the steadying influences of Alex and Neil, but this time, even with the interventions of Ben and David, Geddy was largely on his own with his angst. As Geddy explained, "The responsibility of getting it done and making sure it was done properly and saying: Is this mix good enough? Do we remix this? Do I delay the release date because I have got to do this or I am not happy with this?"

On the upside, while *'My Favourite Headache'* was undeniably Geddy and despite the occasional, evocative jangle of guitar, the album was clearly different than anything his old band would have put together. Like Alex, Geddy had proved that he could work equally well with other parties, and the production experiences he'd gained would stand him in good stead in the future.

Whatever should happen.

'My Favourite Headache' was finally released on 24 October 2000. Despite the understandable pent-up demand from the fans, the album failed to chart – not that it mattered that much. It was enough to be working, and for the songs to be heard by those that wanted to hear them. "Without the support and curiosity of our fans, there wouldn't be the welcoming which all our albums receive when it comes out," said Geddy.

The title track itself, 'Grace To Grace' and 'Home On The Strange' were released as promo singles to US radio, and there was the possibility of a small tour to test out the material live. "It sure would be fun to go out and do some very small venues and have a good time with those guys," said Geddy. "Both Matt and Jeremy have expressed a desire to go do it live, it's just a matter of logistics." But then, everything changed again: Geddy wasn't going to get the chance to go on the road, not like that anyway.

"My day job is calling me back," he said.

Like A Vapor Trail

In two years, Neil had not even considered drumming, or even picked up a drumstick. "Everything that had been the center of my life before was obviously not

Now and Zen

good for me emotionally, so I wanted nothing to do with it," he said. Instead, he had travelled, neither escaping nor arriving, the thousands of miles from Northern Canada to Mexico acting as a buffer to reality. Eventually however, and not before the time was right, reality closed the gap.

Perhaps it was a fax from Liam Birt that was the turning point, sent at the beginning of March 1999. It was "innocent enough" – Liam had been tasked by the others to ask Neil, what to do with the drums he had left in storage. For Neil, this triggered a whole bunch of thoughts. While Neil felt unable to suggest any answers, he was at least prepared to start raising some questions. "Yesterday I was thinking up all the conditions I could demand in return for going to work," he wrote to his friend Brutus, who was still in prison.

In May came another galvanising incident, when Neil had his tarot read. "After great tragedy and tribulation you are trying to build yourself and your life," began the tarot reader, whose complete reading was so accurate and insightful, it was all too much for the grounded, rationalist sceptic. It took another few months before Neil realised that his self-imposed exile was never going to offer a route back to reality. After an ill-fated romantic interlude, Neil found himself without any choices. "I was at the very lowest point. I was so desperate," he said. "It was like, What can I do now? But the answer came to me: I'll play the drums." At the end of June 1999, Neil booked a session at a nondescript Toronto studio, and he took his sticks to his drums once more.

Neil had been visiting photographer and friend Andrew MacNaughtan in Los Angeles, and Andrew had been introducing Neil to the friends he was making. "I had just moved down there when Neil started visiting, it was a new, scary city," says Andrew, who was keen to help Neil mingle. "There is no hill that never ends," went the Masai proverb, and so it was November 1999, that Andrew introduced Neil to Carrie Nuttall, a professional photographer and a native of southern California. "Was I matchmaking?" asks Andrew. "Absolutely - I wanted him to meet people, and I wanted him to meet someone he could fall in love with."

While Carrie could never replace what he had lost, she gave Neil hope for the future. On September 8, 2000, and as predicted by the Tarot reader, the pair were married in "a fairy tale wedding" in Montecito, near Santa Barbara. As a final break with the past, Neil and Carrie decided to stay in California, the land of new beginnings. To Neil, whatever had come before, Carrie was the catalyst for the future.

Shortly before the wedding was to take place, in the early summer of the first year of the new millennium, Neil decided to call Geddy and Alex. "I think it's time that we sat down and started talking about what we're going to do as a band," Neil had said, according to a euphoric Alex. "My heart soared," he said, and not just about the possibility of working together. "It said so much about his recovery, that he was coming back to the world of the living." So they came, and they sat, and they talked. And they decided it was time to make a go of it, to see what developed. They set the timescale for six months, starting in January of the New Year. Over the months, the threesome got their lives in order and worked towards working together once again.

Geddy samples some Vidal Icewine at the Inniskillin Winery, with Daniel Richler and Donald Ziraldo (Inniskillin President)

Publicly anyway, things came together more quickly than anyone could have imagined. By the end of 2000, Rush was officially an item once more and the publicity machine was rolling back into action. The band went official about the regrouping on January 12, 2001. "We are just getting to know each other again," Geddy told reporters. "Everyone's kind of sniffing each other out." The first thing to do was just to spend some time together. "The first two weeks we spent just talking about everything," said Alex. "I don't think we played a single note while we were in the studio." There was a rumour that Geddy was working at a separate studio to the other two, which was quickly dispelled.

The first priority was on ensuring stress levels were as low as possible. Initially, crew members were around to set up equipment, but before long only the three players remained with their instruments. Nobody quite knew what to expect, surmised Geddy, "I would expect the writing sessions to be unlike any we've ever done." There was no timetable, no pressure on anybody apart from the uncertainty: as noted Neil, "Would we really be able to put together enough songs to fill a new album?"

While Geddy and Alex started jamming together, Neil retreated to a back room to see what lyrical content he could assemble. Though he had been away from the drumming, writing was one thing he had kept going. Inevitably the songs that emerged were a lot more personal than they had been in the past. "The old Neil thought the world was a wonderful place and that people were kind of annoying, and the new Neil thinks that the world is a terrible place and that people are beautiful, people are wonderful," says Paul Northfield. These sentiments were reflected as lyrical themes covering loss and re-emergence, and the indifference of the heavens to the trivial to-ings and fro-ings of mankind. There was no overall concept, more a shared feel as Neil fell back on authors such as W. H. Auden, Joseph Conrad and Oscar Wilde for lyrical sustenance.

After a couple of weeks Neil emerged from his room. Geddy took the job of chief arranger, working with Alex to pull the growing pool of musical segments together into

Logic Audio on the computer. Then it was time for all the players to review, rework, rearrange – finally at least, the software and equipment was up to the job. The first song to emerge from this process was 'Out Of The Cradle', closely followed by 'Vapor Trail', 'The Stars Look Down' and 'Earthshine'. "It took a little while to get going, but once we did it took on a life of its own and we were just along for a ride," said Alex. "It felt very much like it was just us getting together and playing and having fun with it."

There were to be no keyboards, however. "Geddy knew full well by the time that we got to this record that I really wanted to get away from keyboards entirely," Alex explained. Geddy wasn't that upset, according to Alex anyway. "His feeling is: if keyboards work for something, fine, let's use them, but if they don't work, fine, I don't care. I really don't want to play them." Neither were there any guitar solos, for that matter. "I'd much rather spend time creating sounds on the guitar that are organic, that would do the same job that keyboards do. It is so much more fun to create these more unusual sounds." To support these textures Geddy added layers of vocal harmony, a process he had developed during *'My Favourite Headache'*. "He used his voice more as an instrument to create those same sort of backdrop sounds that we used keyboards on the past with," said Alex.

Towards the end of the sessions, songs like 'One Little Victory', 'Ceiling Unlimited' and 'Nocturne' started to emerge. "The newer songs started to get weirder," noted Neil, adding that "daring comes out of confidence." 'Ceiling Unlimited' was one of the most optimistic songs on the album. Explained Alex, "Anything is possible, and even out of the darkest darkness there's light. And, just reach for it."

Never Say Never

In May 2001 Alex produced an album for Lifer, a band who he'd picked up on when they'd won the Battle of the Cover Bands competition on MTV. For Lifer, it was a dream come true and the band had an influence on Alex as well – introducing him to Hughes and Kettner amps. The album *'Lifer'* was released on 14 August.

Following a brief yet necessary pause (while Alex produced Lifer's self-titled debut), by June it was time to involve some other people. For an objective ear the band selected engineer-turned-producer Paul Northfield. "He had really got his production shots down and was very much into the guitar-based bands," says Peter Collins. Paul had also worked on the Buddy Rich tribute albums, so clearly he had a broad palette he could offer; most of all however, he was a friend. "I think they wanted someone on this occasion they did know because of all the emotional stuff, they didn't want someone new," says Paul. "I was still very cutting edge which they liked, after 30 years I was still doing records that were relevant and different and unusual so they were quite enthused by that aspect of it."

Paul's first job was to work through the raw arrangements with Geddy – not that they were particularly raw. "They were really quite far in advance," says Paul. "There would be lots of overdubs on there and lots of vocals as well, and sometimes there would be some guitar parts that were inspiring or vocals that were great, or backing vocal layering that Geddy had done." Lorne Wheaton, who had been Max Webster's drum tech many years before, was also brought in to help. "I was Neil's ears in the control room," he says.

The recording process was very different from the past. Rather than writing the cook book then following it assiduously, as they had done for the previous albums, each player developed his parts independently. Every evening the trio would get together (generally after supper) to check how things were going. There were many reasons for this – not least, everyone wanted to keep the pressure on the others to a minimum. "It wasn't because they didn't want to talk to each other, they were trying to allow each other to have lots of space," says Paul. In addition, as Neil remarked, "both Geddy and Alex had produced their own projects, and each of them was used to being the Supreme Boss of Everything." The evening review was very important psychologically – "even if we worked in isolation, we were working together," commented Neil. Not that the threesome were working apart, all the time – "There were some very passionate, very emotional writing sessions," commented Alex.

Lastly of course, whereas Neil would have traditionally recorded his pieces first, this time round he hadn't fully worked out what he was going to play, let alone whether he could play it with sufficient gusto. Paul's role became more hands on than for any past Rush producer: he worked from late morning until tea time with Geddy and then evenings with Neil, while Alex was spending time developing his own material. Once the rhythm section was worked out, Alex took over the evening slot; meanwhile, Neil started to rehearse, tweak and arrange what he'd worked out to play. While he wasn't at his kit Neil started writing a book, collating the many notes, letters and musings of his two-year journey. *'Ghost Rider'*, it would be called, a modern-day *Geisterfahrer*[4].

For Neil, "rehearsing" was like starting from scratch again, requiring all of his single-mindedness and focus to develop the skills he needed. His muscles were far from toned, his rhythmic ear was lacking an edge, his hands lacked the calluses he needed to play for any length of time. Having lain dormant for five years, the muscle memory was still there and before long he started having fun. "He enjoyed himself very much playing, that didn't seem to be too difficult for him," says Paul. Amongst other things, Neil had to learn to rock again – but this was a challenge he was up for. "There's also a new level of freshness for me, coming back to the instrument with a new sense of rededication," he remarked.

After the first, tentative steps, Neil played with enormous energy. Nearly twenty years before, in an interview, Neil had discussed the physical approach to drumming of his friend and mentor Tommy Aldridge. "It's a satisfying thing, it's not something you have to do, but it's something that you really want to do," he had said. "It feels great to hit 'em hard." So hit 'em hard he did, recording all the way and playing back the two or three best takes to the others, after dinner. With the others working in the same way, the final version of a song would represent the first time it had been heard in that exact form, by anyone. "That's something we love about this record," said Alex. "It's so spontaneous and instinctive and it's captured a moment that just happened once."

Slowly, but surely, song by song, it all came together,. "We wanted to make something that was intense," said Geddy – and they had, undeniably so. "By the time we got to the final performances, there was a real intense build up," says Paul, whose influence on the production process was, according to Neil, "strong." He was there for the band as it nurtured its collective soul and felt its way towards an album that would be as dynamic and full of energy as possible. "He saw possibilities that sometimes escaped us (urging 'Ghost Rider' from the verge of abandonment to its glorious realization, for example). He also encouraged our 'eccentricities' in the later emerging songs like 'Freeze' and 'Peaceable Kingdom'."

The isolated production approach isn't always going to be the best way to make an album, admits Paul Northfield. "It's a double edged sword, because sometimes there is a creative tension that comes from kind of rubbing up against each other," he says. In this case it worked, which was as much as anyone could hope for.

The final task was to order the songs. One in particular stood out as the opener – 'One Little Victory', conceived to leave the listener in absolutely no doubt: Neil and the rest of the band were, in his own terms, "ba-a-a-ack!" Neil had originally been working out the in-your-face drum section for towards the end of the song, but Geddy suggested it went right up front. "Frankly, I wouldn't have done it that way," said Neil, "I don't think I would have been so assertive."

Everything was going so well. Mixing started, and then it was time for another break – this time, for Christmas. When the players and producer came back however, nobody was quite as happy as they had been before they left. There appeared to be too much compression in the mix, but even with a change of studio nobody could quite pin down why, or what to do about it. Eventually, tempers started to fray and even Paul was starting to have difficulties seeing the wood for the trees. "We had become too deeply immersed in the material, and we could no longer step back and hear the songs whole," remarked Neil. It was time to sit down and talk, and the conclusion was to get someone else involved, a fresh pair of ears. On the shortlist was David Leonard, fresh from working with Geddy on 'My Favourite Headache', to get the final mixes back on track.

David was available, a major additional factor in his favour considering the short notice. "They had worked on it for so long, and they just needed someone to just come in and put it into perspective without remembering all the baggage that got them to that point," says David. "I just came in and said, oh, I like that and I like that and I like that, and what do you think of that? That's what a mixer often does, anyway."

The troubles weren't over however – everyone was shattered, ground down over the months, and there was still the mastering to go. "We were all so toast," says Paul. Having sent the tapes to a number of people, Geddy and the others opted for mastering engineer Howie Weinberg, who had done such a good job on 'My Favorite Headache'. "The mastering was nightmarish," says David Leonard, who attended the sessions with Geddy. "An ugly distortion appeared on a track. My first thought was that something in the mix was being brought out and aggravated by the mastering process, so I went back to the mix room and recalled the mix. I never found any distortion of that nature. I reprinted the mix at very reasonable levels. There was no distortion in the mix at the time it went back to mastering. But the same thing happened."

Perhaps, put simply, Howie was putting the compression back. Not that he was to know this was the wrong thing to do – it was the fashion of the time, and an aggressive mastering approach befitted the raunchiness of some to the songs. "On certain levels everybody liked it," says Paul. "There was a lot of excitement that it was a powerful record coming out of a very, very difficult time. I didn't hear it until it was all said and done, at which point the record company was over the moon with it, saying it was fantastic, let's get it out there."

While initial reviews of the album were very positive, it took a few weeks for the more careful listeners to feed back. "The audiophiles, amongst the lovers of Rush they started to go, why is it like this? To me it's guilty as charged," says Paul. "All you can say is decisions were made at the time, everybody was just really tired and we did what we felt was right, and then given a month or two's hindsight we found it was wrong."

In some ways, the album served as much as a statement of intent, as a musical piece. When the band came up for air in February 2002, they were overcome by the amount of interest they were getting. Said Alex, "We were barraged with all this press and promotion to an extent we've never done before. It bowled us over. I mean we've been around a long time and we're used to this sort of thing. A little bit out of touch maybe, but we're used to it. But this is just crazy!"

'Vapor Trails' was released eighteen months after the process had started, in July 2002. Who else could there be to produce a cover but Hugh Syme, who once again opted for a painting. Initially the idea was to build on the concept of vapour trails, and everything from the serious to the seriously silly was explored, not least the idea of a dragon. This was quickly rejected: "It kind of tipped the scale way too much into the era of rock music that is 'Wakemanesque', that grand and terribly British folklore kind of thing," says Hugh. Instead, Neil agreed with Hugh that a comet would work, so the cover artist set about putting together a conceptual piece, in oil on canvas. "It was a real quick and dirty rendering," says Hugh, but when Neil and the others saw it, they loved the image. "What was a study became the original for the cover!"

Following the album release, conversation turned inevitably to the idea of a tour. Alex was up for it; Geddy was reluctant, but up for it; Neil was apprehensive. But his musician's instinct to perform outweighed any desire to scuttle back under his rock. "Touring was a difficult concept for him to come to grips with," said Geddy, himself and Alex gently broaching the subject to see what happened.

As the threesome started to discuss set list possibilities, emailing rather than faxing each other this time, the excitement levels grew. Initially Neil agreed to a 38-date tour of the US and Canada, possibly with some overseas dates. As the bookings came in however, the number grew rapidly, reaching 67 shows, and Neil was still up for it. Most of the dates were arenas and ampitheaters, despite the indication that the band could probably fill stadia, if they wanted to.

The bandwagon nearly made it all the way to Europe – but in the end, the trio decided that would be a step too far – they were unsure about interest levels, and left things too late. Half the problem (as ever) was that they were not prepared to put on a cut-down show. However, they did plan some dates in South America for the first time, particularly as their attempts to book dates on the previous tour, had not come off. International agent Neil Warnock had negotiated a few shows – stadium shows at that – and had somehow managed to convince the band that they'd enjoy the experience. So they agreed, not really expecting a

Get Rhythm

In September 2002, Carrie Nuttall showed an exhibition of photos that she had taken of Neil during the creation of 'Vapor Trails', called 'Rhythm and Light', According to the press release, Carrie wanted, "to portray his quiet grace to sheer brute strength, and as a result the images range from the lyrical abstract to stark realism." The photos were released as a book, in May 2004.

'Vapor Trails'

Neil's real-life experiences could never have been predicted in any song, but to cope with his tragedies he became the traveller, not knowing if he was running away or moving towards a goal, concerned only with where his motorbike would take him each day. The possibility of his emergence from this transcontinental journey of the soul was slim indeed; the idea of the threesome getting together to record again was even slimmer. 'One Little Victory' might not be a standard opener, but this is not just any album – this is a triumphant return of a band, and it is reasonable that Neil should take the podium for the first few bars. Guitar and bass follow in an unadulterated heavy blues riff, the Willowdale three reunited in a single purpose, to get out there and do what they do so well.

Equally unsurprising is Neil's desire to document his experiences, though it is slightly unnerving that he wears his heart so openly on his sleeve. Sharing titles with his journeyman's diary, 'Ghost Rider' offers a deep insight into his recent history, as does the title track. Here and everywhere else the drums are at the front of every mix, no more so than 'Vapor Trails', which is not so much a song, as a drum solo with additional parts.

Otherwise, the music suggests a return to base. 'Ceiling Unlimited' is classic Rush, as is 'Peaceable Kingdom'; 'The Stars Look Down' could have fitted on 'Roll The Bones', and 'How It Is' harks back to 'Presto'. None is a complete rehash – the music is unmistakeably new millennium, a return to the post-grunge straightforwardness the band was discovering on the previous album. 'Out Of The Cradle' revisits 'Half The World', and 'Nocturne' starts in a similar way to 'Middletown Dreams', but that is where the similarity ends – back come the guitars, no sign of synthesisers here. Finally, the 'Fear' trilogy gets a fourth part with 'Freeze', this time exploring the symptoms of fear, rather than the causes.

There are some signs of progress, not all of them welcome: 'Secret Touch' continues Geddy's tendency to chant, rather than sing – shame that his melody-making skills sometimes play second fiddle to the textural requirements of the guitars. His still-inimitable vocals could never vanish too far into the mix, however. 'Earthshine' and 'Sweet Miracle' are examples, with short lyrics and heavy guitars, the standardised song structure leaving little room for the melody to shine.

Some have said that the album is once again influenced by whatever is current, in this case nu-metal bands such as Tool. This may be so, but not this time through any active desire to replicate what is going on elsewhere. 'Vapor Trails' does not break too much new ground; rather, and perhaps for the best, it is a restating of past values. It is best to ignore the lack of sonic clarity and to focus on the songs, which are testament to a resilience against tribulations that many would falter before. There's still plenty here to be going on with, and clearly there is a load more where it came from.

huge reaction – the record sales had never been that great in Brazil.

When the band started to rehearse, they realised they had a little way to go before they got their tour legs back. "The first week of rehearsal we sounded like a very bad Rush cover band," said Alex. "There was definitely that period of having to get back on the horse." The issues were as much physical as anything – none of the three had what it took to play a half hour set, never mind one that went on for two or three hours. Family matters were equally important, particularly for Geddy who was finding himself wrenched from his home routines.

Given the intervening years since the last tour, there were some inevitable changes of crew, as past stalwarts had found other bands to work with. In addition, the hiatus had occurred during a period of much development in live sound. Front of House engineer Robert Scovill was not available, so they decided to bring in Brad Madix, who had taken over from Robert for a short while back on the *'Roll The Bones'* tour. On arrival, Brad introduced the use of "line array" speakers (that could project sound much better than traditional speaker configurations), a digital mixing desk and a range of mikes. "We played with different vocal mics in rehearsals until we were all happy and away we went," says Brad.

As well as planning to include an abbreviated '2112' in the set again, the threesome went right back to 'Working Man' as they considered what to play. The band even listened to their fans when it came to deciding the set list, paying attention to what was reported on the website RushPetition.com. "I think we actually looked at that site and took 4 or 5 songs from the Top Ten," said Alex – a job well done for the site instigator: perhaps the Web had its uses, after all. Indeed, the band did everything they could to fit as many songs in as possible, but as they approached the three-hour mark, they had to call it a day. "We have unions to answer to ya know!" laughed Alex.

Like old times, the rehearsals were also the opportunity to work out who was going to trigger which samples. "The samples can be mapped to anything, so it depends on who's convenient for what," says Tony Geranios. In particular, the Roland 5080 samplers could do pretty much everything that used to require an array of equipment. "It's come full circle, from one, to many, to one!" Well, two – the equipment was replicated to minimise the risk of failure. The no-trappings, tech-limited approach was something that appealed to everyone. Remarked Alex, "We've been trapped by the technology for quite a few years and we'd like to feel a little freer and have fun, you know? And feel like we're making a little more contact."

One way to achieve this was through a revamped set of visuals, so Geddy went to Norm Stangl and asked him what he could come up with. "Beyond a doubt, collaborating with Geddy is and has been very rewarding," says Norm. "He is always looking for something different, something more edgy, often with a little tongue in cheek." The dragon idea, rejected from the album cover and with the addition of a cigar, was the perfect icon. Ironically it was called 'Nebbish'[5] – nobody was feeling particularly weak-willed by this stage.

In the spring of 2002, the band and SRO agreed to work with a past collaborator of Jimbo Barton, Dan Catullo, who had proposed making a live DVD of the tour. Larry Jordan, who had directed *'A Show Of Hands'*, was invited to join the team as a consultant[6]. "When I went to meet Geddy, I hadn't seen him in eight years, but I felt there was going to be a comfort level," says Larry. The film shoot was planned for the 8 November performance at the Mohegan Sun casino in Uncasville, Connecticut.

The final gig, at the Maracaña stadium in Rio de Janeiro, was kept as an option for additional footage.

The opening night of the tour was at the Meadows Music Center, in Hartford Connecticut, on 28 June. For the band as for everybody else, it was a truly unforgettable experience. "It was a bit of a blur and things were just so exciting yet tense," said Alex. "I truly had doubted it would ever come again." One by one, the dates passed, every venue filled, every audience rapturous. "I don't think there was one night on the last tour when it felt like a job," remarked Alex. The use of layered vocals caused a bit of a problem on the tour, but Alex picked up some of the harmonic lines, "with the aid of some electronics making his voice sound groovy!" according to Geddy.

In preparation for the video shoot, Larry and Dan went to see the band play in San Diego. As the Uncasville gig approached however, it became clear that the live recording could not go ahead, not there anyway. "Connecticut was all pre-produced, ready to go, but SRO couldn't agree terms with the casino, they wanted to plug the casino," says Dan. There was little time to fix any other venue but one – the last night of the tour and the third date to be spent in Brazil, just 12 days later, at the Maracaña stadium in Rio de Janeiro. "So, we went from a 20,000 capacity casino to the largest stadium in the world!" With no time to spare, the shoot became an order of magnitude greater – more cameras, bigger consoles, better lenses. "In 8 days we had to get work permits and equipment together," says Dan. "The biggest problem was shooting in high definition. We were under the gun, we had one day to find out the equipment for the shipping manifests." In addition the camera crew had to take account of the band's own needs – in particular Neil, who didn't want the distraction of cameramen.

As Larry had shot in Rio a few times before, he was familiar with the location and its special requirements, and he knew how to recruit a crew. "I had some key people I knew," says Larry. Nobody was in any doubt about the logistical issues of working in Brazil, however. "Any show in Brazil is likely to be kind of a mess," says mixing engineer Brad Madix. "Things just don't happen there the way they do in the US, Europe or Japan." It wasn't even clear that there would be much of an audience, as advance ticket sales had been poor. "Everyone was very concerned," admits Larry, but he needn't have worried. "At the last minute they bought thousands and thousands of tickets."

The first night south of the border, things went as well as could be expected. By the second night the tensions were palpable, and that was before they counted on the weather. "We had been through a couple of days of horrible load-ins, load-outs,

> **Undercurrents**
>
> "The carpet that we used on stage got so soaking wet during those days that we had to leave it behind. It was too heavy to ship home. It was so waterlogged that it would have cost way more than it was worth to ship it home, so we just left it there. It's in some Brazilian guy's living room."
>
> Neil Peart

> **Intro Tapes #3**
>
> ...Limp Bizkit, Radiohead, Led Zeppelin, Linkin Park, Tool, The Tragically Hip, Jimi Hendrix, Vertical Horizon, Pink Floyd, Coldplay, Porcupine Tree.

weather, technical difficulties, and so on," says Brad. A final straw was when the monitor console (the one the band uses to hear what it is playing) stopped working due to water in the power supply units. "The crew all got together, got out the hair dryers and blew hot air into the thing until it came on!" Not even the rain could diminish the joy, not to mention the size, of the Brazilian audience: Sao Paolo drew

a crowd of 60,000, and over 40,000 tickets had been sold for the Rio gig, the biggest headline audiences the band had ever played to. "We were completely surprised by it," said Alex, his excitement tempered with apprehension: the next night would be filmed.

After a hard drive

The plan was to start unloading at 8am sharp, with the band arriving at 10, but the previous day's issues had culminated in huge delays leaving Sao Paolo. Further hold-ups on the road meant the crew and equipment didn't reach the stadium until after noon, and still more complications delayed the load-in until 2.30. With brave faces the crew set about constructing the stage, assembling the lighting rigs, unpacking and connecting instruments and backline to desks and PA. At least they didn't have to worry about the rain.

For the video team, things were even more tense. They had gone straight to Rio four days before, but faced no end of technical challenges of their own. "Only about fifty per cent of the planned facilities actually existed," says Larry. "We had four days of utter panic." The team worked day and night, co-ordinating with translators to brief the camera crews, and creating a production facility virtually from scratch using whatever was available. "We built a video control room out of a garbage dumpster, using a chainsaw to cut the windows," says Dan. Also on the scene was Jimbo Barton. "There was a feeling of panic the night before," says Jimbo. "It was a complete mess."

Despite every probability that they would not be able to get things together in time, the video crew and the stage crew brought the two sides together. For the first time anyone could remember there was no time for Rush to have a sound check – the band didn't even arrive until five in the afternoon, and things were not ready in any case. "We didn't get finished until about 20 minutes before the show," says Brad: things were not helped by the fact that the pressure was causing unnecessary mistakes. "The audio cables caught fire at four in the afternoon, because someone put DC down the cables," says Jimbo.

That was just getting things plugged together: there was barely time to test the masses of cabling that linked the trio with the audience. Continues Jimbo, "It was hell! Up until 30 seconds before we rolled tape, someone was on top of the truck trying to gaffer tape the timecode feed[7]." Within the team, stories of heroism were rife.

"Kooster McAllister from Record Plant Mobile was a genius, he single-handedly saved the day," says Jimbo.

Finally, with doors opening three hours late, in front of 44,000 fans and 40 cameras, the band had to get on with the last show of the tour.

No pressure. "We went on dead cold," said Alex. "What was our very comfortable environment up there, suddenly was transformed into this very hectic and tense place so I had to really, really concentrate in the first set." The trio rose to the occasion, riding the pressure like a wave. "Without a soundcheck, and without being totally sure everything was working properly, the show was absolutely great from the first note! It was magical in a way, and a huge relief," says Brad. "I was really prepared for the worst, but it was just... well, maybe the best show of the tour!" Agrees Dan, who was watching backstage with SRO's Pegi Cecconi, "Pegi and I were praying that it would all work, and it did... this thing should never have come together, and it did!"

Of course, the performances of cast and crew would be nothing without the audience, and the Brazilian crowd came up trumps. "We had all these Brazilians who don't speak very much English sing every word to every song and even sing through the instrumentals, it just blew our minds. It's

If You Go Down to the Woods Today...

"After Deborah's great shot on the lake, I'd always wanted to shoot Neil with his drumkit in an exotic location. Sabian shipped the kit down from Toronto, and said why don't we shoot it in a forest or something. I just love that shot where I'm way back and it's just a moment of him playing the drums amongst all the forest. It was so surreal because when he started to play, you could almost see all the squirrels halting and birds flying away, with him playing away! I know Neil got off on it as well, he'll put in the extra effort if its done well, and artistic, and tasteful."

Andrew MacNaughtan

TV Tales

On 1 June 2003, Alex participated in an episode of Canadian TV series 'Trailer Park Boys', titled 'Closer To The Heart'. On 26 January 2004, Geddy made a guest appearance on 'The Monday Report', a political comedy show.

such an amazing thing to watch. There were moments where I just had a lump in my throat. Seeing the audience singing and hearing even through my in-ear monitors how loudly they were singing," said Alex. Agrees Larry Jordan, "40,000 people jumping up and down, it just made them play harder!"

The 'Vapor Trails' tour came to an end with nobody in any doubt where the band stood. The drum-beat announcement to whoever might listen, played at the start of the album – "We're baa-a-ack" – was proven true, 67 times over. "I think the way we feel right now; there's certainly more music in us," said Alex, as he looked back on the experience. "There's certainly more tours."

Moving On

Before making any more plans for the future, the DVD had to be put to bed. Alex travelled down to Dan's place in California to work on the initial stereo mixes, then the project was moved back up to McClear Place in Toronto. "Alex was unhappy with the level of guitar, so off we went," says Jimbo Barton. The sound wasn't helped by the difficulties in recording stadium rock, explains Peter Henderson, who has also recorded at the Rio stadium. "I sympathise completely," says Peter. "The place was terrible! The amount of echo coming back was huge."

Attention
All Planets!
Rush DVDs
accompany
the unmanned
mission
to Mars...

Mars Exploration Rover-2003

Landing Certificate

Presented to

RUSH

On July 12, 2005

Thank you for joining us on this mission of exploration and discovery. DVDs bearing your name are now on Mars at Gusev Crater (Spirit) and at Meridiani Planum (Opportunity).

Our journey of knowledge and wonder continues!

Dr. Edward J. Weiler
Associate Administrator
Office of Space Science

Certificate No. 2672615

Meanwhile, Geddy's brother Allan had set to work on the video. Neil's minicams really hadn't given the results that were hoped, but the footage was too good to waste and Allan decided to lower the quality of the video overall, rather than let Neil's sequences stand out like a sore thumb. To Larry Jordan, the raw nature brought back the exhilaration of the night. "All that comes through and makes it more exciting," says Larry, who went over a couple of times. "I changed a couple of things, but Allan had it covered."

The DVD also incorporated 'bonus footage' in the shape of a documentary of the band, recorded by Andrew MacNaughtan. "I was filming everything, then I came back to the States to start creating a story out of hours and hours of footage," says Andrew. "That was a really hard project for me... I think it gave a unique perspective into the band, I really wanted to try and capture some moments of that."

And it was done. The DVD and accompanying CD were mastered at the beginning of August 2003 by Adam Ayan at Gateway Mastering – where else. "Their attention to detail and desire to maintain the highest quality possible is very impressive," says Adam. "Working with Alex was an absolute pleasure." Unfortunately, some considered that the final result suffered from the same issue as *'Vapor Trails'*. "I was very pleased until the mastering, then someone put very slow compression on it, and crushed the bejeezus out of it!" says Jimbo.

Somebody must have liked it. The DVD debuted at Number 1 in the US DVD charts, and went on to quadruple-platinum status. Back in the homeland, it even picked up a Juno award – the first for many years! Given all the trials and tribulations, that was something nobody expected. "It would probably be overstating the case to call Rio a miracle," says Brad Madix. "But it was remarkable that we did a show at all, let alone that we made an award-winning DVD of it!"

The band were having too much fun, it seemed. As the end of 2003 approached, the trio realised they had spent nearly 30 years together as a unit – Neil had joined on 29 July, 1974, Geddy's birthday, and the anniversary was coming around more quickly than anyone expected. When the idea of an anniversary tour came up, it seemed rude not to agree. In particular, it would enable the band to return to Europe. Geddy was determined the trio would reach the now-alien shores. "He put his foot down saying, the tour would not happen unless it included some European dates," said Alex.

Neil Warnock got to work, ignoring concerns whether there was enough of an audience but ensuring that the amphitheatre sets so popular in the US would work when they were transported to the arenas of Europe. Neil booked two dates at Wembley Arena, though the band only started selling tickets for the first. Before long however, both dates were sold out, as well as dates in Manchester, Glasgow, Milan, Barcelona and a number of other venues. Just as in 1977, the band discovered just how great its following was in the old world.

It was a buoyant band that broke up for the holiday season... but an incident over the break nearly put paid to the whole event. Along with his son, Justin, and his daughter-in-law, Michelle, Alex was arrested for brawling and resisting arrest, following an altercation with the police at a New Year's Eve party at the Ritz-Carlton hotel, near his second home in Naples, Florida. It was unfortunate in the extreme, particularly for mild-mannered Alex who was horrified by the whole situation, not least the police treatment of his son and daughter-in-law. After a night in the cells he walked free, pending a trial. Furthermore, with certain conditions he was allowed to leave the US and move freely within it. Any other decision would have scuppered the possibility of a tour, national or international.

Alex was determined not to let the incident sour the tour preparations, nor the band's desire to get even further back into its groove. The fires were well and truly lit, and the bonds between the players were stronger than they'd ever been. Normally, a tour would follow an album release, but this time of course, there was no album. It felt like there was a space waiting to be filled, an opportunity not to be missed. The idea of a covers album resurfaced, particularly as there had been talk of another tribute album looming. But surely they couldn't... could they?

Neil doing soundcheck at Red Rocks - Howard Ungerleider is in the stalls

Of course they could. Not only was it an opportunity to rock out, but also to go right back to their roots, to play the music the threesome had been playing before they'd even been called Rush, let alone shared a stage together. "It was just a fun little trip down memory lane, to share with our fans the tracks which woke us up to music," said Alex. Together and apart, Alex, Geddy and Neil had all done their time in covers bands, and shared a number of heroes and influences – Cream of course, The Who... before long the band inundated them-selves with ideas on what songs they would like to play. Led Zeppelin was rejected: as they agreed, nobody could outzep the Zep.

The band reunited with producer David Leonard back in Studio A, at Phase 1 studios in Toronto. "Geddy sent me some stuff he'd been doing at home, and we just took it from there," says David. The idea was to take things right back to the earliest days of the band – to record as they used to play, live as a trio, with no click track and with minimal overdubs – the cover of 'Crossroads' was played completely live. A week was spent cutting the drum and bass tracks, then a second week was spent on the guitars. "We got to play with a lot of old guitar sounds," says David. "We went into the little room, just Alex and I, and played with lots of old pedals, and ribbon mikes and stuff like that, it was a blast!"

While the process was short, it was dynamic, liberating and above all, fun. "It was fun for them to do and fun for me to record," says David. "It was freeing because it was some other material that wasn't theirs and they weren't trying to re-invent it. They were just putting their ink on it." The whole process took only two weeks – "That's usually how long it takes to do one song!" laughs fellow Dexter Lou Pomanti.

As usual, Hugh Syme was commissioned to produce a highly psychedelic cover for the disc, called *'Feedback'* due to Geddy and Alex's insistence in

Rush at the Red Rocks Ampitheater, R30 tour

including it on every track. There was barely time to get the EP into production before the tour started, at the end of May 2004, literally thirty years from when the band had first hit the stages of North America. The inclusion of some of the *'Feedback'* covers into the set was seen as a little unusual by some fans, but to the band it made absolute sense – at the end of the thirty years, the songs defined the band as a rock band who were proud to demonstrate their influences. "I think it was an extremely courageous, risky thing for them," agrees friend and collaborator Mendelson Joe.

Rush came to Europe at the now-standard sedate pace, never more than two cities on consecutive days. "They just can't tour like they used to when they were younger, it's too hard on Geddy's vocals," says Andrew MacNaughtan. Neil treated the European leg as a road trip, travelling between gigs on his motorbike with companion and security manager Michael Mosbach. Sometimes Neil would sneak 20 minutes of sleep before going on, and after the gig had ended he would be out of the doors on his bike before the post-encore audience roar had died down.

Throughout the tour, Alex's court case still nagged. The initial date was set bang in the middle of the planned European tour, but one of many legal postponements meant the shows could proceed apace. Alex was determined as ever, not to let the shadow of the case spoil things.

In any case, the guys were just having too much fun.

Made To Last

The tour, like all good things, came to an end on 1 October, 2004. As the threesome went back to the places they called home, it was time for a little retrospective introspection. If Rush was a journey, the travellers were the same people who had set out so many years ago, band and management, crew and collaborators, the line-up had barely changed since the very beginning. "We've been able to play music since we were 15, and we haven't had to grow up," said Alex.

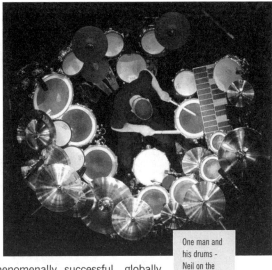

One man and his drums - Neil on the R30 tour

Strip away the layers of the phenomenally successful, globally renowned band, and what is left? Not a great deal, to be frank. "When you eliminate everyone else from the picture, it's just the three of us sitting around," remarked Geddy. Three determined musicians perhaps, but there are plenty of others that share their determination. Three people who put their musicianship first... but they are not alone in that characteristic either. Three people who are somehow able to tap into each other's energies and produce something that is far greater than the sum of its parts? Now we're getting somewhere.

If there's one thing we can learn from the solo efforts of Alex and Geddy, good as they are, they miss that essential Rush-ness, lacking the creative process where each musical and lyrical phrase has been repeatedly selected, moved and in some cases argued over. Somehow this is done without losing track of the fact that the song is more important than the individual words or music. The trio pushed themselves as far as they could in the studio, but their shared heritage of downtown bar blues meant they always knew the resulting songs were to be performed, rather than acting as some demonstration of technique.

Neil, Michael and the art of motorcycle maintenance

There is a personal chemistry between the fellows, that is undeniable. "It's beyond being brothers, it's beyond being a family, it's beyond a marriage," commented Alex recently. However there is also a musical chemistry, a learned ability to balance the right mix of ingredients. At its core, Rush is a power trio, a rock band whose

The band in
action on
the R30 tour

Radio City
Music Hall,
New York

primary purpose is to play it loud. All the same, as the musical landscape has changed, so has Rush, taking on new influences but remaining true to its ideals. "Rush is not so much a mirror, but a satellite dish moving down the road, soaking up different styles, methods, and designs," Neil has said.

Perhaps it is the third kind of chemistry that is the most important, that chemistry between the band and its audience. While Rush's music was never designed to work for the radio-friendly mass market, it has had consistent appeal to a vast fan base, which has been all the more devoted as a result. Rush have touched the lives of many thousands of fans around the world, fans that have stayed with the band through thick and thin. "People always ask me why we were around for so long and sure, it has to do with the fact that the three of us are great pals and we still love writing music together," said Geddy. "But it's also because there's an audience waiting."

None of the contributory factors to Rush's enduring success is unique, not in itself. Rather, it is how the ingredients are combined that gives the band its winning edge, following a mystical formula so secret that even Geddy, Alex and Neil would find it impossible to write down. Ordinary ingredients perhaps, but even the most churlish of journalists would be hard pushed to deny that the resulting three decades, the thousands of live dates played to thunderous applause, the

Something's hurting - Alex and Geddy, R30 Tour

seventeen studio albums, five live albums and numerous compilations have been nothing short of extraordinary.

What of the future? The ill-conceived court case against Alex is now behind him, and the tables are turned – the lamb has become a lion, pressing charges against the law enforcement agencies of Florida. Neil has a new life with Carrie in California, and has even made his peace with the Internet, as demonstrated by his recently published website. Back in Toronto, Geddy has his family, his baseball and his wine.

As the band prepares itself to re-enter the studio, it is worth bearing one thing in mind. Rush is a journey rather than a destination, and the point of the journey is not to arrive. Anything could happen.

Left: Learning to Resist - Geddy and Alex go acoustic
Above: Neil in action, R30 tour

NOTES: **1** The connection was through photographer Andrew McNaughton, who had met *'South Park'*'s Matt Stone at a party. **2** Duke. **3** Jeremy Taggart plays drums for the Toronto-based band Our Lady Peace. **4** Literally "ghost driver" in German, the traditional term has more recently been adopted to refer to cars that drive down the wrong side of the autobahn. **5** Yiddish for a weak-willed or timid person. **6** Not being a guild member, Larry couldn't participate directly. **7** Used to synchronise the digital equipment.

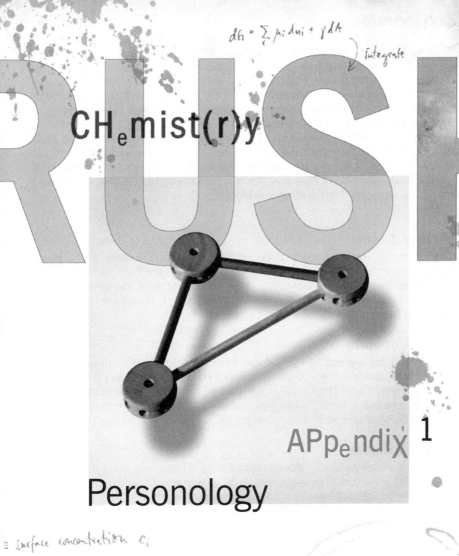

$$dh = \sum_i \mu_i \, d n_i + \gamma \, dA$$

integrate

RUSH

CH$_e$mist(r)y

APP$_e$ndiX 1

Personology

$\equiv$ surface concentration c_i

$$d\gamma = - \sum_i c_i \, d\mu_i \qquad (3)$$

a binary solution in contact with air

$$G_i = \sum_i \mu_i n_i + \gamma A \qquad (4)$$

complete differential

$$\sum_i \mu_i \, dn_i + \sum_i n_i \, d\mu_i + \gamma \, dA + A \, d\gamma \qquad (6)$$

Collaborators

There have been many people involved with Rush over the years, in a variety of capacities. Some have been involved only briefly, provided a service and left to continue their own diverse careers. Others have come and stayed, their close relationships with the band making them part and parcel of the Rush story. Some of the collaborators happen to be family members – this fact was taken as no more reason to exclude them, than to include them.

There's also been a number of people thanked on the albums, among them booking agents and DJ's that supported the band in their earlier years. These people are listed here so, if you've ever wondered what Easy Co was, or who was behind all those animations, read on. Note that this is limited to people who have collaborated with Rush, as opposed to the other way around.

Mostly.

Michael J. Ade

Michael Ade was assistant engineer on *'Hold Your Fire'*, working at The Manor studios with Peter Collins. Later, he worked with Craig Leon (and Nick Davies) on Jesus Jones' debut album, *'Liquidizer'*. More recently Michael has been known for more *avant-garde* production work. In 1999, for example, he mixed the *'_ISM'* project for Jansen Barbieri Karn.

Barry Ainsworth

As a recording engineer for Pye Records, Barry recorded 'Hush' for Deep Purple. He went on to specialise in live production, recording Hawkwind, Slade and The Kinks, the Royal Tournament and *'Oklahoma!'* in his diverse career. While working at the Mobile One mobile recording facility, Barry worked with Andy Rose on the technical set-up of the Rush Glasgow concert that was used on the live album *'Exit...Stage Left'*.

Scott Alexander

Scott Lawrence Alexander, together with Patrick Johnson and Olivia Ramirez, was responsible for the "urban development" on *'Hold Your Fire'*. "I was subcontracted by Hugh Syme and Glen Wexler to build the physical elements, designed by Hugh and then photographed by Glen, for the exterior and interior jackets of the album," he says. "While the overall layout of the interior cover was conceived by Hugh, I designed the buildings themselves. I have never followed the band, to me this was just an opportunity to build some nice models."

Scott co-wrote 'Spaced Invaders' with Patrick Johnson, in 1990.

Colleen Allen

Woodwind player for The Royal Jelly Orchestra, formed for the first Kumbaya festival, and led by Jazz DJ Jaymz Bee (of The Look People). In 1996 the RJO released a lounge lizard version of 'Closer to The Heart'. Colleen was responsible for the horns on Alex's solo project *'Victor'*.

Larry Allen

Larry was a friend of Neil's, brought on board during the *'A Farewell To Kings'* as drum technician. On *'Hemispheres'* he added more general help, continuing in this role through to *'Counterparts'*, where he was referred to as "Official Tour Shravis". He was later replaced by Lorne Wheaton.

Jorn Andersen

Jorn's first band was in the same circuit as Rush and was booked by the same agents: Music Factory and Skinny, where, so he says, a young Ray Danniels worked.

When drummer Greg Critchley left The Dexters, he was replaced by Jorn. "When Greg moved, they called me," says Jorn. "I said sure, I'd be happy!" Jorn knew the other Dexters from the studio circuit, for example Peter Cardinali and Jorn had played with Anne Murray for 6 years.

Joe Anthony

Joe Anthony was a DJ on KISS-FM in San Antonio. He was called "The Godfather" due to his willingness to promote new rock bands, and was a staunch supporter of Rik Emmett's band, Triumph. He did his bit for Rush, and was rewarded with a thank you on *'All The World's A Stage'*; station manager Lou Roney also got a mention.

Joe died of lung cancer on 12 September 1992, at the age of 52.

Adam Ayan

Born in 1975, Adam studied Music Performance and Sound Recording Technology at the University Of Massachusetts at Lowell, graduating in 1997. His instrument was the bass. "As a young bass player I can remember spending hours upon hour trying to learn Geddy's bass lines," he says.

A year after graduating, Adam started working under Bob Ludwig's wing, replacing Brian Lee as apprentice production engineer at Gateway Mastering in Portland, Maine. His first brush with Rush was to make some radio edits of tracks off the *'Different Stages'* live album in 1998. Adam used any gaps in Bob's schedule to build his own experience, eventually picking up some albums of his own. By August 2001 and now a fully fledged mastering engineer, Adam was given his own mastering suite. His first major task was to master *'Collection'*, a greatest hits album for Tracy Chapman; he also been picked up credits with Linkin Park, Martina McBride, Phish, Counting Crows and LeAnn Rimes. In 2003 he was given the *'Rush in Rio'* DVD and CD to master, with Alex in attendance. It was also his wedding in the same week. "Alex called me a few days before the wedding to thank me for my work, and also to wish me well and congratulate me in advance," recalls Adam. "That meant a lot to me."

Val Azzoli

When Val joined SRO in 1982 as General Manager, his role was largely in A&R. He acted as executive producer for *'A Show of Hands'*. When he left SRO, he moved to a similar post in Atlantic Records. In January 1996, he was promoted to co-CEO alongside Atlantic founder Ahmet Ertegun. Within 18 months Atlantic had become the number one record label in America. Val left Atlantic in 2004, a casualty of the reorganisation following Atlantic's acquisition.

Geoff Barton

Sounds journalist Geoff Barton's road to Rush was the same as many youngsters. "I used to devour Moorcock books and Tolkien," says Geoff. "Robert E Howard, *'Conan The Barbarian'*, all that sort of stuff was very wrapped up in that crazy, crazy era." It was the fantasy themes that Geoff picked up when he first heard Rush, as a journalist working for *Sounds* in the UK. "With *'Fly By Night'* and the glorious sword and sorcery visuals, it just was the right thing at the right time," he says.

When Rush caught Geoff's attention, most of the records were only available on import. "In those days even Kiss albums would come out in the UK six months after they came out in the States," says Geoff. "We knew what niche that we were trying to establish in the pages of *Sounds*; it was really important to buy all those import albums and try and persuade your boss to pass your expenses!" Indeed, at the time, Geoff was one of the few journalistic voices that backed bands such as Rush. "99.9% of writers were down the Roxy every night, watching Generation X and the Pistols. I was blithely unaware of punk even though it was all exploding around me. Luckily *Sounds* allowed me to do what I was most interested in."

Without too much forethought, Geoff struck a chord with the *Sounds* readers and established a following of Rush fans. "Like punk, the rock thing was another working class movement that appealed to *Sounds* readers, rather than the slightly cooler, slicker *NME*, *Melody Maker* approach," says Geoff. By the time the band came over to the UK there was a pre-packaged fan base ready to welcome them in – a fact which the band were delighted to discover. "I always remember Alex ushering me out and thanking me," says Geoff. "We did get a lot of bullshit from a lot of musicians and you didn't quite believe them, but Alex was just so genuine, he said, thanks for all the support you've given us in the UK, it's really made a lot of difference."

Geoff went on to coin the phase 'NWOBHM', or the New Wave Of British Heavy Metal, something Rush played their part in inspiring. As the movement grew, in 1981 he launched *Kerrang!* magazine out of *Sounds*, becoming editor of *Kerrang!* in 1984. A few years later he left the music world to write about sport and work on a car magazine, before returning to the fold in 2003 as editor-at-large for UK magazine *Classic Rock*. While his favourite Rush era is pre-*'Kings'*, he will always have a soft spot for the band. "There's not a lot of pretensions about them although ostensibly their music can be pretentious," says Geoff. "As individuals there's a degree of honesty, a tremendous amount of musicality. There's also the feeling that they're still an underground band over here, that people don't know about, even though they play Wembley!"

Let's Party

"My abiding vision of Geddy was the 100th issue anniversary party that we staged for *Kerrang!*, way, way back. It was absolute bedlam; we hired this run-down film studio in Islington and had all these wild British heavy metal bands playing. Geddy turned up with Peter Mensch, which I was amazed about – Geddy wasn't a renowned partygoer at all, and in the UK he liked to have a low profile. He was just standing there looking quite bemused about everything, clearly quite enjoying it in sort of a Geddy style way. It was nice to see him there!"

Geoff Barton

James 'Jimbo' Barton

When Peter Collins' trusted engineer Julian Mendelson found himself moving on to larger roles, he recommended Peter take a look at Jimbo Barton as his replacement. "They had a very similar sort of sound," says Peter. "He had a very hyped-up, hi-tech sound which was perfect for what I was doing in the early 80s." Jimbo assisted Peter on a number of projects, not least with Blancmange and Gary Moore, and when Peter was invited to produce *'Power Windows'* for Rush, Jimbo was his preferred choice for engineer.

Since working on *'Power Windows'* and *'Hold Your Fire'*, Jimbo has worked with a wide variety of artists including Enya, Alphaville, Kiss, Gary Moore (again), Marilyn

Manson, Metallica, Eric Clapton, Queensrÿche (with Peter Collins and Paul Northfield). Jimbo was awarded a Grammy for his efforts on Eric Clapton's *'Unplugged'*. "I've never seen it," he laughs. Jimbo then collaborated with Alex to produce and mix the Dolby 5.1 soundtrack to *'Rush In Rio'*. And indeed, what about Rush? "Astounding musicians, I wish I could say there was a weak one in the bunch," says Jimbo. "The way they do what they do, it's something to be watched. If you can adhere to it they really are great, great people, it goes against the grain."

Jules Belkin

With his brother Mike, in the early seventies Jules ran Belkin Productions, a firm of well-known rock promoters in Cleveland. He was paying attention to Donna's playlist, which led to Rush playing Cleveland for the first time.

Today, Belkin Productions is now part of Clear Channel Entertainment, and Jules is a vice president of CCE Cleveland. Jules Belkin is on the board of Directors of the Rock and Roll Hall of Fame, and was instrumental in getting it located in Cleveland.

Bill Bell

Bill played guitar and provided backing vocals for Tom Cochrane, who supported Rush on a number of tours as a member of Red Rider. More recently, Bill worked with Alex on *'Victor'*. He is married to Canadian singer-songwriter Tara MacLean (who has supported Tom Cochrane), and has co-written some of her songs.

Tom Berry

Tom joined SRO/Anthem before *'A Farewell To Kings'*, 1977, and was managing director until 1985. He subsequently set up his own label, Alert Records, which signed Kim Mitchell.

Liam Birt

Back in 1971, Liam joined Rush's entourage as an assistant to sole crew member at the time, Ian Grandy. By *'Fly By Night'* he was bass technician, and on the tour for the following album he became Alex's guitar tech, or "Stage Right Technician" in Rush-speak, a role which earned him several nicknames: "LeeBee" on *'All The World's A Stage'*, "Elfbjörn" on *'A Farewell To Kings'*, "Leaf" on *'Hemispheres'* and "Punjabi" on *'Permanent Waves'*.

As his role grew, Liam took on an assistant Tony Geranios, and in 1984 he moved over to road managing and handed over his stage right duties to Jim Johnson. Gradually, Liam took over more of the accounts, becoming executive producer on *'Roll The Bones'*, and in 1993 he replaced Nick Kotos as production manager, running the tour accounts, a task he has continued with until the present day. He also co-ordinated the *'Burning for Buddy'* big-band tribute to Buddy Rich, along with Buddy's daughter Cathy.

As Neil has commented, "Liam's professional relationship with Rush was difficult to define, for it was so wide ranging and crucial."

Ira Blacker

Self confessed, "a bit of a PT Barnum," Ira's brash, persuasive style earned him his reputation as someone who could get things done. Ira was in his late twenties when the opportunity to represent Rush came up at ATI, and it couldn't come fast enough.

"At the time, I was enraged by my two partners," he says. These were Jeff Franklin and Sol Saffian, who for different reasons were causing Ira to want to work on his own portfolio. Ira still lacked management experience – "I didn't have any business chops," he says – so he was looking for a band with whom he could cut his teeth.

Ira was already aware of Rush, having been invited by Ray Danniels to watch them play. However, it wasn't until the band started to get US airplay that Ira offered his services to provide US representation. Following "the discovery", Ira remembers things slightly differently from Donna Halper and Bob Roper: "I also arranged the Cleveland airplay, and fixed the performance at the Agora, with Hank Leconti," he says.

At the end of 1974, Ira fell out with Jeff Franklin for the final time. He left ATI and took the US representation for Rush with him. Things turned sour with Anthem however. "One minute, they're saying the best thing they ever did was bring in Ira Blacker," he says. "The next thing I get is a letter from an attorney saying, the contract's over, and please refund twenty thousand dollars. I won, and I would have won more if Jeff Franklin hadn't undermined my case." The process completed at the start of 1977.

Later, Ira was instrumental (sorry) in building Kraftwerk's position in the US. In 1976, he spent some time in the UK, notably running a TV show in Plymouth. He left New York and moved to California – there was nothing really to keep him there. "My mother died, I figured, what the hey," he says. Ira's work with Rush led him to being the manager and executive producer of Savoy Brown.

In 1990, Ira was representing "a bunch of people, including Kraftwerk and Ronnie Lane," when a recession hit the music industry. "I never really hit it after that," he says. The last straw for Ira was a DC-based band, "They had the track 'Put Down The Guns'," he recalls. Ira brought in Barry Richens to do a video, was shipping several hundred a week, a dozen radio stations were playing the record, but it all came to nothing. "We watched MCA blow it," he says.

Today, Ira works for a California-based printing company. Looking back, he has no regrets. "I'm resolved with what I did," he says. "I did it with flair and creativity."

Ken Blair

Ken worked first at Craighall Studios in Edinburgh before moving to Air Studios in Montserrat, where he worked as assistant engineer. As well as working with Rush on 'Hold Your Fire', he worked with Eric Clapton and Sting. In 1989 he returned to Britain and set up his own company, BMP Recording. Today, he is also a visiting lecturer in sound recording, for the University of Surrey's Tonmeister course.

Craig Blazier

In 1975, Craig was working for Kiss as monitor engineer. "Rush was the opening act and I mixed their monitors as well." He did this for a couple of tours, and that was the last he saw of them for 20 years. Having graduated to the role of production manager for the band Chicago, in 1996 he was invited to rejoin the Rush crew as production manager. Craig has continued in this role up to the present day, with partner Karin Blazier as Production Assistant.

Dan Braun

Previously production manager for Metallica and the Allmann Brothers, Dan got involved with Howard Ungerleider when working for Queensrÿche. He arrived on the Rush scene in 1994, taking the role of production stage manager from Nick Kotos.

Dan continued in the role until 1997, when Craig Blazier took his place.

In 1997, Dan was nominated to be 'Road Warrior of The Year' in the Pollstar concert industry awards. More recently, he was executive producer of a Shania Twain DVD, along with Cliff Burnstein.

Rick Britton

Rick was born in 1957, and was indoctrinated from an early age in music. "My mother used to sing and play country guitar," says Rick. "I started playing violin, viola and trumpet, then I picked up the saxophone..." For a while it seemed his destiny was to be a musician, but he was fated never to do any one thing for long. "I got sick of that, and went back to school to do a carpentry apprenticeship," he says. His life as a carpenter met an abrupt end following a back injury, at which point he decided to go back to school again. He studied Music and Electronics for two years, after which he went to work for a number of audio electronics companies, "If you couldn't find it, I'd build it," he explains. "This was pre-MIDI: DMX had just come out."

After a few years of this, Rick was getting itchy feet again. "I was bored and on the bench," he says. "Robert Palmer was in town, and he happened to be looking for a guitar tech." Rick hit the road and has never looked back – he's worked for UB40, the Scorpions (alongside bass tech Russ Ryan) and Barenaked Ladies to name a few, covering all kinds of instruments. He spent over six years as guitar tech for Toto's Tony Spinner and Steve Lukather, before he was approached to join Rush on the 'Vapor Trails' tour.

One of the first things Rick did was redesign Alex's guitar setup. "He re-wired my whole rig," said Alex. "He's a bit of a genius and really good with that sort of thing." Agrees Howard Ungerleider, "He's a brilliant tech, more than people know."

Whatever's next Rick doesn't know but he doesn't think he'll stop adding to his range of skills. "If I could afford it, I'd go back to school for the rest of my life," he laughs.

Doug Brown

Based near Detroit, Michigan, Doug was largely responsible for the launch of Bob Seger's career, having met him in 1964 when he played in Doug Brown and the Omens, then in a band called Southwind. In the seventies, Doug was in Fast Fontaine before becoming a booking agent, and working for Music Shoppe International with Ray Danniels. He is mentioned on 'All The World's A Stage' as the band's responsible agent for Canada.

Terry Brown

Terry couldn't have asked for a better musical education, working in "four of the top independent studios in London" during the height of the UK pop revolution of the sixties. He started at Olympic Studios, where he learned the ropes before tackling 'Substitute' for The Who in his first engineering role, under the careful eye of Pete Townsend. From there he's worked with Procul Harum, Manfred Mann, Joe Cocker, Traffic, The Bonzo Dog Doo Dah Band... you name it, he's worked with them all.

It was a twist of fate that brought Terry to Toronto. At the time he was working at Morgan Studios, "on Willesden High Road, Monty Babson and Barry Morgan, they were very successful," he recalls. A call out of the blue led to his involvement in a series of commercials for Labatts beer, with organist and arranger Doug Riley, who had come over from Canada for the project. Problems with unions ensued – "Labatts were on strike, and the musicians' union were threatening to go out in sympathy because they were not Canadian musicians who played on these commercials, so they were going to have to rerecord it all," he explains. "So I jokingly offered to come over, and he seriously accepted!" Three days later, he was on a plane to Toronto.

It didn't take long for Terry to put down his roots, much to his surprise. "It was so exciting, the energy here was just phenomenal," he explains. "I ended up recording an album with a band called Motherlode, we had a Top 10 hit with 'When I Die', so that kind of cemented it for me." With Doug Riley, Terry saw the opportunity to set up a studio. "The studios over here, when I came over to do the recording, were just that much farther behind the London studios. I think we were eight-track at Morgan, and here it was still four-track," says Terry, who opened the doors of the Toronto Sound Studios in November 1969. "By the time we'd got it finished it was sixteen-track, and then, within a year of starting, we then moved up to twenty-four tracks, so there was this huge jump in the track count. You could really take on a multi-track project, it changed everything."

In the four years that followed, Terry made his name as an engineer and producer of repute. He knew Vic Wilson "from the biz," and when Vic's new band was having troubles with completing their first record, Terry got the call that started his long and highly productive relationship with Rush, lasting until *'Signals'* in 1982. Where the "Broon" nickname came from, Terry does not know. "I'm not really sure who was the king of the nicknames, I think it was Geddy but they were all into it!" he laughs. "Big Bill Broonsie was one that Neil used to sort of throw at me a few times, he was an old blues player, from the Bayou I think, I don't know what the connection was!" Terry collaborated with a number of other bands, including Max Webster and Klaatu, the project of one of his assistant engineers John Woloschuk. Klaatu's second album *'Hope'* earned Terry a Juno award for 'Best Engineer'!

When Terry's time with Rush came to a halt, there were plenty of takers for his skills. In 1986 he produced the first album for Blue Rodeo, *'Outskirts'*. It was a huge success in Canada and spawned the hit single, 'Try'. The following year he worked with Cutting Crew, recording '(I Just) Died In Your Arms' which was a hit all over the world, taking the US *Billboard* Number 1 slot. Later he mixed albums for Fates Warning, Moist, the Killjoys and Matthew Good, and each time, he drew on his experiences with Rush. "There are situations where I work with bands where I have been the producer and I'm still pulling in the input from the band, because I'd always felt that was important, but then that's probably a throwback to those days with the boys anyway." Terry has kept his hand in with the more progressive end of the scale. He worked on Dream Theater's 1999 album *'Scenes From A Memory'*, and in 2004 he produced on the self-titled debut album for Tiles. He's also kept friends with Nick Van Eede of Cutting Crew, co-producing his new project *'Grinning Souls'*.

Jim Burgess

Jim Burgess runs Saved By Technology, a keyboard and synthesizer specialist based in Toronto. He became involved in the period leading up to *'A Farewell To Kings'*, when synthesizers were difficult to operate and even harder to interface!

Since this time and right up to the present, Jim has been helping Geddy with his keyboard rig, helping with configuration and some programming, notably on *'Grace Under Pressure'*, where he assisted Paul Northfield. He also added some synthesiser parts to *'Power Windows'*.

Cliff Burnstein

In 1973 and at the age of 25, the music industry was beckoning for college boy Cliff Burnstein. "The fellowship money was running out," he says. "I looked at lots of different record labels and then I got an interview with Mercury and then I got a job. I kind of sussed it was the only thing I really loved." Just months later, the post of "national head of album promotion" came up, an opportunity Cliff thought was too good to miss. He was in the right place at the right time: young, but so was the label. "I just basically raised by hand and said let me do it," says Cliff.

Album promotion meant dealing with FM radio, as opposed to promotion of Top-40 music to AM. One of Cliff's first tasks was to represent Mercury at a New York Dolls concert in Cleveland. Cliff was instrumental in Mercury's signing of Rush, and a year or so later he took over the band's A&R responsibilities. "At the beginning I was dealing only with Vic Wilson, I did not know about Ray Danniels," he says. "To me Vic was the front guy and Ray was very much behind the scenes." Cliff worked tirelessly for a number of bands, including Rush and also the New York Dolls. "They were kind of a critics band that didn't actually sell very many copies," says Cliff. "I tried the best I could to get them played on the radio, and that wasn't easy."

Five years after Rush, the same approach was adopted for The Scorpions in 1979. "There was another whirlwind thing," he says. "I went to Germany one night, saw the concert, talked to the guys and signed them up immediately. People laughed, they said, I understand you just signed a German rock group, you know these guys don't speak English very well. I didn't care, I thought they were great." As time passed, Cliff found he was increasingly defending the needs of his artists, sometimes against the wishes of the label. "One of my functions much of the time was to tell people not to try to meddle in what the bands were doing," says Cliff. "I thought psychologically or emotionally I would feel better just having a clear cut role being an advocate of the artist."

It wasn't just that – he saw there was more to the economics of the music business than releasing albums and plugging songs. "When Rush played the Palladium in New York in 1979, so many people bought t-shirts. Kiss had been the pioneer of the selling of merchandise, but I saw Rush do it, in front of my eyes," he says. "I can tell you that there were many bands in the 80s that we totally financed off of merchandise sales."

Cliff was friendly with ex-radio programmer Peter Mensch, "a great schmoozer," according to Cliff, and who was now AC/DC's manager. Peter worked for David Krebs, who had such bands as Aerosmith, Ted Nugent and The New York Dolls on his roster. When Cliff left Mercury in January 1980, shortly before Rush toured *'Permanent Waves'*, he joined David Krebs' agency alongside Peter. Together, the pair built up an admirable selection of hard rock bands, adding the Scorpions, Def Leppard and the Michael Schenker Group to their portfolio. Two years later, when Cliff and Peter parted ways with David, the only band willing to come with them was Def Leppard – and that was before the band had made it big. Cliff decided it was worth the risk. "I was willing to make less money in order for the chance to make it on a really big scale," says Cliff. The launch of Def Leppard's *'Pyromania'* in January 1983 was exactly the boost the pair had been looking for. "That really got us up on our feet," he says.

Cliff and Peter's company, Q-Prime, started out with the aim of focusing on long-term success rather than short-term gain. When they later took on Metallica, Cliff approached the situation the same way as he had with Rush. "If you believe in them and think that they have the real ability, then you go with it," says Cliff. "The groundswell built up on Metallica just like it built with Rush and so that felt very comfortable to me, because I knew that there was ultimately a pot of gold at the end of the rainbow." The strategy is one which Cliff and Peter continue to follow, and have built up an impressive roster of clients in the process – not least Muse, Q-Prime's most recent signing for North America. "I feel about Muse the way I felt about Rush," says

Cliff. "People say, Oh man, I am never going to play that Matthew Bellamy on my station, I don't like his voice. I go fine, you are going to wind up playing him sooner or later. I don't know how it will develop exactly, but they are great artists, they are not just about this year or next year or last year, they are going to be around for ages."

Peter Cardinali

A member of The Dexters with Lou Pomanti, Peter also played bass on Alex's solo project *'Victor'*.

Eraldo Carugati

Born in 1921 in Italy, Eraldo Carugati emigrated to the United States after the Second World War, where he went to University on New Mexico. As well as painting the cover for *'Fly By Night'*, Eraldo was later commissioned to produce a number of magazine illustrations for magazines such as *Oui* and *Playboy*. The most famous – and controversial – showed President Nixon as a Russian puppet. In 1978, he painted portraits of each member of Kiss, for their solo covers.

Daniel Catullo

Daniel E Catullo III went into the biz straight after high school. "I became a lighting guy," he says. Before long he was working with artists such as BB King and Extreme. He graduated to tour manager and continued to work the circuit for five years before deciding enough was enough.

Moving to California, Dan set up Ventura, a theatre partnership, with Michael Gross. Two years later, he felt it was time to move on again. He tried his hand in the feature film business, but the call of the road had once again become too great. Paul Geary, one-time band member of Extreme, was now managing Godsmack and agreed for Dan to film a few shows of the tour. And thus, Dan's live video production company, Coming Home Studios, was formed.

"We fund our own shows and distribute our own DVDs, we only do music DVDs," explains Dan, who has worked for Marilyn Manson and Dave Matthews. ("That's the biggest thing I've done, in Central Park this last fall.") It was Jimbo Barton, who Dan had met while working with Marilyn Manson, who helped get the gig to work with Rush by introducing the two sides. "Dan brought to my attention the fact they'd pitched and couldn't get a look in," says Jimbo. "Dan said, if you can get me the meeting, then let's go make the thing. So, I got the meeting."

It was then that Dan found out how little interest there had been from the major labels to produce a Rush live DVD. "This band has consistently sold out venues for 30 years," says Dan, explaining his confidence that a live DVD would do well. He was pleased to get the gig – "we very seldom get to do a stadium," he says. Nobody could have predicted the victory snatched from the jaws of defeat that became *'Rush in Rio'*, which he co-produced with Larry Jordan and Lionel Pasamonte. Says Dan, "Hopefully some day we'll release some extra footage – we've got a couple of hundred hours there!"

Since Rush, Coming Home Studios has not been idle with productions from Matchbox 20, Duran Duran, Nickleback and a repeat performance of Godsmack. "Rush is the most professional band I've ever worked with," says Dan.

Pegi Cecconi

Pegi is the long-time assistant manager at SRO/Anthem. Originally from South Porcupine, her collaborations with manager Ray Danniels go back to way before Rush.

Guy Charbonneau

French-Canadian Guy Charbonneau was born and bred in Montréal, where one of his hobbies was customizing vehicles. "I used to build… I like cars, and I like music. I used to build hi-fi's when I was 12 years old." His first professional foray into music was to set up a Hi-Fi equipment shop, in 1969. "My old hi-fi store still exists, on La Jeunesse street." In 1973, one of his customers – a local radio station called CFGL – was getting into live broadcasting. "I was thinking I could have a live tape to play at the store." So he went along and helped out in the live sessions, the first being classical guitar player André Benichou. The recording turned out better than what the station had recorded before: Guy became an active participant in the live recordings and two years later he sold his retail business and designed and built his first mobile recording truck. "There were so many competitive studios already, I thought a quality mobile facility would be the way for me to get into the business." Of course, this had to be built into the truck, from scratch.

Guy first worked with Terry Brown on a jazz recording of Moe Koffman, *'Live At George's'*, in 1975. It was the first of many projects with Terry, including Klaatu (with John Woloschuk), Rush and BB Gabor. "Working with Terry is like working with a friend," says Guy. "We almost did a project together 10 years ago, but the budget was not there. I offered for Terry to stay at my house! Anything to try to do the project with him. He is the nicest guy."

By 1977, Guy had established himself an enviable reputation, as well as a recording truck to die for. He impressed producer Phil Ramone enough to land a job recording Paul Simon's album *'One Trick Pony'*. In 1980 he moved to New York and two years later, he set himself up in California with a rehearsal studio, which could be plugged into his truck to provide a complete recording facility.

In 1986, Guy was asked to record the Canadian leg of what would become *'Exit Stage Left'*, together with Terry Brown. In 1988, Guy was brought back to engineer for *'A Show of Hands'*. Since then, Guy's mobile recording business has continued to go from strength to strength. As well as recording some of the biggest names in the industry (not least Gwen Stefani and No Doubt, The Pretenders, Aerosmith, the Bee Gees, Cher, Deep Purple, Eric Clapton, The Eagles and Fleetwood Mac), he has been involved in projects as diverse as the *'The Doors'* movie, *'Spy Kids II'* and *'About Schmidt'*.

Today, Guy is still at it – recording artists and customising his truck, just like he has always done. Like his truck, the clients get a little bigger than they used to be, that's all. "With each project that I do, no matter what it is, I want my clients

No Tricks

"While working at Carnegie Hall in New York for CBC, I called my friend Bruno Hochstrasser at Studer and said, 'Where does Phil Ramone work?' And he said, 'A&R Studio.' I called them under the guise of visiting their studio and said, 'I'm down from Montreal, doing a recording for CBC at Carnegie Hall, I'd like to see your studio.' I drove Le Mobile to their front door. They asked if they could see what I had inside. They walked in, saw a Neve console like theirs, but they saw a new Studer A800 that they didn't have. I had the first Studer A800 24-track recorder in North America. I never saw their studio.

"A month later, I got a call from Phil, and I came and recorded *'One Trick Pony'*."

Guy Charbonneau

happy with the best sound possible," says Guy. The blend of today's new technology with the knowledge acquired over the years would enable me to go further than ever before. I always want to do better every time, that's all it is. Going back to work with Rush would be like seeing old friends, I would love to record them again."

Sam Charters

Sam Charters started as a journalist, and worked up to editor of Canadian rock mag *Stage Life*. While he was recovering from a car accident, he was approached by Howard Ungerleider to help out on tour. "Howie asked if I'd like a gig with the band, although at the time they weren't too clear on what it would be," he recalled in a 1979 interview. The undefinable role that he undertook on the *'Permanent Waves'* tour became known as "Shreve" (Screvato), in practice this meant doing whatever needed to be done.

'A Show of Hands' was dedicated to his memory.

Bruce Cole

"I grew up in the flower child era – we were taught as teenagers that, you can be whatever you want to be, and there is no obstacle you cannot overcome," says Bruce Cole, who was a student at the University of Buffalo in 1970, "the year after the riots." After graduation and in the absence of a job, Bruce returned to Toronto and started taking pictures for an underground newspaper. "I decided I enjoyed it, so I offered my services to the record companies for PR photography," he says. "Back then, you took four guys, you throw them together, you gave them a name and you took a picture and all of a sudden you've got a band to market."

Before long, Bruce's reputation was growing and he landed a couple of good contracts, including for Gordon Lightfoot, Bachman Turner Overdrive and Mendelson Joe. "A lot of the pictures I took for the record companies went to *Billboard*, *RPM* or *Record Week* – the rags that covered the music industry in Canada." In 1972 he set up his first company, BIC Photography. "BIC – the initials of my name," he says. "It was just myself and a full-time assistant darkroom technician." It was BIC that got the call from SRO, for some publicity shots that would eventually make it to the cover of *'Rush'* as well as a number of live sessions, at gigs and in the studio. "I was just a young photographer, I was learning my craft just as much as they were learning their music craft," he says. "We had a good time." It didn't last however – at quite a young age, he discovered the vagaries of the music business. "When Canadian bands signed with US companies, the A&R guys would say, oh, you gotta use my photographer, you gotta use my album designer," he says. "When Rush signed with Mercury I was kicked out the door!" Sometimes an artist would fight Bruce's corner however, such as Randy Bachman from BTO. "Randy said, you know what, we've got a photographer in Toronto. We'll let you pick whatever image you want for the front of the cover, as long as I get to pick the images for the back of the cover. So they hired a photographer from California to shoot the front cover, and Randy called me up and

Picture Perfect

"When Anne Murray moved to Toronto, I did a lot of photography for her. When she got interviewed by *Macleans* magazine she refused to allow their photographer to take pictures of her, and demanded that I be the photographer, otherwise they couldn't run her on the front cover. The reason was that she didn't trust anybody to pick the right picture – by hiring me, we sat down together to decide which was the best image. She couldn't guarantee the picture they would pick would be the one she liked, so she only sent them one!"

Bruce Cole

I did all their liner note photographs."

In October 1977 BIC changed its name to Plum Studios, and Bruce's photography business was going well. Despite being the official photographer for the Juno awards however, by the early eighties he could see the writing was on the wall. "I remember I walked into the office of the new Ontario promo guy for Polygram, and he said, aren't you kind of too old to be doing this? I just told him the reason I had grey hair was because rock 'n' roll made it that way! He couldn't have been a day over 19..." It was time to think of something else to do, and he turned his hand to conferences and trade shows. "I learned the hard way, made a lot of mistakes and spent a lot of money the wrong way," he says. "But I'm a firm believer – as long as you only make a mistake once and you learned from it, and as long as you make more right decisions than wrong decisions, then you're going to get ahead!"

Bill Collins

Bill Collins was "One of the original riggers in the business," says his son Brian. His job was to design and configure the lighting trusses, "the rigger's in charge of everything above peoples heads, all 45 thousand pounds of it." Known for his lack of fear, Bill worked with Rush from the *'Permanent Waves'* tour through to *'Test for Echo'*.

Brian Collins

Whatever destiny held for Brian, it became clear early. "I've been out on tour since I was seven," he says, describing how he would travel with his father Bill Collins to gigs. As he grew up, he tried a few other things before joining his dad on the circuit. "I needed a job, he said, come work with me," says Brian. "We were the first father and son to be riggers in the business."

Brian has worked for a variety of artists, not least he worked on the *'Lord of The Dance'* for seven months, and more recently he accompanied Green Day on their world tour. Always, however, he likes to come back to Rush. "The band's so great," says Brian. "I've known them all my life, and they've always treated me with respect."

As for the travel, "It's interesting living on a bus," says Brian. "Ten people, I knew none of them, their traits and idiosyncrasies..." Of course it is total coincidence that Brian wants to write "a screenplay about a serial killer who tours with a band." Probably.

Peter Collins

Despite appearing an odd choice to produce a rock album, "pop producer" Peter Collins was very comfortable in that genre. "My background was in the actual British folk revival of the sixties and seventies," he says. "I was a singer song writer and that's where my taste lay." By the mid-seventies, however, he found he was getting more enjoyment out of bringing the best out of others, than recording for himself.

In 1979 Peter had his first hit as a producer. He worked with a number of artists including Tracey Ullman, Musical Youth and Nik Kershaw, on which he was joined by a very junior apprentice engineer, Dave Meegan. "The main thing I tried to learn from Peter was his interaction with people, and getting the best out of artists, which is 50% of production anyway," says Dave. "Everybody that

Gonna Go Far

"I had been smoking cigars since I was about 20. When I was a fledgling producer, all the major producers came in with Cuban cigars, and I made the association with successful producer and Cuban cigars very early on."

Peter Collins

worked for him, worked absolutely to the best – artists, tape ops, engineers, everyone." Neil Peart explained the other fifty percent in an interview. "Peter holds himself aloof from the technique and technology, and rightly considers these things to be the domain of the musicians and the engineer," explained Neil. "His job is to keep the project moving, and to ensure that craft is not allowed to interfere with art – the song. That's his secret, if he has one." When circumstances dictated he was no longer able to work with his preferred engineer Julian Mendelson, Peter started working with Jimbo Barton. The first collaboration was Gary Moore, following which the pair went to work with – or on – Rush. Peter did more than produce *'Power Windows'* and *'Hold Your Fire'* – he restored the band's faith in their own abilities. He felt unable to work on what became *'Presto'* – this privilege fell to Rupert Hine. Peter did, however, come back on board for *'Counterparts'* and *'Test For Echo'*.

In between his first two Rush productions, Peter worked on *'Enough Is Enough'* with Billy Squier. The project was less than successful – "It went really, really, very badly," says Peter. "My confidence was really undermined at that point. God bless Rush, they called me back to work on *'Hold Your Fire'*. It was an incredible experience and after making that record I felt back in the game again."

Today Peter is based in Nashville. Over the years he has worked with Queensrÿche and Alice Cooper, The Indigo Girls, Nanci Griffith, Leann Rimes and Elton John. His hobbies include flying model aeroplanes.

Fin Costello

Brought up in Cork and trained as a sail maker in London's docks, Fin Costello started in photography in 1968, when he was invited by a friend to come and snap some shots at a gig. He tried covering different kinds of camera work, including sport, before settling back with bands in 1971.

Gradually, better and better opportunities came his way. "My 'break' was the Stones' *'Exile On Main St'* tour," he says. Another of his pictures was also used for the cover of *'Made In Japan'* by Deep Purple, following which he was invited to work with other big names such as Kiss and Aerosmith. Before long it was Rush's turn. "I met Rush in the USA in 1975 when they were supporting Foghat," he explains. "I shot their show and had the pics published in *Circus*." Based on that experience, Geddy asked Fin to work with the band some more. Fin contributed the liner photos for *'A Farewell To Kings'*, and the inner sleeve and poster photography for *'Hemispheres'*. Later, he took the photos of the girl and the man waving for the cover of *'Permanent Waves'*, at Deborah Samuel's studio in Toronto and Morin Heights respectively. His final contribution was to *'Moving Pictures'*, though his images have been used frequently since then, for example on the *'Different Stages'* live album.

There are few rock bands that Fin has not taken pictures for, and his name will always be associated with some of the best.

Dalbello

Lisa Dal Bello was born in 1958. She toured for the first time when she was 13, and by her late teens she had already achieved pop star status in her native Canada. In 1984 she recreated herself as Dalbello, working with former David Bowie guitarist Mick Ronson. Shortly after she moved to England, and continued working with Mick until he died of cancer in April 1993.

Returning to Toronto, Dalbello has been involved in a variety of collaborations, not least singing the vocals on the song 'Start Today' on Alex's 1996 album, *'Victor'*.

Ray Danniels

Ray may well be the youngest person ever to go into band promotion and management. He dropped out from school and worked for other promoters, before forming his own agency, Music Shoppe International. This company merged with Vic Wilson's own agency to become SRO, whose most successful act became, and has remained, Rush. "He tried to expand the stable a couple of times," says old contemporary Don Shafer; other bands in the past have included Mendelson Joe and Kim Mitchell's Max Webster, but time and priority always came back to the trio. "I attribute almost all popstars' successes to the manager (whom I refer to as 'pimp' on occasion), because without a pimp no-one saw Van Gogh, nor heard Elvis north of the Mason-Dixon line," says M. Joe. "Selling is everything and, once in a while, the product sold has real sustaining value! Ray Danniels deserves huge credit. He has the gift, anything that he decides he's going to give it 110% will succeed, it won't matter who it is."

In the nineties, Ray also managed Van Halen through until November 1997, and since then, Rush has given him plenty to be getting on with. "He hasn't lost his stride," says Don Shafer. "He's a dedicated, passionate manager."

Ben Darlow

Ben was son of Denys Darlow, professor of music at the Royal College of Music in London. He was assistant engineer at Nomis Studios, London, where he was involved in the mixing of *'Roll The Bones'*. Ben has also assisted Erasure, Paul Weller and more recently Mike Oldfield, creating the mix for *'Tubular Bells 2003'* at Roughwood Studios.

Robert Di Gioia

Robert was assistant engineer to Peter Henderson on *'Grace Under Pressure'*, along with Frank Opolko. He has also worked with Kim Mitchell, and more recently, he was producer for Jerrycan.

Harry Dilman

Harry was a projectionist, working with the band from earlier times up to *'Power Windows'*. One of the more effusive members of the crew, Harry was noted (along with Skip Gildersleeve) for bar-hopping, earning a "keep the change" credit on *'Hemispheres'*.

Mike Donegani

Mike was tape operator and engineer at Trident Studios, where he assisted on *'Hemispheres'*. In 1978 Mike worked with Reno Ruocco on *'Masques'* by Brand X, which was engineered by Stephen Tayler. Mike later moved to Vancouver, where he worked with Vince R. Ditrich on *'Supertonic'*, released in 2002.

Pye Dubois

Pye was a "member" of Canadian band Max Webster, though he never played or sang a note. Rather, his role was inspirational and lyrical input. His first collaboration with Rush was to provide the words to 'Tom Sawyer', ostensibly as a thank-you for the band's participation on Max Webster's *'Battlescar'*. Following Kim's departure from the band, Pye wrote the lyrics for Kim's first four solo albums.

Pye later wrote 'Between Sun and Moon' and contributed to the songs *'Force 10'* and

'Test For Echo'. Neil valued his sometimes unorthodox ideas, which counterbalanced Neil's own sense of structure. "I always like working with him because it takes the boat to a place that we wouldn't get on at home," said Neil. "A lot of imagery comes from him and I try to impose order on it. My sense of structure, I guess, around his kind of street poetry." The elusive Pye Dubois is also a registered psychologist. He is "listed as missing in action." To support the collaborations, he co-owns Pysart Music Publishing with Neil.

Anne Dudley

Born in Kent, England in 1956, Anne Dudley qualified as a classical music performer with a master's degree from King's College, and Performer's Diploma from the Royal College of Music. Despite this background, Anne refused to be pigeonholed as a classical performer. She moved into the pop world, working as a session musician and getting involved professionally with Trevor Horn, working with both ABC and Frankie Goes To Hollywood.

Anne has worked with artists across the board, from Rod Stewart and Elton John, to Pulp and the Spice Girls. She was also a founding member of The Art Of Noise, and has been involved in a number of more esoteric projects such as the North-African-influenced *'Songs from A Victorious City'*, co-written with Jaz Coleman.

Between Us

Pye read the original poem for 'Between Sun and Moon' at the second Kumbaya festival, on 4 September 1994.

There is a lake between sun and moon
Not too many know about
Some go there for their high noon
Some go there for their midnight moon
It is a moment between silence and shout
Maybe you, might as well me
Why the sun, why the sun

Say yes, say yes, ahh say yes to self-esteem

We want to escape because we don't want to fall in
The signs are clear and so is the fear
We do not trust the firmness of the ground

Then say yes, say yes, ahh say yes to self-esteem

There is a fine place between actor and audience
This is the fine line
The fine line of living
This moment experienced
This fine deliverance
Do what you want to do in no ordinary way
Say what you need to say in no ordinary way
And sing what must be sung in no ordinary way

Say yes, ahh please, please say yes to self esteem

Some go there for their high noon
Some go there of their midnight moon

It is the moment between silent and shout
This is a fine place
Faces face to face
These bonfire eyes
In the lake of the sky
It is our light to land and leave
Never so dark to unravel the weave
Never give up and never say die

Do what you need to do in no ordinary way
Say what you need to say in no ordinary way
And sing what must be sung in no ordinary way

With Rush, "wonderful arranger" Anne (according to Geddy) arranged and conducted strings on *'Power Windows'*, at Abbey Road Studios in London. Meanwhile, bigger arrangements started to catch Anne's eye, including working with Michael Flatley on the music to *'Lord of The Dance'*. Anne composed film scores including *'Buster'*, *'The Crying Game'* and *'American History X'*, and it was for her 1997 score to *'The Full Monty'* that she was awarded an Oscar.

More recently Anne scored the music for *'Monkeybone'* and is currently working on *'Tristan and Isolde'* with director Kevin Reynolds.

Edwin

Toronto-born Edwin formed I Mother Earth in 1990 with jamming friend Jagori Tanna. Alex spotted Edwin on IME's *'Dig'* tour (in support of Rush's *'Counterparts'* tour) and invited him to participate on his solo production.

Following *'Victor'* and the *'Scenery and Fish'* album, Edwin decided to leave I Mother Earth. In 1999, he released the solo album *'Another Spin Around The Sun'*. Today, he has his own band, Edwin and The Pressure.

Jon Erickson

Sound engineer Jon Erickson worked with the band on the *'Signals'* and *'Power Windows'* tours before moving back into the studio. He co-produced the 'Big Money EP' single in 1988, then at Elora Sound, he was pre-production engineer for *'Grace Under Pressure'* and *'Hold Your Fire'*. He did go back on the road for this, latter tour, before being replaced by Robert Scovill.

As well as working with Rush he worked on two albums for Pat Travers, *'Whiskey Blues'* and *'Born Under a Bad Sign'*. He also produced Bart Davenport's second album. Later, Jon engineered the 'Pieces of Eight' drum piece for Neil.

Charlie Fach

Charles E Fach Jr headed Mercury subsidiary Smash Records in 1961, signing James Brown in 1963, as well as Roger Miller who penned 'King of The Road'. He is credited with discovering Jerry Lee Lewis when he was VP of A&R for Mercury, and he was instrumental in bringing BTO's classic song 'You Ain't Seen Nothing Yet' to the masses.

Charlie was head of Mercury Records at the time Rush was signed. He was thanked on the re-issued first album. He later signed Kool and The Gang, Shania Twain and Rod Stewart, before going on to set up the Compleat record label.

Richard Fegley

As well as the photography on *'Fly By Night'*, Richard Fegley worked as a highly successful glamour photographer for *Playboy* from 1971 to 1994. He died 15 September 2001, aged 64.

Scott K Fish

"My interest in drums started very early – about age 5 – and continues to this day," explains Scott K Fish, former managing editor of *Modern Drummer* magazine. Scott was a professional drummer and drum teacher for about seven years while living in Iowa, New York, and Connecticut – before and after his association with *Modern Drummer*.

Scott first started freelance writing for *Modern Drummer* in 1976. In 1980 he was hired as managing editor, co-ordinating MD's freelance writers and photographers. At *Modern Drummer* Scott started working with columnist Neil Peart. "I don't remember the exact moment Neil and *Modern Drummer* developed a column-writing arrangement," says Scott, "but I know Neil loved writing and he was a very good writer."

Scott left *Modern Drummer* in October 1983 to become Northeast District sales manager for the Gretsch company. Between 1976 and 1980, Scott had written almost 50-percent of *Modern Drummer*'s feature pieces.

Today, Scott remains active in studying music history and also in Maine politics. Scott owns and edits Maine's premier political website – As Maine Goes – online since 1998.

Eugene Fisher

Eugene is a widely published and award-winning photographer best known for his landscape photography, and his images of traditional and aboriginal peoples. Some of his pictures of the Arctic north of the American continent were used on *'Test For Echo'*. In January 2000 he had an exhibition of the same, entitled "Nunavut – Jewel of the Arctic."

Kevin Flewitt

Kevin became involved with the band in the early eighties, acting as "Shreve and Factotum" on the *'Moving Pictures'* tour. He continued in this role through to *'Hold Your Fire'*. Today, Kevin plays bass guitar, runs his own computer business and lives in downtown Toronto.

Jeff Franklin

Following Action Talent, which managed two big name artists: Brooklyn Bridge and Stevie Wonder, Jeff formed American Talent International in 1970 with Wally Meyrowitz and Sol Saffian, and acted as Rush's agent with Ira Blacker in the early days. Howard Ungerleider also worked at ATI as an office junior. Jeff sold ATI in February 1985 and moved into the film industry as a screenwriter and director, later becoming executive producer for *'Casper'* and *'Stuart Little'*.

Anthony Frederick

Photographer Anthony Joseph Frederick worked with the band on *'Test For Echo'*, and some of his pictures were also used on *'Different Stages'*.

In 2004, Anthony Frederick was charged with the murder of model and porn actress Taylor Summers (real name Natel King), who he had met via the Internet. He pleaded guilty to one count of third degree murder, on 28 February 2005.

John Friesen

John is a classical cellist, based in Vancouver and working out of Mushroom Studios. He worked with K. D. Lang (and therefore Ben Mink) on a number of her albums. The Ben Mink connection led to John's involvement on *'My Favorite Headache'*, where he played cello on 'Working at Perfekt'.

Tony Geranios

"Music was the first thing that affected my senses in a positive way," says New Yorker Tony Geranios, who used to go to sleep listening to his older brother's doo-wop collection. In his teens Tony started learning to play instruments, but he graduated towards doing the sound for local bands. "It was easier to do that, than to get round some of the egos," he says. Night after night for several years he learned on the job, ploughing the local circuit. Meanwhile, his brother had also become a technician, but at a more professional level. It was through his brother's gig with Blue Öyster Cult that Tony got to work on bigger stages, when the opportunity came up to be a guitar and keyboard tech.

Before long, Tony realised there was a bitter pill in his chalice. The guy he replaced had been well liked by band and crew alike, and Tony was never quite allowed to fill his shoes. Not only this, but the spirit of camaraderie was sadly lacking. "It was very competitive among the crew," says Tony. "The circumstances of me coming in did not help my cause, I found myself being taken advantage of." The band didn't help matters – "They're the ones who set the tempo."

It was through Blue Öyster Cult that Tony first met Rush, and it didn't take him long to realise that things were very different in the Rush camp. "They opened several times in '75 and '76, I got to know them pretty well," he says; before long, they were talking about how he could join them. "They had to make a position for me," he says. Indeed, they needed his help. "The backline was expanding, they had Taurus pedals and keyboards and no one wanted to deal with them."

Tony joined the crew on the *'A Farewell To Kings'* tour, as assistant to technician Liam Birt, with whom he was said to have a passing resemblance. "We both had long black hair and moustaches, we were both working stage right, we were both young, beautiful and thin!" As keyboards became more and more part of the act, for the *'Hold Your Fire'* tour Tony and Liam (who moved on to stage managing) handed guitar duties over to Jimmy Johnson. "By that time, my guitar tech duties pretty much came to an end," says Tony. "The keyboards were so complex and bigger than anything else, they took up all my time."

By now an engineer of standing, Tony was invited back to tour with Blue Öyster Cult on more even (and friendly) terms. In 1988, he contributed growling vocals, "this 'seven, seven, seven, seven' thing," to the album *'Imaginos'* and in 2001 he worked on two songs for a tribute to Blue Öyster Cult stalwart Helen Wheels, who had died prematurely the year before.

Skip Gildersleeve

Russell "Skip" Gildersleeve is a crew veteran of many bands. He was brought in for the *'Caress of Steel'* tour to replace Jimmy Johnson, and he often used to introduce the band. Skip, a.k.a. "Slider", became Geddy's bass technician, and by Counterparts he graduated to a stage management role. When not touring with Rush, he worked for Steely Dan (with Lorne Wheaton) as equipment manager, and guitar tech for Bob Seger and the Silver Bullet Band.

Skip is no mean guitar player himself. He guested on Japanese artist Venus Fly Trapp's debut CD *'Shakunetsu'*, which means "red heat".

Shelley Grafman

Sheldon Grafman was founder and owner of St Louis radio station KSHE. He opened the station in 1967, and until he left in 1984 he had the reputation of giving his DJ's scope and freedom to play what they wanted to play. He was thanked on *'All The World's A Stage'* for his services to the band.

Shelley died in 1997.

Neal Graham

Neal Graham started out as a music educator and performer, then in the early 1970s he set up a teaching studio in Fort Wayne, which also sold a few drum-related items. The retail business was a victim of its own success, becoming The Percussion Center and establishing a reputation both locally and nationally. Fortuitously, more than once Rush tours happened to start in Indiana, and The Percussion Center was called upon to service equipment and provide consumables. "We serviced them in Fort

Wayne a couple of times and they developed a relationship from this contact," says Neal. "They didn't want to bring consumable items like heads and sticks with them from Canada and have the hassles of the border crossings."

Before long, The Percussion Center had become Neil Peart's *magasin du choix* for drums and percussion equipment: when he wanted a new kit, or to try a different manufacturer, he would come to Fort Wayne. In 1986, prior to the recording of *'Hold Your Fire'* Neil conducted a bake-off of six drum kits. Before the testing began Neil ran his first ever drum clinic, for the Center. "I had promised Neal Graham for years," he said. "Though the idea of speaking in front of a crowd seemed a lot more intimidating than just playing drums."

After 22 years of business, the Percussion Center was closed so that Neal could give his full attention to XL Specialty Percussion Inc., a manufacturing and distribution company that produces drum cases under the trademark Protechtor Cases, and accessories for marching percussion products.

Ian Grandy

Ian helped the band with its kit since 1969, when he was Rush's first roadie – this is not to say the boys didn't do their own share of lifting and driving, but they were grateful for the help! He was joined by Liam Birt in 1971. By the *'Caress of Steel'* tour, Ian was well ensconced in his role as drum technician and sound engineer, and by *'2112'* he was co-ordinating the crew and running the tour accounts.

During the *'Exit Stage Left'* tour, Ian was Security Chief. It was around this time that he and the band parted ways.

George Graves

School wasn't the first love for Los Angeles-born George Graves. "I went for music and lunch," he says. George started in mastering in the sixties, first at Century Records in Newhall, CA, then at RCA Hollywood on Sunset Boulevard. "This was a large turning point in my career," says George. "I now was working with artists whose music I enjoyed hearing such as Henry Mancini, Harry Nillson, and The Monkees." It was at RCA that George first met Jack Richardson, who was producing The Guess Who at the time.

After he finished his military service in 1971, George took another step up in his mastering career, at The Mastering Lab, again in Hollywood. "The artists were super heroes of the industry," he explains. "Some of the ones I worked with were Neil Diamond, Seals & Croft, Ike & Tina Turner, Kenny Rogers, Three Dog Night and Steppenwolf. The best part of this job was working with fellow engineers that knew that they made a great difference to this music that people loved." In 1974 George was approached by Jack Richardson to help start Just Another Mastering Facility (JAMF) in Toronto. At JAMF George mastered first *'2112'* and then *'A Farewell To Kings'*. "Terry Brown was the producer at the time for Rush and he brought *'2112'* to me at JAMF," says George. "Terry was the contact person with these projects and came to all the mastering sessions. All the decisions that were made concerning the Rush projects were made through him." Eventually, Rush took their business to US-based studios. "Rush became popular worldwide and their Canadian complex prevailed where the thought was it had to be better across the border," says George. "Like so many Canadian artists when they have money their thought is, it must be better in the USA. I don't blame the artist completely for this decision as usually it's their management or record company that pushes them towards something different."

In 1978 he moved to The Lacquer Channel (TLC), originally part of Phase One recording studios. Today, George is Chief Mastering Engineer at TLC where he's worked "with artists just starting out as well as more established ones." Bigger names include Peter Gabriel, Alice Cooper and Cirque du Soleil. "I now have been in Canada for 30 years," George says.

Gerry Griffin

Gerald D. Griffin started working for NASA in 1960 and retired in 1986. His full career included flight director for the Apollo space program, including responsibility for the flight controllers who were co-ordinating the safe return of the astronauts of Apollo 13.

Gerry served as deputy director of the John F. Kennedy Space Center in Florida, and later Director of the Lyndon B. Johnson Space Center in Houston. When at Florida, he invited the band to the launch of the Space Shuttle, prior to 'Signals' – with Lee Scherer. He has acted as technical advisor for the films 'Apollo 13', 'Contact' and 'Deep Impact'. Today, Gerry lives in Hunt, Texas and works as a management consultant.

John Halfpenny

Animator John Halfpenny's first job was to work on the Canadian production of Sesame Street. He worked for Nelvana and Canimage, on a wide variety of productions including mainstream titles such as 'Scooby Doo' and 'Inspector Gadget'. After a short foray into illustration, he returned to the world of animation, picking up projects for Labatts beer and for Rush. John created the opening sequence for 'A Show Of Hands', the characters were known as the "rockin constructivists". He also worked on 'Force 10'.

Back at Nelvana, John worked on the animated version of 'Beetlejuice', as art director. Most recently, he worked on a project called 'Angela Anaconda', which was nominated for an Emmy and earned a prize at the Annecy International Animation Festival.

Donna Halper

Donna Halper started her career as an English teacher in Boston, but left the post in late 1973, shortly before qualifying for her tenure... the music was calling her. "I was offered a full-time radio job in Cleveland," she explains. "I had been doing part-time announcing at a local station about 5 miles from Boston, but my heart was in radio and I wanted to be in broadcasting full-time. I left Boston in late 1973, much to my parents' surprise and that of my students."

It was in her role at Cleveland's WMMS, as music director and assistant programme director, that Donna first came across Rush. In this role, she worked with record promoters from all over, and indeed outside, the country. "We had a couple of promoters who were obnoxious, but most were very kind to me and they treated me well," says Donna. "But I don't delude myself – they befriended me not because of my winning smile or my charm, but because I was the music director at one of the most influential album-rock stations in the USA."

Donna was not like other program directors, which presented a bit of a dilemma to some of the less scrupulous promoters. "I was a non-smoker, non-drinker, non drug user," she laughs. "I'm the only person I know who got fired for not smoking dope!" Her actions were not so much frowned upon, as confusing. "One [A&R man] welcomed me by bringing me some weed, for example, and when I refused it, he interpreted my refusal as rejecting the quality of his marijuana which, he assured me, was top of the line..." In addition she was a woman, which helped not at all. "The General Manager hated me – he expected me to type his letters and do office work – something he never expected the man who was the music director before me to do, plus he refused to give me equal pay to what that guy had gotten." Few would disagree however, that Donna could give as good as she got: she didn't become chair of the Prisoners' Rights Project of the American Civil Liberties Union in Ohio by accident. "It kept me busy and helped me to feel useful," she explains.

Donna had a good working relationship with several promoters, not least Bob Roper at A&M – "He would send down stuff, so we started to play Canadian music," says Donna. It was this contact that led to Rush being played on WMMS – "the rest shall we say is history," says Bob. Continues Donna, "Rush probably saved my career in a way. I took a lot of heat from certain people at the station. But when I discovered Rush and got their career started in the States, suddenly everybody thought I was marvellous!" Donna's early intervention earned her "big sister" role with the band, in particular with Geddy and Alex.

At the end of March 1975, Mercury Records hired Donna as East Coast director of A&R, so she moved to New York, continuing to spread the word to the best of her ability. In 1980 Donna formed her own radio programming and management consultancy, and has since written several books on the history of radio programming and the role of women therein.

Donna will always be remembered as the person who "discovered" Rush.

Ronnie Hawkins

Referred to by Bob Dylan as "my idol," rockabilly star Ronnie Hawkins fronted the band The Hawks in the fifties, garnering a reputation of one of the wild men of rock and roll. Having been told Canada was "the promised land" for a singer, he emigrated in 1958. It wasn't long before he'd bought a farm to house his equipment. "I had to have a place, I'm into old cars and old tractors, and I needed somewhere for them," he says, of his place at Stony Lake, Ontario. As for the barn, fellow musician Lonnie Mack was the first to give it a whirl. "He played in it, he said it sounded really great," says The Hawk, whose own band was soon rehearsing in the barn – at which point Ronnie Hawkins decided to fit it out for musical equipment. Rush rented the entire farm on a number of occasions (Ronnie and his wife moved out of the farmhouse for the duration), including to develop ideas for 'Moving Pictures'.

Over the years, Ronnie Hawkins has recorded over twenty albums and innumerable singles, has acted and has hosted his own TV show. "To this day he's a good friend and a great leader, with an uncanny ability to pick the best musicians and build them into first-rate bands," says drummer Levon Helm, who played with The Hawks. "He was immediately likable, trustworthy, and just naturally an entertainer; one of the funniest guys I ever met."

To his doctors he's also a miracle – as documented in 'Ronnie Hawkins: Still Alive and Kickin'', in 2002 Ronnie fought against pancreatic cancer, and won.

Peter Henderson

Peter Henderson started his musical career as assistant engineer, at George Martin's Air Studios. He worked for Geoff Emerick – engineer of some of The Beatles' most famous albums, including 'Revolver' and 'Sergeant Pepper'. "He was my mentor," says Peter. Having cut his teeth assisting Geoff on Paul McCartney's

'Wings at The Speed of Sound', in 1977 Peter was offered the opportunity to engineer 'Even In The Quietest Moments' for Supertramp. "It was very cool at the time!" he agrees.

Clearly they liked what he did, as it forged a 5-year partnership co-producing three albums, not least 'Breakfast in America' and the live disc 'Paris'. His most notable efforts included 'The Logical Song' and 'Breakfast in America' which picked up a Grammy in 1980 for Best Engineered Recording, Non-Classical. His final collaboration with the band was 'Famous Last Words', in the autumn of 1982.

Skating Away

While working on 'Grace Under Pressure', Peter had an unfortunate incident of food poisoning. "The chef served skate," he says. "For three days I was so cold, with tunnel vision!" Everyone rallied round, and did what they could to make him more comfortable. "Neil drew me a picture of the skate…"

Peter was drafted in at a late stage as co-producer for 'Grace Under Pressure', assisted by Frank Opolko and Robert Di Gioia. In August 1983 he was invited to come and meet the band in Toronto. "Rupert Hinc was first choice I believe. At the time I was totally unfamiliar with their music, I have to say I was very impressed with Neil's drumming," he says. At the end of the project, he was asked if he could record a live project for Rush. "For some reason it didn't happen," he says. "Maybe my management asked for too much money!"

Peter returned to the UK to work on a number of projects with Paul McCartney, including the 1989 album 'Flowers In The Dirt' and its live follow-up 'Tripping The Live Fantastic', as well as working with a number of grungier bands across the pond. "As time went on, I wasn't Division 1 anymore," Peter says, explaining why he decided to turn to other things including designing a number of TV productions. As a sideline, he interviewed a number of artists (including Roger Waters) for *Mojo*.

Recently Peter has been working on a virtual drum kit follow-up to the popular 'Drumkits from Hell'. "It's called Superia Custom and Vintage," he says. "We recorded 5 sets of drums, and we had 100,000 drum samples to edit!" He's also remixing Harry Smith's seminal 'Anthology of American Folk'. "It was the blueprint for Dylan, Cohen, those New York artists," says Peter.

Rob Higgins

Geddy's nephew Rob Higgins played in a number of bands – Change Of Heart, then Tristan Psionic, before in 1999 he became vocalist/bassist with The Royals, then Rocket Science with whom he was bassist/vocalist. In 2001 he recorded the latter band's debut album 'Foolscap' at his Uncle's home studio, Signal to Noise Studios. Geddy produced the album and sang backing on one track, 'Space Suit'.

In 2003 Rob helped out with Our Lady Peace.

Rupert Hine

Born in 1949, Rupert released his first single, 'The Sound of Silence' when he was only 16 years old. It failed to chart, and it wasn't until five years later that Rupert released his first album, 'Pick Up A Bone', followed by 'Unfinished Picture' some two years later. While he continued to develop as an artist, fronting Quantum Jump in the 70s, and then releasing his best-known solo album in 1980, 'Immunity'. He was also developing as an arranger/programmer and producer. He honed his skills with bands that needed broad production skills, such as Camel, Saga and Chris De Burgh; with co-conspirator and engineer Stephen Tayler, in 1981 he turned his hand to pop, recording Howard Jones's debut album 'Humans Lib' and Tina Turner's comeback

'Private Dancer' in close succession. It was nothing unexpected for him to switch genres at the drop of a hat – "I always liked each project to be different to the last, and ideally to anything I'd done before,", he says. Rupert continued to make his own solo albums, 'Waving Not Drowning' (1982) and 'The Wildest Wish to Fly' (1983) and 1986's concept album 'Thinkman', a fictional account of musicians against media manipulation. "They were supposed to be media terrorists," says Rupert, "righting wrongs in the classic Robin Hood tradition, inside global companies." In reality, the band was made up of trained actors who played their part in press interviews. Much to everyone's astonishment, the ruse was taken seriously. "We were never actually asked, 'is this true?'" says Rupert. "My own theory is that it was such a great story, why should they worry about it? They wanted it to be true!"

> ### I Think Therefore I Am
>
> To support Rupert Hine's 'Thinkman' tour, three black vans were built, supposedly transport for the media warriors but in fact transport for the kit. Unfortunately not everybody believed it was just a story, particularly in Germany where drivers were arrested and jailed overnight as suspected terrorists. "They were really road crew going between gigs!" laughs Rupert. "So we got on the front page of a couple of newspapers. That was a fantastic help, I mean, now we were believed 10 times more. It's a good ploy!"

Following work with The Thompson Twins, The Fixx, Saga (again), his then-partner Stevie Nicks and others, in 1989 Rupert was invited to produce two albums for Rush, namely 'Presto' (on which he supplied additional keys and vocals) and 'Roll The Bones'. In 1995 he recorded his most recent solo album, 'The Deep End'. More recently, Rupert has worked with Suzanne Vega ("trying to bring groove back to her, like the DNA remix of 'Tom's Diner'," he says), Duncan Sheik and Teitur, and has taken an executive producer role with Martin Grech. "I'm only interested in what it is the artist has to say, and therefore they're the only artists that I'm attracted to. I cannot possibly make a record that's simply entertaining," he says. "I can't be responsible for adding one jot of meaningless music."

Ever the maverick, Rupert has very clear views on the way music is going. "The entire record industry is merely rearranging the deck chairs on the Titanic," he says, "but then there's the music business. What I'm interested in is the stripped down next generation, which will be all about scaling back down to the kind of models that started each of the cycles of over fifty years of popular music."

Mike Hirsch

Mike worked for Concert Sound Inc., who first worked for Rush on the 'Caress of Steel' tour. Mike was very tall, and he had a very deep voice, earning him the nickname "Lurch". "He had only to walk into a room and any troublemakers around would do a double take and instantly quieten down," reported Brian Harrigan.

By 'A Farewell To Kings' Mike had joined the band's own payroll, as stage manager. He had a reputation for arriving with the first truck and leaving with the last, covering every aspect from load-in to load-out. Mike decided to step down at the end of the 'Moving Pictures' tour, informing his successor Nick Kotos at the end-of-tour party.

Dan Hudson

Canada-born artist Dan Hudson first came to Neil's attention when he sold Neil a painting, having met the drummer at a Toronto party. Neil proposed that some of his works were included on the 'Retrospective' cover. Dan currently works out of Canmore, Alberta, Canada: he supplements his income by writing and photographing for snowboarding magazines.

Yosh Inouye

Yosh was responsible for the majority of the pictures on *'2112'*, together with band photography by Gérard Gentil. He took the cover photos for *'A Farewell To Kings'* (sleeve photo by Roger Stowell) and *'Hemispheres'* (inner sleeve photo by Fin Costello).

Today, as a professor of the Faculty of Business and Creative Arts, Yosh teaches graphic design at George Brown College, in Toronto.

Andrew Jackman

Andrew Bryce-Jackman was born in 1946. In 1965 he joined a band, The Selfs, with Chris Squire, then a year later, he went on with Chris Squire and Pete Banks to form The Syn, which played Tamla Motown covers. Chris and Pete went on to form Yes in 1967, and Andrew turned his attentions to more orchestral work, though he continued to collaborate with his old friends, for example on Chris Squire's 1974 solo album *'A Fish Out Of Water'*. He also started a long and fruitful collaboration with Peter Skellern, with whom he worked on 3 albums.

Andrew contributed to the 1978 Yes album, *'Tormato'*, and in the same year, he became conductor of the London Symphony Orchestra. It was perhaps inevitable that the orchestra should release an album of rock classics shortly after, which went to Number 3 in the UK charts. It was the first of ten.

Just before working for Rush in 1985, Andrew worked with Elkie Brooks, on her album *'Screen Gems'*. For *'Power Windows'* he arranged tracks including 'Marathon' for a choir, which was recorded at Angel Studios, London. Then, he arranged and conducted The William Faerey Engineering Brass Band's contribution to the *'Hold Your Fire'* track 'Mission', recorded at Mirage Studio, Oldham. Additional *'Hold Your Fire'* arrangements were by Steve Margoshes. After Rush, Andrew worked on Barclay James Harvest's album *'Face to Face'*.

Andrew later turned his attention to film scores, working on both *'American Werewolf in London'* and *'The Great Rock and Roll Swindle'*. Andrew Jackman died in late 2003 of a heart attack, shortly after featuring on *'Elements'* by Steve Howe's Remedy.

Jim Johnson

J.D. "Jimmy" Johnson was one of the original road crew for the *'Rush'* and *'Fly By Night'* tours, along with Ian Grandy and Liam Birt. He replaced David Scace as guitar technician, and was himself replaced by Skip Gildersleeve on the *'Caress of Steel'* tour.

He returned for *'Grace Under Pressure'* as stage right technician, taking over from Liam Birt who was moving into stage management duties. Essentially, Jimmy was looking after Alex's guitars once again, aided and abetted by George Steinert. He continued this role through to *'Counterparts'*. Following this, he went to work for Styx, and was succeeded on the *'Vapor Trails'* tour by Rick Britton.

Patrick Read Johnson

With Scott Alexander and Olivia Ramirez, Patrick developed the models used on the album inner for *'Hold Your Fire'*.

Lawrence Jordan

Larry started in film as soon as he graduated from college. He moved to New York and joined a music video company, quickly working his way up to editor, where he edited videos for Godley and Creme and David Bowie, before wanting more. "I got so tired of editing," says Larry. "I was fed up of fixing other people's problems. So, I got into directing." He accepted a post with Calhoun Productions, who had a reputation for recording major live music events. "I worked with all English crews," said Larry.

Larry's work with Calhoun included recordings of Pink Floyd in Versailles and an Amnesty movie for US broadcaster HBO – "the project of which I am most proud," he says; he has also worked with Christina Aguilera, Maria Carey and Eddie Izzard. When Calhoun won the contract to record Rush at Birmingham NEC, on the *A Show of Hands'* tour, Larry's name was in the frame to direct.

The band were pleased with the results, to the extent that they wanted Larry to work on more projects with them, but as happens so often in music, the schedules got in the way. "Geddy called me personally and asked me to work on the videos, but it didn't really work out, it didn't happen. Larry was plenty busy with other projects, travelling all over the world and building his reputation for stadium work. Indeed, it was over a decade before the two sides managed to hook up again, for what became *'Rush in Rio'*.

Michael Kamen

New Yorker Michael Kamen was a highly accomplished musician, first turning his hand to the piano at the age of 2 and later picking up the guitar, clarinet and oboe. He helped found the New York Rock 'n' Roll Ensemble in the late sixties, and soon after he began to arrange music for ballet, all the while keeping his hand in on the popular music scene, becoming a highly respected composer and arranger. With his work on *'The Wall'* he began a long series of collaborations with Pink Floyd and Roger Waters, becoming one of the few people to work with both David Gilmour and Roger Waters following Roger's departure from the band. As well as working on the film score for *'The Wall'*, he also scored the music for films as wide ranging as *'Brazil'*, *'Lethal Weapon'* and *'Die Hard'*.

Following a diagnosis of multiple sclerosis in 1996, Michael died suddenly in November 2003, aged 55.

Yousuf Karsh

Yousuf Karsh was born in 1908, moving to Canada in 1924. When he was commissioned as portrait photographer on *'Grace Under Pressure'*, Yousuf Karsh was one of the most famous photographers of his time, having photographed the Pope, Andy Warhol, Albert Einstein and innumerable kings and queens. All the same, said Geddy, "It looks a little like a bar mitzvah photo, doesn't it?" He died in 2002.

Allan King

Allan Winton King was born 6 February 1930, in Vancouver. He became a film director and gained a reputation for his leading edge documentary work. In 1973 he directed *'Come On Children'*, which featured an Alex Zivojinovich and his partner, Charlene McNichol. In 1985 Allan directed an episode of *'The Twilight Zone'*. He has won several awards, mostly for documentaries.

Roger Kneebend

An action figure ("replete with flippers and wet suit") belonging to Julian Weinrib, Roger was de facto producer on *'Grace Under Pressure'*, before Peter Henderson was brought in. According to legend Roger has also toured with the band, later appearing on Geddy's keyboards on the *A Show of Hands'* video.

Gilbert Kong

Gilbert worked for Jim Shelton at Mercury Sound Studios in New York, where he mastered the band's debut album *'Rush'* for its Mercury release, as well as *'Fly By Night'*. After Mercury Sound Studios became Masterdisk, Gilbert also worked with artists such as Rod Stewart, Thin Lizzy and The Velvet Underground.

Joe Kotleba

Joe worked for AGI, Chicago, which was the company Mercury used for its album packaging and printing. He had worked on a number of BTO covers, and was brought in with Jim Ladwig to design the cover for *'Fly By Night'*. Twenty years later Jim was responsible for the package design for Dave Edmunds' 1994 album *'Plugged In'*.

Nick Kotos

Nick was born 1949 in Flint, Michigan. He got into concert lighting when he was doing his degree course in Television Production at UCLA. "I started doing lighting for concerts to pick up extra $$s," he says. In the mid-seventies he took a job with See Factor, Rush's lighting contractor, and in 1978 he joined the Rush crew as Master Electrician. Nick's fellow crew members called themselves Easy Company. "This was not an actual group, more of a mind set or attitude," says Nick. "It was a take-off from a 50s-60s comic book *Sgt. Rock and The Easy Company*, an army company of hardened veteran soldiers who would do anything under the most difficult conditions." At the end of the *'Moving Pictures'* tour, Nick's colleague and stage manager Mike Hirsch told him he wanted to step down. "About 5 minutes later the Band and the Tour Manager asked me if I wanted to become the Production Stage Manager," says Nick, who quickly accepted the offer. He continued in this role until 1993 when he was enticed away, to operate the largest outdoor amphitheatre in the USA, based in Los Angeles, and his Rush role was taken by Dan Braun. His time with Rush was a learning experience "Personally, I made a lot of lasting friendships," says Nick. "Professionally, I honed my skills and reputation."

After nine years, he found the call of the road to be too great once again, so back he went.

These days Nick is a freelance event coordinator and production manager. He is currently working on a tour based on a video game, called *'GameRiot'*. "It merges new video games and game technology to an entertainment environment," he says. "The industry and touring aspect of it are in the same place that the music industry was in the early 70s." So, how easy is it to transfer the skills from music to gaming? "I never learned to play a musical instrument and I can't play any video games, but that's not why they hire me!"

Bernie LaBarge

Bernie was born March 11, 1953 in Ottawa, Ontario. He was a teen guitarist, as he explains, "I saw The Beatles on *Ed Sullivan* in 1964 and started learning guitar soon after. I was playing professionally at age 13." Having spent most of his career performing in bars across Canada and the USA, it was the 80s before Bernie cut his own recordings, for one of which he was nominated for a Juno. "I had an album and a bunch of singles in the 80s," he says. "I sang on a few tracks with Kim Mitchell and I played the guitar on a track on one of his albums too."

When Lou Pomanti called Bernie about joining Alex's house band in November

1994, "I was in Portage La Prairie, Manitoba (Canada) playing with Cassandra Vasik in 1994. I had just walked into my hotel room after an all-night drive." It seemed like a good idea, and Bernie has been in the band ever since, just carrying on what has turned out to be quite a journey. "Playing with many, many heroes of mine keeps me going," says Bernie. "From Boxcar Willie to Gordon Lightfoot to The Irish Rovers to Domenic Troiano to Alex Lifeson to John Sebastian, etc... It's a very long list and it's still growing."

Bernie reserves some of his finest praise for Alex. "I wish I had known Alex all my life," he says. "We have a very special connection. I feel as if I've known him forever. We both have the same inherent feeling about guitar playing and music (and life) in general. I can only say that about a handful of people I have met over the years. He is completely humble, very giving, ridiculously creative, and drop-dead hilarious. He'd give you the shirt off his back." It's a mutual feeling, according to Orbit Room co-owner Tim Notter. "Alex has enormous respect for Bernie," he says.

Brian Lee

Born in 1970, Brian went to Berklee College of Music in Boston from 1988-1992, majoring in Music Production and Engineering under notable engineers Bill Scheniman and Carl Beatty. "When I graduated college, as luck would have it I heard that the great mastering engineer Bob Ludwig was moving to Portland, Maine which is where I was living at the time," says Brian. "I called in all my favors and got my professor Bill Scheniman to make a few calls for me." Bill used his own contacts to fix a meeting between Brian and Bob – "You have to hire this guy," Bill said. So, Bob did.

Brian acted as Bob's assistant at Gateway Mastering Studios for about a year, before he started to be given mastering projects of his own. His first major task for Rush was to remaster the earlier Rush albums, from 'Rush' to 'Hold Your Fire'. "They wanted to use the latest digital technology to capture the original analog tapes," says Brian. "The masters were in excellent condition, actually not much work had to be done because they already sounded so great. Some of the early albums needed more work than the others, but that is a testament to the engineers that put together the original albums."

In 1998 Brian stopped mastering and started working on DVD Authoring, video editing and graphic design. "Selected DVD artists that I have authored are Blue Man Group, Loreena McKennitt, Bruce Springsteen, Madonna, Eric Clapton, Nine Inch Nails and Frank Sinatra," he says.

Geddy Lee

Bass and vocals. And keyboards.

David Leonard

David was never really a musician, not in his eyes anyway. "Prior to being an engineer at high school I played bass and clarinet," he says, however, "I don't consider myself a player." As for Rush, "I grew up listening to their music – I'm from the North East and they're huge up here." He started in the music business as soon as he left high school. "The day after I graduated I went on the road as front-of-house mixer and roadie for Chick Corea," he says. "After my stint on the road I moved to LA and was on staff at Sunset Sound. There were no big breaks, just lots of hours."

Over his career, David has developed an enviable portfolio of acts – "I have worked with Prince, Paul McCartney, Sugar Ray, Barenaked Ladies, Avril Lavigne, Rush,

Dwight Yoakam, Duran Duran, John Mellencamp, Indigo Girls, Tony Bennett, Toto and many, many other wonderful musicians," says David.

David first got involved with the band when he mixed and engineered Geddy's solo project *'My Favourite Headache'*. He was later brought in at the end of *'Vapor Trails'* at Metalworks Studios, Mississauga (December 2001 to February 2002). "I found great recordings ready to mix," he says. "I believe they all had worked long and hard and were so very close to it that maybe it was time for a fresh perspective."

He was asked back again, for *'Feedback'*. "I assume because we have developed a good working relationship," he says. "The whole experience was exhilarating and joyous." As for plans for the future, "One never knows until the phone rings."

Michael Letho

An Australian engineer, Michael worked for Split Enz before acting as mixing engineer for *'Counterparts'*.

Alex Lifeson

Guitars. Lots of guitars.

Bob Ludwig

Bob is a renowned mastering engineer, working on a huge number of famous albums including U2's *'Joshua Tree'* which had been engineered by Dave Meegan. "When you get him to master an album, when he leaves the room it isn't finished – he takes it home, checks it out, comes back the next day and changes things that he found were wrong at home," says Dave. "He was the instigator of that school, he had a very unique way, he was one of three people that made everyone want to go to America to master."

While at Masterdisk, NY, the first album Bob worked on for Rush was *'Permanent Waves'*. Soon after he left Masterdisk and set up his own facility at Gateway Mastering Studios, Portland, Maine, attending first to *'Exit...Stage Left'*. For *'Grace Under Pressure'* and *'Hold Your Fire'* he was assisted by Brian Lee. He has since been involved in mastering every Rush album until *'Vapor Trails'*, usually accompanied by Geddy who would review the masters before they went to acetate. In 1997, Bob and Brian also worked on remastering the Rush series.

Bob is known for taking on apprentices, of which Brian is one. A more recent student was Adam Ayan, who went on to master *'Rush in Rio'*. Bob has also mastered just about everybody, indeed there are far too many to list, but they include *'Scooby Doo'*.

Pat Lynes

Pat was the driver of Rush's tour bus. He died shortly before *'Counterparts'*, which was dedicated to his memory.

Robin McBride

Robin was a Chicago based music producer, who worked initially for Columbia records. One of his claims to fame was in 1964, when he signed and worked with Barry and The Remains. A musician himself, he provided keyboards for the Buddy Miles album *'Them Changes'*.

When Rush arrived on the scene, Robin was head of A&R for Mercury Records. He passed *'Rush'* to Cliff Burnstein, and took the executive producer role for Rush's debut album, as well as for *'The Man Who Sold The World'*. Later in 1974, Robin produced a three-and-a-half minute single version of Kraftwerk's *'Autobahn'*, which was instrumental in the success of the associated album. Kraftwerk's US representation at the time was handled by Ira Blacker.

Michael and Patrick McLoughlin

Michael McLoughlin ran a theatre in Toronto's Summer Gardens. As sometimes happens, he was approached one day to help out a band in difficulties – The Bay City Rollers were in need of someone to cover their merchandising. Why not, he thought to himself, and so he headed off for a week to fill the gap. "He came back and said to Mum, I've found my new job," recalls his son Patrick, who remembers as well how Michael sold his theatre interests and set up as a purveyor of show merchandise. It wasn't long before he reached the attention of Ray Danniels, who asked him to do the same for Rush. "Why not," agreed Michael.

Before long, this relationship with Rush grew to mean not only the merch but also running the backstage club and fan club activities on behalf of SRO. Michael moved the business to Las Vegas for family reasons, and as the operation in the mid-nineties he brought in family members Shannon and Patrick to help.

Michael died in December 1998, but the family business lives on. His role was taken over by Patrick, who opened another office back in Toronto and has been managing things ever since.

Andrew MacNaughtan

"I wanted to be involved in music in some way," says Toronto-born Andrew MacNaughtan, whose first knowledge of Rush came from his sister – she gave him *'A Farewell To Kings'* when he was 14 years old. "I only could play Side One, not Side Two, it was too loud, too heavy metal or something," he says. "I eventually flipped over to Side Two and I was hooked!" Hooked enough to run off a few issues of a Rush newsletter, a year later. "It was me wanting to be entrepreneurial, I was never really a fanatical fan," he says. "I loved the music, it definitely shaped my teenage years." Before long Andrew had moved on to publish a more broad-based music magazine, distributed to the local record stores. "It was garbage, it wasn't done well at all!" he laughs. "Then, I needed to do photos for my magazine. I would borrow a camera from a friend. I wasn't great but I got by, eventually I bought a camera."

Through a lucky break when his magazine was bought by a publishing corporation, Andrew found himself with nothing but his camera. Despite his lack of education in photography, he decided that was enough and started touting his services around the contacts he had made through his magazine. In 1984 and when Andrew was in his early 20s, the opportunity came up to shoot a Rush concert. "I photographed *'Grace Under Pressure'*," says Andrew. "I shot one of the concerts in Toronto." Sadly however, the pictures were never used.

Meanwhile, Andrew needed to pay the bills. Some friends were in a band called The Spoons who were signed to SRO, and Andrew was asking around for part-time work. SRO's Pegi Cecconi offered him a job answering phones and sorting out the tape room, and a conversation with Geddy's wife Nancy led to Andrew helping out in her fashion business, Zapata, as well. "They were designers, they had a fashion studio and then they would sell their clothes to various retailers," he says. "It was a very exclusive line which was so beautiful." Andrew also got work as a waiter.

A chance meeting with Howard Ungerleider led to a discussion about the photos he had taken – little did Andrew know, but SRO was having difficulties getting pictures together for the *'Power Windows'* tour book. "I'm going, that's awesome, my childhood heroes, it would be so great to have them use my pictures," says Andrew. To his surprise they asked to use 14 of them. "I got a little note from Neil thanking me for the beautiful pictures, and a photo credit in the tour book, I was like, this is so exciting, I really do want to be a photographer!"

In July 1985, after running errands for Nancy (and on occasion Geddy), Andrew plucked up the courage to show his portfolio to Geddy and asked if he could take his portrait. "He said, absolutely, so he came down to my studio and I did those portraits in 'Presto'. He loved it so much, he asked the other guys if it would be OK if I did their portrait. I was actually a little nervous – this was an incredible opportunity for me as a photographer, but also I had a lot to prove, this was the first time I shot such a hugely successful band." Andrew was asked to take some more shots – of the video of 'The Pass', and then some more portraits. "It was all Geddy, basically, Geddy was very supportive of my work and my ability," says Andrew. "We'd become good pals and there's an interesting dynamic too, he sort of took me under his wing in a way."

As time passed Andrew ended up taking on more and more of the Rush portfolio. When offered the opportunity to act as band assistant on the 'Presto' tour, of course he jumped at it. "Of course I said yes!" Doing it meant he had to close his studio for the duration of the tour. "I said, you know what, for 6 months, it's the chance of a lifetime. I got to see America!" He also got to see Europe on the following tour – but it wasn't all roses. "Being on the bus was one of the most dreadful experiences of my life! I don't know how crew can do it," he says. "In hindsight I probably shouldn't have done the 'Bones' tour, I really felt that being away from home for so long was a bit of a mindfuck for me."

Meanwhile, however, Andrew had been developing his own skills with other bands, and had a growing reputation as a video director. "One of the bands I did an album cover for – the Gandharvas – asked me if I'd do a music video for them," he says. "By chance, the guys who did the special effects for the 'Hellraiser' movies, they happened to be in town. I basically had these incredible hooks and stuff going through the singer's skin…" The resulting video was very well received, becoming the number one video on Canadian channel MuchMusic. "It launched my video career!"

Following a number of successful videos, Andrew joined Deborah Samuel as a video director at the Revolver film company, which at the time was being run by Allan Weinrib. Andrew had learned his lesson from the road trip – next time, he would stay at home. "Also at that point my career was starting to take off in photography," he says. "I was away for 8 months and clients were starting to use other photographers!"

Having worked with the likes of Alanis Morissette and Tom Cochrane, Andrew moved to California in the late nineties, "I got burnt out in Toronto," he says. "I needed to shake things up, personally, spiritually and creatively. I was sick of being stuck in my studio for 6 months of the year, in winter, being limited on low-paying budgets." Los Angeles was a fresh start, full of new opportunities, but that didn't make the change any easier. "I started to meet a bunch of Canadian expatriates – John Kastner from the Dough Boys, my friend Dave Foley (of the Kids In The Hall comedy troupe). I started to get to know Matt Stone from South Park, we like to think of him as being Canadian!"

Through some twist of fate, Andrew's new domain offered a kind of sanctuary for Neil, who at the time was biking through his dual tragedies. "I don't think LA really held any special memories for him, that's why he sort of gravitated to it," says Andrew. "We just started hanging out together – I was in charge of his social calendar, I would take him to my friends' houses or we all would go for dinner. They're wonderful people and great friends, and I think he recognised that. As well as anonymity I think it was a win win situation for everybody!"

At some of his photo shoots, Andrew had been employing an assistant by the name of Carrie Nuttall. "One day we were driving home from one of the shoots, and she was saying, 'I just broke up with somebody, I'm tired of dating all these superficial gym bunnies, I wish I could meet someone a little older, someone really interesting and articulate'," says Andrew. "I said, 'I just might know somebody, but he's been through a lot...' To cut a long story short, we all went out on a double date and they hit it off. I think they had a lot in common, Carrie is very articulate, she was well travelled, speaks French, lived in Paris, she's just a smart, beautiful woman."

Currently living back in Toronto, Andrew remains Rush's photographer, most recently taking the pictures for *'Feedback'* and working with Neil on his Sabian drum video. "It's weird... being in my parents' living room, listening to *'A Farewell To Kings'*, and then, me introducing Neil to his new wife – weird!" he says. "Life is so strange, I've done such incredible things and seen so many things and learned so many things, I'm very, very fortunate."

Barry McVicker

At the time that Barry was involved in the photography on *'Caress of Steel'* with Terrence Bert and Gérard Gentil, he ran a studio called Montclair Sound near Toronto. Barry also did some of the photography for *'2112'* and *'Permanent Waves'*, for which he was uncredited. Today he runs a studio called Cedar Valley Studios Inc., just north of Toronto.

Brad Madix

A native of San Francisco, Brad played keyboards in High School and had a PA that he "rented out to other bands occasionally." Deciding on an interest in recording, he went to the Berklee College of Music in Boston to major in Music Production and Engineering, and played out his spare time in a band. "Banditt, we were called... two 't's... how 80s!" he laughs. "I also worked in a little recording studio – it did teach me that the studio can be a very boring place."

One night, events transpired that would set the scene for Brad's career. "Banditt was a covers band, but we were going to try to write and record some originals and send them off in hope of a record contract. We borrowed some recording gear from a sound company called Scorpio Sound, and packed it all in a truck to drive up to New Hampshire for a week long gig at some bar there. We were going to record in the day, and gig at night, and see what happened. I parked the truck around the corner from the apartment and locked it up. When I got up in the morning... well, it was gone. All of my gear, all of the sound gear... everything. Gone."

The moment came to explain what had happened. Gary King, who ran Scorpio Sound, was more than fair. "He offered to let me work it off, so I started doing shows for his sound company for cheap or even free. I think I did two shows actually unpaid, but after a month or so, he started sending me out on things and paying me. I was making more money doing that than playing in the band. And it was way more fun than working in the studio."

Having "kicked around in the clubs and college circuit for a while," Brad landed some bigger gigs, notably assisting Robert Scovill on Def Leppard's *'Hysteria'* tour in 1987-88. "That's when I started stealing his tricks," he says. Brad met with Howard Ungerleider when both were working for Queensrÿche, and he first joined the Rush crew on the *'Presto'* tour, back in support of Robert Scovill. "Part of my job was to mix the opening act, a band called Mr Big," he explains. While the main act was on, Brad used his time wisely. "I learned a lot of my technique from watching Robert," he says. "I had never mixed a big tour to that point and watching Robert was very instructive." With his new-found knowledge, Brad went off to mix the live sound for Queensrÿche, before being called back at the end of the *'Roll The Bones'* tour to take over from Robert. "He had a scheduling conflict, so I came in and took over for about the last six weeks or so," says Brad. "All I did was, continue to run the show as Robert had set it up."

This was the last he would see of Rush for some time. Brad's experience helped him to develop as a mixing engineer, ultimately leading to taking FOH roles for Def Leppard, Bruce Hornsby and Marilyn Manson. When Robert was once again unavailable for Rush, for the *'Vapor Trails'* tour, Brad's name was in the frame. "I suppose I must have made a good impression," he says. Brad brought his hard rock experiences to bear, appealing to fans and crew alike. "I think the thing I added was a somewhat more "in-your-face" sound, maybe a harder edge," he says. Fellow crew member Tony Geranios concurs. "Brad is one of the most amazing sound guys the band's ever had, he's made the band sound like a rock band again," says Tony. "A fan came up to me, said they'd never heard the band sound better."

Despite acknowledging the prestige attached to mixing Rush, Brad is typically understated about his role. "Not only is the band particular about their sound, so are the fans," he says. "Also, within the industry, they are regarded as a good sounding band. As it happens, they are great players, so making them sound good isn't the hardest thing in the world!"

David Mallet

Director David Mallet worked for Blondie, Queen, Iron Maiden and Peter Gabriel, before directing *'Distant Early Warning'*, and the *'Grace Under Pressure'* tour video. Other videos from the album were directed by Rocky Morton and Tim Pope.

Blake Manning

A good friend of Bill Bell, Blake has toured with Bill and with his partner Tara McLean. He provided drums on Alex's solo project *'Victor'*, with Bill and with Edwin from I Mother Earth.

Steve Margoshes

Steve was well known for his work with Jim Steinman, notably with Meatloaf on *'Bat Out Of Hell'*, specifically on 'For Crying Out Loud'. It was the Jim Steinman link that resulted in Steve conducting string arrangements on the song 'Mission'. "He must have recommended me," says Steve.

Later, Steve composed the music for *'Fame, The Musical'*. "The movie was an unexpected hit," says Steve. "David Di Silva always envisioned it as a theatre piece, he held the rights as it was his own score."

David Marsden

Nicknamed "The Mars Bar" when he was a CHUM-FM DJ alongside Don Shafer, David Marsden was one of the first people to play a Rush song on the radio, when he spun 'Finding My Way' to the delight of young listener Alex Lifeson.

David was later recruited as programme director at what was to become the 'Spirit of Radio' station, CFNY. Today, David is back to DJ'ing, hosting an evening show at the Toronto station "The Rock."

Dave Meegan

When a young Dave Meegan was at school in the late seventies, his heart was already set on having something to do with music. He ran his own pirate radio station, playing mainly punk but Rush was ever-present. "My best mate had a few bands that he just tried to jam down my throat and one of them was Rush," he says. "I couldn't be found dead with a Rush tape, even though I was tempted to listen I would always refuse to!"

Having set up his own recording studio in his Dad's garage, Dave got a job as a tape operator at Sarm East Studios in London. He worked mainly for Peter Collins, assisting Peter's engineer Julian Mendelson. "I was Julian's assistant of choice most of the time," says Dave, who learned a great deal under Peter's wing. "Peter let me do things that I felt confident enough to do," says Dave. "He had a Fairlight at the time, he used to let me borrow it at weekends, and I would try and learn on it. I never wanted to be just a tape op, I wanted to get into as much as possible." Dave needn't have worried. "One evening I asked Dave to come up with some ideas for the basic groove of Nik Kershaw's 'The Riddle', he came up with an amazing programme," says Peter Collins. "I am very aware he was much more than just an assistant."

Peter was Dave's mentor. "I was three years working on sessions for him," says Dave. "He could give you a hard time over things as well, like smarten yourself up. He acted like my dad a couple of times, but at the right time, and he sorted me out otherwise I would have fucked things up in my career if it wasn't for a couple of things he said."

Most of the projects Dave was involved in were pop-oriented, despite the occasional opportunity to work with artists such as Gary Moore and Phil Lynott. "English pop things was not where my heart and soul was really," says Dave. "When something like Rush came in, it's just exciting when you love the music just as much as the work and it sounded great as well."

When Dave started working with Rush, he was just starting to pick up engineering roles. "That's why, half way through *'Power Windows'*, Heff Moraes took over from me, because I had to go engineer for Trevor Horn," he says. "It would have been to do an in-house, ZTT project."

Dave's portfolio went from strength to strength from this point on, with his big break coming with engineering U2's *'The Joshua Tree'*, back in Dublin. He earned his producer's stripes in the US, and more recently has been working with Marillion in the UK where he has a "sixth member" reputation. He is still in touch with his roots, developing new acts such as Carrie Tree and Pave. "It's all down to home production, luck and hard work!"

Frankie Says

"There's a story, and I was there the minute it happened. We were working on Yes, the *'90125'* album, in Sarm East, I was in the control room with Trevor Horn, and the guitar tech of Yes was down in the lobby watching Channel 4's *'The Tube'*. Frankie came on, they were doing that dancing in the boxing ring, and doing their version of 'Relax', and the roadie came running in saying, 'you've gotta see this, you've gotta see this!' Trevor ran out, saw it, he was blown away by it, got on the phone straight away to Andy Moorley and said, 'I've gotta see these guys by Monday!' – and that is how it happened! The roadie probably got no credit, ever!"

Dave Meegan

Mendelson Joe

"The reason I played music and did it for a living was because that's all I ever wanted to do since I was a kid," says Mendelson Joe, who first caught the bug at the age of 10, when he heard Little Richard on the radio. "I played my sister's guitar at eleven, and still do." In his late teens Joe started playing with a band called Mainline and recorded his first album when he was 24, in 1968. His second album, again with Mainline, was recorded in London, UK.

In 1972, Joe left Mainline and became a solo artist, and shortly afterwards he met a budding agent called Ray Danniels. "I never felt part of a sound or scene or trend," he says. "I made my first recording for Nobody/GRT in 1972 (I played all the instruments). The album was a collage of idioms and sillinesses titled *'Mr. Middle of The Road'*. Humor is a medium I've employed since song #1."

By 1974 Ray had started to book gigs for Joe, and after a year he became his manager, representing Joe for four albums. "I'm very, very fussy about my music, I don't do what people want me to do ever," says Joe, who nonetheless recognised the role that Ray could play. "I attribute to almost all peoples' successes, as much as Eric Clapton has an ability to play the guitar, or Jeff Beck, or David Gilmour, these guys wouldn't be anywhere without managers at some point."

Characterised as a "folk satirist", Joe's 1979 *'Not Homogenized'* album included a guest slot for Ben Mink on violin, and in 1988 Geddy persuaded Anthem to release the Mendelson Joe album *'Born To Cuddle'*. Geddy played on *'Women Are The Only Hope'*, "an unreleased album from 1992," says Joe. "He adapted his style well for 'Joe' songs."

In April 1992, Joe started Artists Against Racism with Lisa Cherniak. Neil was the second person to join the campaign. "All art is political," says Joe. "Honesty is about truth and as an artist, I've tried to write, sing, paint and guitar my truth my way. There is little or no market for truth in any form. Few people want the truth; fewer would recognize it; that is the truth!"

All You Have To Do

"At a certain point, when you're in the music business, the dream is to make records. Then the dream is to make a living; then the dream is to have success. Then the dream is to make more money than you did at the last job, because you were playing in a toilet. And before you know it you want to be playing in better venues. At that point, that's when you have to make some decisions. Do you want to play in what you call football arenas, or do you want to play in sit-down concert halls that only hold 2,500 people? So, it's when the dream starts to make money that is the toughest time, because you have to make a decision — what do you want? Do you want to do it purely for music, and do it for an aesthetic reason, or do you want to make more money, and more money?"

Mendelson Joe

For the past few years, Joe has been living in Muskoka, in Northern Ontario. "I live in the woods because I embrace nature and loathe most humans," he says. "I avoid computers/faxes but I confess I enjoy computer-mixing and appreciate the website in my name. I'm actually a contradiction because I love the technology of motorcycles (I own an R1 Yamaha)." As well as his music, he is recognised for his landscape and portrait painting. "I think he went into painting because he gave up on the music industry," says friend and collaborator Bruce Cole. "If you don't dot your I's and cross your T's, someone will come up and screw ya." Having photographed him as an artist, Bruce also worked with Joe as a painter. "He would give me a painting and I would shoot some postcards for him, as a matter of fact he even did a portrait of me!" Joe freely admits that Rush's music doesn't do much for him. "I know that many people do not get my music and/or my paintings; It's about taste and inclination," he says. "Neil's lyrics do not speak to me but his letters are graceful, sometimes hilarious communications. His books are almost as good as his letters."

With a total of 24 albums under his belt ("Not all of them were released, but many have been," he says), Mendelson Joe is living proof that there's more to life than the beaten track would suggest. "He's very much the eccentric gentleman," says Bruce. "Instead of going with the flow and hiding who he is, he wears who he is on his sleeve. He's a gentleman, he's a genuine man."

Wally Meyrowitz

Wally was co-owner of American Talent International (ATI) together with Jeff Franklin and Sol Saffian, which was the booking and signing agent for Kiss, and which (with Ira Blacker) took on Rush's US interests in the early days. Wally was quite a personality by all accounts. "He reinvented the definition of a signing agent" according to Rod Light, speaking at the 10th Annual Concert Industry Consortium.

Ben Mink

Ben is known for his experimentation with a wide variety of esoteric instruments. He first met the band in the early eighties as violinist with FM, who took over the support slot for Rush when Kim Mitchell left Max Webster during the *'Moving Pictures'* tour.

Ben first collaborated with Rush on the *'Signals'* track 'Losing It', on which he played electric violin. Ben had developed a broad repertoire – he was involved in country music, as well as writing material for such artists as K. D. Lang and Barenaked Ladies. He later collaborated with Geddy on *'My Favorite Headache'*.

Heff Moraes

Heff was Assistant Engineer at Sarm East studios in London and Paul Wright. He took over from Dave Meegan half way through production of *'Power Windows'*. He has also worked with Roxy Music, Paul McCartney (*'Flowers In The Dirt'*, assisting Peter Henderson), Chris Squire and Annie Lennox.

Pat Moran

Pat produced The Searchers in the early 1960s. As resident engineer at Rockfield Studios, he supported Terry Brown on *'A Farewell To Kings'* and *'Hemispheres'*. He also engineered for Van Der Graaf Generator and the Grateful Dead. Later he worked with Robert Plant on his 1983 album *'The Principle of Moments'*.

Rocky Morton

A co-founder of Cucumber Productions with his wife Annable Jankel, with whom he produced a number of animations for TV commercials, as well as for a number of TV shows including *The Tube*. Their first music video was 'Accidents Will Happen' for Elvis Costello. Rocky did the animations for the live show prior to *'Grace Under Pressure'*. He also directed *'The Body Electric'* and *'The Enemy Within'*.

A few years later, Rocky and Annabel collaborated with Steve Roberts to create the character Max Headroom.

Michael Mosbach

Michael Mosbach is no ordinary director of security. Having started his career as a systems analyst, he found that he enjoyed the investigative elements of his work the most and he joined the State of Hawaii as an Investigator, developing his capabilities in computer forensics – searching data for evidence of computer crime. On moving to Los Angeles in 1998, Michael formed his own security consultancy company, conducting what is known as "threat assessment management" for high profile clients – securing everything from physical presence, to personal privacy. In parallel he completed a philosophy degree, and spent his summers studying percussion at Berklee College of Music in Boston. "Music always was and will always be my first love," he says.

Michael had already met Andrew MacNaughtan on the Los Angeles circuit, and Andrew introduced Michael to Neil, who was looking to take advantage of such services; before long, the pair had found they had plenty to talk about. "Although my philosophy training was formal, and his informal, he seemed to know and comprehend everything I had spent so much money on in school!" laughs Michael. "We seemed to always have something pleasant to talk about whether it be intense subject matter, like Kant or Hegel, or the latest *South Park* episode." Michael was quick to realize that Neil's private persona was very different to the image he presented in public. "Fans think he is reclusive and unappreciative, but this is far from the truth," says Michael. "He does appreciate his fans; he just wants his fans to appreciate his music, not him personally."

Michael was employed as Director of Security for the *'Vapor Trails'* and 30th anniversary tours. Not only this, but Michael's love of motorcycles made him a suitable partner for Neil's unique approach to travelling between gigs – when offered, he jumped at the chance to travel the world. "I had worked with many bands before, but never stayed for an entire tour," he says. "This time I would get to ride my motorcycle with a friend and get paid for it, and tour with one of the greatest bands that ever was. After about .0001 seconds of thought, I accepted the job!"

Most recently, Michael has been instrumental in putting together Neil's website.

Paul Northfield

When the 17-year-old Paul Northfield applied for a post at Advision Studios in London, he didn't expect to get it. "I was miserable at school, I found out about studio life from hanging out with bands," he says. "I found a copy of *Beat Instrumental* with addresses in it and I wrote to three studios. Trident didn't reply, CTS in Wembley gave me a form letter saying we will get in touch and Advision sent me an interview." For some reason Paul was chosen over the 40-odd university graduates that had also applied. "It was very much an apprenticeship, they wanted somebody they could mould," he says. "Your first year or so is setting up microphones and making tea."

In March 1973, Paul started engineering for Greg Lake, his first project being to assist on Gentle Giant's album *'In A Glass House'*. He worked with Gentle Giant on and off for a number of years, becoming their preferred engineer – Paul went freelance from the studio so he could work wherever they went. When in 1977 the band wanted to produce an album at the renowned Canadian studio in Morin Heights, he was the logical choice – and was offered a job at Le Studio for his efforts. "The owner kept the offer open for a year or so," says Paul. For the 22-year-old, to be back in a salaried post was attractive, so in July 1978 he took it. "I went from London to the mountains of Quebec."

In the autumn of 1978 Paul engineered for Terry Brown on *'Permanent Waves'*, assisted by Robbie Whelan. *'Moving Pictures'* followed – "in many respects, the highlight of my career and in some ways the highlight of Rush's career," says Paul. "It is not a question of peaking, I think that everything came together on that record, the arrangements, the sound, the songwriting, performance, it all gelled in such a way that it made a record that stands the test of time. Those things I don't think you can plan, they just happen." Paul also participated on *'Signals'*, then *'Grace Under Pressure'*, assisting Jim Burgess with the PPG synthesiser programming. When Peter Collins brought with him Jimbo Barton there was no role for Paul, but when Jimbo was no longer available as Peter's engineer, Geddy set Paul up with Peter. "Jimbo and his wife were having a baby, so Peter called me up and asked me if I would do the

Queensrÿche album," says Paul. "I have done five or six records with him."

Meanwhile, Paul's own career went from strength to strength, including spending a month engineering with Marilyn Manson. "I had done a lot of what I call 'gorilla recording', where we go and set up a studio on the spot," says Paul. "They were going to work in the old Houdini mansion, we had to build a recording space. Dave Sardie (co-producer) had never done anything like that and Manson really wanted to work in the house, so they had me go in and do the bed track recording." Paul was also firming up his producer's skills, working in more of a production capacity on albums for I Mother Earth, Suicidal Tendencies and GZR with Black Sabbath's Geezer Butler.

Paul retained close links with the band, working on the two 'Burning for Buddy' tributes to Buddy Rich, with Neil. He was brought back in to co-produce 'Different Stages' with Geddy Lee, then 'Vapor Trails', joined by David Leonard for the mixing. Straight after 'Vapor Trails' came the Porcupine Tree album 'In Absentia', co-produced with Porcupine Tree frontman Steven Wilson. "That was the opposite end of the spectrum for me," says Paul. "Going from spending seven or eight months with Rush, to doing an album a month in New York with Steve, it was quite an amazing shift of gears. It was a very beautiful record to do and probably just what I needed."

By coincidence, Neil mentions 'In Absentia' as one of his favourite albums, in his book 'Travelling Music'. "I get an e-mail from Neil saying its funny, I have been listening to this record, its been on my turntable for the past two months, its my favourite record, and today I picked it up and I see your name on it," says Paul. "It was a wonderful confirmation, suddenly out of the blue he wrote this absolutely wonderful letter to say that it was a wonderful piece of work." Paul has been involved in engineering the latest Porcupine Tree album 'Deadwing', as well as producing the debut album for Pure Reason Revolution.

Tim Notter

Born in 1950, Tim was already a bartender back in the early seventies, at the same time as Rush were starting and a time when live music was rife in downtown Toronto. "We grew up knowing what good musicians are," he says, recalling how he used his evenings off to go watch the band. "I saw them at high schools, Abbey Road, Piccadilly, The Gasworks, you name it..."

His interest led him to write for the Toronto rock press, but his day job continued and before long he had a bar of his own. One bar was in the East End of Toronto, "A regular was Alex," says Tim, who became firm friends with the guitar player. A decade or so later, when Alex was looking for other things to do than just music, he came to see Tim. "They were going to take some time off anyway, so Alex was knocking around looking for something to do," explains Tim. The pair agreed to go into partnership, to set up a restaurant bar with a little live music on the side, just like old times. "The original intention was a little lounge that served food and cocktails. The band was to play Saturdays so that Alex would have someone to play with."

Tim's first challenge was to find a band. "I phoned up the only other musician I knew – this was Lou Pomanti." Lou took the job of putting a band together, and Tim got on with creating The Orbit Room – the Room first opened its doors in November 1994, with musical accompaniment by The Dexters. Over the months that followed, the restaurant gave way to a bar where live music was the centrepiece. "It's been refitted a few times to get to the situation it is in now," says Tim. "By year two we had live music every night."

Tim is relaxed about Alex's association with The Orbit Room. "If we owned it anywhere in the US it would be an enormous success, but here in Toronto, it's just a bar."

Carrie Nuttall

Carrie Nuttall is an established portrait photographer working out of Santa Barbara. She met Neil through Andrew MacNaughton in 1999, and the pair married in September 2000. Carrie provided additional photography on 'Rush in Rio', together with M. Rossi. She produced a book with Neil called 'Rhythm and Light', containing photos taken during the recording sessions leading up to 'Vapor Trails'.

Frank Opolko

With Robert Di Gioia, Frank was assistant engineer at Le Studio to Peter Henderson on 'Grace Under Pressure'. Frank started out as a bass player at the age of 14, playing "in a number of Toronto bands with derivative names like The Buddy Beck Blues Band or The Corporation," he says. He studied music at university, at night working as a musician to cover his fees.

Frank's big break came when he worked with Hugh Padgham, notably on 'Tonight' for David Bowie. "I learned a lot on that session," he says, not least how unrelenting music can be, earning $300 Canadian for 6 weeks work. "I worked 16 hours a day 7 days a week for 6 weeks yet I never received an album credit!" he exclaims. Again with Hugh, he worked on 'Synchronicity' for The Police, then 'Dream of The Blue Turtles' with Sting. "This was the first time I realized just what a brilliant songwriter he was," he says. "Also what a kind soul he was when the stress of The Police was removed."

Frank was brought in to Le Studio to support Robbie Whelan as a second assistant engineer. "There was so much work booked that I was hired to give Robbie a break," he says. Tragically, Robbie was killed in a car crash, at which point Frank had to take over his role.

Neil Peart

Percussion. And chocolate.

Lou Pomanti

When Lou Pomanti turned 18 in 1976, there was no dispute about what he wanted to do – music. He quickly learned that if he wanted to keep working he had to be prepared to do anything – within reason. "Living in a city like Toronto, you have to be versatile if you want to have a career," he says. "Even though it's a big city, it's not London and it's not New York and it's not L.A."

Lou's first big break came in 1980, when he was called by David Clayton-Thomas of Blood, Sweat and Tears, to join the band on their world tour. Using this experience as a springboard, Lou has played with the rollcall of Canadian performers, including Anne Murray, Triumph and Platinum Blonde. In the late eighties he became acquainted with bar owner Tim Notter, and he played keyboards with Kim Mitchell from 1992 to 1994. "I played on his album called *'Itch'*, I also wrote a song on it." Itch was recorded at Reaction Studios, later the location for *'Test For Echo'*.

In 1994, Lou was invited by Tim Notter to form a band for Tim and Alex's joint venture, the Orbit Room. "It was Labor Day, I was playing with Kim Mitchell at an old forties dance pavilion in Muskoka, the cottage country of Toronto," remembers Lou. "Tim called me, he said that him and his old buddy, Alex Lifeson, were starting a club. He wanted me to be the band leader, and he wanted me to model it after Booker T. and The MGs. I thought, if I get six weeks out of this it will be sweet!"

Lou set about putting a band together, and one of the first people he called was guitarist Bernie LaBarge. "The phone rang and it was Lou Pomanti on the other end," explains Bernie. "He figured it would be a six-month long stint. I said, sure thing. I hung up the phone and immediately said to myself, 'The Dexters'." And the band had a name.

Lou has been Musical director of the Juno Awards; "I've done a number of television movies and I just completed my first theatrical release feature film — *'Bailey's Billions'*, recorded March 2004, at Angel Studios in London," he says. "I kind of like being the guy who is the musical director at the Gemini awards this year and can conduct the band live on national television, and then stay in my basement for three months and score a feature film, and then go play a gig with the Dexters at the Orbit Room, it's all kind of, it's cool. It is the spice of life.

"The older I get, when I still get to do a first, its really exciting," says Lou, but there also has to be a last. Joined by Alex, The Dexters (with Lou on keys, Danish born Jorn Andersen on drums, Peter Cardinali on bass and Bernie on guitar and vocals) played their last gig as a house band of The Orbit Room ten years to the day after they had started, in November 2004. "The tenth anniversary gig was so spectacular, it was great," says Lou. "Doing it for ten years was a nice round number."

Tim Pope

Previously having worked with Talk Talk and The Cure, Tim directed *'Afterimage'*. Other videos from *'Grace Under Pressure'* were directed by Rocky Morton and David Mallet. Tim later worked on *'The Crow: City of Angels'*.

Simon Pressey

Simon was born in 1961, in Dartford, UK. His enjoyment of singing (though, he says, "I didn't have as much talent musically as I would have liked") led him to want to do something in music, a path which eventually led to Canada. He emigrated from the UK in 1986, to work as an in-house engineer at Le Studio at Morin Heights.

Simon assisted on *'Presto'* and *'Roll The Bones'*, and quickly became known for his careful handling of situations. "My nick name is 'We' as in 'Royal'," he says. "It came from Neil, laughing at part of my butlering diplomacy." With an attitude like that and his solid engineering skills, he was asked to assist on numerous projects, hired freelance by Peter when he no longer worked at Morin Heights. He helped Michael Letho mix *'Counterparts'*, assisted on *'Test For Echo'* and helped mix and edit the live album *'Different Stages'*.

He was also brought in for solo projects and others, including *'My Favourite Headache'* and the Geddy-produced *'Rocket Science'*, as well as the Buddy Rich tribute albums and a number of other collaborations with Paul Northfield. Simon also worked with Mutt Lang and Shania Twain (one of the highlights of his career, he says, "for the confidence it gave me.") as well as Celine Dion and A-Ha.

In January 2000, Simon moved to UbiSoft Montreal, to work on the music for video games. In 2003 he won the GameAudio Network Guild award for Audio Director/Producer of the year, and recently he was working on the music for the game 'Myst 4', along with Peter Gabriel. "I am very proud of it, it's a real bar raiser for the 'Myst' series," he says. "I haven't worked with Rush for a while, but my secret ambition is to produce a Rush album."

Robert Quartly

Considered to be one of Canada's most prominent rock video directors, in 1983, Rob picked up a "Best Video" Juno for Corey Hart's 'Sunglasses At Night'. Robert directed the video for 'Big Money'. It was produced by Allan Weinrib. Robert has also worked with Platinum Blonde, and on TV commercials for Labatts beer, Ikea, Chrysler and Kodak.

Olivia Ramirez

One of the team responsible for the urban development on *'Hold Your Fire'* on behalf of Hugh Syme, with Patrick Johnson and Scott Alexander.

Andy Richards

Andy was a "specialist" synthesizer player, who previously played with art-rock band The Strawbs (replacing Rick Wakeman) and who worked with Frankie Goes To Hollywood, with Trevor Horn. Andy was introduced to Peter Collins by Dave Meegan, who brought him in on *'Power Windows'* for programming and some keyboards. "I cannot remember if it was Rush, but they were looking for a keyboard player," says Dave. "I said, Trevor has been using this great guy Andy Richards on all the Frankie stuff, you should try him out."

Jack Richardson

As producer, Jack choreographed Max Webster and Rush in the recording of 'Battlescar'. Jack set up Just Another Mastering Facility (JAMF) with George Graves.

Rick Ringer

A CHUM-FM disc jockey who was mentioned on the liner notes for *'All The World's A Stage'*, Rick interviewed Geddy in 1981 at the time of the *'Moving Pictures'* release. In 1995 Rick took a dual role, as a DJ at CKPT and as programme director at CKQM, both based at Peterborough, Ontario, Canada.

Bob Roper

Bob Roper has worked for over thirty years in the music industry of Canada and North America. He was born in November 1947, in downtown Toronto.

His first job was with Capitol-EMI; after a couple of years, in the early seventies he was headhunted by A&M, working with bands such as Supertramp, Nazareth, Cat Stevens and (Andy Richards' band) The Strawbs. "I promoted new releases on A&M to radio, newspaper, and other media," explains Bob. "It is the promo rep's job to 'break' the artist through the media and hope that the public will then buy the records." Bob was one of the first people to come across Rush, and was instrumental in the Rush discovery story in early 1974, when he was working as regional promotion representative for A&M.

Bob left A&M in 1977 and went back to Capitol-EMI, moving to Vancouver as their "West Coast promotion man," he explains. "I always liked that gig because it reminded me of the old Rolling Stones track of the same name."

He then moved to Warner, to run their A&R division. He was then "headhunted" to manage a famous children's act, Sharon, Lois and Bram – famous for kids, that is. "They had a North American TV show and sold a million CDs per year!" Despite claiming that "It was a wonderful education," it was two years in this job however, that left Bob wondering what he was doing it for. "I couldn't handle not doing rock music," he says. "Had I heard 'She'll Be Comin' Round The Mountain' one more time, I would have needed a straitjacket!" In 1993, looking to get back to real music, Bob contacted Ray Danniels, who by coincidence had just lost Val Azzolli to Anthem as general manager of A&R. Bob's main job was to manage Anthem artist Lawrence Gowan. He stayed in the post for two years, before Ray decided to trim down some of Anthem's acts at the same time as he landed Van Halen's management. "Gowan and I had an inkling that our days at SRO/Anthem were numbered," says Bob. "When Gowan didn't generate huge commissions it was time for Ray to move on. Van Halen was certainly a much bigger payday for Ray both financially and prestigiously." Bob nonetheless saw his firing as an opportunity. "It did work out because it forced me into self-employment which I now regret not having done much sooner in life," he remarks. Meanwhile, Gowan fell on his feet when the position came up to replace Dennis DeYoung as the keyboardist/vocalist of Styx.

Bob has been running his own artist management company for 13 years now, and he is a director at The Harris Institute For The Arts, which provides training for careers in the music industry. Bob is also on the board of the Metronome foundation, a music charity.

Andy Rose

Andy started working for Mobile One in 1977 at the age of 22, graduating to the mixing desk. He was responsible for recording the Glasgow performance that was used on the *'Exit…Stage Left'* live album. His technical assistant was Barry Ainsworth.

In 1983 Andy formed his own mobile studios, known as Fleetwood Mobiles, and developed his main expertise in recording live TV shows. Fleetwood eventually became part of Sanctuary Mobiles. More recently, Andy worked with Oasis in the production of a DVD.

John Rutsey

John was a school friend of Alex and drummer on the debut album. He wrote a large number of the lyrics early on. John did try to find another band after Rush but to no avail.

Reno Ruocco

Trident engineer Reno Rucco was tape operator on *'Hemispheres'*. In 1978 he worked with Mike Donegani on *'Masques'* by Brand X, engineered by Stephen Tayler.

Russ Ryan

Toronto born and raised, Russ saw out the seventies playing the downtown bar circuit. However, he developed a reputation for fixing guitars, not playing them. "A sound man, Ross Tuskey watched me fix guitars, he gave me a call to work with Boy's Brigade as monitor engineer," says Russ. Unfortunately his monitor skills were not as apparent as his guitar skills. "I graduated to guitar," he says... "they fired me and re-hired me!" He went from there to another SRO band, this time Coney Hatch, and also worked with Honeymoon Suite, Platinum Blonde and Lou Pomanti. While he was aware of Rush, he wasn't a fan and never saw them live. "Great musicians but not my cup of tea," he says. "I was seeing George Benson!"

Following many years on the live circuit, Russ started with Rush as bass tech on the second half of the 'Test For Echo' tour, following a call from Jimmy Johnson. The timing could have been better – going on tour was the last thing he wanted to do at that point. "I'd just finished with the Scorpions," he explains. "It didn't sell well, the band was miserable, I had to decide, did I want to get straight back?" A second call from Liam was followed up with another from Jimmy. "Trust me, do it," they said, so Russ decided to bite the bullet. Not once has he regretted the decision. "These guys just don't get any better," he says. "There's a family vibe, like a whole bunch of buddies that like to get together and tour, and have a great time. You don't even see arguments among the crew!"

> **Totally Vending Machine**
>
> "It's full of knick-knacks Geddy has found on tour. We have lots of fun trying to fill the stuff. Nobody knows but the band – it's for us! Bobbleheads of Sammy Davis Junior and Mr T, a toy dog, a rubber dragon and Lady Penelope's car. Rock and Roll."
>
> Russ Ryan

In particular, Russ was surprised at the simplicity of the bass rig. "Is this ever simple," he thought. Geddy's bass is piped through a speaker simulator, and even the sound levels are pretty much fixed. "Any EQ will not change the rest of the tour," says Russ. "We set it up on Day 1 and that's the way it stays!" Russ is also responsible for the washing machines and vending machine, set up to fill the gaping hole left by Geddy's amps. If nothing else, the appliances offered a perfect opportunity to wind up journalists who asked what they were for. "Geddy looks for the dry, clean sound," they would explain, then try to keep straight faces as the humour slowly dawns...

Russ picked up a credit for studio work on Geddy's solo album 'My Favorite Headache'. "I did a lot of guitar maintenance for Ben Mink," he says.

Dimo Safari

Toronto-based photographer Dimo Safari has had a long-standing collaboration with Hugh Syme, which led to his involvement on 'Power Windows', 'A Show Of Hands', 'Test For Echo' and 'Different Stages'. "Dimo and I enjoyed both a long term camaraderie and respect on a creative level," says Hugh, who particularly enjoyed the experience of working with Dimo on 'Power Windows'. "That was the most profound and most enjoyable collaboration I have ever had in my career. Dimo was the true Jekyll for this Mr Hyde on many occasions. He's a great travel companion, and a terrible fisherman!" Dimo worked with many other artists, including Platinum Blonde.

Sol Saffian

Sol was a booking agent at American Talent International with Jeff Franklin and Ira Blacker, and later at Buddy Lee Attractions, Inc. He was thanked on the first album, and was a good friend of Howard Ungerleider. Later he picked up acts such as Willie Nelson and Tammy Wynette, retiring in 1996.

Sol died of cancer in July 2005.

Deborah Samuel

Deborah joined as photographer in October 1979, brought in to do band photography on *'Permanent Waves'* at Le Studio, as well as her studio being used by Fin Costello. She later worked with Hugh Syme on *'Exit...Stage Left'*, *'Moving Pictures'* (on which she makes a cameo appearance, as Joan of Arc) and *'Signals'* for which she photographed the cover.

David Scace

David was guitar tech on the first Rush tour.

Lee Scherer

Lee R. Scherer was a Captain in the Navy when he started working with NASA, and he joined formally in 1965 following 25 years flying in the Navy. He worked as an Apollo programme director and manager of the Lunar Orbiter Program from its inception in 1963 through its successful completion in 1967.

In October 1971 Lee became Director of Dryden Space Center, a post he held until 1975, where he went on to direct the Kennedy Space Center. During his tenure there was the Apollo Soyuz Test Project and the early developments that became the Space Shuttle programme. In 1979, he took up an external relations post at NASA Headquarters, during which he co-ordinated Rush's visit to the Space Shuttle launch with Gerry Griffin. Following his tenure he moved to become senior executive at General Dynamics commercial services group, a post he still occupied in 2000.

Peter Schliewen

Peter was the proprietor of Record Revolution, the first shop in Cleveland to import copies of *'Rush'*. Peter passed away in the mid-eighties, but his shop is still going strong.

Flip Schulke

Flip was involved in the photography on *'Permanent Waves'*, with Fin Costello and Deborah Samuel.

Robert Scovill

While he started out as a musician, it wasn't long for the young Robert to realise he could have more fun in front of the stage. "At a Supertramp concert at the ripe age of 13, I kind of had an epiphany," he says. "The show's audio production was simply sensational, I distinctly remember thinking, wait, there is something more happening here than just the band playing their instruments on stage." As his musical tastes developed, one of the bands Robert discovered was Rush. "I was a pretty passionate fan during my teen years. I never in my wildest dreams could have imagined I would one day end up working with them."

Robert did indeed go into pro audio, working his way up that ladder until he was working with bands such as Def Leppard. At one gig, at CNE stadium in Toronto, the band's manager (and Cliff Burnstein's partner) Peter Mensch made a comment to Robert in passing. "Hey Bob, Ged is coming down to hear you mix tonight because they may be looking for a mixer for their upcoming tour." No pressure – as it happened, it was one of those gigs... the baseball game played in the stadium during the day went into extra time. "The game ended about 30 minutes before the doors were scheduled to open," remembers Robert. "Needless to say there was a mad scramble to get everything just thrown into place. The show was started on time, we were totally flying by the seat of our pants." Against all odds, the show came together and Geddy liked what he heard.

Robert joined the Rush crew as sound engineer on the *'Presto'* tour, replacing John Erickson. "It was so surreal for me," he says. "My first day at rehearsal was really special in that I was embraced as if I had been around for 20 years with them. The first night's performance was really grand as well. I still pinch myself every now and then when I think back at that night." Robert continued to work with Rush on the *'Roll The Bones'*, *'Counterparts'* and *'Test For Echo'* tours, selecting from the latter the shortlist of shows for what would become the *'Different Stages'* album. In the Rush hiatus, he found himself working more and more for other bands, including Tom Petty and The Heartbreakers. He was offered the opportunity to re-join Rush on the *'Vapor Trails'* tour, but conflicts of schedule forced him to hand over the reins to Brad Madix. "I was heartbroken," he says. Who wouldn't be.

Paul Seigel

Along with Rob Wallis at Bearsville Studios, Paul worked with Neil on his instructional video *'A Work In Progress'*. See Rob Wallis entry for more details.

Rod Serling

'Caress Of Steel' was dedicated to Rod, the creator of the *'Twilight Zone'*, writing 92 of the 156 episodes himself. One of the episodes was directed by Allan King. Rod died on 28 June 1975, due to unexpected complications following a heart bypass operation.

Don Shafer

Born in 1956 in Pittsburgh, Don Shafer started in radio in 1969 following time as a cryptologist and communications specialist working for the US Military and the NSA. After moving to Canada in the early 70s, Don worked as programmer and DJ for a number of radio stations including Toronto's CHUM-FM (which he joined in 1972, working with David Marsden), and he was a contemporary of Ray Danniels. "I am distinguished in this regard, only in that I was the first announcer in Canada to play Rush on CHUM FM in the early 70s," he says. "Ray Danniels and I have been friends for a very long time. He was a struggling manager/promoter and I was cutting my teeth on rock radio." Don was thanked for his efforts to promote the band, picking up a mention on the cover of *'Fly By Night'*.

Don worked his way through a number of radio stations in both the US and Canada, as a programme director and manager. He later founded the Rock Radio Network in Canada, a pioneer in radio syndication, and has worked in both TV and the printed media before moving back into radio in 2003. Today Don works for Standard Radio, managing a group of 21 radio and 2 TV stations in British Columbia. "I am fortunate to work for an owner who asks what it sounds like first, then how we're doing financially second," he says. Don has seen many changes over the years, particularly in how Canadian bands are perceived in the wider world. "We used to criticise Canadian music for eating their young," he says. "We turned our backs on the talent, but not now."

Jim Shelton

James P. Shelton was studio manager at Mercury Sound Studios, and acted as mastering consultant on Rush's first album. Mastering was done by Gilbert Kong: "Gilbert actually worked with the client, while I managed the studio," says Jim. Jim remained in charge when the studios were spun off from Mercury and bought by Lee Hulko of Sterling Sound, who named the new organization Masterdisk. "After Masterdisk was sold off, I moved on," says Jim. In 1977 he started a company, Europadisk Plating Ltd., to be the first in North America market to use Swedish company Europafilm's plating equipment and process for electroforming vinyl stampers from lacquer masters. Europadisk has prided itself on its adoption of new technologies when they became available, from Direct Metal Mastering of vinyl up to the present day addition of DVD replication.

Kevin Shirley

As well as playing guitar and studying composition, South African born Kevin "Caveman" Shirley cut his engineering teeth in his home country before deciding that the apartheid regime wasn't for him. He moved to Sydney, and found he had to build his reputation all over again. His big break came when an album he had engineered in New York for The Baby Animals hit the big time, prompting Kevin to move to the Big Apple and try his luck. Of course, this meant he had to build his reputation all over again... fortunately, one fan of The Baby Animals' album was Peter Collins, who invited Kevin to Morin Heights as his engineer, for *'Counterparts'* – assisted by Simon Pressey.

Following a few more collaborations with Peter, Kevin returned to Australia. His inimitably raw producing style was instrumental in the success of the debut album by Silverchair. Having cemented a reputation as a leading edge producer, he has gone on to produce Journey, Aerosmith, the Black Crowes, Iron Maiden, Dream Theater and his childhood heroes, Led Zeppelin.

Jason Sniderman

Rush first met Jason Sniderman at the 1977 Juno awards, when he was Vice President of the 100-store Sam The Record Man music chain – a friendship with Geddy developed which has lasted to this day. Jason provided additional keyboards on *'Presto'* and in 1990, he presented the band with the CARAS Artists of The Decade award. More recently Jason contributed keyboards again, this time to Geddy's *'My Favorite Headache'* solo outing.

Norman Stangl

Born thirty miles outside Toronto, Norm Stangl studied animation at Sheridan College in Oakville in the mid-70s, a brave move at the time. "I originally planned to go into photography, but I kind of fell into animation during a tour of the college when I happened upon a screening of some animation that the students had produced," he says. "I loved the concept of making things move. I loved to draw, it all fit."

When he qualified, Norm went to work for an animation shop called Nelvana Ltd, before moving to Mammoth Pictures to work on "animated FX for commercials." In 1981 he returned to Nelvana to work on the feature film *'Rock 'n' Rule'*, and it was there that he took the call from Rush. "That was the first time that I met Geddy and Howard," he explains. "We met, our minds connected and we were off to a brilliantly long working relationship."

Shortly afterwards, Norm started Keen Pictures as an independent and took his Rush business with him. "Geddy was gracious enough to grant the loyalty of production and I continued to produce animated and live action work for the band's tour films," he says. After Keen, it was back to Nelvana for four years, before Norm joined SPIN Productions as a partner in 1992. Once again, he brought his loyal customers along. "Rush has stayed with me through all of my career path changes," he says.

While it is not working for Rush, SPIN Productions currently works mainly for advertisers and broadcasters. "I am also developing some computer animated series for broadcast in 2006," says Norm. It wasn't such a bad career decision. "Animation was hardly considered a reliable career path 30 years ago," he comments. "People would scratch their heads and question how anyone could make a living in animation. Today, the idea doesn't seem so far out there. Call it dumb luck!"

George Steinert

George and the band go way back – living in St Catherine's since the seventies, George knew Neil since he was in his late teens, and was around in 1974 when Neil joined the band.

George trained as a carpenter and started working in several theatres in the St Catherine's area, working on props, making repairs and so on. In 1984, as the band were preparing for the *'Power Windows'* tour, he got a call from Liam Birt who was living in St Catherine's at the time. "They started doing a lot of prop work," says George, whose first task for Rush was building a set of four ramps that were part of the live set. His calm demeanor quickly made George a welcome member of the crew, and he found his role did not stop with the carpentry – during shows, he would support Jim Johnson on stage right.

David Stock

A past employee of SRO and the original producer of *'Rush'*, the production of which was taken over by Terry Brown.

Roger Stowell

Roger took the sleeve photograph used on *'A Farewell To Kings'*. Today, he specialises in cookery photography.

Chris Stringer

Chris was engineer at Reaction Studios, Toronto. He added percussion to *'My Favorite Headache'*, and assisted the recording of *'Vapor Trails'*.

Hugh Syme

Called "manic" by Neil, Hugh Syme spent 5 years at grammar school in the North of England, at the same time as a young Dave Stewart. "I went to school in Sunderland but ended up finishing in Canada for the last year," says Hugh. "We all joked about that little twit of a red head, thinking he was going to be a rock star later..." Hugh came back to Europe to study for a degree, but he left before the end of the course when he was invited to play keyboards for his friend, Ian Thomas' band. "Music always called on me," he says.

The Ian Thomas Band signed to SRO, and Hugh's grounding in graphic arts was sufficient for him to put together a cover for one of their albums. He didn't think that much of stablemates Rush, however. "I didn't anticipate them to be a real force to be reckoned with," says Hugh. "I was a pretty committed Genesis, Supertramp, 10CC kind of snob and didn't understand Rush at the time." All the same, he accepted the opportunity to design a cover for *'Caress of Steel'*, kicking off a professional relation-ship that has lasted three decades.

Hugh also picked up a number of keyboard credits, his visits to the studio to discuss cover designs often resulting in him jamming with the band and adding something musical to the album. "We jammed on a version of 'Rough and Ready' for quite a few hours, I believe aided by their ever present cellar of good wines," says Hugh. "We did as many versions as we could think of." He played keys on 'Tears' and 'Witch Hunt', and grand piano on 'Different Strings'.

In 1979, Hugh left the Ian Thomas Band and turned his attention to album design, for a number of reasons, not least the lack of support for Canadian artists. "There was some notable stuff coming out of Canada but we were a long way from Celine Dion, Bryan Adams, Avril Lavigne and all the other good stuff," says Hugh. "I think I made the right decision to have a visual career because it is a bit more controllable."

In making the decision, he was able to ride the wave of heavy metal album covers. "I was asked to create some very indulgent and extravagant productions by a whole slue of people, a lot of whom became my friends and clients," he says. Hugh has done covers for Iron Maiden (not to mention a full scale mockup of the band's icon, Eddie, which the band's record company deemed too scary to be used on the album cover) and Queensrÿche, having to overcome the dangers of being typecast along the way. "The people at Q-Prime called and said they thought I was a Rush guy," said Hugh, who was quick to point out he held no strict allegiances. In 1986 Hugh moved to Los Angeles, where he met Glen Wexler, Patrick Johnson, Scott Alexander and Olivia Ramirez. "Scott, Patrick (though a seldom used talent) and the wonderfully gifted Olivia were an oft hired group in a lot of my work in subsequent years," he says. Hugh spent a total of 11 years in LA, before moving back to Toronto.

Over the years, Hugh has seen many changes, including the technologies available for graphic art. "Albums such as *'Hold Your Fire'* involved lengthy processing. It was all dye transfer," says Hugh. "You collect the elements from your suppliers, you then knit together the final image, the final concept." The knitting process was a long-winded routine known as emulsion stripping, which involved many stages of cutting, removing, and retouching before the final image was reached. "You are left with this new piece of imagery, really rough around the edges," says Hugh. "It needs a lot of bleaching and dying and retouching by hand, on what's known as a dye transfer, which is a 700 dollar print. If you screw it up you need to buy another one."

By *'Presto'* and *'Roll The Bones'* computers were starting to replace the manual processing, but while these might have been easier, they were no cheaper. "When you wanted to do any kind of colour editing or editing you would rent time in places that had multi-million dollar equipment known as Quantel Paintbox," says Hugh. "You would spend 350-700 dollars an hour with your well planned manoeuvres."

With *'Counterparts'* came the arrival of digital technology, and by *'Test For Echo'* in 1997, the entire cover was done digitally. The relative ease of use was a double-edged sword, however. "You had the latitude to perfect and delve deeper," says Hugh. "In that respect it becomes anything but easier. Like good music it has to be somewhat spontaneous, there is a dance, a rhythm, a spontaneity that you need to respond to as well." All the same, the new was infinitely preferable to the old. "I have t-shirts bearing the statement, *'Command Z means you never have to say you are sorry'*. I am very grateful for never having to smell another bottle of potassium permanganate or bleach."

Over the years, Hugh has never stopped pushing the boundaries, but he's never complacent about his role with Rush. "It's my nature not to believe in my own press, I like to remind myself every once in a while that you are (as they say) only as good as your last piece," he says. "When I do get the call, I am always able to hang up and feel that same similar sense of glee and excitement and gratitude for their including me."

Jeremy Taggart

Jeremy Taggart was born on 7 April 1975. Straight after high school he joined the band Our Lady Peace. He collaborated on *'My Favorite Headache'*, adding drums to 'Home On The Strange'.

Peter Talbot

A friend of Neil's, Peter was co-writer of 'Closer To The Heart'.

Stephen Tayler

Despite an in-depth musical education, Stephen Tayler decided he'd rather be a recording engineer than follow a directly musical career. "I didn't want to go into the recording industry and be perceived as a frustrated musician, so I actually played it down," he says. "I never wanted to come across as the know-it-all musician!" All the same, he could not help bringing his musical knowledge into his engineering. For a number of years he worked at Trident studios as a staff engineer, which at the time meant being very much tied to the studio. "There was the Trident school of thought and the Air Studio school of thought, each had an identity," says Stephen, who was on occasion assisted by Reno Ruocco and Mike Donegani. Unknown to Stephen, Rush also worked at Trident during his time there, mixing *'Hemispheres'* in 1978.

Having worked with such artists as Brand X, Bill Bruford and Peter Gabriel, Stephen formed a lasting alliance with musician/producer Rupert Hine. "He knew that I was very musical," says Stephen. "Our first collaborations were testimony to both sonic and musical experimentation." These included Howard Jones' *'Human's Lib'*, released in 1984 and the first of many chart albums for the pair, including for Tina Turner and The Thompson Twins. In the late eighties and early nineties respectively, Stephen worked with Rupert on *'Presto'* and *'Roll The Bones'* for Rush, at Le Studio in Morin Heights. "He was very, very important to those albums," says Rupert. "He is an astonishing engineer." While continuing to engineer, Stephen started to consider once again how he could make his own music, in particular as technology had started to lower the bar for production facilities. With his partner, Canadian-born Sadia, the pair released an album *'Equa'* in 1996. "We are talking the early days of sampling and assimilating different styles of music," says Stephen. "I started to realise that there was going to be more and more integration, it wouldn't do to just be a blinkered specialist anymore." His experience diversified into a wide spectrum of world music and fusion styles, notably working on the soundtrack for the film *'The Fifth Element'*.

Today, Stephen runs a production company Chimera Arts with Sadia. In 2003 the pair worked on music for the documentary *'The Noon Gun'*, and they have recently recorded a live DVD for Howard Jones, and visited Australia with Sadia's video and sound installation *'The Memory of Water'*. Despite the levelling aspect of technology, Stephen is sanguine, indeed positive about the future. "At some point all things are possible to everybody," he says. "What do you have to offer any more, other than your specific talent – it is coming back full circle."

Lee Tenner

Lee was projectionist for all tours from *'Moving Pictures'* though to *'Hold Your Fire'*. *'Counterparts'* was dedicated to his memory.

Dave Thomas

With Rick Moranis, Dave was the other half of the comedy duo, Bob and Doug Mackenzie. Dave is also brother of Ian Thomas, of the Ian Thomas Band.

Howard Ungerleider

Howard started out playing in a band when he was at college, but he also worked for the Student Union. "I was always the guy who put the lighting together," he says. In this role he happened to cross paths with Sean Laroche, a big-shot agent who included The Who on his roster. "I asked him what it took to get a deal." A short while later, Howard quit University and went to New York in search of a record deal for his band. The first place he targeted was Sean's offices, but he couldn't even get past the reception desk. He waited for his opportunity, watching for when the secretary took her breaks. It was this, second meeting with Sean that really set Howard on the right track. "You're never going to get a deal," said Sean, "Knuckle down and learn the business." Sean gave Howard six names of people in the business; one of these was Jeff Franklin, who ran a company called Action Talent.

Howard called Jeff and he was offered a job, right at the bottom of the stack. He quite literally worked in the mail room and made the tea. Audacious as ever, he took his chance at a big break when he overheard Jeff trying to book a certain date for Fleetwood Mac. A few phone calls later, Howard had secured a spot at the Fairleigh Dickinson University in New Jersey, for double the money, and his agency career was on its way.

Howard went on to book a number of bands, including Blue Öyster Cult, through whom he met Elliott Krowe of See Factor. Officially he was working on the contractual side, but he kept his hand in on the lighting, learning on the job from the old hands that he met in the venues. When Rush was signed with ATI, Howard was sent to Toronto by Ira Blacker to work with Ray Danniels on the band's very first tour. Before long Howard left the agency and went to do the lighting for Rush. By *'Fly By Night'* he was referred to as "Road Master", and the following tour he earned the nickname "Herns" and took the dual roles of road manager and lighting director.

> ### You're Nicked
>
> In the early seventies, Howard was working as tour manager for English jazz artist Brian Auger, and his band Oblivion Express. "I was always barking orders," says Howard, recalling how this reminded Brian of a British TV character called Sergeant Herns. "One day he walked in and said, hey, Herns! The guys heard it, and it went on from there!"

From 1981, Howard started managing the band Boys Brigade which later signed to SRO (and had Geddy as producer for their 1983 debut album, *'Into The Flow'*). After the *'Presto'* tour, Cliff Burnstein's company QPrime offered Howard the opportunity to work with Def Leppard (on the design of the *'Hysteria'* tour), Queensrÿche and Tesla. "Howard is fantastic", says Cliff. "I always loved Howard."

At this point Howard left Rush's books and set up his own company, Production Design International (PDI www.pdifx.com), to take the Queensrÿche gig, working with Brad Madix (sound engineer) and Dan Braun (production manager) amongst others. Unexpectedly Queensrÿche had a hit single 'Silent Lucidity' in the middle of the tour, which immediately was extended, from seven to what eventually became 16 months – Howard's Rush tour management role was taken by Liam Birt. Meanwhile, Howard continued to sub for QPrime between Rush tours, including being tour manager for Metallica's *'Ride The Lightning'* tour. "I wanted to do lighting for them but they wouldn't let me – their loss!" When working with Def Leppard, he met with Robert Scovill.

Howard has carried on as lighting designer and director for Rush until the present day. He is also managing a band called Transient Noise. "Alex has produced three tracks for me last year," he says.

Michael Vander Veldt

Michael was the boy on the cover of *'Roll The Bones'*, and in the associated video.

Rich Vinyard

Rich works for Howard Ungerleider in charge of the four people in the lighting crew. "Howard designs it, I put it up," he says. His first tour as a paid-up member of the Rush crew was *'Vapor Trails'*, prior to which he would accompany the tour on behalf of the lighting company.

Rob Wallis

Rob Wallis and his partner Paul Siegel are both drummers, co-owning a drum school. "It's a kind of drummers' collective," says Rob. "We had a desire to educate musicians and modernise education a bit." The pair started DCI Video to produce drum tuition videos in 1982, with an aim to bring in influential drummers. "Neil had always been at the top of the list," says Rob, whose collaborators included Steve Smith and Freddie Gruber, who the pair had introduced. "We came to learn we couldn't really call Neil, so we used to write letters to him. We wrote one or two times a year, for six to eight years. He said his schedule didn't allow him time to take on an outside project. He'd write back, 'not the right time, check back down the road', but he always left the door open. One day, he said we'd finally worn him down and he'd finally caved in."

Meanwhile, DCI Video had been sold to Columbia Pictures Publications, back in 1992 – but Rob and Paul's services had been retained.

It took a further two years before the pair finally managed to pin Neil down, shortly after *'Test For Echo'* and it was agreed to work at Bearsville. "We wanted to incorporate some of the surrounds," says Rob. "Paul knew the studio manager." The video *'A Work In Progress'* was shot in May 1997, and several months of editing followed. "Every so often, we'd send it to Neil and he'd send his critique," says Rob. "Neil was involved every step of the way, to say the least. It was a great, very satisfying experience."

The next collaboration was *'Burning For Buddy'*: Neil asked whether Rob and Paul could film the recording sessions, as unobtrusively as possible. "Neil didn't want to impose with a full crew," says Rob. "We went out and bought a couple of Canon cameras – not very expensive, but they were decent at the time, and small." The pair spent every day for two weeks recording the sessions, the result being the video *'The Making of "Burning for Buddy"'*. "Neil was totally involved every day," says Rob. "It was very intensive – set up, tune and do a take, break down the kit and get the next one in, it was cool!"

Rob and Paul have remained in fairly regular communication with Neil, even during his travels. "He came to New York to see Paul and I one night," says Rob. "Neil's a great, great guy."

Michael Wargo

Michael directed *'A Work In Progress'*, Neil's instructional video (1996), filmed and edited by Paul Siegel and Rob Wallis.

Neil Warnock

In 1962 and at the tender age of sixteen, Neil Warnock saw his first band using electric guitar at his local youth club, and he was hooked. He bought a drum kit, and while he quickly discovered he was an absolutely hopeless drummer, he became fascinated in the work surrounding bands, how they rehearsed, how they put on a gig, and so on.

His day job was as an apprentice compositor (a typesetter, when type was still set by hand), but he started promoting bands, 'The Emeralds' for example, for his local youth club. "My dad was the bouncer on the door, and I think my mum took the money," he recalls. Soon he was doing the same for his college, the London College of Printing, his biggest coup being to book The Who for £70 to play the day after 'I Can't Explain' was released.

Neil set up his first agency 'South Bank Artists' at the age of eighteen, joining forces with another agent who was successfully promoting British bands in Germany, which enabled Neil to develop an enviable network of London Colleges where he could place bands. "I started to put artistes into University College, Imperial College, Kings College on the Strand – so much so that the major agencies had to come through me to put their bands into the colleges," says Neil.

Neil stuck with his apprenticeship in parallel with the agency work until he was 21, after which he "resigned honourably". "It meant that I could always go back and get my ticket again," he says. Not that he ever would – within a year the pressure to work for one of the major agencies became too great. He chose to work at the Beatles' agency Nems Enterprises, but it was when Nems acquired the more contemporary Bryan Morrison Agency (representing Pink Floyd, Tyrannosaurus Rex, Fairport Convention and the like) that Neil really learned what it took to be a good agent. "The education their agents gave me, changed me from being an old style agent where you always looked after the promoter, to realising that the band, the artist is the reason why everybody else is making a living," he explains.

Having worked his way up to becoming a director of Nems, in 1973 Neil moved to Bron Agency as joint managing director, working with Pink Floyd, Jeff Beck and Deep Purple. "I was picking up the heavier acts," says Neil. "By the time we got to '75 we had Uriah Heep, we had Blue Öyster Cult, we had Aerosmith, Kiss..." Through such bands Neil had a good relationship with Jeff Franklin's company, ATI; through this connection he first heard about Rush and almost immediately, he set about becoming their international agent by putting a call in to SRO. "They told me that they couldn't believe that there was any market whatsoever for Rush in the UK; I said, if you want to come over we can do two dates at Hammersmith, we can do Manchester, Birmingham, four or five shows," he says. "I had already spoken to John Curd at Straight Music, a promoter with brilliant ears who picked up on a lot of music very early on." SRO said yes – and the first UK tour for the band was set – as well as Neil earning the role of international agent, which he carries on today. "Every single show they've played outside of America I have been the agent for – Japan, Brazil, everything."

All the same, Rush could never be his only band. "If I was going to set my income for life based on this band touring over here, I would have been a pauper a long time ago!" Over the years, Neil has worked doggedly to get Rush to tour outside North America. Things haven't been helped by the disinterest of the band's recording label.

"If I took notice of what the label were telling me in terms of sales we would never have brought the band in and we would certainly never have brought the band back."

The international presence of Neil Warnock's agency – The Agency Group – has taken many years to establish. "As I got bigger bands, and as the bands started to spread out around the world then I learnt to book around the world," he says. "My two favourite trail blazers are Status Quo and Deep Purple, they have got the crews that can deal with it and they have also got the bands that can deal with it." Today, the company has a number of offices worldwide and represents over a thousand acts but Neil still insists on having his own roster of artists – Rush included. "It is a fairly mixed up, eclectic roster," he says. "George Benson, Motorhead, Lisa Stansfield and Rush, it's all over the place. I have a mezzo Soprano, Katherine Jenkins, who is going to be selling 300,000 albums by Christmas – I like to push myself to do different things as well."

Back at Rush, Neil has learned through the years how best to satisfy the band's demands, at the same time as enabling them to reach out internationally. His efforts culminated in Rush's agreement to play Brazil for the first time, on the 'Vapor Trails' tour. "They never believed there was an audience for them there," says Neil, who left no stone unturned in his quest. "I kept going back to them and saying I got this now, yeah but we need all our stuff taking down there in a 747 freighter, yeah I got that, we have all got to be in 25 star hotels. Everything is like, which argument have you got now that we can't go, give me an argument because I have covered everything that you said you wanted to have covered! The best thing that happened in Europe and in South America was that the band enjoyed it. The band are at the stage now where, if they don't enjoy doing it they are not going to repeat it."

Howie Weinberg

Howie mastered 'My Favorite Headache' for Geddy, at Masterdisk in New York City. "He is a savant in terms of mastering," says Paul Northfield. "One day he will get out of bed and what he does is stunning and the next day he will get out of bed and it won't be very good at all. Getty had a fantastic experience with him on his solo record." He also mastered 'Vapor Trails', supported by Roger Lian.

Allan Weinrib

Geddy Lee's brother, Allan at one time ran The Revolver Film Company, a Toronto-based production company for music videos. Past customers include David Bowie, Marilyn Manson and The Cranberries. In 1985 Allan produced the 'Big Money' video, directed by Robert Quartly. He produced a number of other Rush videos, particularly in the eras of 'Counterparts' ('Stick it Out' and 'Nobody's Hero') and 'Test For Echo' ('Half The World' and 'Driven'). He was also co-producer on the 2003 DVD 'Rush in Rio', notably making the decision not to do anamorphic encoding of the DVD, due to the poor image quality of Neil's drumming.

Photographer Andrew McNaughtan is a video director at Revolver.

Paul Weldon

Having trained as an architect in the early 1960s, Toronto-based keyboardist Paul Weldon formed a band in 1966 with jamming partner Larry Evoy, bringing in guitarist

Danny Marks. They called the band Edward Bear after the bear that inspired Winnie the Pooh, and signed to Capitol Records in 1969. "Once we began playing regularly I had to take a break from architecture and I decided to pursue another interest, graphic design," he says. "I found a lot of work designing all sorts of things for music groups, recording studios, record companies and so on." Indeed, the band's first single off their second album, *'You Can't Deny It'*, included a cover designed by Paul. In 1971 and 1972 Paul designed covers for the Crowbar album *'Bad Manors'*, for Everyday People's debut album, and for the *'America Eats Its Young'* cover for Funkadelic.

Through mutual contacts Paul was contacted by Ray Danniels and Vic Wilson, who asked if he could design a logo for the newly created Moon Records. He went on to produce a cover for Rush's first album. "We agreed on a concept and an approach," he says. "In Rush's early days they didn't have much money and so I kept it to a 2 colour job (black and red)."

Since then, Paul has expanded his portfolio to include corporate and industrial graphics, and he has lived through the many evolutions of media, not least the advent of digital techniques and the rise of the now-ubiquitous Internet. He's kept his hand in music – these days, Paul plays piano in the T. O. Trio, a jazz combo with Alan Sumpter on bass and Craig Barrett on drums. "We play for events and clubs in Toronto," he says.

Glen Wexler

Los Angeles resident Glen first set up his own photographic studio in 1978. He met Hugh Syme in 1986, through a mutual acquaintance. "A close friend of mine, Chuck Wright, at the time was the bass player in Quiet Riot," explains Glen, "Hugh had recently completed painting album covers for Quite Riot and Whitesnake." Both had good experience of album covers, which led to Hugh using Glen for the cover of *'Hold Your Fire'*. "At the time, both Hugh and I had a lot of album cover work behind us," says Glen. "We shared similar conceptual sensibilities and an interest in pushing the boundaries of photographic images." Agrees Hugh, "Glen was a patient and always gracious host when we chose to work in his studio – and he shared my determination to pursue excellence."

Having developed his own reputation on the LA circuit, Glen was a source of many contacts. "I had established an elaborate network of resources for creating my work," he says – not least Patrick Johnson, Scott Alexander and Olivia Ramirez. Together, and involving other collaborators they worked on covers for other bands, including Slaughter (*'Stick It To Ya'*) and Michael Schenker (*'Perfect Timing'*). "There were several photography-based album packages, recording industry ads, and a fashion account," says Glen. An early advocate of digitally altered photography, today Glen continues to work from his busy studio in Los Angeles. His web site is www.glenwexlerstudio.com

Lorne Wheaton

Lorne first knew of Rush when they played his high school (the George Vanier) in the early seventies, and it wasn't long before he'd headed down the same track. The overriding desire to work in the biz was tempered by pragmatism, which drew him away from the stage and into the technician role. "I quickly realized it paid better!" he laughs. Not much better however – taking a variety of roles, "drum tech, guitar tech, stage manager, drove truck," it would be few years before he really made any money.

By the mid-seventies he established himself as drum tech for Max Webster and Godot, and it was through the Max connection in 1978 that Lorne hooked up with the trio once again, when the Websters were supporting Rush, through until they split in 1979. By then he had established a reputation on the circuit. "I manage to get along with most people," he says, and he never really looked back from this point. In the early eighties, Lorne went to work with Steve Smith in Journey, not to mention Robert Palmer and Bryan Adams. He also worked (together with Skip Gildersleeve) for Steely Dan.

When Rush decided to go back into the studio again for what was to become 'Vapor Trails', the band needed a tech and Lorne happened to be in the right place at the right time. At Neil's suggestion, Liam Birt called Lorne and asked him in to look after the guitars, basses and drums required for recording the album. "I looked after the guitars, basses and drums," recalls Lorne. This was no small job – "Alex has 35 guitars, he likes to get them restrung quite often…" After this experience, Lorne was the logical choice as Neil's drum tech for the 'Vapor Trails' tour, a role he has continued to the present day.

Robbie Whelan

Robbie was a resident engineer at Le Studio, assistant to Paul Northfield. "He was loved by all the clients and especially by Neil," says colleague Frank Opolko. "Nothing was impossible for Robbie – any request, legal or otherwise!"

Robbie worked with Terry Brown on 'Permanent Waves', 'Moving Pictures' and 'Signals', shortly after which he died in a car crash. "Tragically one morning, on his way to work and during The Asia sessions," says Frank. 'Grace Under Pressure' was dedicated to him.

Vic Wilson

Vic was born and bred in Ontario, and decided early on that he wanted to work in the music industry. In 1969, he moved to Britain for a couple of years, where he played in a band. He returned to Canada to form his own management company, called Concept 376. Eventually he merged companies with Ray Danniels to form SRO Productions. As SRO grew, Vic managed a widening roster of bands, including Downchild, a band he later joined as baritone sax player.

When Vic left SRO in 1981, he sold his share of the company to Ray but remained active in the music industry. He was president of CIRPA (Canadian Independent Record Production Association) from 1981-1986. In 1993 he was invited to join the line-up of Little Caesar and The Consuls, hastily reformed to make the album 'Since 1956', with previous members Steve Macko on vocals, Norm Sherrat on saxophone, Tom Wilson on bass, Gary Wright on drums, and new boy Tony Crivaro. Also in 1993, Vic formed an indigenous label, First Nation Records, in partnership with Lawrence Martin.

John Woloschuk

As well as working as assistant engineer on 'Fly By Night' with Terry Brown, in the early seventies John was in a number of bands with ex-school friends Terry Draper and Dee Long. Notably, John took on lead vocals and piano in Klaatu, which took its name from the alien in 'The Day The Earth Stood Still'. Terry Brown was "fourth member", but really acted more as producer than performer. He supported the band's first album, '3:47 EST', which was recorded over three years at Toronto Sound Studios, released in 1976. Terry was also involved on 'Hope' and 'Sir Army Suit', which were released over the two years that followed.

Klaatu deliberately set out to make a statement of anonymity, refusing to say who was in the band. This being the hype-ridden record industry however, the idea backfired somewhat when journalist Steve Smith speculated the band were the reformed Beatles. One of their songs, 'Calling Occupants of Interplanetary Craft' was covered by The Carpenters in 1977.

In 1981 Klaatu released *'Magentalane'* and set off on its first and last tour. Keyboard player Gerald O'Brien was brought in, to be replaced in 1982 by Max Webster keyboardist Terry Watkinson. The band came to an end in 1984, as the band members went their separate ways: John went to train to be an accountant, qualifying in 1986.

Brett Zilahi

Brett assisted Michael Letho in the final mix of *'Counterparts'*. Today he is based at Metalworks Studios.

Adrian Zivojinovich

At the age of 14 Adrian decided he wanted to get into music, but the last thing he wanted to do was bask in his father's projected limelight. "I don't get a chance to hear him much," remarked Alex at the time. "He's very secretive about his playing, but I sneak around the house and catch him when he's practising."

When he left school Adrian played in some local bands and worked as an assistant engineer in a Toronto recording studio, but ultimately he wanted to produce material of his own. He left in the summer of 1999 to work on his own, techno/ambient music at the Lifeson home studio. "He's written some stuff that just blows my mind. I mean, he's got a handle on creating moods and colors with music that is overwhelming. I think that he has a future in music, and I know that's what he wants to do. I support him and stand by him 100%."

Adrian participated on *'Victor'*; more recently, Alex has been helping Adrian put a demo together to try for a record deal, adding the occasional piece of material. "I've been doing a fair amount of work with him lately, he's asked me to come in and do guitar on some of the things he does," said Alex. "So we're having a lot of fun... to be in that environment with your kid, where you're both creative and I feel like a kid still."

Charlene Zivojinovich

Charlene is Alex's wife, *née* McNichol. She participated on Alex's solo album *'Victor'*, contributing voice parts for 'Shut Up Shutting Up'.

Justin Zivojinovich

Justin was Alex and Charlene's first son, born in 1971 when Alex was just 18. Justin worked at the bar of The Orbit Room. He took some of the pictures for the *'Test For Echo'* tour book, and in 1998 his photography earned him a Juno award for Best Album Design, for the cover to *'Songs of A Circling Spirit'* by Tom Cochrane.

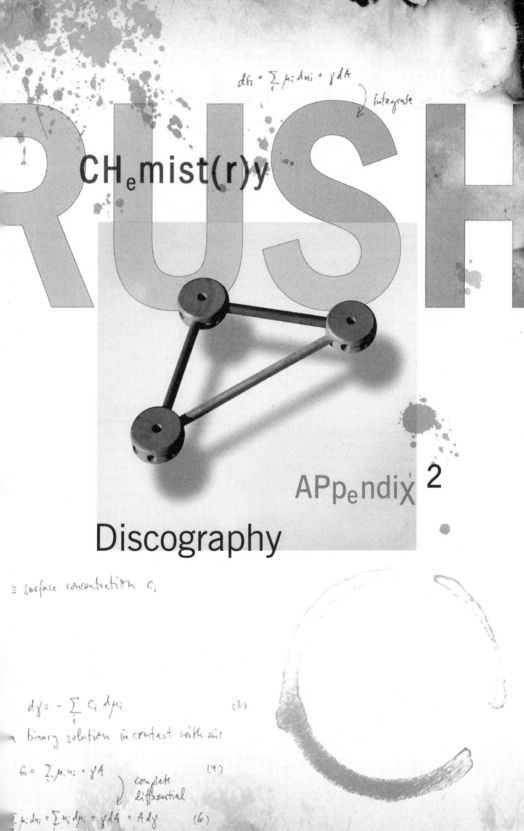

CH$_e$mist(r)y

APp$_e$ndix ^{2}

Discography

Rush have released 17 studio albums, 5 live albums and a number of compilations, not all of the latter with the band's blessing. The information below was collated with an enormous dollopful of thanks to Eric Hansen at the Power Windows website, which can be found at **www.2112.net**

Music by Lee/Lifeson, lyrics by Peart, except where stated otherwise.

■ *Rush*

For best results play at maximum volume. With Special Thanks to Donna Halper of WMMS in Cleveland for getting the ball rolling.
Released Moon Records, March 1974.
Re-released Mercury/Polygram, July 1974.

Finding My Way	(5:06)
Need Some Love	(2:19)
Take A Friend	(4:24)
Here Again	(7:35)
What You're Doing	(4:22)
In The Mood	(3:34)
Before and After	(5:34)
Working Man	(7:10)

Geddy Lee - Lead Vocals/Bass.
Alex Lifeson - Guitars/Vocals.
John Rutsey - Drums/Vocals.
Produced by Rush.
Remix Engineer: Terry Brown.
All songs by Lee/Lifeson except:
'In The Mood' by Lee.

■ *Fly By Night*

For Best Results... Play This Album.
Released Mercury/Polygram,
15 February, 1975.

Anthem	(4:22)
Best I Can	(3:25)
Beneath, Between and Behind	(3:02)
By-Tor and The Snowdog	(8:37)
I. At The Tobes of Hades	
II. Across The Styx	
III. Of The Battle IV. Epilogue	
Fly By Night	(3:21)
Making Memories	(2:58)
Rivendell	(4:57)
In The End	(6:47)

Geddy Lee - Bass/Acoustic Guitar/Vocals.

Alex Lifeson - Acoustic & Electric Guitars.
Neil Peart - Drums/Percussion.
Produced by Rush and Terry Brown.

■ *Caress of Steel*

*Dedicated to the memory of
Mr. Rod Serling.*
Released Mercury/Polygram,
September 1975.

Bastille Day	(4:37)
I Think I'm Going Bald	(3:37)
Lakeside Park	(4:08)
The Necromancer	(12:30)
I. Into Darkness	(4:12)
II. Under The Shadow	(4:25)
III. Return of The Prince	(3:52)
The Fountain of Lamneth	(19:59)
I. In The Valley	(4:18)
II. Didacts and Narpets	(1:00)
III. No One At The Bridge	(4:19)
IV. Panacea	(3:14)
V. Bacchus Plateau	(3:13)
VI. The Fountain	(3:49)

Geddy Lee - Bass/Acoustic Guitar/Vocals.
Alex Lifeson - Acoustic & Electric Guitars.
Neil Peart - Drums/Percussion.
Produced by Rush and Terry Brown.

■ *2112*

Released Mercury, April 1976.

2112	(20:34)
I. Overture	(4:32)
II. Temples of Syrinx	(2:13)
III. Discovery	(3:29)
IV. Presentation	(3:42)
V. Oracle: The Dream	(2:00)
VI. Soliloquy	(2:21)
VII. The Grand Finale	(2:14)
A Passage To Bangkok	(3:34)
The Twilight Zone	(3:17)
Lessons	(3:51)
Tears	(3:31)
Something For Nothing	(3:59)

Geddy Lee - Bass/Vocals.
Alex Lifeson - Guitars.
Neil Peart - Drums/Percussion.
Additional Musician:
Hugh Syme - Keyboards (Track 5).
Produced by Rush and Terry Brown.
Engineered by Terry Brown.

Lyrics by Peart, except: 'Lessons' by
Lifeson and 'Tears' by Lee.

■ All The World's A Stage

Recorded live at Massey Hall,
Toronto, 11, 12 & 13 June, 1976.
Released Mercury/Polygram,
29 September, 1976.

Bastille Day	(4:59)
Anthem	(4:57)
Fly By Night/In The Mood	(4:05)
Something For Nothing	(4:04)
Lakeside Park	(5:06)
2112	(16:51)
I. Overture	
II. The Temples Of Syrinx	
III. Presentation	
IV. Soliloquy	
V. Grand Finale	
By-Tor and The Snowdog	(12:01)
In The End	(7:15)
Working Man/Finding My Way	(14:20)
What You're Doing	(5:41)

Geddy Lee - Vocals/Bass.
Alex Lifeson - Guitars/Vocals.
Neil Peart - Drums/Percussion.
Produced by Rush and Terry Brown.
Engineered by Terry Brown.

■ A Farewell To Kings

*Dedicated to Nancy, Charlene and
Jacqueline.*
Released Mercury, September 1977.

A Farewell To Kings	(5:51)
Xanadu	(11:08)
Closer To The Heart	(2:53)
Cinderella Man	(4:21)
Madrigal	(2:35)
Cygnus X-1	(10:25)
Prologue	(5:01)
1.	(0:45)
2.	(1:34)
3.	(3:05)

Geddy Lee - Bass/Accoustic. Guitar/Mini-
   Moog/Bass Pedals/Vocals.
Alex Lifeson - Accoustic and Electric
   Guitars/Bass Pedals.
Neil Peart - Drums/Percussion.
Produced by Rush and Terry Brown.
Engineered by Pat Moran and Terry Brown.

Tracks 1, 2, 5 & 6 lyrics by Peart.
Track 3 lyrics by Peart and Talbot.
Track 4 lyrics by Lee.

■ Archives

Released Mercury, April 1978.
Triple LP repackaging of the following
albums in unique gatefold picture sleeve.

Rush (1974)
Fly By Night (1975)
Caress of Steel (1975)

Geddy Lee - Vocals/Bass.
Alex Lifeson - Guitars/Vocals.
Neil Peart - Drums/Percussion.
John Rutsey - Drums/Vocals (on *Rush*).

■ Hemispheres

Released Mercury, 29 October, 1978.

Cygnus X-1 Book II: Hemispheres	(18:08)
I. Prelude	(4:27)
II. Apollo: Bringer of Wisdom	(2:35)
III. Dionysus: Bringer of Love	(2:05)
IV. Armageddon: The Battle of	
Heart and Mind	(3:06)
V. Cygnus: Bringer of Balance	(4:50)
VI. The Sphere: A Kind of	
Dream	(1:05)
Circumstances	(3:41)
The Trees	(4:46)
La Villa Strangiato (instrumental)	(9:35)
(An Exercise in Self-Indulgence)	
I. Buenos Nochas, Mein	
Froinds!	(0:00)
II. To sleep, perchance to	
dream...	(0:27)
III. Strangiato Theme	(2:00)
IV. A Lerxst in Wonderland	(3:16)
V. Monsters!	(5:49)
VI. The Ghost of The Aragon	(6:10)
VII. Danforth and Pape	(6:45)
VIII. The Waltz of The Shreves	(7:26)
IX. Never Turn Your Back on A	
Monster!	(7:52)
X. Monsters! (Reprise)	(8:03)
XI. Strangiato Theme (Reprise)	(8:17)
XII. A Farewell to Things	(9:17)

Geddy Lee - Bass/Accoustic Guitar/Mini-
   Moog/Bass Pedals/Vocals.
Alex Lifeson - Acoustic and Electric
   Guitars/Bass Pedals.

Neil Peart - Drums/Percussion.
Produced by Rush and Terry Brown.
Engineered by Pat Moran and Terry Brown.

■ *Permanent Waves*

Released Mercury, 1 January, 1980

The Spirit of Radio	(4:57)
Freewill	(5:23)
Jacob's Ladder	(7:28)
Entre Nous	(4:37)
Different Strings	(3:49)
Natural Science	(9:16)
I. Tide Pools	(2:21)
II. Hyperspace	(2:47)
III. Permanent Waves	(4:08)

Geddy Lee - Bass/Mini Moog/Oberheim
    Polyphonic/Taurus Pedals/Vocals.
Alex Lifeson - Acoustic & Electric
    Guitars/Taurus Pedals.
Neil Peart - Drums/Percussion.
Additional Musician: Hugh Syme -
    Piano (Track 5).
Produced by Rush and Terry Brown
Engineered by Paul Northfield.
Lyrics by Peart, except:
    'Different Strings' by Lee.

■ *Moving Pictures*

Released Mercury, 12 February, 1981.

Tom Sawyer	(4:33)
Red Barchetta	(6:06)
YYZ (instrumental)	(4:24)
Limelight	(4:19)
The Camera Eye	(10:56)
Witch Hunt (Part III of Fear)	(4:43)
Vital Signs	(4:43)

Geddy Lee - Bass/Mini Moog/Oberheim
    Polyphonic/Taurus Pedals/Vocals.
Alex Lifeson - Acoustic and Electric
    Guitars/Tarus Pedals.
Neil Peart - Drums/Percussion.
Additional Musician: Hugh Syme -
    Synthesizers (Track 6).
Produced by Rush and Terry Brown.
Engineered by Paul Northfield.
Assisted by Robbie Whelan.
Lyrics by Peart, except lyrics to 'Tom
    Sawyer' by Peart/Dubois.

■ *Anthology*

Made in Holland by Mercury, distributed
by Phonogram, 1981.
Made in Mexico by Mercury, distributed
by Polygram Records Mexico, SA de CV,
1981.

Fly By Night	(3:21)
Making Memories	(2:58)
Bastille Day	(4:37)
Something For Nothing	(3:59)
Cinderella Man	(4:21)
Anthem	(4:22)
2112	
I. Overture	(4:32)
II. Temples of Syrinx	(2:13)
The Twilight Zone	(3:17)
Best I Can	(3:25)
Closer To The Heart	(2:53)
In The End	(6:47)

Geddy Lee - Bass/Acoustic Guitar/Vocals.
Alex Lifeson - Acoustic & Electric Guitars.
Neil Peart - Drums/Percussion.

■ *Exit... Stage Left*

Released Mercury, 29 October, 1981.
Recorded 27 March, 1981, except:
Tracks 4-7 recorded 10-11 June, 1980.

The Spirit of Radio	(5:12)
Red Barchetta	(6:48)
YYZ (instrumental)	(7:44)
A Passage To Bangkok	(3:47)
Closer To The Heart	(3:09)
Beneath, Between and Behind	(2:34)
Jacob's Ladder	(8:47)
Broon's Bane	(1:37)
The Trees	(5:50)
Xanadu	(12:10)
Freewill	(5:33)
Tom Sawyer	(5:01)
La Villa Strangiato (instrumental)	(9:38)

Geddy Lee - Bass/Vocals/Synthesizers/
    Bass Pedals/Rhythm Guitar.
Alex Lifeson - Acoustic & Electric Guitars/
    Taurus Pedals.
Neil Peart - Drums/Percussion.
Produced and Engineered By Terry Brown.

■ *Signals*

Mercury/Polygram, 9 September, 1982.

Subdivisions	(5:33)
The Analog Kid	(4:46)
Chemistry	(4:56)
Digital Man	(6:20)
The Weapon (Part II of Fear)	(6:22)
New World Man	(3:41)
Losing It	(4:51)
Countdown	(5:49)

Geddy Lee - Bass/Synthesizers/Vocals.
Alex Lifeson - Acoustic & Electric Guitars/
    Taurus Pedals.
Neil Peart - Drums/Percussion.
Additional Musician:
    Ben Mink - Electric Violin (Track 7).
Lyrics by Peart, Music by Lee/Lifeson,
    except Track 3 lyrics by Lee/Lifeson/
    Peart.
Produced by Rush and Terry Brown.
Engineered by Paul Northfield.
Assisted by Robbie Whelan.

■ Grace Under Pressure

In Memory of Robbie Whelan.
Released Mercury, 12 April, 1984.

Distant Early Warning	(4:59)
Afterimage	(5:04)
Red Sector A	(5:10)
The Enemy Within (Part I of Fear)	(4:34)
The Body Electric	(5:00)
Kid Gloves	(4:18)
Red Lenses	(4:42)
Between the Wheels	(5:44)

Produced by Rush and Peter Henderson
Engineered by Peter Henderson

■ Power Windows

Released Mercury, 29 October, 1985

The Big Money	(5:36)
Grand Designs	(5:05)
Manhattan Project	(5:05)
Marathon	(6:09)
Territories	(6:19)
Middletown Dreams	(5:15)
Emotion Detector	(5:10)
Mystic Rhythms	(5:54)

Additional Musicians:
Jim Burgess - Synthesizer Programming.
Andy Richards - Keyboards/Synthesizer
    Programming.

Produced by Peter Collins and Rush.
Engineered by Jimbo Barton.

■ Hold Your Fire

Released Mercury, 8 September, 1987.

Force Ten	(4:28)
Time Stand Still	(5:07)
Open Secrets	(5:37)
Second Nature	(4:35)
Prime Mover	(5:19)
Lock and Key	(5:08)
Mission	(5:15)
Turn The Page	(4:53)
Tai Shan	(4:14)
High Water	(5:32)

Additional Musicians:
Jim Burgess - Synthesizer Progamming.
Aimee Mann - Vocals (Track 2).
Andy Richards - Keyboards/Synthesizer
    Programming.
Produced by Peter Collins and Rush.
Engineered by Jimbo Barton.
Lyrics by Peart, except lyrics to 'Force
    10' by Peart/Dubois.

■ A Show of Hands

Released Mercury, 10 January, 1989.
Recorded 21, 23 & 24 April, 1988
    except: Track 5 recorded 27 January,
    1988. Tracks 6 & 12 recorded 1
    February, 1988. Track 7 recorded 3
    February, 1988. Tracks 9 & 10
    recorded 31 March & 1 April, 1986.

Intro	(0:53)
The Big Money	(5:52)
Subdivisions	(5:19)
Marathon	(6:32)
Turn The Page	(4:40)
Manhattan Project	(5:00)
Mission	(5:44)
Distant Early Warning	(5:18)
Mystic Rhythms	(5:32)
Witch Hunt (Part III of Fear)	(3:55)
The Rhythm Method (drum solo)	(4:34)
Force Ten	(4:50)
Time Stand Still	(5:10)
Red Sector A	(5:12)
Closer To The Heart	(4:53)

Additional Musician: Aimee Mann -
Vocals (Track 13).

Produced by Rush.
Engineered by Guy Charbonneau.

■ *Presto*

Brought to you by the letter "D".
Released Atlantic/Anthem,
21 November, 1989.

Chain Lightning	(4:33)
The Pass	(4:51)
War Paint	(5:24)
Scars	(4:07)
Presto	(5:45)
Superconductor	(4:47)
Anagram (for Mongo)	(4:00)
Red Tide	(4:29)
Hand Over Fist	(4:11)
Available Light	(5:03)

Produced by Rupert Hine And Rush.

■ *Chronicles*

Released Mercury/Anthem,
4 September, 1990.

Disc One:

Finding My Way	(5:08)
Working Man	(7:12)
Fly By Night	(3:21)
Anthem	(4:24)
Bastille Day	(4:39)
Lakeside Park	(4:10)
2112 (Overture/Temples of Syrinx)	(6:48)
What You're Doing (live)	(5:41)
A Farewell To Kings	(5:53)
Closer To The Heart	(2:54)
The Trees	(4:41)
La Villa Strangiato (instrumental)	(9.34)
The Spirit of Radio	(4:57)

Disc Two:

Freewill	(5:23)
Tom Sawyer	(4:37)
Red Barchetta	(6:10)
Limelight	(4:22)
A Passage To Bangkok (live)	(3:47)
Subdivisions	(5:35)
New World Man	(3:42)
Distant Early Warning	(5:59)
Red Sector A	(5:13)
The Big Money	(5:35)
Manhattan Project	(5:07)
Force Ten	(4:34)
Time Stand Still	(5:10)
Mystic Rhythms (live)	(5:42)

Show Don't Tell	(5:01)

Additional Musicians:
Aimee Mann - Vocals (Disc 2; Track 12);
John Rutsey - Drums (Disc 1; Tracks 1
& 2).

■ *Roll The Bones*

Atlantic/Anthem, 3 September, 1991

Dreamline	(4.38)
Bravado	(4:56)
Roll The Bones	(5:30)
Face Up	(3:54)
Where's My Thing? (instr.)	(3:49)
(Part IV, "Gangster Of Boats" Trilogy)	
The Big Wheel	(5:15)
Heresy	(5:26)
Ghost Of A Chance	(5:19)
Neurotica	(4:40)
You Bet Your Life	(5:00)

Additional Musician:
Rupert Hine - Keyboards/Backing Vocals.
Produced by Rupert Hine And Rush.
Engineered by Stephen Tayler.

■ *Counterparts*

Released Atlantic/Anthem,
19 October, 1993.

Animate	(6:03)
Stick It Out	(4:30)
Cut To The Chase	(4:48)
Nobody's Hero	(4:54)
Between Sun And Moon	(4:37)
Alien Shore	(5:45)
Speed Of Love	(5:02)
Double Agent	(4:51)
Leave That Thing Alone! (instr.)	(4:05)
Cold Fire	(4:26)
Everyday Glory	(5:11)

Additional Musician:
John Webster - Keyboards.
Produced by Peter Collins and Rush.
Lyrics by Peart, except lyrics to 'Between
    Sun And Moon' by Pye Dubois.

■ *Test For Echo*

Released Atlantic/Anthem,
10 September, 1996.

Test For Echo	(5:56)
Driven	(4:27)
Half The World	(3:43)
The Color Of Right	(4:49)
Time And Motion	(5:01)
Totem	(4:58)
Dog Years	(4:55)
Virtuality	(5:44)
Resist	(4:24)
Limbo (instrumental)	(5:29)
Carve Away The Stone	(4:05)

Produced by Peter Collins and Rush.
Lyrics by Peart, except lyrics to 'Test For Echo'/'Between Sun And Moon' by Peart/Dubois.

■ Retrospective I: 1974-1980

Released Mercury/Anthem, 6 May, 1997.

The Spirit of Radio	(4:57)
The Trees	(4:41)
Something For Nothing	(3:59)
Freewill	(5:23)
Xanadu	(11:05)
Bastille Day	(4:37)
By-Tor and The Snowdog	(8:37)
Anthem	(4:21)
Closer To The Heart	(2:53)
2112	
I. Overture	(4:32)
II. Temples of Syrinx	(2:13)
La Villa Strangiato (instrumental)	(9.34)
Fly By Night	(3:21)
Finding My Way	(5:08)

■ Retrospective II: 1981-1987

Released Mercury/Anthem,
3 June, 1997.

Red Barchetta	(6.09)
Subdivisions	(5.33)
Time Stand Still	(5.09)
Mystic Rhythms	(5.53)
The Analog Kid	(4.47)
Distant Early Warning	(4.57)
Marathon	(6.09)
The Body Electric	(5.00)
Mission	(5.16)
Limelight	(4.19)
Red Sector A	(5.09)
New World Man	(3.42)
Tom Sawyer	(4.33)
Force Ten	(4.31)

Additional Musicians:
Jim Burgess - Synthesizer Programming.
Aimee Man - Vocals (Track 4).
Andy Richards - Keyboards/Synthesizer Programming.

■ Different Stages

In loving memory of Jackie and Selena.
Released Atlantic/Anthem,
10 November, 1998.
Disks 1 & 2 recorded 14 June, 1997, except:
Disk 1 Track 4, 30 April, 1994.
Disk 1 Track 6, 27 February, 1994.
Disk 1 Track 7, 24 May, 1997.
Disk 1 Track 10 & Disk 2 Track 7, 23 June, 1997.
Disk 2 Track 2, 22 March, 1994.
Disk 2 Track 6, 2 July, 1997.
*Japanese release only, Disk 2 Track 10, 4 June, 1997.

Set One:

Dreamline	(5.34)
Limelight	(4.32)
Driven	(5.16)
Bravado	(6.23)
Animate	(5.29)
Show Don't Tell	(5.29)
The Trees	(5.28)
Nobody's Hero	(5.01)
Closer To The Heart	(5.13)
2112	
I. Overture	(4.32)
II. The Temples of Syrinx	(2.20)
III. Discovery	(4.17)
IV. Presentation	(3.40)
V. Oracle: The Dream	(1.49)
VI. Soliloquy	(2.07)
VII. Grand Finale	(2.39)

Set Two:

Test For Echo	(6.15)
Analog Kid	(5.14)
Freewill	(5.36)
Roll The Bones	(5.58)
Stick It Out	(4.42)
Resist	(4.27)
Leave That Thing Alone (instr.)	(4.46)
The Rhythm Method (drum solo)	(8.19)
Natural Science	(8.05)
Force Ten*	(4.47)
The Spirit of Radio	(5.00)
Tom Sawyer	(5.18)
YYZ (instrumental)	(5.25)

Set Three (Hammersmith Odeon, 20 February, 1978)**:**

Bastille Day	(5.07)
By-Tor and The Snowdog	(4.59)
Xanadu	(12.32)
A Farewell To Kings	(5.53)
Something For Nothing	(4.01)
Cygnus X-1	(10.23)
Anthem	(4.47)
Working Man	(4.00)
Fly By Night	(2.04)
In The Mood	(3.34)
Cinderella Man	(5.09)

Produced by Geddy Lee and Paul
  Northfield.
Mixed by Paul Northfield.
Disc Three Engineered by Terry Brown.

■ *Vapor Trails*

Brought to you by the letter "3".
Released Atlantic/Anthem,
14 May, 2002.

One Little Victory	(5:08)
Ceiling Unlimited	(5:28)
Ghost Rider	(5:41)
Peaceable Kingdom	(5:23)
The Stars Look Down	(4:28)
How It Is	(4:05)
Vapor Trail	(4:57)
Secret Touch	(6:34)
Earthshine	(5:38)
Sweet Miracle	(3:40)
Nocturne	(4:49)
Freeze (Part IV of "Fear")	(6:21)
Out Of The Cradle	(5·03)

Music by Lee and Lifeson.
Lyrics by Peart.
Produced by Rush and Paul Northfield.

■ *The Spirit of Radio:*
Greatest Hits (1974-1987)

Released Mercury/Anthem,
11 February, 2003.

Working Man	(7:12)
Fly By Night	(3:21)
2112 (Overture/Temples of Syrinx)	(6:48)
Closer To The Heart	(2:54)
The Trees	(4:41)
The Spirit of Radio	(4:57)

Freewill	(5:23)
Limelight	(4:22)
Tom Sawyer	(4:37)
Red Barchetta	(6:10)
New World Man	(3:42)
Subdivisions	(5:35)
Distant Early Warning	(5:59)
The Big Money	(5:35)
Force Ten	(4:34)
Time Stand Still	(5:10)

Additional Musicians:
Aimee Mann - Vocals (Track 17).
John Rutsey - Drums (Track 1).

■ *Rush In Rio*

Released Atlantic/Anthem,
21 October, 2003.
Recorded 23 November, 2002, at
Maracana Stadium, Rio de Janeiro,
Brazil, except: 'Between Sun & Moon'
recorded at Phoenix, Arizona, Cricket
Pavilion on 27 September, 2002, and
'Vital Signs' recorded at Quebec City,
PQ, Colisee on 19 October, 2002.

Disc One:

Tom Sawyer	(5:10)
Distant Early Warning	(4:48)
New World Man	(4:03)
Roll The Bones	(6:03)
Earthshine	(5:42)
YYZ (instrumental)	(4:35)
The Pass	(4:50)
Bravado	(6:15)
The Big Money	(5:58)
The Trees	(5:07)
Freewill	(5:32)
Closer To The Heart	(3:01)
Natural Science	(8:34)

Disc Two:

One Little Victory	(5:32)
Driven	(5:05)
Ghost Rider	(5:36)
Secret Touch	(7:00)
Dreamline	(5:04)
Red Sector A	(5:12)
Leave That Thing Alone! (instr.)	(4:59)
O Baterista (drum solo)	(8:18)
Resist (acoustic)	(4:24)
2112 Overture/Temples of Syrinx	(6:52)

Disc Three:

Limelight	(4:24)
La Villa Strangiato (instr.)	(10:05)

The Spirit of Radio   (4:59)
By-Tor and The Snowdog   (4:35)
Cygnus X-1 (prologue)   (3:12)
Working Man   (5:35)
THE BOARD BOOTLEGS
Between Sun & Moon   (4:48)
Vital Signs   (4:59)

■ *Feedback*

Released Atlantic, 29 June, 2004.

Summertime Blues (Eddie Cochran)
Heart Full of Soul (The Yardbirds)
For What It's Worth (Buffalo Springfield)
The Seeker (The Who)
Mr. Soul (Buffalo Springfield)
Seven And Seven Is (Love)
Shapes Of Things (The Yardbirds)
Crossroads (Robert Johnson)

Produced by David Leonard and Rush.

SOLO ALBUMS

■ Alex Lifeson - *Victor*

In Memory of Randy Knox.
Released Atlantic/Anthem/Lerxt Music,
9 January, 1996.

Don't Care   (4.04)
Promise   (5.44)
Start Today   (3.48)
Mr. X (instrumental)   (2.21)
At The End   (6.07)
Sending Out A Warning   (4.11)
Shut Up Shuttin' Up (instrumental) (4.02)
Strip And Go Naked (instrumental)   (3.57)
The Big Dance   (4.14)
Victor   (6.25)
I Am The Spirit   (5.31)
Bill Bell - Guitars.
Edwin - Vocals.
Alex Lifeson - Guitars/Bass/Keyboards/
   Programming/Vocals.

Blake Manning - Drums.
Additional Musicians:
Peter Cardinali - Bass (Tracks 7 & 10);
Les Claypool - Bass (Track 9);
Dalbello - Vocals (Track 3);
Adrian Zivojinovich - Programming
   (Tracks 5 & 9).
Produced and Mixed by Alex Lifeson.
Assisted by Bill Bell.

■ Geddy Lee - *My Favourite Headache*

Released Atlantic/Anthem,
14 November, 2000.

My Favorite Headache   (4:44)
The Present Tense   (3:25)
Window To The World   (3:01)
Working at Perfekt   (4:59)
Runaway Train   (4:31)
The Angels' Share   (4:34)
Moving To Bohemia   (4:25)
Home On The Strange   (3:47)
Slipping   (5:05)
Still   (4:29)
Grace To Grace   (4:57)

Geddy Lee - Basses, Voices, Piano,
   Guitar, Programming, Percussion,
   Whining.
Ben Mink - Electric & Acoustic Guitars,
   Violins & Violas, Programming,
   Wheezing.
Matt Cameron - Drums on all tracks
   except:
Jeremy Taggart - Drums on Track 8.
John Friesen - Cellos on Track 4.
Chris Stringer - Additional Percussion.
Waylon Wall - Steel Guitar on Track 3.
Pappy Rosen - Backward vocals Track 9.
Duke - Dog.
Lyrics - Geddy Lee.
Music - Lee and Mink.
String Arrangements - Mink and Lee.
Produced by Geddy Lee, Ben Mink and
   David Leonard.
Mixed and Engineered by David Leonard.

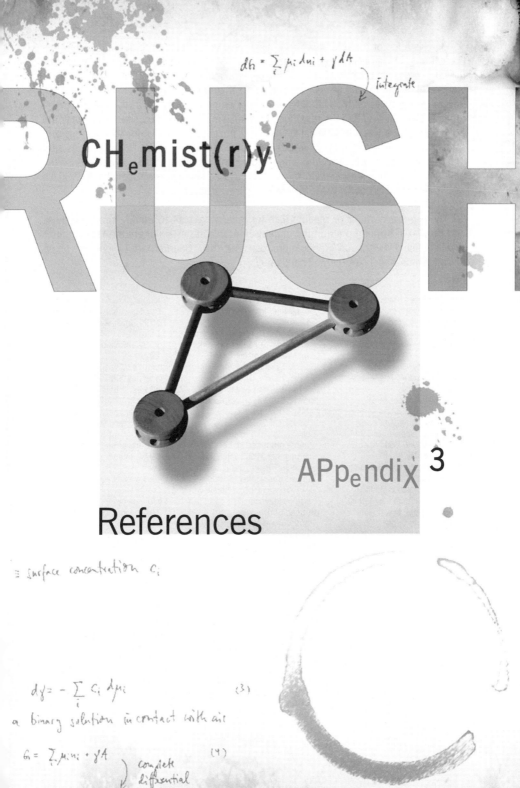

CH$_e$mist(r)y

$$dh = \sum_i \mu_i \, dn_i + \gamma \, dA$$

integrate

APp$_e$ndix 3

References

$\equiv$ surface concentration c_i

$$d\gamma = - \sum_i c_i \, d\mu_i \qquad (3)$$

a binary solution in contact with air

$$G_i = \sum_i \mu_i n_i + \gamma A \qquad (4)$$

complete differential

$$\sum_i \mu_i \, dn_i + \sum_i n_i \, d\mu_i + \gamma \, dA + A \, d\gamma \qquad (6)$$

Here is a list of the references that were used in compiling the quotes used in this book. Many of the articles are available on the Web, the more recent ones appearing directly, older interviews transcribed painstakingly by fans. The Web is quite wonderful, for all the old interviews, but also dangerous as much information has been passed around like myth, without necessarily being checked. A useful starting point for any fan is www.2112.net which links to a number of fan sites, not least the Power Windows website which I have found inordinately useful for tour listings and transcriptions. A great, quirky website is MUSICinTheABsTrAcT's Rush Oddities site, and equally useful was www.nmsmirror.com, linking to all those old editions of the online fanzine, the *National Midnight Star*. Other sources and useful links will be available from the book's website, www.rushchemistry.com.

There are a number of mailing lists for fans, I have been quietly scanning these and they have turned up a number of gems. Notable in particular are the Hemispheres mailing list (THML) on Yahoo! groups, and the Counterparts message board www.rushmessageboard.com. Thanks guys.

'Roll The Bones' Radio Special, Interview with Neil Peart

Harris, Paul A., *The St Louis Post-Dispatch*, 31 October 1991, Interview with Neil Peart

Aledort, Andy, *Guitar World*, February 1994, Interview with Alex and Geddy

Allstar, 31 October 1996, Interview

Armbruster, Greg, *Keyboard* magazine, September 1984, Interview with Geddy Lee and Tony Geranios

Atlantic promo, Interview with Geddy Lee

Ayers, Chris, Music Monitor 'Backstage' club newsletter, 1988, Interview with Neil Peart

Baktabak picture disc, 1987, Interview with Alex Lifeson

Banasiewicz, Bill, "Rush Visions", 1 June 1990

Barton, Geoff, *'Hemispheres'* tour book

Barton, Geoff, *'The Words and The Pictures'* tour programme, 1979

Bashe, Philip, *Circus* magazine, 30 November 1982, Interview with Geddy Lee

Bass Player, Nov/Dec 1988, Interview with Geddy Lee

Batten, Steven, *The Scene* magazine, 31 October 1996, Interview with Alex Lifeson

Billboard magazine, August 3, 1996, Interview with Alex Lifeson

Bradley, Simon, *Guitarist* magazine, Interview with Alex Lifeson

Britt, Bruce, *The San Francisco Chronicle*, 9 February 1994, Interview with Neil Peart

Brophy, Stephen M., *The Salt Lake Tribune*, 16 May 1997, Interview with Geddy Lee

Brown, G., *The Denver Post*, 21 May 1997, Interview with Geddy Lee

Bullock, Scott, "Profile: A rebel and a drummer", *Liberty*, September 1997, Interview with Neil Peart

Buttner, Christopher, *Bass Frontiers*, c.1997, Interview with Geddy Lee

Buttner, Christopher, *Mackietone News*, Interview with Alex Lifeson

Buttner, Christopher, *Music Gear Review*, Interview with Alex Lifeson

Campbell, Mary, *The Greenville News*, 17 February 1990, Interview with Geddy Lee

Canadian Musician, December 2000, Interview with Geddy Lee

Cantin, Paul, *Jam! Showbiz*, 12 January 2001, Interview with Geddy Lee

Cantin, Paul, *Jam! Showbiz*, 8 November 2000, Interview with Geddy Lee

Caputo, Salvatore, *The Arizona Republic*, 29 November 1996, Interview with Neil Peart

Chappell, Jon, *Guitar for The Practicing Musician*, February 1994, Interview with Alex Lifeson

Christgau, Robert, *Village Voice*, 1977

Chum TV, May 6 2002, Interview with Alex Lifeson c.1993, Interview with Kevin J. Anderson

Circus magazine, 14 February 1977, Interview with Geddy Lee

Circus magazine, 27 October 1977, Interview with Geddy Lee

Circus magazine, Interview with Geddy Lee

Circus magazine, October 27 1977, Interview with Geddy Lee

Cockerton, Paul, *Manchester Online*, 1 September 2004, Interview with Alex Lifeson

Cohen, Scott, Frost, *Circus* magazine

Collins, Brian, Editor's note to "A Port Boy's Story" written by Neil Peart, St *Catharines Standard*

Coryat, Karl, *Bass Player*, December 1993, Interview with Geddy Lee

D., John, Gonzalez, *The Grand Rapids Press*, 23 October 1996, Interview with Neil Peart

Deggans, Eric, *The St Petersburg Times*, 6 December 1996, Interview with Neil Peart

Derringer, John, 'Roll The Bones' Radio Special, 1992, Interview with Neil, Alex and Geddy

Dome, Malcolm, *Metal Hammer*, 25 April 1988, Interview with Neil Peart

Double Agent 5150, Counterparts message board, 2002, Interview with Alex Lifeson

Downes, Steve, *Rockline*, 1996, Interview with Alex Lifeson

Downes, Steve, *Rockline*, 24 January 1994, Interview with Geddy and Alex

Fish, Scott K., *Modern Drummer*, April 1984, Interview with Neil Peart

Fish, Scott K., *Modern Drummer*, January 1986, Interview with Neil Peart

Flohil, Richard, "Canadian Gold Rush", *Canadian Composer* magazine, Winter 1991

Fricke, David, *Circus* magazine, 1 April 1980

Frost, Debra, "A Canadian Rush", *Circus* magazine, 14 February 1977

Gehret, Ula, *The Aquarian Weekly*, 9 March 1994, Interview with Neil Peart

Gett, Steve, "Rush – Success Under Pressure", 1984

Gill, John, "THE RUSH 'UNS ARE COMING", *Sounds*, 5 May 1979, Interview with Rush

Gilray, Stewart, *Spirit of Rush* fanzine, July 1994, Interview with Alex Lifeson

Graff, Gary, *The Detroit Journal*, 26 October 1996, Interview with Neil Peart

Green, Tony, *The St Petersburg Times*, 4 March 1994, Interview with Neil Peart

Guitar Player, 1980, Interview with Geddy Lee

Guitar Player, July 1987, Interview with Alex Lifeson

Guitar World, January 2001, Interview

Halper, Donna, "The Rush Discovery Story", Rushweb, 2000

Harrigan, Brian, "Rush", 1982, Interview with Geddy, Neil and Alex

Harrison, Tom, *The Vancouver Province*, 10 November 1998, Interview with Geddy Lee and Alex Lifeson

Haymes, Greg, *The Albany Times Union*, 12 December 1991, Interview with Neil Peart

Haymes, Greg, *The Albany Times Union*, 17 October 1996, Interview with Neil Peart

Helm, Levon, Ronnie Hawkins official website

Hogan, Richard, "Vital signs from Rush", *Circus* magazine, 30 December 1981

Howell, Peter, *The Toronto Star*, 1 October 1996

Iero, Cheech, *Modern Drummer*, April 1980, Interview with Neil Peart

In Concert, Interview with Geddy Lee

In The Studio, 1981, Interview with Geddy Lee and Alex Lifeson

Issue 25, *Seconds*, 1994, Interview with Geddy Lee

Jam magazine, February 8 1996, Interview with Alex Lifeson

Jam! Music News, February 27 1997

Jam! Music, 11 August 2000, Interview with Geddy Lee

Jim DeRogatis, *The Chicago Sun Times*, 27 March 1994, Interview with Neil, Geddy and Alex

Johnson, Howard, *Raw* magazine, 27 October 1993, Interview with Geddy Lee

Jones, Tim, *Short Takes*, Interview with Geddy Lee June 24/25 1994

Kava, Brad, & Claudia, Perry, *The San Jose Mercury News*, 20 November 1996, Interview with Neil Peart

Kerrang!, 18 April 1992, Interview with Alex Lifeson and Geddy Lee

Kerrang!, May 1992, Interview with Geddy Lee

Kirkman, Jon, *Rock Ahead*, 17 October 2003, Interview with Alex Lifeson

Knippenberg, Jim, *The Cincinnati Enquirer*, 31 August 1974, Interview with Geddy Lee

Kot, Greg, *The Chicago Tribune*, 1 November 1991, Interview with Neil Peart

Krewen, Nick, *Canadian Composer*, April 1986, Interview with Neil Peart

Krewen, Nick, *Canadian Musician*, April 1990, Interview with Geddy Lee

Krewen, Nick, *The Hamilton Spectator*, 25 October 1991, Interview with Neil Peart

L., Kira, Billik, *The San Diego Union-Tribune*, 3 February 1994, Interview with Neil Peart

L., Robert, Doerschuk, *Keyboard* magazine, March 1989, Interview with Geddy Lee

Lancaster, Frank, 19 August 1991, Interview with Geddy Lee

Laskosky, Lance, *Only Music*, December 1987, Interview with Geddy Lee

Lee, Geddy, Barnes and Noble Chat, 13 November 2000

Lee, Geddy, 'Counterparts' tour book

Lee, Geddy, MSN Chat, December 20, 2000

Lee, Julian, Email to Ben Clifford, THML 6651 – thanks!, April 16 2001.

Letter from Neil Peart, *Modern Drummer*, August 1996

Levine, Robert, *The San Francisco Chronicle*, 17 November 1996, Interview with Geddy Lee

Lifeson, Alex, AT&T Celebrity chat, 10 February 2003

"Living in A Big Rush", *Rochester Times Union*, 24 October 1991, Interview with Neil Peart

MacDonald, Dan, *The Jacksonville Times-Union*, 2 March 1994, Interview with Neil Peart

MacDonald, Dan, *The Jacksonville Times-Union*, 21 February 1992, Interview with Neil Peart

MacGregor, Roy, *Macleans*, 23 January 1978, Interview with band and Ray Danniels

Mack, Bob, *LA Weekly*, 8 December 2000, Interview with Geddy Lee

Makowski, Pete, *Sounds*, December 18th, 1982

Manson, Marilyn, Autobiography

McCollum, Brian, *The Buffalo News*, 5 March 1994, Interview with Geddy Lee

McCollum, Brian, *The Detroit Free Press*, 25 October 1996, Interview with Neil Peart

McCollum, Brian, *The Philadelphia Inquirer*, 6 November 1996, Interview with Neil Peart

Melody Maker, 1983, Interview with Geddy Lee

Metal Hammer, 25 April 1988, Interview with Neil Peart

Mettler, Mike, *Mobile Entertainment*, 2004, Interview with Geddy Lee and Alex Lifeson

Milano, Brett, *The Boston Globe*, 19 November 1987, Interview with Neil Peart

Miles, Barry, "Rush: Is Everybody Feelin' all RIGHT? (Geddit...?)", *NME*, March 1978, Interview with Geddy, Neil and Alex

Miller, William F., "The Fire Returns", *Modern Drummer* magazine, September 2002, Interview with Neil Peart

Miller, William F., *Modern Drummer*, December 1989, Interview with Neil Peart

Miller, William F., *Modern Drummer*, February 1994, Interview with Neil Peart

Milwaukee Journal, 1984, Interview with Alex Lifeson

Mitchell, Don, *Epiphone News*, 29 July 2004, Interview with Alex Lifeson

Mitchell, Mark, "Magic Man", *Guitar School*, May 1990, Interview with Alex Lifeson

Mizejewski, Gerald, *The Washington Times*, November 1996, Interview with Alex Lifeson

Morgan, Jeffrey, *Creem* magazine, 1983, Interview with Hugh Syme

Muchmusic, 1990, Interview with Geddy Lee

Musique Plus, Interview with Geddy Lee

'My Favorite Headache' world premiere, Interview with Geddy Lee

Myers, Paul, *Canadian Musician*, December 1996, Interview with Alex, Geddy and Neil

Near, Dan, 11 February 1994, Radio Interview with Geddy, Neil and Alex

Niester, Alan, *Toronto Globe & Mail*, 17 November 1998, Interview with Geddy Lee

Nooger, Dan, "Rush goes into Future Shock", *Circus* magazine, April 27 1976

Obrecht, Jas, *Guitar Player* magazine, April 1986, Interview with Alex Lifeson

Online chat with Geddy Lee, December 21 2000

Pantsios, Anastasia, *Creem* magazine, 25 November 1976, Interview with Neil Peart

Parks, Ed, Rush Job, *Sounds*, 4 June 1983

Pearce, Tralee, *Ottowa Sun*, February 27 1997

Peart, Neil, "A Port Boy's Story", *St. Catharines Standard*

Peart, Neil, "A Real Job", *Modern Drummer*, February 1987

Peart, Neil, "Another Drumset Giveaway!", *Modern Drummer*, March 1987

Peart, Neil, "Behind the Scenes", Tour of the *'Hemispheres'* tour book

Peart, Neil, "Creating the Drum Part", *Modern Drummer*, August 1988

Peart, Neil, "For Whom the Bus Rolls"

Peart, Neil, "Into Africa", Maclean's, 3 April 1995

Peart, Neil, "Scissors, Paper, Stone", *'Presto'* tour book

Peart, Neil, "Starting Over", Modern Drummer, November 1995

Peart, Neil, "The Quest for New Drums", *Modern Drummer*, May 1987

Peart, Neil, Answers to readers' questions, *Modern Drummer*

Peart, Neil, *'Counterparts'* tour book

Peart, Neil, Editorial on Satanism, *The Daily Texan*

Peart, Neil, "Ghost Rider"

Peart, Neil, *'Grace Under Pressure'* tour book

Peart, Neil, "Masked Rider: Cycling in West Africa"

Peart, Neil, *'Moving Pictures'* tour book

Peart, Neil, *'Permanent Waves'* tour book

Peart, Neil, Rush *'Backstage'* Club mailing, July 1985

Peart, Neil, Rush *'Backstage'* Newsletter, January 1994

Peart, Neil, *'Rush Profiled!'* CD Interview

Peart, Neil, *'Test For Echo'* tour book

Peart, Neil, Travelling Music

Peart, Neil, *'Vapor Trails'* Album Bio, 2002

Penfield, Wilder III, *Network*, January 1989, Interview with Geddy and Neil

Pipher, Geneen, CNN, 2002, Interview with Alex Lifeson

Popoff, Martin, "Contents Under Pressure", 2004, Interview with Geddy, Neil and Alex

Provencher, Norman, *The Ottawa Citizen*, 26 February 1997, Interview with Geddy Lee

Reynolds, Bill, *Canadian Musician*, February 1989, Interview with Geddy Lee

Reynolds, Bill, *Canadian Musician*, February 1989, Interview with Geddy Lee and Val Azzoli

Robert, Pierre, WMMR, 18 December 2000, Interview with Geddy Lee

Roberts, Michael, *Westword* magazine, 15 May 1997, Interview with Geddy Lee

Robicheau, Paul, Interview with Neil Peart

Robinson, Jill, Rock 103.5 in Chicago, 5 September 1996, Interview with Geddy, Alex and Neil

Rockline, 2 December 1991, Interview with Neil Peart

Rockline, 5 October 1987, Interview with Geddy Lee

Rockline, 6 February 1989, Interview with Alex Lifeson

Rowland, Hobart, *The Houston Press*, 5 December 1996, Interview with Neil Peart

Rush Hour, *Muchmusic*, 1987, Interview with Geddy Lee

Sakamoto, John, *Jam! Showbiz*, October 16 1996, Interview with Neil Peart

Schulte, Frank, *Canadian Musician*, October 1991, Interview with Geddy Lee

Schwartz, Jim, *Guitar Player* magazine, June 1980, Interview with Alex Lifeson

Scott, Jane, *The Plain Dealer*, 15 November 1991, Interview with Alex Lifeson

Sculley, Alan, *The St Louis Post-Dispatch*, 5 June 1997, Interview with Neil Peart

Seconds, Issue 25, 1994, Interview with Geddy and Neil

Semel, Paul, *huH* magazine, September 1996, Interview with Geddy and Alex

Sept 2002, Interview with Geddy Lee and Alex Lifeson

Simmons, Sylvie, *Sounds* magazine, 5 April 1980, Interview with Neil Peart

Smith, Fred, *Rolling Stone* magazine, May 1801, Interview with Alex Lifeson

Smith, Jeric, 1997, Interview with Neil Peart

Smolen, Michael, *Circus* magazine, 31 July 1984, Interview with Alex Lifeson

Source unknown, 1979, Interview with Sam Charters

St. Catharines Standard, June 24/25 1994, Interview with Neil Peart

St. Paul Pioneer Press, Interview with Geddy Lee

Stern, Perry, *Network* magazine, November 1993, Interview with Geddy Lee

Stern, Perry, *Network* magazine, November 1996, Interview with Geddy Lee

Stevenson, Jane, *Jam* magazine, September 12 1996, Interview with Alex Lifeson

Stevenson, Jane, *Toronto Sun*, 5 July 1998

Stix, John, *'Guitar for The Practicing Musician'*, December 1991, Interview with Geddy Lee

Stix, John, *'Guitar for The Practicing Musician'*, May 1991, Interview with Alex Lifeson

Stories from *'Signals'*, Interview with Neil Peart

Surkamp, David, *The St Louis Post-Dispatch*, 1 March 1990, Interview with Neil Peart

Swenson, John, *'Chronicles'* liner notes, Interview with Geddy Lee

Tan, Gerald, *BigO* magazine, October 1998, Interview with Alex Lifeson

The Arizona Republic, 8 May 1997, Interview with Geddy Lee

The Fuze, Interview with Fin Costello

Titus, Christa, *Billboard* magazine, 15 May 2004, Interview with Alex Lifeson

Tolleson, Robin, Bass Player magazine, November 1988, Interview with Geddy Lee

Toronto New Music, Interview with Geddy Lee

Toronto Star, 6 January 2002, Interview with Dave Bidini of The Rheostatics

Turner, Mary, *'Off the Record'*, 1984, Interview with Neil Peart

Turner, Mary, *'Off the Record'*, 1987, Interview with Geddy Lee

Turner, Mary, broadcast 1984, Radio Interview with Neil Peart

Turner, Mary, Interview with Geddy and Alex

Van, Lynn, Matre, *The Chicago Tribune*, 30 March 1980, Interview with Neil Peart

Vancouver Radio, 4 December 1998, Interview with Geddy

Veitch, David, *Calgary Sun*, October 29 1998, Interview with Alex Lifeson

Veneman, Ted, Harmonix, January 1983, Interview with Alex Lifeson

VH1, 16 August 2000, Interview with Geddy Lee

Warden, Steve, World Premiere of *'Counterparts'*, 14 October 1993, Interview with Neil, Alex and Geddy

Weiss, Wieslaw (translated by Goss, Philip), *Tylko Rock*, November 1996, Interview with Geddy Lee

Weitzman, Steve, "Rush wrap up five-month tour", *Circus* magazine, August 31 1981

Welch, Chris, *Rock World*, November 1993, Interview with Geddy Lee

Welch, Ernie, *Boston Globe*, 5 December 1985, Interview with Neil Peart

Widders-Ellis, Andy, *Guitar Player*, December 1993, Interview with Alex Lifeson

Widders-Ellis, Andy, *Guitar Player*, November 1991, Interview with Alex and Geddy

Wiederhorn, Jon, "Rush Rolls Again", *Onstage* Magazine

Zildjan, www.zildjian.com/zevents.asp Interview with Neil Peart

Zulaica, Don, *LiveDaily*, 7 November 2000, Interview with Geddy Lee

Drawing by Alex. Sometimes the fun just had to stop!

Marillion: Separated Out
by Jon Collins
Paperback ISBN   1-900924-49-8
352pp 234x156mm b/w illustrated
throughout
UK £14.99 US $19.95
From Marillion's current line-up with
Steve Hogarth right back to its first
players, Marillion have fashioned a
career as an original, accomplished
and enduring rock band.
Originally fronted by the charismatic
singer Fish, with 1983's *'Script
for A Jester's Tear'* Marillion
ushered in a post-punk progressive
rock renaissance.
Starting with early pub gigs and
regular spots at Aylesbury Friars,
through the pioneering days of
'Market Square Heroes', to the chart
topping 'Kayleigh'-era and on to the
Steve Hogarth incarnation in 1989,
Marillion have continued to make
groundbreaking and innovative music
and retain a furiously loyal and
dedicated following, who have
even gone so far as to directly
bankroll a US tour and the making
of an entire album.
Drawing on fresh interviews with all
the major players in the Marillion
story, *'Separated Out'* is not only the
most extensively researched,
comprehensive and factual history
of the band since their earliest days.
It also captures, as a series of
anecdotes and memories, what
Marillion continues to stand for in the
hearts and minds of its fans and
supporters: the tens of thousands of
people who know, despite what
others may think, that they are
a part of something greater than just
a band and its music...

True Faith: An Armchair Guide To New Order

by Dave Thompson

The first ever book to focus on the music of New Order, one of the key rock groups of the 1980s. Formed from the ashes of Joy Division after their ill-fated singer Ian Curtis hanged himself, few could have predicted that New Order would become one of the seminal groups of the 80s, making a series of albums that would compare well with anything Joy Division had produced, and embracing club culture a good ten years before most of their contemporaries. From the bestselling 12-inch single 'Blue Monday' to later hits like 'Bizarre Love Triangle' (featured in the *'Trainspotting'* movie) and their spectacular world cup song 'World In Motion' the band have continued making innovative, critically revered records such as their 2001 hit 'Crystal' that have also enjoyed massive commercial success. This book is the first to treat New Order's musical career as a separate achievement, rather than a postscript to Joy Division's and the first to analyse in-depth what makes their music so great. New Order release their eighth studio album in 2005: *'Waiting For The Sirens' Call'*.

'Not only is this exhaustingly thorough …it's actually interesting as well… Fascinatingly comprehensive, this will be ambrosia for fans of New Order and contains enough juice to keep even the most lax fan occupied.' *NME*

Paperback ISBN 1-900924-94-3
256pp 234x156mm 8pp b/w photos
UK £12.99 US $19.95

Brian Jones: Who Killed Christopher Robin - The Truth Behind The Murder of A Rolling Stone

by Terry Rawlings

The basis for Stephen Wooley's new feature film *'The Wild and Wycked World of Brian Jones'* due in cinemas August 2005, this first ever paperback of an out-of-print classic includes new photos of the movie set, new evidence and a deathbed confession. In 1969, The Rolling Stones' founder Brian Jones was found dead in the swimming pool of his home, Cotchford Farm, AA Milne's former residence. Through exhaustive research, Terry Rawlings has amassed evidence contradicting the official Accidental Death verdict and in this book he names Jones' murderer. While Brian was initially the Stones' leader and creative driving force, by the mid-60s, his drink and drug intake began to spiral out of control and his resulting unreliability led to rifts within the band; Brian left the Stones in 1969. Three weeks later the 27-year-old rock star was found dead in his swimming pool - a verdict of misadventure was recorded. Terry Rawlings has interviewed in depth those who were present during Brian's last days and with the benefit of a deathbed confession he has solved the mystery of the tragic premature death of a Rolling Stone in this highly gripping page-turner.

Paperback ISBN 1-900924-81-1
288pp 234x156mm 8 b/w photos
UK £12.99 US $19.95

Belle and Sebastian: Just A Modern Rock Story

by Paul Whitelaw

First ever biography of the ultimate reclusive cult band – drawing on extensive interviews with band members. Formed in 1996, this enigmatic Glasgow band has risen to become one of Britain's most respected groups. For years, Belle and Sebastian were shrouded in mystery - the 8-piece ensemble led by singer-songwriter Stuart Murdoch refused interviews and the band scarcely toured. Their early singles though built them a strong and committed cult following. Their debut mail-order only album *'Tigermilk'* sold out within a month of its release and the follow-up, *'If You're Feeling Sinister'*, with its Nick Drake-influenced melodies and dark, quirky lyrics, found favour in alternative circles as far afield as San Francisco, Japan, South America and especially France. Oddly, for a band that sings about kinky sex and S&M, Stuart Murdoch lived above a church hall, sings in a choir and reads the bible. Such idiosyncratic contradictions are rife in this fascinating and curious tale. This is not only the first biography ever written on the band, but the most official that might ever hit the market. The band has agreed to participate in the project and to give the author extended interviews, paraphernalia and both personal and publicity still photos. Stuart Murdoch himself has agreed to design artwork for the cover. Paul Whitelaw is an arts writer from Glasgow who has met and interviewed Belle and Sebastian on several occasions and he was the first journalist to champion the band in print. Paperback ISBN 1-900924-98-6 288pp 234x156mm 16pp b/w photos UK £14.99

The Who By Numbers
by Alan Parker and Steve Grantley
From 'My Generation' and 'Substitute' to 'Pinball Wizard', 'Won't Get Fooled Again' and 'Who Are You' - the stories behind all The Who's songs. The Who are one of the few truly legendary rock 'n' roll bands. Backed by wild man drummer Keith Moon and the more stolid bassist John Entwistle, fronted by classic rock vocalist Roger Daltrey and powered on by the playing and composing of 'windmilling' guitarist Pete Townshend, they emerged from the mid-60s R'n'B world with a furious sound and a series of great anthems like 'My Generation' and 'Substitute'. Unlike many of their rivals who fell by the wayside, the band forged a more mature body of work in the late 1960s and the 1970s with the first successful rock opera *'Tommy'* and the later *'Quadrophenia'*. Even after the death of Keith Moon in 1978, the band reconvened on a number of occasions for sold out tours and remain one of the classic live bands. Though renowned for Keith Moon's madcap antics and for incendiary live shows, The Who are best known for and best judged by their songs. This is an anecdote-packed, richly detailed album-by-album song-by-song commentary on the songs of one of the classic rock bands by acclaimed author and Sid Vicious biographer, Alan Parker and professional rock drummer and Stiff Little Fingers member, Steve Grantley. Paperback ISBN 1-900924-91-9 256pp 234x156mm 16pp b/w photos UK £14.99 US $19.95

Kicking Against The Pricks: An Armchair Guide to Nick Cave
by Amy Hanson
Complete career retrospective of one of the most important singer-songwriters of the last twenty-five years. Nick Cave is the only artist to emerge from the post–punk era whose music and career can truly be compared with legends such as Bob Dylan or Van Morrison, with a

string of acclaimed albums including *'Junkyard (Birthday Party)'*, *'Tender Prey'*, *'The Boatman's Call'* and his most recent epic, *'Abattoir Blues/The Lyre of Orpheus'*. Cave left Australia to become part of a maelstrom unleashed to awestruck London audiences in the late 70s: the Birthday Party. Miraculously, Cave survived that band's excesses and formed the Bad Seeds, challenging his audience and the Godfather-of-Goth tag: as a bluesman with a gun in one hand, a Bible in the other; a vamp-ish torch singer with echoes of Vegas-era Elvis and a sensitive writer of love songs. *'Kicking Against The Pricks'* chronicles in depth these diverse personalities and the musical landscapes that Cave has inhabited, with a penetrating commentary on all his themes and influences. Cave's memorable collaborations and forays into other media are covered too: duets with Kylie Minogue, PJ Harvey and Shane MacGowan, the acclaimed novel And *'The Ass Saw The Angel'*, film appearances such as in Wim Wenders' *'Wings Of Desire'*, and his stint as Meltdown 2000 curator. Ultimately, it reveals Cave as the compelling and always-relevant musical force he is.
Paperback ISBN 1-900924-96-X
256pp 234x156mm 16pp b/w photos
UK £14.99 US $19.95

In Between Days: An Armchair Guide to The Cure
by Dave Thompson
The Cure's complete career, chronicled for the first time. The Cure are one of the most respected and well-loved of rock's survivors, traceable right back to punk's fabled 'Bromley Contingent'. The band's labyrinthine story has at its centre the enigmatic, charismatic frontman Robert Smith, forever shuffling personnel, themes and styles to make enduring music without losing an iota of credibility. *'In Between Days'* is the first book to make sense of a uniquely versatile band who are far more than the Goth band, documenting their development from the new wave attack of 1979's *'Boys Don't Cry'*, the existential rock of *'Seventeen Seconds'*, the near-religious angst of 'Faith', the joyous pop of *'Wish'*, the dark beauty of 'Disintegration' - right up to the majesty of *'Bloodflowers'* and 2004's *'The Cure'*, consecutive 21st century masterpieces. In Between Days also studies Robert Smith's brilliant interweaving literary influences from Mervyn Peake and Coleridge to Albert Camus and Jean Cocteau. Album-by-album, track-by-track study of the extraordinarily popular and enduring post-punks behind hits such as 'Love Cats' and 'In Between Days'.
Paperback ISBN 1-905139-00-4
256pp 234x156mm 16pp b/w photos
UK £14.99 US $19.95

From The Velvets To The Voidoids
by Clinton Heylin
Exhaustively researched and packed with insights to give a detailed and all-encompassing perspective of American punk rock's 60s roots through to the arrival of new wave - this is the definitive story. Long overdue, fully revised and updated edition of the definitive account of the rise of US punk and the 'new wave' movement, led by acts such as Richard Hell, Television, The Ramones, Blondie and Talking Heads. Also includes more obscure acts of the era, as well as legendary venues like CBGB's and Max's Kansas City. This was originally published by Penguin in the early 90s. Clinton Heylin is the acclaimed author of a number of books

including highly regarded biographies of Bob Dylan, Van Morrison and Orson Welles.

'No other book or account succeeded so well in accurately bringing the period to life.' Richard Hell

'This is a great story, and before Heylin no one saw it whole.' Greil Marcus

Paperback ISBN 1-905139-04-7
288pp 234x156mm 16pp b/w photos
UK £14.99

On The Road With Bob Dylan

by Larry Sloman

In 1975, as Bob Dylan emerged from 8 years of seclusion, he dreamed of putting together a travelling music show that would trek across the country like a psychedelic carnival. The dream became a reality, and *'On The Road With Bob Dylan'* is the ultimate behind-the-scenes look at what happened. When Dylan and the 'Rolling Thunder Revue' took to the streets of America, Larry 'Ratso' Sloman was with them every step of the way.

'The War and Peace of Rock and Roll.' Bob Dylan

Paperback ISBN 1-900924-51-X
288pp 198x129mm
UK £12.99

I'm With The Band: Confessions of A Groupie

by Pamela Des Barres

Long overdue return to print for the ultimate story of sex, drugs and rock 'n' roll - The definitive groupie memoir from the ultimate groupie. From the day she peeked at Paul McCartney through the windows of a Bel Air mansion, Pamela was hooked. Graduating high school, she headed for the sunset strip and rock and roll. Over the next ten years, she dallied with Mick Jagger, turned down a date with Elvis Presley, had affairs with Keith Moon, Noel Redding and Jim Morrison, and travelled with Led Zeppelin as Jimmy Page's girlfriend - he had 'dark chilling powers' and kept whips in his suitcase. She hung out with Cynthia Plastercaster, formed the all-girl group the GTOs, and was best friends with Robert Plant, Gram Parsons, Ray Davies and Frank Zappa.

'Ah, those were the days, and this is still one of the most likeable and sparky first-hand accounts.' ****Q

'Pamela's mixture of hippy enlightenment and teenage lust is terrific.' *The Guardian*

Paperback ISBN 1-900924-61-7
320pp 198x129mm 16pp b/w photos
UK £9.99

Rainbow Rising: The Story of Ritchie Blackmore's Rainbow

by Roy Davies

Blackmore led rock behemoths Deep Purple to international, multi-platinum, mega-stardom. He quit in '75, to form Rainbow, one of the great live bands, with Ronnie James Dio and enjoyed a string of acclaimed albums and hit singles, including 'All Night Long' and 'Since You've Been Gone' before the egos of the key players caused the whole thing to implode. A great rock 'n' roll tale. Already in a reprint, this is a surprise hit that proves the enduring appeal of one of the great rock bands of the 1970s.

'A thorough and detailed history.' *Classic Rock***

Paperback ISBN 1-900924-31-5
255pp
UK £14.99 US $19.95

Wheels Out Of Gear: 2-Tone, The Specials and A World On Fire

by Dave Thompson

Fascinating study of the 2-Tone ska revival of the late 70s and early 80s that plots the sounds of the remarkably successful scene against a backdrop of a Britain beset by unemployment, racial tension and large scale rioting. Taking its roots from Jamaican ska, rock steady and reggae, the 2-Tone sound was honed into a modern urban multi-racial mix by bands such as The Specials and The Selecter. Coming on the back of punk, 2-Tone was remarkably successful. The Beat and The Selecter also enjoyed strings of chart hits and groups born out of the same era such as Madness and UB40 forged their early success.

'Thompson recounts the rise of The Specials, Madness, The Selecter, The Beat et al with a tangible passion and also sets the music in the political and social context of those strange and disturbing times...a fine book that is as much social history as musical biography.' *Uncut* *** Top 30 Books for 2004
Paperback ISBN 1-900924-84-6
256pp 234x156mm 16pp b/w photos
UK £12.99 US $19.95

Electric Pioneer: An Armchair Guide to Gary Numan
by Paul Goodwin

The first ever book to concentrate on the music of Gary Numan, 80s icon turned cult hero - adored and reviled in equal measures with a foreword from the pioneer himself. From selling 10 million records in 2 years, both with Tubeway Army ('Are "Friends" Electric?') and solo ('Cars' *et al*), to more low key and idiosyncratic releases through subsequent decades, Gary Numan has built up an impressive body of work and retained a hugely devoted cult following. *'Electric Pioneer'* is the first ever guide to his recorded output, documenting every single and album and featuring sections on his live shows, memorabilia

and DVD releases.

'Nothing will alter the fact that I think he has written a couple of the finest things in British pop music.'
David Bowie
'Gary Numan is a man who deserves respect for his songwriting and dedication to electronic music... Sometimes it takes a real fan to do it properly and I'm glad this one did.'
DJ Magazine
Paperback ISBN 1-900924-95-1
288pp 234x156mm 16pp b/w photos
UK £14.99 US $19.95

Sex Pistols: Only Anarchists Are Pretty
by Mick O'Shea

What *'Backbeat'* was to The Beatles, *'Only Anarchists Are Pretty'* is to The Sex Pistols! Drawing both on years of research and creative conjecture, this book, written as a novel, portrays the early years of the Sex Pistols. Giving a fictionalised fly-on-the-wall account of the arguments, in-jokes, gigs, pub sessions and creative tension, it documents their day-to-day life – chaos, rancour and a strange innocence. Before singles like 'Anarchy In The UK' and 'God Save The Queen', tabloid outrage and the recruitment of Sid Vicious, back in the years 1974-1976, the band were a bunch of rock 'n' roll obsessed street urchins and petty crooks, hanging around Malcolm McLaren's shop Sex [*'Only Anarchists'* takes its name from one of McLaren's shirt slogans] listening to his war stories of managing The New York Dolls; arguing, fighting, and forming a band to relieve the boredom.

'The idea alone is genius...an antidote to the self-important toss that is generally written about punk rock...'Only Anarchists Are Pretty' is unexcelled.' **** Classic Rock
'Engaging...true or not, this is the real

story of the Sex Pistols.' ***Uncut*
Paperback ISBN 1-900924-93-5
256pp 234x156mm
UK £12.99 US $19.95

Psychedelic Furs: Beautiful Chaos

by Dave Thompson
Rise and fall of glamorous post-punk pioneers best known for US hit 'Pretty in Pink.' The Psychedelic Furs were the ultimate post-punk band - combining singer Richard Butler's hoarse rasping vocals, reminiscent of Johnny Rotten, with the Bowie-esque glamour of his angular cheek bones, and a blistering futuristic wall of sound that merged distorted guitars with saxophone and synths. When John Hughes wrote a movie based on their early single 'Pretty in Pink' the Furs hit the big time in the US with a re-recorded, though inferior, version of the song. The now-leather jacketed Butler and co became MTV darlings and appeared poised to join U2 and Simple Minds in the premier league. Then just as quickly, they withdrew behind their shades. Recently reformed and playing energising live shows in the US, the Furs are one of the few 1980s rock bands to have survived with their mystery and integrity intact.
'Charts in an engaging and sardonic manner the rise and fall of the Psychedelic Furs...a loving portrait of a ramshackle bunch of visionaries that is well-written and informative...' ***
Classic Rock
Paperback ISBN 1-900924-47-1
256pp 234x156mm b/w illustrated throughout
UK £14.99 US $19.95

Bob Dylan: Like The Night (Revisited)

by CP Lee
Fully revised and updated edition of the hugely acclaimed document of Dylan's pivotal 1966 show at the Manchester Free Trade Hall. Documenting the most legendary concert and tour in rock history, this is a riveting eyewitness account of the controversial concert where fans called Dylan Judas for turning his back on folk music in favour of rock 'n' roll. Having been out of print for a number of years, this new edition covers the release of the official album and the resulting controversy over the emergence of the Judas accuser, as well as featuring additional previously unseen photographs.
'A terrific tome that gets up close to its subject and breathes new life into it... For any fan of Dylan this is quite simply essential.' Time Out
Paperback ISBN 1-900924-33-1
224pp 198x129mm b/w illustrated throughout
UK £9.99 US $17.95

Steve Marriott: All Too Beautiful

by Paolo Hewitt and John Hellier
Definitive account of the Small Faces and Humble Pie main man: Mods, clothes, hit records, drugs, booze, mafia, bankruptcy, schizophrenia, classic rock 'n' roll, premature death and one of the great, great voices! Following his childhood debut as a street urchin in the original stage production of Oliver! Marriott became the world mod icon and prime mover behind 60s chart-toppers, The Small Faces, who scored a string of top ten singles including the classics 'All Or Nothing' and 'Tin Soldier'. They lived together in millionaire style at their chic Pimlico home, travelled by limousine, dated models and actresses and frequented London's most fashionable clubs. In 1968 Marriott and his band mates released a number one classic album Ogden's Nut Gone Flake and the world beckoned. But it was with Humble

Pie, formed with Peter Frampton, that Steve and his blistering rock 'n' blues guitar playing achieved legendary status in the USA. After years in seclusion, Marriott's plans for a comeback in 1991 were tragically cut short when he died in a house fire. He continues to be a key influence for generations of musicians from Paul Weller to Oasis and Blur.
'Revealing...sympathetic, long overdue.'
****Uncut
Hardback ISBN 1-900924-44-7
288pp 234x156mm 8pp b/w photos
UK £20.00 US $29.95

This Is A Modern Life
compiled by Enamel Verguren
Pictorial and anecdotal documentation of the 1980s London Mod scene.
Lavishly illustrated guide to the mod revival that was sparked by the 1979 release of 'Quadrophenia'. This Is a Modern Life concentrates on the 1980s, but takes in 20 years of a Mod life in London and throughout the world, from 1979 to 1999, with interviews of people and faces who were directly involved, loads of flyers, posters and a considerable amount of great photos.
'Good stuff ... A nice nostalgic book full of flyers, pics and colourful stories.'
Loaded
Paperback ISBN 1-900924-77-3
224pp 264x180mm b/w illustrated throughout
UK £14.99 US $19.95

Everybody Dance -
Chic and The Politics of Disco
by Daryl Easlea
The life and times of one of the key partnerships in musical history who were best known as the quintessential disco band Chic. Led by Black Panther activist Nile Rodgers and family man Bernard Edwards, Chic released or produced a string of era-defining records: 'Le Freak', 'Good Times', 'We Are Family', 'Lost In Music'. When disco collapsed, so did Chic's popularity. However, Rodgers and Edwards individually produced some of the great pop dance records of the 80s, working with Bowie, Robert Palmer, Madonna and ABC among many others until Edwards's tragic death after a Chic reunion gig in Japan in 1996. 'Everybody Dance' puts the rise and fall of the emblematic disco duo at the heart of a changing landscape, taking in socio-political and cultural events such as the Civil Rights struggle, the Black Panthers and the US oil crisis. There are drugs, bankruptcy, up-tight artists, fights, and Muppets but, most importantly an in-depth appraisal of a group whose legacy remains hugely underrated.
'Daryl Easlea's triumphant 'Everybody Dance' is the scholarly reappraisal the "black Roxy Music" deserve.' Time Out
'A lovingly crafted account of how Nile Rodgers and Bernard Edwards lovingly crafted some of the most sophisticated music of all time.' **** The Observer
Paperback ISBN 1-900924-56-0
288pp 234x156mm b/w illustrated throughout
UK £14.00 US $19.95

ISIS: A Bob Dylan Anthology
edited by Derek Barker
Second outing for the acclaimed anthology, oral biography, reference book and listening guide from the ultimate Dylan experts. ISIS is the bestselling, longest lasting, most highly acclaimed Dylan fanzine. This fully revised and expanded edition of the ultimate Dylan anthology draws on unpublished interviews, further rare photos and

research by the *ISIS* team together with the best articles culled from the pages of the definitive Bob magazine.

'This book is worth any Dylan specialist's money.' Ian MacDonald **** *Uncut*
Paperback ISBN 1-900924-82-X
352pp 198x129mm 16pp b/w photos
UK £9.99 US $17.95

Smashing Pumpkins, Tales of A Scorched Earth
by Amy Hanson

Initially contemporaries of Nirvana and Pearl Jam, Billy Corgan's Smashing Pumpkins outgrew and outlived the grunge scene with hugely acclaimed commercial triumphs like 'Siamese Dream', which legitimised heavy metal, and Number One album *'Mellon Collie and The Infinite Sadness'*. Drugs, the death of a band member and other problems led to the band's final demise. Seattle-based Hanson followed the band for years and this is the first in-depth biography of their rise and fall.

'Extremely well-written - a thrilling and captivating read.' *Classic Rock*
Paperback ISBN 1-900924-68-4
256pp 234x156mm 8pp b/w photos
UK £12.99 US $18.95

Got A Revolution: The Turbulent Flight of Jefferson Airplane
by Jeff Tamarkin

Acclaimed music journalist Jeff Tamarkin chronicles the band's long, convoluted history - they were on the scene before the Grateful Dead, Janis Joplin, or Santana. Rendered in crisp, engaging prose and informed by scores of insider interviews with former band members, friends, lovers, crew members and fellow musicians this is their fascinating full-length story.

'This book brings it all back: the music by turns powerful and puzzling; the dysfunctional family-as-rock band!'
Rolling Stone
Paperback ISBN 1-900924-78-1
408pp 234x156mm 8pp b/w photos
UK £14.99

Love: Behind the Scenes - On The Pegasus Carousel With The Legendary Rock Group Love
by Michael Stuart-Ware

Their masterpiece *'Forever Changes'* still regularly appears in critics' polls. Yet the band never truly fulfilled their potential and broke through to the LA premier league inhabited by Crosby, Stills and Nash and The Doors. Michael Stuart-Ware, Love's drummer, shares his inside perspective on the band's recording and performing career and tells how drugs and egos thwarted the potential of one of the great groups of the burgeoning psychedelic era. As one fellow band member tells him: 'There wasn't any love in that group. It had nothing whatsoever to do with love. It was all about hate. That should have been the name of the band.'
Paperback ISBN 1-900924-59-5
256pp 234x156mm
UK £14.00 US $19.95

The Fall: A User's Guide
by Dave Thompson

Album-by-album, track-by-track guide to the extensive, highly idiosyncratic 25-year oeuvre of one of rock's most enduring cult acts.
Paperback ISBN 1-900924-57-9
256pp 234x156mm b/w illustrated throughout
UK £12.99 US $19.95

Be Glad: An Incredible String Band Compendium

edited by Adrian Whittaker

The ISB pioneered an eclectic, 'World music' approach on 60s albums like *'The Hangman's Beautiful Daughter'* - Paul McCartney's favourite album of 1967! - taking in experiments with theatre, film and lifestyles along the way and even inspiring Led Zeppelin. Featuring interviews with all the ISB key players, as well as a wealth of background information, reminiscence, critical evaluations and arcane trivia, this is a book that will delight any reader with more than a passing interest in the ISB.

Paperback ISBN 1-900924-64-1
288pp 234x156mm b/w illustrated throughout
UK £14.99 US $19.95

In Search of The La's – A Secret Liverpool

by Matthew Macefield

With timeless single 'There She Goes', Lee Mavers' La's briefly overtook The Stone Roses as the great hopes for British guitar rock and paved the way for Britpop. However, since 1991, The La's have been silent, while rumours of studio-perfectionism, madness and drug addiction have abounded. The author sets out to discover the truth behind Mavers' lost decade and subsequently gets drawn into the musical underground of a secret Liverpool before finally gaining a revelatory audience with Mavers himself.

Paperback ISBN 1-900924-63-3
192pp 234x156mm 8pp b/w photos
UK £10.99 US $17.95

The Clash: The Return of The Last Gang In Town (revised)

by Marcus Gray

A revised edition of the exhaustively researched, definitive biography of the rock band whose instantly memorable hits 'London Calling,' 'Should I Stay or Should I Go' and 'Rock the Casbah' made them the greatest rock 'n' roll band of the post-60s era. The book vividly evokes the mid-70s environment out of which punk flourished, as the author traces their progress from pubs and punk clubs to US stadiums and the Top Ten. This edition is further updated to cover the band's recent induction into the Rock 'n' Roll Hall of Fame, band members' post-Clash careers and the tragic death of iconic frontman Joe Strummer.

'Revised edition of the superb band biography. A fascinating, fiery read.'
**** Q

Paperback ISBN 1-900924-62-5
448pp 234x156mm 8pp b/w photos
UK £14.99

Surf's Up: The Beach Boys on Record 1961-1981

by Brad Elliott

A detailed chronicle of the group's extensive recording history replete with a 385-entry chronological discography, an extensive discussion of unreleased material including studio outtakes and radio and television appearances and over 100 photographs.

Paperback ISBN 1-900924-79-X
512pp 234x156mm 16pp b/w photos
UK £25.00

Get Back: The Beatles' Let It Be Disaster

by Doug Suply and Ray Shweighardt

A singularly candid look at the greatest band in history at their ultimate moment of crisis. It puts the reader in the studio as John cedes power to Yoko; Paul struggles to keep things afloat, Ringo shrugs and George quits the band.

'One of the most poignant Beatles books

ever.' *Mojo*
Paperback ISBN 1-900924-83-8
352pp 198x129mm
UK £9.99

Hit Men: Powerbrokers and Fast Money Inside The Music Business

by Fredric Dannen

Hit Men exposes the seamy and sleazy dealings of America's glitziest record companies: payola, corruption, drugs, Mafia involvement and excess.

'The best book ever written on the business side of the music industry... Unreservedly recommended.' *Music Week*
Paperback ISBN 1-900924-54-4
416pp 234x156mm
UK £14.99

The Big Wheel

by Bruce Thomas

Thomas was bassist with Elvis Costello and The Attractions at the height of the band's success. Though names are never mentioned, *'The Big Wheel'* paints a vivid and hilarious picture of exactly what it is like touring the world with Costello and co, sharing your life 24 hours a day with a moody egotistical singer, a crazed drummer and a host of hangers-on. Originally published by Viking in 1990, Costello sacked Thomas for writing it.

'Laugh-out loud tales pepper the pages...conveys a wit that readers of Motley Crue's *'The Dirt'* will find hard to fathom.' *Q* ****
Paperback ISBN 1-900924-53-6
192pp 235x156mm
UK £10.99

Pink Floyd: A Saucerful of Secrets

by Nicholas Schaffner

From the psychedelic explorations of the Syd Barrett-era to 70s superstardom with *'Dark Side of The Moon'*, and on to the triumph of *'The Wall'*, before internecine strife tore the group apart, Schaffner's definitive history also covers the improbable return of Pink Floyd without Roger Waters, and the hugely successful *'Momentary Lapse of Reason'* album and tour.

'Schaffner succeeds ...this remains all but definitive.' *Q*****
Paperback ISBN 1-905139-09-8
352pp 197x129mm 8pp b/w photos
UK £10.99

Waiting For The Man: The Story of Drugs and Popular Music

by Harry Shapiro

Fully revised edition of the classic story of two intertwining billion dollar industries. From marijuana and early jazz, through acid-rock, speed-fuelled punk, to crack-driven rap and ecstasy and the Dance Generation, this is the definitive history of drugs and pop.

'Wise and witty.' *The Guardian*
Paperback ISBN 1-900924-58-7
304pp 198X129mm
UK £10.99 US $18.95

The Buzzcocks: Harmony in My Head - Steve Diggle's Rock 'n' Roll Odyssey

by Terry Rawlings and Steve Diggle

First-hand account of the punk wars from guitarist and one half of the songwriting duo that gave the world three chord punk-pop classics like 'Ever Fallen In Love' and 'Promises'. Diggle dishes the dirt on punk contemporaries like The Sex Pistols, The Clash and The Jam, as well as sharing poignant memories of his friendship with Kurt Cobain, on whose last ever tour, The Buzzcocks were the support act.

'As a first hand account from the punk front lines, it's invaluable, but it works best as a straightforward sex, drugs and

rock 'n' roll memoir.'**** *Uncut*
Paperback ISBN 1-900924-37-4
304pp 235x156mm
UK £14.99 US $19.95

The Dark Reign of Gothic Rock: In The Reptile House with The Sisters of Mercy, Bauhaus and The Cure
by Dave Thompson
From Joy Division to Nine Inch Nails and from Siouxsie and the Banshees to Marilyn Manson, gothic rock has endured as the cult of choice for the disaffected and the alienated. During the mid-80s it was the underground alternative to the glossy throwaway pop of the day. The author traces the rise of 80s and 90s goth from influences such as Hammer Horror movies and schlock novels, through post-punk into the full blown drama of Bauhaus, The Cure and the Sisters of Mercy.
Paperback ISBN 1-900924-48-X
288pp 235x156mm
8pp b/w photos
UK £14.99 US $19.95

Back To The Beach: A Brian Wilson and The Beach Boys Reader
edited by Kingsley Abbott
Revised and expanded edition of the Beach Boys compendium *Mojo* magazine deemed an 'essential purchase.' This collection includes all of the best articles, interviews and reviews from the Beach Boys' four decades of music, including definitive pieces by Timothy White, Nick Kent and David Leaf. New material reflects on the tragic death of Carl Wilson and documents the rejuvenated Brian's return to the boards.
'Riveting!' **** *Q*
Paperback ISBN 1-900924-46-3
288pp 235x156mm
UK £14.00 US $18.95

Serge Gainsbourg: A Fistful of Gitanes
by Sylvie Simmons
Rock press legend Simmons' hugely acclaimed biography of the French genius tells the story of the classy, sleazy, sexy, funny, hard-drinking, chain-smoking Gallic icon who invented French pop and inspired a new generation of louche wannabes.
'I would recommend *'A Fistful of Gitanes'* [as summer reading] which is a highly entertaining biography of the French singer-songwriter and all-round scallywag.' JG Ballard
Paperback ISBN 1-900924-40-4
288pp 198x129mm
UK £9.99

Blues: The British Connection
by Bob Brunning
Former Fleetwood Mac member Bob Brunning's classic account of the impact of blues in Britain, from its beginnings as the underground music of 50s teenagers like Mick Jagger, Keith Richards and Eric Clapton, to the explosion in the 60s, right through to the vibrant scene of the present day.
'An invaluable reference book and an engaging personal memoir.' Charles Shaar Murray
Paperback ISBN 1-900924-41-2
288pp 198x129mm
UK £14.99 US $19.95

Al Stewart: Lights, Camera, Action - A Life in Pictures
by Neville Judd
A collection of photographs, most never published before, from both the public and private life of Al Stewart, Scottish cult folk hero behind chart hit 'Year of The Cat' who enjoyed Top Ten success in the US.
Paperback ISBN 1-900924-90-0

310x227mm All 192pp photos, 16pp of colour
UK £25.00 US $35.00

King Crimson: In The Court of King Crimson

by Sid Smith

King Crimson's 1969 masterpiece *'In The Court Of The Crimson King'*, was a huge US chart hit. The band followed it with further albums of consistently challenging, distinctive and innovative music. Drawing on hours of new interviews, and encouraged by Crimson supremo Robert Fripp, the author traces the band's turbulent history year by year, track by track.
Paperback ISBN 1-900924-26-9
288pp 234x156mm b/w Illustrated throughout
UK £14.99 US $19.95

A Journey Through America with The Rolling Stones

by Robert Greenfield

Featuring a new foreword by Ian Rankin. This is the definitive account of The Stones' legendary '72 tour.
'The Stones on tour in '72 twist and burn through their own myth: from debauched outsiders to the first hints of the corporate business - the lip-smacking chaos between the Stones fan being stabbed by a Hell's Angel at Altamont and the fan owning a Stones credit card.' Paul Morley #2 essential holiday rock reading list, *The Observer*
Paperback ISBN 1-900924-24-2
256pp 198x129mm
UK £9.99 US $17.95

Ashley Hutchings: The Guvnor and The Rise of Folk Rock - Fairport Convention, Steeleye Span and The Albion Band

By Geoff Wall and Brian Hinton

As founder of Fairport Convention and Steeleye Span, Ashley Hutchings is the pivotal figure in the history of folk rock. This book draws on hundreds of hours of interviews with Hutchings and other folk rock artists and paints a vivid picture of the scene that also produced Sandy Denny, Richard Thompson, Nick Drake, John Martyn and Al Stewart.
Paperback ISBN 1-900924-32-3
256pp 234x156mm
UK £14.99 US $19.95

Firefly Publishing: An Association between Helter Skelter and SAF

The Nirvana Recording Sessions

by Rob Jovanovic

Drawing on years of research, and interviews with many who worked with the band, the author has documented details of every Nirvana recording, from early rehearsals, to the *'In Utero'* sessions. A fascinating account of the creative process of one of the great bands.
'Manna from heaven for the completists ...A painstakingly exhaustive catalogue of every track at every session.... The author's determination to concentrate purely on the music is admirable... If you're planning to invest in the box set, this will make an excellent companion piece.' *Kerrang*
Hardback ISBN 0-946719-60-8
224pp 234x156mm b/w illustrated throughout UK £20.00 US $30.00

The Music of George Harrison: While My Guitar Gently Weeps
by Simon Leng
Santana biographer Leng takes a studied, track by track, look at both Harrison's contribution to The Beatles, and the solo work that started with the release in 1970 of his epic masterpiece 'All Things Must Pass'.
Hardback ISBN 0-946719-50-0
256pp 234x156mm 8pp b/w photos
UK £20.00 US $26.00

The Sensational Alex Harvey
by John Neil Murno
ISBN 0-946719-47-0 224pp
UK £20.00 US $30.00

Poison Heart: Surviving The Ramones
by Dee Dee Ramone and Veronica Kofman
ISBN 0-946719-48-9 224pp
UK £9.99

Blowin' Free: Thirty Years of Wishbone Ash
by Gary Carter and Mark Chatterton
ISBN 0-946719-33-0 224pp
UK £12.99 US $18.95